Criminal Justice
in Canada

Third Edition

a reader

Julian V. Roberts
Universities of Oxford and Ottawa

Michelle G. Grossman
University of Oxford

NELSON / EDUCATION

NELSON / EDUCATION

Criminal Justice in Canada: A Reader

by Julian V. Roberts and
Michelle G. Grossman

**Associate Vice President,
Editorial Director:**
Evelyn Veitch

**Editor-in-Chief,
Higher Education:**
Anne Williams

Senior Marketing Manager:
Lenore Taylor-Atkins

Senior Developmental Editor:
Rebecca Rea Ryoji

**Senior Content Production
Manager:**
Tammy Scherer

Production Service:
GEX Publishing Services

Copy Editor:
GEX Publishing Services

Proofreader:
GEX Publishing Services

Production Coordinator:
Ferial Suleman

Design Director:
Ken Phipps

Interior Design:
Johanna Liburd

Cover Design:
Ken Phipps

Cover Image:
J. Christopher Lawson/Getty Images

Compositor:
GEX Publishing Services

Printer:
Webcom

**Library and Archives Canada
Cataloguing in Publication Data**

Criminal justice in Canada :
a reader / [edited by] Julian V.
Roberts, Michelle G. Grossman. —
3rd ed.

Includes bibliographical
references.
ISBN-13: 978-0-17-642409-1
ISBN-10: 0-17-642409-1

1. Criminal justice, Administration
of—Canada. I. Roberts, Julian V.
II. Grossman, Michelle G.

HV9960.C2C75 2007   364.971
C2006-906049-5

The editors dedicate their work on this book to the memory of Mary K. Roberts (1917–2005)—a scholar in all but name.

PREFACE

Julian V. Roberts, Ph.D., and Michelle G. Grossman, M.A., M.S.W.

Welcome to the new, improved third edition of *Criminal Justice in Canada!* A decade ago, teachers in the field of criminology and criminal justice who sought a text for their students had few Canadian works from which to choose. That has since changed: several excellent books are now available. Finding a collection of readings, however, remains a challenge. Although several good readers exist, they deal with crime rather than criminal justice or specific topics, such as crime control policy. Instructors looking for a more general collection of primarily introductory readings are often forced to cobble together a collection of readings and package them through commercial or university print shops.

Our reader simplifies this task. The third edition is aimed at any course with a primary or secondary focus on the criminal justice system. We designed this book to accompany standard criminal justice and criminology texts by providing a diversity of views: some articles take a critical approach to criminal justice; others report findings from a more "mainstream" perspective. Most readings have been commissioned especially for this new edition. In addition, this edition includes an expanded section comprising the writings of people who are working in or who have passed through the criminal justice process, because the voice of practical experience has greater value than mere theory.

Furthermore, we have attempted to address two concerns in this reader: discrimination within the criminal justice system and variability of treatment. Whatever the merits of our system (relative to the criminal justice systems of other jurisdictions), certain elements of the population receive disproportionate attention from the police and thereafter inequitable treatment at the hands of other criminal justice professionals. This fundamental lack of equity is the single most important issue to bring to the attention of students of criminal justice. As for variability, it is important to note that the justice system accords criminal justice professionals a high degree of discretion, which inevitably results, rightly or wrongly, in variable treatment.

ACKNOWLEDGMENTS

First and foremost, we thank the contributing authors whose work is represented here and the copyright holders for their permission to reprint material. We would also like to acknowledge the important contributions of Joanna Cotton and Rebecca Rea from Thomson Nelson. We are also grateful to the following individuals for reviewing the second edition and making suggestions for improvement: John Anderson, Malaspina University-College; Elizabeth Hibbard, Mohawk College; Heather A. Kitchin, Acadia University; Anthony Miccuci, Memorial University; and Larry White, Mohawk College.

Julian V. Roberts and Michelle G. Grossman
At Oxford, June 1, 2006

A Note from the Publisher

Thank you for selecting *Criminal Justice in Canada*, eds. Julian V. Roberts and Michelle G. Grossman. The editors and publisher have devoted considerable time to the careful development of this book. We appreciate your recognition of this effort and accomplishment.

CONTENTS

ABOUT THE CONTRIBUTORS

EDITORS

Julian V. Roberts holds a Ph.D. from the University of Toronto and is currently a Professor of Criminology in the Faculty of Law at the University of Oxford and the Department of Criminology at the University of Ottawa. His recent books include *Understanding Public Attitudes to Criminal Justice* (2005, with M. Hough; Open University Press) and *The Virtual Prison: Community Custody and the Evolution of Imprisonment* (2004, Cambridge University Press).

Michelle G. Grossman has graduate degrees in criminology and social work from the University of Toronto. In addition, she has worked in a clinical capacity at the Toronto Child Abuse Centre. Most recently, she has worked in a policy/research capacity for the Government of Canada, at the Department of Justice and Solicitor General, with a particular focus on the issue of victims. She has published a number of articles in the area of sexual aggression. She is currently completing a doctoral thesis in the Faculty of Law, University of Oxford.

CONTRIBUTING AUTHORS

Shereen H. Benzvy Miller, M.A. LL.B, is a human rights lawyer by training and inclination. She has taught courses in law, criminology, and sociology at Carleton University, the University of Pennsylvania, and York University. She is a trained mediator and has written on restorative justice and governance. Previously a criminologist and criminal defence lawyer, she worked on a multitude of law reform files, including development of the statement of purpose and principles of sentencing for inclusion in the Criminal Code of Canada, and with the Correctional Law Review, which drafted the Corrections and Conditional Release Act. While her focus has been primarily in criminal justice and human rights, she views the essence of her work as contributing to the support of democratic processes and values that improve Canada for Canadians.

Gillian Blackell is Senior Legal Counsel with the Family, Children and Youth Section of the Department of Justice Canada. She has worked on legal policy issues related to violence against women and children for ten years, has been involved in the development of legislative reforms and has had the privilege of participating in negotiations at the United Nations.

Paul Burstein started his own practice in 1992 specializing in criminal and constitutional litigation. He has argued appeals before the Supreme Court of Canada, the Ontario Court of Appeal, and the Federal Court of Appeal. Paul has appeared before Parliamentary Committees dealing with various criminal legislative proposals and has been the Director of Osgoode Hall Law School's Criminal Law Intensive Programme since 1999. He is also involved with the Trial Advocacy courses offered by the Law School to both students and practitioners and is an adjunct professor at Queen's Law School, teaching both trial and appellate advocacy.

Kathryn Campbell is a faculty member in the Department of Criminology at the University of Ottawa. She is an expert in the field of youth justice and the editor of *Understanding Youth Justice in Canada*, published by Pearson Canada in 2005.

Mary E. Campbell is the Director General of Corrections and Criminal Justice Directorate in the Department of Public Safety Canada. She has a B.A. from the University of Toronto, an LL.B. from Queen's University, and an LL.M. from McGill University. Ms. Campbell also teaches at the university level. She has particular criminal justice expertise in the areas of sentencing, corrections, and community reintegration.

Carla Cesaroni is an assistant professor at the University of Ontario Institute of Technology. She received her Ph.D. from the Centre of Criminology, University of Toronto. Her interest in youth in custody began while she was a volunteer at a secure custody facility for high risk, violent youth. She has worked with and interviewed over 300 male youth in facilities throughout the province of Ontario. Her current research is on the stress and adjustment of youth in detention.

Judge David P. Cole was appointed to the Ontario Court of Justice in 1991. He currently presides at Metro West court in Toronto. From 1992 to 1996, Justice Cole was seconded to the Commission on Systemic Racism in the Ontario Criminal Justice System. Justice Cole teaches the law of sentencing and penal policy at the Faculty of Law and the Centre of Criminology, both at the University of Toronto. He is the co-author of *Release from Imprisonment: The Law of Sentencing and Parole* and the co-editor of *Making Sense of Sentencing*. Justice Cole also is a member of the editorial board of the *Canadian Journal of Criminology and Criminal Justice*.

Myriam Denov is currently an Associate Professor in the School of Social Work at McGill University. She holds a PhD from the University of Cambridge, where she was a Commonwealth Scholar. Her current research and teaching interests lie in the areas of human rights, war and political violence, and at-risk youth. She is currently writing a book on child soldiers which will be published by Cambridge University Press.

Anthony N. Doob is a professor at the Centre of Criminology, University of Toronto. He has written extensively on a wide range of topics, including public knowledge and attitudes about sentencing and other aspects of the youth and criminal justice system, the operation of the youth justice system, the deterrent effect of sentencing, trends in imprisonment in Canada, and the processing of cases in the criminal courts. His work in the area of youth justice began in the mid-1970s with research on police discretion in the handling of young offenders. He co-authored *Responding to Youth Crime in Canada*, with Carla Cesaroni, in 2004 (University of Toronto Press).

Liz Elliott is Assistant Professor and Co-Director of the Centre for Restorative Justice in the School of Criminology at Simon Fraser University. Her teaching and research interests are in the areas of restorative justice, prisons, crime prevention through social development, and criminological theory.

Thomas Gabor is a Professor of Criminology at the University of Ottawa. He received his Ph.D. from Ohio State University in 1983 and has published over 100 works in the field, including books on armed robbery, the prediction of criminal behaviour, and on crime by the public. He has just completed a concise textbook for introductory criminology students, entitled *Basics of Criminology*. He has served on the Editorial Committee of the *Canadian Journal of Criminology and Criminal Justice* for over 15 years. He has also served as a consultant to the United Nations, foreign governments, and various federal departments in Canada.

Holly Johnson is Chief of Research at the Canadian Centre for Justice Statistics at Statistics Canada. She is currently on secondment to the University of Ottawa. She was principal investigator on Statistics Canada's national surveys on crime victimization and violence against women and is the author of many publications in this field. She also provides advice to community-based researchers and governments internationally on the development and design of surveys to measure violence against women and acts as advisor to the International Violence Against Women Survey, a multi-country project coordinated through the United Nations. She received her Ph.D. from the University of Manchester.

Catherine Kane is Director of the Policy Centre for Victim Issues and Acting General Counsel, Criminal Law Policy Section, Department of Justice, Canada. She joined the Department of Justice, Criminal Law Policy Section in 1982. Her work has focused on a range of criminal law reforms, particularly those dealing with sexual assault, victims and witnesses of crime, impaired driving, and mentally disordered offenders. She is actively involved in many intra- and inter-departmental committees, Federal Provincial and Territorial Committees, and the Uniform Law Conference of Canada, and has served as secretary to the Criminal Section since 1996 and served as chairperson of the Section in 2004.

Rebecca Kong graduated from Carleton University in 1994 with an honours degree in law and criminology. She has worked as an analyst and survey manager for the Canadian Centre for Justice Statistics at Statistics Canada in Ottawa for 13 years. During that time, she has authored several publications on crime and victimization and has developed new data collection in the areas of victim services and fraud.

Carol La Prairie received her M.A. from the Centre of Criminology, University of Toronto, and her doctorate from the University of British Columbia. She has worked as a researcher for the federal Ministry of the Solicitor General and the Department of Justice. She has also conducted a great deal of research and published extensively in the area of Aboriginal justice. In 2005, she co-authored *Will the Circle be Unbroken: Aboriginal Communities, Restorative Justice and the Challenges of Conflict and Change* (University of Toronto Press).

Barry N. Leighton is a criminologist specializing in policing in Canada. He teaches or has taught at a number of universities, including Carleton University and the University of Ottawa.

Brian Manarin is an Assistant Crown Attorney prosecuting criminal matters in Windsor, Ontario, after many years of practice with the Ministry of the Attorney General in the Greater Toronto Area. He was called to the Ontario Bar in 1988, and his prosecutorial experience has run the gamut of matters criminal. An internationally published author, he has written numerous articles on various legal topics.

Julius Melnitzer is an author living in Toronto. His books include *Maximum, Minimum, Medium: A Journey through Canada's Prisons* (1995) and *Dirty White Collar* (2002).

Karen Middlecoat graduated from University of Toronto with a B.A.H. with a double major in criminology and psychology and a minor in English. She started working in the Ministry of Correctional Services as a correctional officer, then spent a year at the Metropolitan Toronto Forensic Services (METFORS), working with psychiatric staff to conduct assessments on individuals to determine their fitness to stand trial. She became a probation and parole officer in 1985 and worked in the field till 1997, when she was asked to work at the Toronto courts as the administrative probation liaison.

Andrea McCalla is a doctoral student at the Centre of Criminology, University of Toronto. Her thesis explores the relationship between race, perceptions of social injustice, and criminal activity among Toronto high school students. Her research interests include youth crime and victimization and discrimination within the Canadian justice system.

Karen Mihorean obtained her master of arts degree in criminology from the University of Ottawa in 1991. She is currently the Chief of the Integration, Analysis and Research Program at the Canadian Centre for Justice Statistics at Statistics Canada, where she has worked for the past 15 years. With extensive experience in the analysis of criminal justice data surveys, she has written a number of publications on criminal victimization, family violence, and violence against women. She has also made numerous presentations, both nationally and internationally, on the nature and extent of spousal violence and violence against women in Canada, and on methods of measuring these sensitive experiences.

Sheldon Schwartz received a bachelor of arts degree from York University, majoring in economics. He then worked in the field of public accounting and auditing for several years before entering the field of social work. After three years of working for an agency providing supervision services under contract to the Correctional Service of Canada (CSC), he was hired by the Government of Canada for another department (Human Resources Development Canada, formerly Employment and Immigration). After six years in various HRDC roles, he transferred back to CSC in 1996, where he has been ever since. He has received a bachelor of social work degree from York University and a masters in social work from the University of Toronto and is now a registered social worker.

Jane B. Sprott is an associate professor in the Department of Sociology and Anthropology at the University of Guelph. Her research interests include risk and protective factors for juvenile delinquency, the operation of the youth and adult justice systems in Canada, and public perceptions of crime and justice.

Simon Verdun-Jones is a Professor of Criminology at Simon Fraser University. His major interests are criminal law, mentally disordered offenders, plea bargaining, sentencing, victim participation in the criminal justice system, the International Criminal Court of Justice, and violence and aggression in mental health facilities. Among his recent books are *Introduction to Criminal and Civil Law* (2006); *Criminal Law in Canada: Cases, Questions and the Code*, 4th ed. (2007); and *Canadian Criminal Cases: Selected Highlights*, 2nd ed. (2007).

Richard Weisman is Associate Professor in the Law and Society Program at York University in Toronto. He is currently completing a book on the role of remorse in law using cases and other data from Canada, the United States, and South Africa.

Scot Wortley is a professor at the Centre of Criminology, University of Toronto. He is also the Justice and Law Domain Leader at the Centre of Excellence for Research on Immigration and Settlement (CERIS). His research interests include street gangs, the relationship between immigration and crime, sentencing outcomes, racial differences in police stop and search practices, and the depiction of racial minorities and immigrants in the Canadian print media. He has made numerous presentations at international conferences and has published in many journals.

PART ONE
Introductory Readings

CHAPTER 1

Criminal Justice in Canada: An Overview

INTRODUCTION

This introductory chapter provides context for the rest of the volume. It begins by noting two conflicting models of criminal justice in Canada and then reviewing research on public opinion about crime and criminal justice. Many Canadians believe they know how the criminal justice system works (and have strong opinions about how it should work); but as we shall see, there is often a considerable gap between public ideas about how the system works and the actual functioning of the system. One of the primary functions of any course or text in the field of criminology is to correct public misperceptions. A good place to start, therefore, is to document the extent of public knowledge of crime and justice. The chapter concludes by noting some of the current priorities for criminal justice in Canada, many of which are subsequently explored in later chapters in the volume.

Julian V. Roberts, University of Ottawa and Oxford

THE COMPLEXITIES OF CRIMINAL JUSTICE

Criminal justice in Canada—as elsewhere—involves a complex system of checks and balances, in which responsibility for a criminal case is divided among many different decision makers. To complicate matters further, these decision makers are guided by somewhat different mandates. Judges are guided by the *principle of proportionality* when they impose a sentence. This means that they attempt to ensure that the severity of the sentence imposed reflects the seriousness of the crime committed (and the offender's level of culpability). Parole boards, on the other hand, have a different mandate. When deciding whether inmates should be allowed out of prison to spend the remainder of their sentences in the community under supervision, parole boards are concerned about whether the offenders will benefit from release on parole and whether they represent risks to the community. The seriousness of the crime plays little role in the decision, unless it sheds light on the issues of rehabilitation or risk to the community. Thus, the length of the sentence is determined largely by the seriousness of the crime, while the portion of the sentence served in prison is often determined by other criteria. This is just one example illustrating the complexity of the system.

The justice system is also complex because it must respond to a wide diversity of human behaviour. If crime were to comprise only a limited number of proscribed acts, the system could develop a far more focused (and predictable) response. But the variability in criminal conduct is immense, and the system needs to vary its response accordingly. The criminal justice system must be able to respond to cases of premeditated murder, minor acts of vandalism committed by bored teenagers, and all forms of offending between these two extremes. In addition, even if they have been convicted of the same category of crime, no two offenders are ever alike. Two people convicted of burglary may have very different backgrounds, and one may be more blameworthy than another. Consider a case of break and enter in which one offender is 35 years old and has 4 previous convictions for breaking into houses; whereas the other offender is 18 years old and has no previous convictions. Even if they committed the crime together, their cases would be very different, and it is surely appropriate that the justice system treat them differently.

The criminal justice system is the subject of both intense media coverage and great public interest. Crime and criminal justice stories—especially the most publicized cases—fascinate the public. For example, over 100 million people in North America watched the television coverage of the verdict in the O.J. Simpson trial. In fact, the Simpson trial received more coverage than any other news story that year. Canada also has criminal justice stories that attract similar amounts of attention. When Saskatchewan farmer Robert Latimer was convicted of the murder of his severely disabled daughter, the case became the source of heated discussion across the nation. Few Canadians were unaware of the verdict and subsequent sentence. Similarly, there was widespread and intense coverage of the Karla Homolka case.

MODELS OF CRIMINAL JUSTICE

Two competing perspectives underlie our criminal justice system. These perspectives are closely associated with the research of Herbert Packer, who coined the terms *crime control model* and the *due process model* (see Packer, 1968). As the name implies, the **crime control model** stresses the importance of controlling crime and favours providing the community with criminal justice professionals with considerable powers for responding to crime, such as police. In contrast, the **due process model** prefers to place limits on the powers of the criminal justice system. How are these limits established? One example is to require police to obtain permission from a court prior to placing a wiretap on a suspect's telephone line. Similarly, police officers cannot stop a person and search him or her without grounds. In these and many other ways the due process model prevents the State from having unlimited power over the lives of suspects and accused persons. The due process is therefore more concerned with protecting the rights of the accused and following correct legal procedure. For almost every important issue in criminal justice, one can find crime control as well as due process approaches.

For example, when determining the limits on the powers of the police, crime control advocates argue that the police should have wide powers to gather evidence and to question and interrogate suspects and accused persons. Due process advocates, on the other hand, want such powers limited in order to ensure that individual rights are not compromised and that innocent people are not stopped and detained by the police. The conduct of criminal trials also provides many examples of the conflict between due process and crime control models of criminal justice. During a criminal trial, an accused person is not obliged to take the stand and testify in his or her own defence. The onus is on the state, through the prosecutor, to establish the guilt of the accused beyond a reasonable doubt, without any help from the testimony of the accused. The due process model defends this procedural rule by arguing that the accused should not have to cooperate with the state's case. In contrast, crime control proponents would argue that the accused *should* have to testify because this may be the only way to get to the truth.

A criminal justice system founded exclusively on one perspective or the other would be problematic. Pursuing crime control to the exclusion of due process considerations would inevitably result in an increase in the number of persons wrongfully convicted, because due process procedural safeguards provide the innocent with a strong defence against a false accusation. However, a system that stresses due process considerations to the extreme would result in a higher number of wrongful acquittals: guilty people would evade punishment because the police would be hampered in their search for incriminating evidence. For this reason, the Canadian justice system has elements of both perspectives. But even a balanced approach can result in miscarriages of justice. As we shall see later in this volume, wrongful convictions can—and do—occur, resulting in the imprisonment of innocent people, sometimes for many years.

The ultimate arbiter of conflicts between the two models of criminal justice is the Supreme Court of Canada, the decisions of which are binding upon Parliament and all courts in Canada. The Supreme Court frequently hears arguments regarding the constitutionality of specific pieces of criminal justice legislation and decides whether a particular law is consistent with the rights guaranteed by the *Canadian Charter of Rights and Freedoms*. A law that goes too far in the direction of controlling crime may violate one of the provisions of the *Charter of Rights and Freedoms*.

PUBLIC OPINION AND CRIMINAL JUSTICE

People in Canada (as elsewhere) tend to be quite critical of their criminal justice system. Many view it as being overly lenient and biased more toward the interests of the offender than toward those of the victim. However, this is often a false perception. The media also increasingly report that Canadians have lost confidence in their criminal justice system. But is this true? What do the polls say about the issue? Two surveys, both conducted in 2002, asked Canadians to express their degree of satisfaction or confidence in the justice system (see Roberts, 2006). In one of these surveys, respondents rated the degree of confidence that they had in "the justice system in Canada," using a 7-point scale, where 7 represented a great deal of confidence and 1 no confidence at all. Leaving aside the 22 percent in the midpoint category (4), 46 percent of the respondents expressed confidence in the system, while 32 percent expressed little or not confidence—a difference of 14 percent. On balance, this poll suggests that Canadians are more positive than negative about their justice system. The other survey conducted that same year asked respondents to express their level of satisfaction with the system. The response options were "very satisfied," "satisfied," "dissatisfied," or "very dissatisfied." This range of options permits a comparison of the proportion of respondents with positive or negative views. Just over half (54 percent) were satisfied, and 41 percent were dissatisfied. Thus, the surveys suggest that more Canadians are positive than negative about the system.

But how do confidence trends for criminal justice compare to those for other public institutions? Table 1.1 shows that compared to other public institutions, the justice system attracts somewhat lower confidence ratings. However, the proportion of respondents expressing a great deal or quite a lot of confidence in the justice system is not significantly lower than the proportion expressing similar levels of confidence in the education system. Moreover, confidence levels in criminal justice are significantly higher for the justice system than for Parliament.

We should also not lose sight of the fact that the health care or educational systems have mandates very different from that ascribed to the justice system. The health care system exists for the benefit of the health consumer: the patient. Its activities are directed toward one goal: improving the well-being of the patient, without any competing interests. In contrast, the justice system has a more complex mandate to fulfill, responding to the interests of multiple parties. Offenders, victims, and the families of both groups have rights and needs that sometimes conflict. It is therefore unreasonable to expect confidence levels to be comparable for the justice and health systems. In addition,

Table 1.1 *Public Confidence in Selected Public Institutions, Canada, 2003*

	A great deal of confidence	Quite a lot of confidence	Not very much confidence	No confidence at all
Local business	19%	61%	11%	1%
Banks	19%	49%	21%	6%
Health care system	19%	48%	24%	4%
Educational system	17%	48%	21%	3%
Justice system	14%	43%	27%	7%
Corporations	8%	38%	33%	10%
Parliament	8%	35%	35%	10%
Welfare system	9%	32%	29%	9%

Source: Adapted from Roberts (2006).

the health care and educational systems share a mandate to help members of the public. In contrast, the mission of the criminal justice system is not *primarily* to help victims, but rather to promote public safety and impose appropriate punishments. Judges must discharge multiple mandates, one of which is ensuring that defendants receive a fair trial. Similarly, prosecutors must act in the public interest, which may mean discontinuing a prosecution or not launching an appeal against acquittal or sentence. Predictably, nurses, educators, and military personnel receive higher ratings from the public than lawyers, judges, or members of the parole board (see Roberts, 2007). The public may lose sight of the complexity of the justice system mandate, which may explain why justice professionals receive somewhat lower ratings of public confidence.

Levels of Confidence in Branches of Criminal Justice

The public may be more positive than negative about the justice system as a whole, but it reacts very differently when asked to rate the performance of or express confidence in specific branches of the justice system. In general, the public has a great deal of confidence in the police and far less confidence in other criminal justice professionals. For example, a survey conducted in 2002 found that over two-thirds of respondents rated the police as doing an "excellent" or "good" job, whereas only half expressed the same level of support for judges (Roberts, 2002). Table 1.2 summarizes findings from this survey of public ratings of four criminal justice professions. As the table shows, people rate the police more positively than they rate other criminal justice professionals. Moreover, this finding is not restricted to Canada: similar trends emerge in all other countries in which such surveys have been conducted (see Roberts, 2006).

Table 1.2 *Public Evaluations of Criminal Justice Professions in Canada*
....

	Excellent or Good	Average	Poor or Very Poor
Police	67%	25%	7%
Defence Counsel	56%	36%	6%
Prosecutors	53%	40%	5%
Judges	50%	31%	17%

Source: Roberts (2002).

Explaining Variations in Confidence Levels

Several explanations can account for this hierarchy of confidence. With respect to Packer's (1968) two models of criminal justice, the public is more sympathetic to crime control than due process. Support for this proposition can be found in the results of a number of surveys. A British poll found that four out of five respondents agreed with changing the law to permit the state to retry individuals who have been found not guilty (Observer, 2003). An American survey found that nearly half of those interviewed believed that the criminal justice system treats defendants better than victims (National Crime Center, 1991). Although these issues have not been explored by pollsters in Canada, it is likely that many Canadians share these views.

The public is equally intolerant of obstacles to prosecuting (and convicting) defendants. The judicial system can make two kinds of "classification" errors: it can convict innocent people and it can acquit guilty parties. The aphorism is well engrained in legal thinking that it is better to acquit ten guilty individuals than allow an innocent person to be convicted. In other words, one kind of error is considered much worse than the other. The desire to ensure that the innocent are acquitted explains the many criminal procedures designed to avoid such a judicial mistake. The public, however, appears to be less concerned about the occurrence of wrongful convictions. A British Attitudes Survey asked people whether it was worse to convict an innocent person or let a guilty person go free. Almost half (42 percent) of the sample believed that letting a guilty person go free was worse (Dowds, 1995, Table B.3). This finding reflects the crime control orientation of the public. Although it was a British survey, research on related issues makes it clear that Canadians would respond in the same way. In short, most people favour a justice system that allows police and prosecutors significant powers rather than a system that follows procedural safeguards to ensure that due process is maintained.

Thus, the police are more closely allied in the public mind with a crime control mandate and for this reason receive higher ratings. While the police have to observe constitutionally based rules regarding the surveillance of suspects and the collection of evidence, police practices are ultimately regulated by the courts through constitutional challenges. The judiciary has a more complex mandate. Unlike their counterparts in the continental justice system, judges in common law jurisdictions must remain neutral while the parties to the proceedings conduct the case. In the popular mind, judges are probably associated far more closely with a due process model of justice, one that, as we have seen, attracts less support from members of the public.

In popular opinion, therefore, the mandate of the police is closer to the crime control model of justice. Judges, on the other hand, must strive to protect the rights of the accused during a trial, and prosecutors must consider the interests in justice, not simply pursue the conviction of the defendant. The public is seldom aware of the true nature of the prosecutorial role. Research has shown that many people see the prosecutor as the "victim's lawyer" (Roberts, 2002), and they may be disappointed when Crown Counsel take a position at odds with the opinion of the crime victim. Members of the public are less familiar with and have less sympathy for these elements of justice; and this lack of familiarity may be reflected in their perceptions of the courts and prosecutors.

One final explanation for the higher public approval ratings of the police is more mundane than theoretical. From many perspectives, the police are the most visible of all criminal justice professionals: they wear uniforms, drive (usually) marked vehicles, and perform their duties in public, on the streets of the nation. The public nature of policing contrasts the work of other professionals, such as judges or lawyers, whose duties are discharged out of the public eye. A significant proportion of the population has contact with a police officer at some point; the MORI poll in the United Kingdom found that almost one third of the respondents reported having some contact with the police in the previous year. Yet how many people have contact with a judge, a member of a parole board, or a probation officer? Higher levels of exposure to the police likely promote confidence in the policing branch of criminal justice. The movement towards community policing in recent years reflects this relationship between exposure and confidence. The premise underlying community policing is that increasing the visibility of the police in the community promotes public confidence.

Public Knowledge of Criminal Justice Practices

This section summarizes findings from a review of public opinion polls in Canada about crime and criminal justice issues. I start by discussing one of the most important public misperceptions affecting attitudes toward the justice system. For the sake of brevity, full bibliographic citations for works cited in this section of the chapter are omitted here but can be found in Roberts (1995) or Roberts and Hough (2005).

Perceptions of Crime Trends

Public opinion surveys in several nations show that the public always thinks that crime rates are rising, regardless of whether crime is going up or down or remaining stable. Public perceptions of crime trends are generally unrelated to actual trends. Thus in the 1980s, most people were correct when they responded to polls by saying that crime rates were rising. However, throughout the 1990s, crime rates declined significantly; yet polls revealed that most Canadians still believed that crime was on the rise. Police statistics and victimization surveys tend not to reach the general public because downward or stable trends are not particularly newsworthy. The resulting misperception has important consequences for public attitudes to the criminal justice system: if most people believe that crime rates are steadily increasing, then they may well also believe that the system has failed in its principal function—namely to prevent crime. This misperception of crime trends, then, is probably responsible for much of the public criticism of the criminal justice system.

Finally, most members of the public believe that a relatively large proportion of crime involves violence when in reality violent crime accounts for a relatively small percentage of crimes reported to the police. Most crime involves non-violent criminal conduct, but people tend to focus primarily on the most serious offences, namely those involving violence.

Sentencing

Opinion polls often ask the public to rate the court system and, specifically, the severity of sentences imposed. The percentage of Canadians who feel that sentences are too lenient has been high for more than 20 years. In 1970, approximately two-thirds of Canadians endorsed the view that sentences were not harsh enough. In 1992, the proportion expressing this view was 85 percent. The most recent poll (conducted in 2005) found that 73 percent of Canadians felt that the justice system was "too soft" toward people convicted of crimes (Roberts, Crutcher, and Verbrugge, 2006). However, this perception is often founded upon inaccurate knowledge of the actual severity of sentences imposed. People tend to underestimate the severity of sentencing practices. For example, approximately 90 percent of offenders convicted of robbery are sent to prison; yet fully three-quarters of respondents to a representative survey of the public estimated the incarceration rate for this crime to be under 60 percent (Canadian Sentencing Commission, 1987). Similar results emerged for other offences. Thus, the perception of leniency in sentencing at the trial court level is based upon a misperception of the actual severity of sentences imposed.

Many people also mistakenly believe that increasing the severity of penalties will have an appreciable impact on crime rates. The reality is that such a small percentage of offenders are actually sentenced that the ability of the sentencing process to reduce crime is very restricted. This point has been made repeatedly in the sentencing literature. Ashworth (2005) notes that judges deal with no more than about 3 percent of the offences actually committed. Statistics Canada reports similar trends in this country: a sentence is imposed in fewer than 5 percent of crimes committed because of *case attrition* in the criminal justice process. The term *case attrition* simply means that cases drop out of the criminal justice system. Only some crimes are reported to the police and, of these, only some are deemed by the police to be *founded*. Of the founded incidents, some do not result in the laying of a criminal charge. Of the charges actually brought to court, some are dropped or stayed, and the remainder do not all end in the conviction of an accused. If such a small percentage of crimes result in the imposition of a penalty, the nature of the sentence will have little impact on the overall volume of crime. Clearly, then, the sentencing system is limited in its ability to affect the crime rate.

Use of Incarceration as a Sanction

Despite the difficulty of comparing international sentencing because of the differences between criminal justice systems (e.g., offence definitions and early release provisions), statistics show that incarceration rates in Canada are high relative to those in most other countries. Even with the incarceration rates declining in recent years (see Chapter 2), in 2005 the incarceration rate in Canada was still significantly higher than that in many other western nations (Public Safety and Emergency Preparedness Canada, 2005). Commissions of inquiry as well as the federal government have long acknowledged that Canada relies too heavily on the use of imprisonment as a sanction. Yet the public is often unaware of this reality. In 1999, a poll asked Canadians whether the incarceration rate in this country was higher, lower, or the same as that in most other western countries. Only 15 percent of respondents knew that the incarceration rate was higher here than elsewhere. Most respondents believed that the incarceration rate was lower in Canada (Roberts, Nuffield and Hann, 2000).

Corrections

There is a significant gap between public perception and the reality of prison life. Many Canadians feel that an inmate's life is an easy one and are not aware of the privations and difficulties suffered by incarcerated offenders. Most people are also unaware of the high rates of homicide, suicide, and assault in correctional institutions. One Gallup survey conducted in 1991 found that half the respondents felt that conditions in penal institutions were "too liberal," although fewer than 5 percent reported any firsthand experience in a correctional institution.

In addition, many members of the public believe that if prison conditions were much harsher, prisoners would be less likely to reoffend and risk reincarceration. However, research has shown that making prisons more austere and taking away privileges may make prison life more unpleasant, but it does not result in lower re-offending rates. Simply put, making a prison a very inhospitable place to live will not mean that prisoners will be less likely to return to a life of crime. Preventing reoffending involves ensuring that ex-offenders get jobs and have a stake in the community.

Parole Grant Rates

The correctional issue that generates most public criticism concerns early release from prison. Most Canadians believe that too many inmates are released from prison too early. This view is based to a large extent on misperceptions about the purpose of the parole system. In general, the public believes that most prisoners are granted release on parole and that parole is easy to obtain. One survey found that half the respondents overestimated the federal parole rate. In reality, less than half the applications for full parole release at the federal level are approved (Public Safety and Emergency Preparedness Canada, 2005). In addition, prisoners applying for parole must convince the Parole Board that they are not a risk to the community, and that their progress towards rehabilitation would be assisted by release.

Success Rates of Parolees

The gap between public perception and reality is probably greater for parole and early release issues than for any other criminal justice topic. Intense media coverage of the small number of cases in which a parolee is charged with a serious offence likely contributes to widespread public concern about prisoners released on parole. High-profile incidents influence public knowledge about parole and subsequently affect public attitudes toward early release programs. Moreover, the public tends to believe that a significant percentage of these parolees commit further offences. In fact the failure rate of offenders on parole tends to be quite low. Public misperceptions regarding parole recidivism may also fuel public opposition toward the early release of inmates serving terms of imprisonment for violent crimes.

Costs of Incarceration versus Supervision in the Community

A Gallup survey found that fewer than 20 percent of respondents were able to accurately estimate the cost of keeping an offender in prison. Few Canadians realize that it costs over $80,000 to house an offender in a penitentiary for a year (Public Safety and Emergency Preparedness, 2005). Most people believe that it costs less than this amount. At the same time, just as people underestimate the cost of incarceration, they also overestimate the cost of supervising an offender in the community. On average, it costs approximately $20,000 to supervise an offender in the community—one fifth the cost of imprisonment Public Safety and Emergency Preparedness, 2005). If the public knew how much money the system could save by punishing offenders in the community rather than in prison, they would probably be more supportive of community-based sentences and parole.

SUMMARY

Most people have a great deal of interest in criminal justice issues. However, this does not mean that they are necessarily well informed about the system. While expecting the public to have accurate views of all aspects of crime and justice would be naïve, and while there are areas in which public awareness has increased in recent years, there remain important issues for which further public education is imperative. Crime is a serious problem in Canadian society, one that provokes a great deal of concern and debate over the nature of appropriate crime control policies. However, when evaluating public support for these policies, criminologists should bear in mind what people actually know about crime and criminal justice. Only when the public has a realistic understanding of crime and justice can an informed debate over crime control policies take place.

CURRENT PRIORITIES FOR CRIMINAL JUSTICE IN CANADA

Aboriginal Justice

One current priority in the Canadian criminal justice system concerns the treatment of Aboriginal offenders, who have long been overrepresented in correctional statistics in several provinces. For example, although Aboriginal Canadians represent only about 2 percent of the general population, they account for fully 16 percent of admissions to federal penitentiaries or provincial institutions (Public Safety and Emergency Preparedness, 2005). As Chapter 16 shows, the problem of overrepresentation is far worse in certain parts of the country. Accordingly, there has been a concerted attempt to reduce the number of Aboriginal persons entering custody.

A number of solutions to this problem have been proposed, including the creation of a separate Aboriginal justice system. In 1996, Parliament implemented several sentencing reforms, one of which was directed at the problem of high rates of Aboriginal admissions to prison. A provision in the *Criminal Code* urges judges to consider all possible alternatives to prison and diversion programs, particularly when sentencing Aboriginal offenders. In addition, some parts of the country use sentencing circles with Aboriginal offenders. These circles involve meetings with representatives of the community as well as friends and family members of the offender and victim. Together the participants attempt to devise a satisfactory sentence, which often may involve a sentence served in the community rather than prison. However, as of 2002, these solutions have not reduced the rate of Aboriginal admissions to custody.

Aboriginal peoples are not the only minority group disproportionately represented in criminal justice statistics. The 1995 report of the Commission on Racism in Ontario showed that black suspects were more likely to be denied bail than whites with similar profiles. More recently, in 2002, allegations were made that police officers in Toronto use racial profiling. The treatment of minorities by the criminal justice system is likely to remain a priority for a long time.

Youth Justice

In April 2003, the *Youth Criminal Justice Act* became law, replacing the *Young Offenders Act (YOA)*, which had been in force since 1984. Over the 1990s, no legislation had come under as much public criticism as the *YOA*. Central to the criticism had been the allegation that as a result of the *YOA*, youth court judges imposed very lenient sentences, and that this leniency itself became a cause of youth crime. Meanwhile, during the same period, criminologists were arguing that Canada was using custody for young offenders more often than was necessary. The *YCJA* attempts to address these criticisms as well as a number of other issues relating to youth justice in Canada. As discussed in Chapter 19, the new legislation has had an important impact on the punishment of young offenders in Canada.

Conditional Sentencing

The conditional sentence of imprisonment was created in 1996 to reduce the number of admissions to custody. To many people, a conditional sentence is a paradox: an offender is sentenced to a term of custody but is then allowed to spend it at home, provided he or she complies with a number of conditions. The disposition was created to reduce the number of admissions to custody. Analyses have demonstrated that the conditional sentence has had an important impact on admissions to prison, which have declined significantly since 1996 (Roberts, 2004). Yet the sentence has been used for some serious crimes, such as sexual assault or manslaughter, leading to calls for amendments to the provision. In 2006, the newly elected Conservative government introduced reform legislation which, if passed, would restrict the use of conditional sentences to a narrower range of offences than at present.

Mandatory Sentencing

The federal government has also introduced legislation to amend the mandatory sentencing provisions of the **Criminal Code**. This legislation reflects widespread public concern about gun crime. Residents of Toronto have been particularly affected by gun-related crimes in their city, culminating in the tragic killing of a young woman on Boxing Day, 2005. Regardless of whether mandatory sentencing is an effective and appropriate response to such crimes, it is very popular with voters and politicians. For example, in the last federal election, which directly followed the Boxing Day shooting, the three major political parties all called for the introduction of more or more severe mandatory sentences of imprisonment. In the Spring of 2006 the government introduced new legislation to increase the number and severity of mandatory sentences of imprisonment (Bill C-10).

Mediation and Other Alternatives to the Criminal Justice System

The traditional way to deal with a crime is to use the criminal process. The system uses police to locate the alleged offender, who may then become an accused and face a criminal proceeding. If found guilty to a specified legal standard (beyond a reasonable doubt), the accused will be sentenced. However, this process is not necessarily the best way to resolve the problem. Victims are not always satisfied by the criminal justice response, and offenders are sometimes stigmatized by the conviction in a way that increases, rather than decreases, their likelihood of further offending.

Third-party mediation is an alternative way of addressing the problem. Mediation can take many forms, but it usually involves a face-to-face meeting between the victim and the suspect or accused in the presence of a third party. An agreement may arise out of this meeting that will result in some tangible benefit for the victim (perhaps restitution or reparation). Mediation can also be advantageous for the offender who, as a result of this meeting and the expression of remorse, may end up with a less severe penalty or even no penalty at all if the victim is satisfied with the outcome. Society benefits by saving the expense of a criminal trial as well as the costs of incarcerating the offender. Although mediation does not work in all cases; and there are dangers in giving the victim more influence over the disposition of a case, in many instances, mediation is a more positive response to criminal conduct than the conventional criminal process.

Mediation is a part of a broader response to crime, called **restorative justice**, that is beginning to attract a great deal of attention internationally. Unlike the conventional criminal justice system, restorative justice attempts to build something positive following the commission of the crime. Restorative justice advocates claim that it can do a better job of helping victims and rehabilitating offenders than the criminal justice system, which tends to ignore the former and simply punish the latter.

Problem-Solving Courts

Canada has followed the United States example of creating "specialty" courts that deal almost exclusively with one category of offence. By specializing in the treatment of drug offenders, for example, criminal justice professionals such as judges and prosecutors will become more knowledgeable about "what works" for this category of offender These courts are sometimes called *problem-solving courts*, because they attempt to address the social or medical problems giving rise to the offending behaviour—rather than simply punish the offender for the crime. Specialized courts now exist for domestic violence offenders, Aboriginal offenders, and drug offenders.

Offenders with substance abuse problems represent a unique challenge to the criminal justice system. If the system's response to these offenders is the same as its response to offenders without addictions, drug offenders are likely to return to crime, either as a means of supporting their drug habits, or through associating with others with drug problems. One solution involves the creation of Drug Treatment Courts that now exist across the United States. These courts attempt to respond to drug offenders with both punishment *and* treatment. Offenders who are processed through Drug Treatment Court follow a strict regime of treatment accompanied by urinalysis to ensure that they are refraining from further illegal drug use. Unlike a conventional criminal court, in Drug Treatment Court, offenders are encouraged and praised for taking steps to solve their drug dependency problems. Drug Treatment Courts now exist in Vancouver and Toronto, and there are plans for others elsewhere across Canada.

Role of the Victim in the Criminal Process

Criminal justice systems in western nations are paying increasing attention to the needs of victims, and Canada is no exception to this trend. Although the criminal process remains a dispute between two parties, the accused and the state, the victim should not be ignored. Victims need information about the case, assistance to pursue their interests, and compensation for their losses. In this country, the criminal justice system has introduced a number of reforms at the provincial and federal levels to help victims. For example, victims have the right to submit an impact statement at sentencing and to deliver the statement orally at sentencing. This statement describes the effect of the crime on the life of the crime victim and must be considered by the court when sentence is imposed. This is only one example of the many rights of crime victims in the criminal justice system.

PLAN OF THE THIRD EDITION

This third edition of *Criminal Justice in Canada: A Reader* provides a diverse collection of contemporary readings in criminal justice. The goal of the book is to supplement textbooks in criminal justice by providing readings on selected critical issues. The focus is upon the justice system, rather than on crime statistics or theories of crime. Almost all the chapters have been written or rewritten for this volume and reflect the latest research findings policy developments. For example, Chapter 2 provides an overview of very recent criminal justice trends based on analyses of national statistics collected by Statistics Canada.

Part Two contains contributions from participants in the criminal justice system. These chapters feature criminal justice professionals commenting on the system based on their own experiences. Textbooks in criminal justice and even the most carefully conducted research cannot replace the experience of those actually participating in the criminal process. (This is why I have always encouraged students in Criminology to observe the practice of the system directly whenever possible by going on "ride alongs" with the police or by attending court.) This section of the reader was conceived with this purpose in mind: to provide a view of the justice system drawn directly from the participants themselves.

The text concludes with chapters addressing some of the most important criminal justice issues being discussed in Canada today and which have attracted widespread media attention.

FURTHER READINGS

Goff, C. 2004. *Criminal Justice in Canada*. 3rd ed. Toronto: Thomson Nelson.

Griffiths, C. 2007. *Canadian Criminal Justice: A Primer*. 3rd ed. Toronto: Thomson Nelson.

Paciocco, D. 2000. *Getting away with Murder: The Canadian Criminal Justice System*. Toronto: Irwin Law.

Roberts, J.V. and Hough, M. 2005. *Understanding Public Attitudes to Criminal Justice*. Maidenhead: Open University Press.

REFERENCES

Ashworth, A. 2005. *Sentencing and Criminal Justice*. 4th ed. Cambridge: Cambridge University Press.

Canadian Sentencing Commission. 1987. *Sentencing Reform: A Canadian Approach*. Ottawa: Supply and Services Canada.

Dowds, L. 1995. *The Long-eyed View of Law and Order: A Decade of British Social Attitudes Survey Results*. London: Home Office.

National Victim Center 1991. *Citizens' Attitudes about Victims' Rights and Violence*. New York: National Victim Center.

Observer, The. 2003. *Crime Uncovered*. 27 April, 2003.

Packer, H. 1968. *The Limits of the Criminal Sanction*. Stanford: Stanford University Press.

Public Safety and Emergency Preparedness Canada. 2005. *Corrections and Conditional Release Statistical Overview*. Ottawa: Public Safety and Emergency Preparedness Canada.

Roberts, J.V. 1995. *Public Knowledge of Crime and Criminal Justice*. Ottawa: Department of Justice Canada. (Available on the Department of Justice Web site: http://canada.justice.gc.ca).

Roberts, J.V. 2002. *Public Evaluations of Criminal Justice Professionals in Canada*. Ottawa: Department of Justice Canada.

Roberts, J.V. 2004. *The Virtual Prison*. Cambridge: Cambridge University Press.

Roberts, J.V. 2006 (in press). Exploring public confidence in criminal justice in Canada. *Canadian Journal of Criminology and Criminal Justice*.

Roberts, J.V., and Hough, M. 2005. *Understanding Public Attitudes to Criminal Justice*. Maidenhead: Open University Press.

Roberts, J.V., Crutcher, N., and Verbrugge, P. 2006 (in press). Public attitudes to sentencing in Canada: Some recent findings. *Canadian Journal of Criminology and Criminal Justice*.

Roberts, J.V., Nuffield, J., and Hann, R. 2000. Parole and the public: Attitudinal and behavioural responses. *Empirical and Applied Criminal Justice Research*, 1: 1–29.

CHAPTER 2
Criminal Justice Trends in Canada[1]

INTRODUCTION

This chapter provides some statistical context for the remainder of the book. It is important to have a basic understanding of the stages of the criminal process. For example, how much does the criminal justice system cost? Which sentence is imposed most often? How often do prisoners released on parole successfully complete their sentences in the community? The agency responsible for the collection and dissemination of information about the justice system in Canada is the *Canadian Centre for Justice Statistics*, a sub-unit of Statistics Canada. Publications by the Centre include *Juristat*, which summarizes statistical information about key elements of the justice system in Canada. Karen Mihorean and Rebecca Kong draw upon the latest statistics to answer some of the most fundamental questions about Canada's criminal justice system.

Criminal Justice Trends in Canada
Karen Mihorean and Rebecca Kong, Canadian Centre for Justice Statistics, Statistics Canada

STRUCTURE OF CRIMINAL JUSTICE IN CANADA

The criminal justice system in Canada involves multiple levels of government and comprises three key sectors: the police, the courts, and corrections. Each of these sectors makes certain decisions, ranging from determining whether a crime actually took place to imposing sentence and deciding whether to release a prisoner on parole.

For an act to enter the criminal justice system, it must be perceived as criminal by either the victim or a witness who contacts the police (Figure 2.1). The police must then decide whether or not the incident is in fact a crime. If they believe the act was an attempted or committed crime, they deem the incident *founded*. In contrast, an *unfounded* incident is one for which there are no reasonable grounds to believe that a crime has taken place, and the police take no further official action. If an incident is classified as founded, the police decide whether to lay a charge against a suspect or to deal with the individual less formally by employing an alternative measure. For example, the police may resolve the matter by asking the suspect to write a letter of apology to the victim.

If a formal charge is laid against the suspect, the case enters the criminal court system. At this stage in the process, the courts may decide to deal with the suspect informally through an *alternative measures program*. However, if the case goes to court, it can either be *plea bargained* to avoid the formal court process or be taken to trial. Once the case goes to trial, the lawyers and accused must decide whether to proceed by judge alone or by judge and jury. From there, three results can occur: the judge or judge and jury can find the accused guilty or not guilty, or the judge can stay the proceedings.[2]

Depending on the seriousness of the crime, an accused found guilty can be sentenced to a term of incarceration, a conditional sentence of imprisonment, a period of probation, a fine, or some combination of these sentencing options. If the offender is sentenced to a term of incarceration, a conditional sentence, or a period of probation, he or she enters the corrections and parole system. If sentenced to incarceration, depending on the length of the sentence, the offender will either serve their time in a provincial/territorial institution (for terms of less than two years) or federal institution (for terms of two years or more). Prior to the termination of their sentence, inmates can be paroled to serve part of their sentence in the community. For example, most prisoners are eligible for day parole after serving one-sixth or six months of their sentence, for full parole after completing one-third of their sentence, and for statutory release after completing two-thirds of their sentence. The goal of these release options is to assist prisoners to re-integrate into society.

COSTS OF THE CRIMINAL JUSTICE SYSTEM

In 2002/03, the most recent year for which spending data are available for all sectors, over $12 billion was spent on administering policing, courts, legal aid, prosecutions and adult corrections in Canada, amounting to $399 per Canadian. Among the five sectors, policing represented the largest expenditure at 61 percent, followed by adult corrections (22 percent), courts (9 percent),

Figure 2.1 *Flow through the Canadian Criminal Justice System*

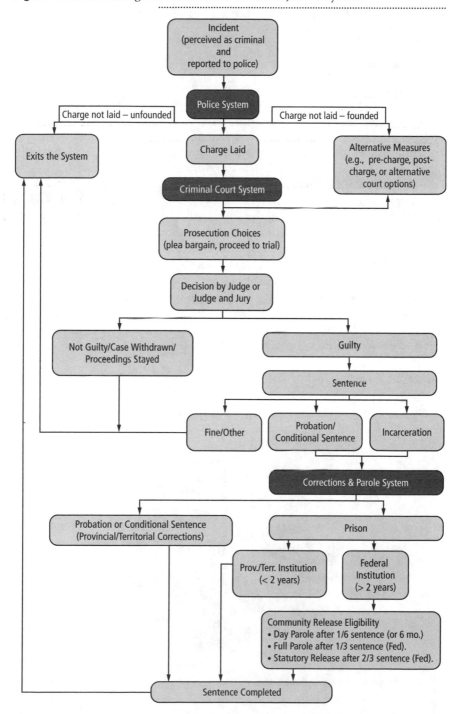

legal aid (5 percent), and criminal prosecutions (3 percent). The distribution of justice spending among the sectors has remained relatively unchanged over the past number of years (Figure 2.2).

DIVERSION AND ALTERNATIVE MEASURES

Diversion and alternative measures programs are alternatives to the formal criminal justice process. These programs can be invoked by criminal justice officials at various stages of the criminal justice system, from the point of first contact with the police through to sentencing by the courts. Such programs are administered differently from one jurisdiction to another, and these differences can include variations in the types and number of programs available and the criteria which make an individual eligible for alternative measures.

Acts of Parliament have formalized diversion programs for both youths and adults. Up to April 1, 2003, the *Young Offenders Act (YOA)*, the legislation governing the youth criminal justice system, provided for alternative measures for teenage offenders. On April 1, 2003, this legislation was replaced with the *Youth Criminal Justice Act (YCJA)*. The new legislation incorporates alternative measures into the *extrajudicial measures scheme*, which aims to provide greater guidance on the use, type, and objectives of diversion. Alternative measures for youths are currently known as *extrajudicial sanctions*. The *YCJA* also includes other diversionary measures, namely police warnings and referrals and Crown cautions. The proclamation of *Bill C-41* in 1996 established an

Figure 2.2 *Criminal Justice System Costs by Sector, 2002/03*

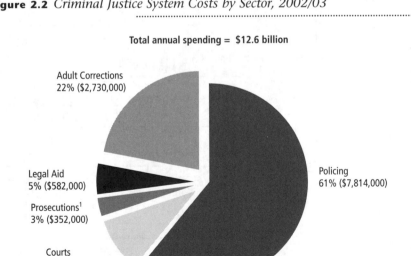

Total annual spending = $12.6 billion

Adult Corrections
22% ($2,730,000)

Legal Aid
5% ($582,000)

Prosecutions[1]
3% ($352,000)

Courts
9% ($1,048,000)

Policing
61% ($7,814,000)

[1]Prosecutions costs exclude British Columbia.

Source: Canadian Centre for Justice Statistics, Statistics Canada.

alternative measures program for adults. Examples of formal diversion programs include community service, personal service, or financial compensation to the victim, and apologies. Depending on the province or territory, the administration of formal diversion programs to adults and youth is carried out by three types of agencies: governmental agencies (e.g., probation services), non-governmental organizations, and Youth Justice Committees.

In 2002/03, about 24,500 youths were assigned to alternative measures (Reitano, 2004). The most common alternative measure was a community service order. The next most common measures were a verbal or written apology (17 percent) and social skills improvement (15 percent). Interventions involving counselling (3 percent), essay/presentation (2 percent), education program (2 percent), personal service (2 percent), referral (less than 1 percent), and supervision by a probation officer (less than 1 percent) were less frequently ordered.

POLICING

The primary mandate of the police is to serve and protect the public. As agents of the state, police officers are granted special powers of search, arrest, and detain. Among their principal duties, police personnel are responsible for enforcing laws, maintaining the peace, preventing crime, responding to emergencies, and assisting victims of crime. The police are also involved in community support and outreach efforts (e.g., drug awareness programs and impaired driving campaigns). They are employed by municipal, provincial, and federal governments.

While the federal government is responsible for criminal law, under the *Constitution Act*, each province and territory assumes responsibility for its own policing at the provincial, territorial, and municipal levels. Further, many First Nations communities also administer their own police service. The federal government, through the Royal Canadian Mounted Police (RCMP), is responsible for enforcing federal statutes in each province and territory, and for providing services such as forensic laboratories, identification services, the Canadian Police Information Centre (CPIC), and the Canadian Police College.

Provincial policing involves enforcement of the *Criminal Code* and provincial statutes within areas of a province not served by a municipal police service (i.e., rural areas and small towns). In some cases, police boundaries may overlap. For example, in some areas, provincial police perform traffic duties on major provincial thoroughfares that pass through municipal jurisdictions.

The RCMP provides provincial/territorial policing and community policing services in all provinces and territories except Quebec and Ontario. These two provinces maintain their own provincial police services: the Sûreté du Québec and the Ontario Provincial Police. In Ontario and Quebec, the RCMP provides policing only with respect to federal matters. Where a provincial policing contract is granted to the RCMP, the RCMP automatically assumes the provincial policing powers.

Municipal policing consists of enforcement of the *Criminal Code*, provincial statutes, and municipal bylaws within the boundaries of a municipality or several adjoining municipalities that comprise a region (e.g., Durham Regional Police in Ontario) or a metropolitan area (e.g., Montréal Urban Community). Municipalities have three options when providing municipal policing services: to form their own police force, to enter into a service-sharing agreement with an existing municipal police force, or to enter into an agreement with a provincial police force or the RCMP to have them assume policing responsibilities for the municipality. Newfoundland and Labrador, Yukon, the Northwest Territories and Nunavut, are the only areas in Canada without municipal police services.

In addition to federal, provincial/territorial, and municipal policing, there are also various types of First Nations policing agreements for Aboriginal communities in place across Canada. The First Nations Policing Policy (FNPP), announced in June 1991 by the federal government, was introduced in order to provide First Nations across Canada with access to police services that are professional, effective, culturally appropriate, and accountable to the communities they serve. The FNPP is implemented across Canada through tripartite agreements negotiated among the federal government, provincial or territorial governments, and the First Nations communities. Depending on the resources available, the First Nation may develop and administer its own police service, as is the case in most of Quebec and Ontario, or it may enter into a Community Tripartite Agreement (CTA). Under such agreements, the First Nation has its own dedicated contingent of officers from an existing police service (usually the RCMP). Efforts are made to staff these police services with Aboriginal police officers. Demand for more such policing agreements has grown dramatically in recent years. The program currently serves 315 communities through 130 agreements that cover 60 percent of the on-reserve population.

Policing Costs → increases

Controlling for inflation, spending on policing rose almost 4 percent in 2004 (Sauvé and Reitano, 2005). This marks the eighth straight year in a row that constant dollar (meaning adjusted for inflation) spending on policing has increased. In 2004, expenditures for policing amounted to $8.8 billion or $276 per Canadian. In constant dollars, the annual figure is 6 percent higher than spending in 2003.

Number of Criminal Incidents

The workload of the police is largely influenced by the volume of recorded crime. While the nature of police work has evolved to include activities such as community policing and crime prevention, the majority of police work can still be characterized as reactive in nature. The police respond to public calls when a crime has occurred or is in the process of occurring. Even calls for service that are eventually deemed unfounded require police intervention. In addition, the growing complexity of crime influences the amount and type of police intervention.

In 2004, police reported more than 2.5 million *Criminal Code* incidents *but not all crime is reported* (non-traffic), including about 302,300 violent incidents, over 1.2 million property crimes, and almost 1 million "other *Criminal Code*" offences[3] (Sauvé, 2005). That year, the national crime rate of 8,051 incidents per 100,000 population represented a slight decrease (–1 percent) from 2003, when Canada witnessed its first increase in the crime rate in over a decade. Overall, the rate of violent crime fell by 2 percent, and property crime dipped 3 percent. The rate of "other *Criminal Code*" offences grew by 2 percent.

Longer trends show a mix of slight increases and decreases in the national crime rate. Since 1994, the rate of police-reported incidents has generally declined in most major crime categories. The police-reported crime rate in 2004 was 13 percent lower than that of a decade earlier. Compared to 1994, the 2004 rate of property crimes (which normally account for about half of all reported offences) was 24 percent lower. Violent crimes usually account for roughly one in ten reported crimes, but due to their nature, they often require more intensive investigation than other crimes. From 1994 to 2004, the rate of violent crimes decreased by 10 percent. Contrary to these declines, "other *Criminal Code*" offences—such as mischief, prostitution, arson, weapons offences, probation, and bail violations—increased by 10 percent over the last decade. These "other *Criminal Code*" incidents typically account for almost four in ten crimes.

Criminal Incidents Solved by Police

The extent to which police can clear or solve a case by laying a charge is an important measure of the effectiveness of the police in solving crime. In 2004, approximately one-quarter (23 percent) of the 2.8 million incidents reported by police were cleared by charge, and a further 13 percent were cleared otherwise.[4] However, the clearance rate varies depending on the type of crime. For example, crimes that have direct victims and/or witnesses and which are reported in a relatively timely fashion are the ones most likely to result in the police being able to clear the offence. For these reasons, violent crimes tend to have higher clearance rates than property crimes. In 2004, 69 percent of violent crimes and only 20 percent of property crimes were cleared.

Within the broad groupings of violent and property crimes, certain offences are considered more serious by the public because of the level of violence or monetary loss involved. These offences include homicide, sexual assault, assault, robbery, breaking and entering, motor vehicle theft, and theft over $5,000. Among these offences, clearance rates for 2004 were highest for homicide (74 percent), followed by assault (72 percent), sexual assault (59 percent), and robbery (36 percent). Clearance rates were lowest for motor vehicle theft (11 percent), breaking and entering (15 percent), and theft over $5,000 (16 percent). Overall, police clearance rates have remained relatively stable over the last few decades, with annual clearance rates for all *Criminal Code* incidents (excluding traffic violations) ranging from 32 percent to 37 percent.

LEGAL AID

It is important that people charged with a crime receive legal assistance. Accused persons who appear in court without legal representation are at a great disadvantage. However, some people charged with a criminal offence lack the financial resources to pay for the services of a lawyer. For this reason, legal aid programs in all provinces and territories assist low-income Canadians to retain professional legal counsel. In most jurisdictions, legal aid coverage is available for those charged with serious criminal offences. Civil cases, such as family law matters, are also eligible for legal aid everywhere in Canada, although the types of services and coverage vary from one province or territory to another.

Legal Aid Expenditures

In 2004/05, legal aid plan expenditures in Canada amounted to almost $608 million (Besserer, 2006), a figure virtually unchanged from the previous year. In 2004/05, 82 percent of the total legal aid plan budget, or $497 million, was spent nationally on direct legal aid services, of which approximately one-half (52 percent) went towards cases involving civil matters, with the rest going to criminal matters. Direct legal services include the provision of legal advice, information, referrals to other agencies, and representation, including payments made to private lawyers, as well as service delivery by legal aid plan staff. The remaining 18 percent of expenses incurred by legal aid plans were for central administrative costs and other expenditures, including external projects, legal research, public legal education, and grants to other agencies.

Lawyers Providing Legal Aid

Across Canada, approximately 11,000 lawyers provided legal aid assistance in 2004/05 (Besserer, 2006). This represents about one in five lawyers practicing in Canada. Ninety percent of lawyers who provided legal aid services were private lawyers, and the remainder were legal aid plan staff lawyers. Compared to 2003/04, the number of staff in legal aid offices grew 5 percent in 2004/05 to reach 3,192.

While the number of legal aid applications received by provinces and territories can be seen as a measure of the need for services, the fact that applicants are screened prior to applications being filed means the number of applications does not necessarily reflect the demand for service. Changes in coverage and eligibility criteria can affect the number of applications over time. In 2004/05, 755,300 applications for legal aid were submitted in Canada. This represents a 1 percent decrease from the previous year. After peaking at about 1.2 million in 1992/93, applications for legal aid services decreased steadily, falling to roughly 802,000 in 1997/98. Factors such as changes in pre-screening procedures, changes in legal aid coverage, and stricter eligibility criteria may have contributed to this decrease. Following these decreases, the number of applications rose for four years straight. Since then, there have been three consecutive declines.

COURTS

Responsibility for Canada's courts is shared among the federal, provincial, and territorial governments. There are essentially four levels of court (Figure 2.3). The first and lowest level of courts comprises the provincial and territorial courts. These are found in all provinces and territories except Nunavut, and they hear the majority of cases that come into the system. These lower courts are administered exclusively by the provinces and territories. The second level includes the provincial and territorial superior courts that deal with more serious crimes and handle appeals of judgments rendered in the provincial/territorial courts. While judges for these courts are appointed to and paid for by the federal government, the courts are administered by the provinces and territories. The second level also includes the Federal Court, which deals with civil matters relating to federal laws only.

The provincial/territorial courts of appeal and the Federal Court of Appeal make up the third level of Canada's court system. Each province and territory

Figure 2.3 *Court Structure in Canada*

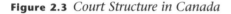

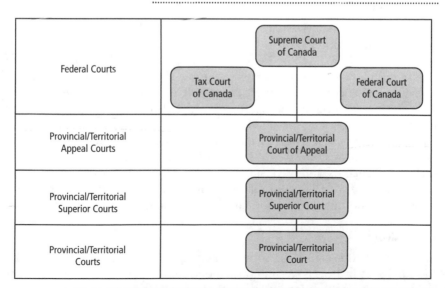

Source: After diagram by Sandra Besserer and R. Craig Grimes in *Crime Counts*, eds. Leslie W. Kennedy and Vincent F. Sacco, 1996, as cited in Snowball (2002a):6.

has a court of appeal that hears appeals of decisions of the superior courts and provincial/territorial courts. Like those in the superior courts, appeal court judges are appointed and paid for by the federal government, but court administration is the responsibility of the provinces and territories.

The Supreme Court of Canada is the highest level of court in Canada and represents the final court of appeal from all other courts. It has jurisdiction over disputes in all areas of law, such as criminal, administrative, and constitutional law. *(handwritten: precedent setting + binding precedent on all lower courts)*

PROSECUTIONS

In the Canadian criminal justice system, *Crown prosecutors* (also called *Crown counsel* or *Crown attorneys*) are lawyers authorized to represent the state before the courts. Responsibility for overseeing these activities is divided between the Attorney General of each province and the Attorney General of Canada. Relative to courts and legal aid expenditures, the cost of criminal prosecutions has seen significant increases in recent years. According to the Prosecutions Personnel and Expenditure Survey, in 2002/03, a total of $352 million was spent on criminal prosecutions, or $13 per capita. Controlling for inflation, this represents a 20 percent increase over 2000/01 per capita expenditures. Similar to other sectors, the majority of expenditures (79 percent) went towards salaries and benefits paid to staff. A further 12 percent was for other operating expenditures, including witness costs, purchases of transcripts, and office supplies. The remaining 9 percent of expenditures covered ad hoc or per diem lawyers.

Youth Courts

Like other countries, Canada has a long-standing history of dealing with young offenders differently than adults, including court hearings and sentencing. In April 2003, the *Youth Criminal Justice Act (YCJA)* became law. The goal of this new legislation is to replace the use of youth courts for less serious, nonviolent offences with *extrajudicial sanctions* (or *alternative measures*, as they were known under the previous law). The *YCJA* also seeks to reduce the use of incarceration, especially for nonviolent offences, and to reinforce the importance of non-custodial sentencing alternatives. The *YCJA* includes several new sentencing options for youth. Non-custodial alternatives to sentencing include reprimands, intensive support and supervision program orders, and attendance orders. New custodial sentences include deferred custody and supervision and intensive rehabilitative custody and supervision orders.

Court Costs

According to the Courts Personnel and Expenditure Survey, in 2002/03, Canada spent just over $1.1 billion[5] to operate the court system, or $37 per Canadian. Controlling for inflation, this represents a 2 percent increase in spending compared to 2000/01 expenditures. Unlike the large increase in police spending, controlling for inflation, spending on the court system has remained relatively stable, fluctuating between $28 and $31 per capita from 1996/97 to 2002/03. Almost 91 percent of court costs go towards provincial and territorial courts. This is not surprising, given the fact that the lower and provincial superior courts process the greatest number of cases in Canada. Federal courts, including the Supreme Court, Federal Court, Tax Court, and the Office of the Commissioner for Federal Judicial Affairs, make up the remaining 9 percent of expenditures. Salaries and employee benefits comprised the greatest proportion of court expenditures, representing 82 percent of total expenditures.

Adult Courts versus Youth Courts

Of the 445,650 cases heard in adult courts in 10 provinces and territories in 2003/04, 27 percent involved crimes against the person (as the most serious offence in the case), while 23 percent involved crimes against property, and 18 percent involved administration of justice offences (e.g., breach of probation or failure to comply with an order).[6] The remainder of adult court cases were made up of other *Criminal Code* offences (e.g. weapons offences, prostitution, and disturbing the peace) at 7 percent, *Criminal Code* traffic offences at 13 percent, and offences against federal statutes other than the *Criminal Code* (e.g., *Controlled Drugs and Substances Act*) at 12 percent.

In contrast, youth courts in Canada dealt with 70,465 cases in 2003/04, the most frequent of which were crimes against property (36 percent), followed by crimes against the person (29 percent). While crimes against the administration of justice accounted for 10 percent of cases, other *Criminal Code* offences made up 6 percent (Thomas, 2005). Not surprisingly, *Criminal Code* traffic offences were less common in youth court (2 percent) than in adult court (13 percent), whereas offences against other federal statutes were more common (18 percent), largely due to administrative offences against the *Youth Criminal Justice Act*.

Number of Cases

The number of cases being heard in court has decreased in recent years, most likely as a result of lower crime rates and changes to the legislation governing young offenders. During 2003/04, 380,978 cases were heard in adult criminal courts in the eight provinces and territories with trend data. This number marks the first decrease (–4 percent) after two years of increases. Although the number remains higher than the low recorded in 2000/01, it is still 13 percent below the 1994/95 caseload volume. The long downward trend in caseload volume between 1994/95 and 2000/01 generally corresponds to the decline in Canada's crime rate and the number of persons charged (Thomas, 2004).

The number of cases processed through youth criminal courts has also fallen. The youth court system heard 70,465 cases in 2003/04, a 17 percent decline from the previous year and a 33 percent drop since 1991/92. This downward trend is mainly the result of fewer cases of crimes against property appearing in youth criminal courts. The decrease in 2003/04, however, is largely attributable to the introduction of the *Youth Criminal Justice Act* in April 2003, which was intended to reduce the use of youth courts for less serious offences (Thomas, 2005).

Length of Court Cases

[handwritten margin note: prelude to Charter + speedy trial]

Despite fewer cases appearing in court, cases are taking longer to process, likely as a result of the increasing complexity of the cases. In adult court, the average number of court appearances per case increased from four appearances in 1994/95 to six in 2003/04 (Thomas, 2004). This has naturally increased the amount of time required to complete a case. On average, adult court took seven and a half months to complete a case in 2003/04, compared to four and a half months in 1994/95. Similarly, youth court took an average of almost five months to complete each case in 2003/04, the longest time ever recorded since data became available in 1991/92. The jump in 2003/04 for youth court cases may have resulted from the police and Crown relieving the courts of less serious cases through the *YCJA*'s extrajudicial measures, leaving the courts with a higher proportion of complex, serious cases (Thomas, 2005).

Conviction Rates

In 2003/04, the accused was found guilty in 58 percent of adult criminal court cases, and another 3 percent ended in an acquittal. A further 36 percent of cases were stayed, withdrawn, or dismissed, meaning that the court stopped or interrupted the proceedings against the accused (Thomas, 2004). In the remaining 4 percent, a variety of other decisions were rendered, such as finding the accused not criminally responsible for the crime or deciding to waive the case in or out of the province or territory.

  Criminal Code traffic offences (e.g. impaired driving offences) were those most likely to end in a conviction (76 percent). In comparison, convictions were recorded in only 62 percent of offences against property (e.g. theft, break and enter) and 48 percent of crimes against the person (e.g., violent crimes such as assault, sexual assault, and robbery).

  Trends are similar in youth court. In 2003/04, 57 percent of youth court cases ended in a finding of guilt, and 1 percent ended in acquittal (Thomas, 2005). Compared to adult court, a higher proportion of youth court cases were stayed, withdrawn, or dismissed (41 percent), and 1 percent ended due to a variety of other reasons, such as transfer to adult court, transfer to another province or territory, or declarations that the accused was unfit to stand trial or not guilty by reason of insanity. As in adult court, youth court cases involving *Criminal Code* traffic offences had the highest conviction rates (69 percent), followed by property crime and crimes against the person (57 percent each).

Incarceration and Probation

In adult court, prison and probation are the most frequent and most severe sentences imposed by the courts.[7] In 2003/04, 35 percent of convicted cases handed down a term of imprisonment (as the most severe sentence), and 30 percent gave a term of probation. About one-quarter (26 percent) imposed a fine, and very few ended in a *conditional sentence* of imprisonment (5 percent) or in other types of sanctions (3 percent), such as restitution, compensation, or an absolute discharge. From 1994/95 to 2003/04, there has been a marked increase in the use of probation and a decrease in the imposition of fines.

CORRECTIONAL SERVICES

Several responsibilities fall within the jurisdiction of adult and youth correctional services in Canada. Some of these responsibilities lie with the provincial or territorial governments, while others lie with the federal government. Provinces and territories have exclusive responsibility for young offenders (persons aged 12 to 17 at the time of the offence) who are convicted in a youth court. Sanctions for youth are determined by the *Youth Criminal Justice Act*. Correctional services provided to youth include *remand* (i.e., detention prior to or during court trial), secure and open custody, and programs administered within the community, such as probation and community service work.

For adult offenders, six primary responsibilities fall under the umbrella of adult correctional services in Canada. These are custodial remands; custodial sentences (i.e., imprisonment); conditional sentences; supervised probation; conditional release; and, parole boards. Some of these responsibilities fall to the provinces and territories and some to the federal government. Persons in custodial remand and offenders serving conditional sentences or on supervised probation are the responsibility of the provincial and territorial governments. Conditional sentences allow offenders sentenced to a term of custody to serve their time in the community under supervision. These offenders must comply with a number of conditions. If the offender violates the court-ordered conditions, he or she may be committed to custody for the remainder of the sentence.

The length of a custodial sentence determines which level of government is responsible for the offender during his or her term. Adult offenders sentenced to a term of imprisonment less than two years are the exclusive responsibility of provincial or territorial correctional services. The *Criminal Code* stipulates that all offenders sentenced to an aggregate custodial sentence of two years or more shall be imprisoned in a federal penitentiary. In Canada, all penitentiaries are the responsibility of the federal Correctional Service Canada (CSC). Most prisoners will leave prison before the end of their sentence as a result of *conditional release programs*. Conditional release is the planned and gradual release of inmates back into the community. The best-known release program is full parole, but prisoners also leave prison through temporary absence passes, day parole, and statutory release.

Quebec, Ontario, and British Columbia operate parole boards that have jurisdiction for all offenders in their provincial institutions, whereas the National Parole Board has jurisdiction over all adult offenders serving a sentence in a federal penitentiary (those who receive a sentence of two years or more) as well as those in provincial/territorial correctional institutions where no parole board exists. Parole boards are administrative tribunals that have the authority to grant, deny, terminate, or revoke parole in their jurisdiction. The National Parole Board also has the authority to terminate or revoke offenders on statutory release, detain certain offenders, and grant unescorted temporary absences for some offenders in penitentiaries.

Federal versus Provincial System Costs

Housing an inmate in the federal system is more expensive than housing one in the provincial/territorial system. For example, in 2003/04, the average daily amount spent on keeping an inmate in a federal institution was $240.18 compared to $141.75 for housing a provincial/territorial inmate. A number of factors contribute to the difference in costs, including higher levels of security required in the federal system, higher costs of incarceration associated with housing the relatively small number of female offenders (Johnson, 2004), and the greater number of treatment programs available to offenders serving longer sentences associated with federal custody.

Adult Corrections Institutions

In 2003/04, there were 186 correctional institutions for adult offenders in operation in Canada. Of these, 116 were provincial/territorial facilities (99 secure facilities and 17 open facilities such as halfway houses), and 70 were federal institutions (Statistics Canada, 2005). The federal institutions comprised 16 community correctional centres, 16 minimum-security institutions, and 15 medium- and 8 maximum-security prisons, as well as 15 prisons with multi-level security. The total capacity for provincial/territorial institutions was 23,657 individuals, and federal prisons had a capacity for 14,660 offenders.

On an average day in 2003/04, there were 154,606 adults in custody or under community supervision (Beattie, 2005). The majority (79 percent) were being supervised in the community on probation (100,993), conditional sentence (13,632), or community release (7,974). The remaining 21 percent were either serving a sentence of imprisonment (9,844 in provincial custody and 12,641 in federal custody), were remanded to custody (9,160), or were in temporary detention (361).

Canada's Incarceration Rate

The ratio of the number of people in custody to the Canadian population aged 18 years and older, also known as an *adult incarceration rate*, is a statistic that measures Canada's use of imprisonment. In 2003/04, the adult incarceration rate was at its lowest since 1981/82—130 persons in custody per 100,000 population. This marks a 3 percent decrease from the previous year. The 2004/05 figure was relatively unchanged from 2001/02 (133 per 100,000) and represented a 16 percent decrease from 1994/95 (155 per 100,000). These declines coincide with the general drop in crime rates in Canada.

Offenders in Sentenced Custody versus Pretrial Detention

While the number of offenders serving custodial sentences has been decreasing for both provincial/territorial and federal custody, counts for remand and community supervision have been rising. From 1994/95 to 2003/04, the overall adult correctional population grew by 5 percent, with the average daily count of offenders on community supervision growing by almost 8 percent and the population in any type of custody falling 5 percent. Although the numbers of offenders serving sentences of imprisonment in the federal or provincial/territorial correctional systems have decreased (–9 percent and –31 percent, respectively) in the 10-year period, the number of offenders remanded into custody for pre-trial detention has climbed 72 percent from 5,327 in 1994/95 to 9,160 in 2003/04.

The number of persons in remand has grown for several reasons: the 1997 amendments to the *Criminal Code* which widened the grounds for justifying pretrial detention; the increased proportion of violent crime offenders compared to nonviolent offenders; and the longer court processing times which lead to increased durations in remand (Johnson, 2003).

Parole Grant Rate

Due to the declining average number of offenders in custody, the number of applications for parole has decreased, as have the number of offenders on parole. However, there is also evidence that in some jurisdictions, the rate at which parole is granted by parole boards is down. For instance, the rate (though not the total number) at which full parole is granted by the provincial parole board in Quebec fell steadily from 66 percent in 1999/00 to 47 percent in 2003/04 (Statistics Canada, 2005). The grant rate for full parole by Ontario's parole board has slid from 28 percent to 22 percent during this same time period.[8] The National Parole Board, which is responsible for federally sentenced offenders as well as provincially sentenced offenders outside of Quebec, Ontario, and British Columbia, has changed its grant rates for day and full parole less dramatically. The grant rate for full parole for federal offenders has remained relatively stable, moving from 43 percent in 1999/00 to 45 percent in 2003/04, while the rate for provincial offenders has inched up from 61 percent to 65 percent. There has also been little fluctuation in grant rates for day parole by the National Parole Board (from 72 percent to 74 percent for federal offenders, and from 76 percent to 73 percent for provincial offenders).

Parole Success Rates

The vast majority of offenders released on parole complete their parole successfully. For instance, in 2003/04, 76 percent of full paroles granted by Quebec and Ontario Parole Boards were terminated simply because their term expired, meaning the offenders were successful parolees who did not have their paroles terminated because of a breach of conditions of their release or because of reoffending (Statistics Canada, 2005). This is referred to as the parole *success rate*. At the federal level, 75 percent of provincially sentenced offenders whose full parole ended in 2003/04 completed their parole successfully, whereas 23 percent had their parole revoked because they breached conditions of their parole, as well as another 2 percent for commission of a criminal offence. The success rate for provincially sentenced offenders on day parole was 80 percent. For federally sentenced offenders, 73 percent completed their full parole successfully, 18 percent had it revoked due to breach of conditions and another 9 percent due to commission of an offence; and a further 83 percent were successful in completing their day parole.

Youth Corrections

The *Youth Criminal Justice Act*, which came into force April 1, 2003, emphasizes diverting youth from the criminal justice system and reserves sentences of custody for only the most serious offenders. The new law has had a dramatic effect on the number of youth in prison. In 2003/04, the number of youth aged 12 to 17 years admitted to correctional services dropped 25 percent overall compared to the previous year (Calverley, 2006). This includes a 46 percent decrease in the number admitted to open custody and a 43 percent decline in youths admitted to secure custody. Admissions to remand (–13 percent) and to probation (–40 percent) also fell. Other factors have also contributed to the decline of youth in the correctional system, such as overall declines in the crime rate and the number of youth charged with criminal offences (Sauvé, 2005). On an average day in 2003/04, there were 23,400 young persons either in custody or on supervised probation. Nine out of ten young persons in correctional services (91 percent) were on probation, while 6 percent were in sentenced custody, and 3 percent were in pretrial detention (i.e., remand). The rate at which Canada incarcerates youth has been declining. In 2003/04, the youth incarceration rate stood at 9 per 10,000 youth. This represents a 30 percent decrease from the previous year and a 55 percent drop from 1994/95.

DISCUSSION QUESTIONS

1. *How does this overview of trends in criminal justice differ from your perceptions? That is, is there any specific finding which surprised you more than the others?*
2. *Women are still underrepresented in the police services across Canada, accounting for fewer than one officer in five. In your view, what explanations account for this gender imbalance?*

FURTHER READING

Gannon et al., 2005. *Criminal Justice Indicators, 2005*. Catalogue 85-227-XIE. Ottawa: Statistics Canada.

REFERENCES

Beattie, K. 2005. Adult correctional services in Canada, 2003/04. *Juristat*, 25 (8). Catalogue 85-002XIE. Ottawa: Statistics Canada.

Besserer, S. 2006. *Legal Aid in Canada: Resource and Caseload Statistics 2004/05*. Catalogue 85F0015XIE. Ottawa: Statistics Canada.

Calverley, D. 2006. Youth custody and community services in Canada, 2003/04. *Juristat*, 26 (2). Catalogue 85-002XIE. Ottawa: Statistics Canada.

Gannon, M. et al., 2005. *Criminal Justice Indicators, 2005*. Edited by Rebecca Kong. Catalogue 85-227-XIE. Ottawa: Statistics Canada.

Johnson, S. 2004. Adult correctional services in Canada, 2002/03. *Juristat*, 24 (10). Catalogue 85-002XIE. Ottawa: Statistics Canada.

Sauvé, J. 2005. Crime statistics in Canada, 2004. *Juristat*, 25 (5). Catalogue 85-002XIE. Ottawa: Statistics Canada.

Sauvé, J., and Reitano, J. 2005. *Police Resources in Canada*. Catalogue 85-225-XIE. Ottawa: Statistics Canada.

Statistics Canada, 2005. *Adult Correctional Services in Canada*. Catalogue 85-211-XIE. Ottawa: Statistics Canada.

Thomas, J. 2005. Youth court statistics, 2003/04. *Juristat*, 25 (4). Catalogue 85-002XIE. Ottawa: Statistics Canada.

Thomas, M. 2004. Adult criminal court statistics, 2003/04. *Juristat*, 24 (12). Catalogue 85-002XIE. Ottawa: Statistics Canada.

ENDNOTES

[1] This chapter is adapted from Gannon et al. (2005).

[2] *Stay or withdrawn* includes stay of proceedings, withdrawn, dismissed, and discharged at preliminary inquiry. These decisions all refer to the court stopping or interrupting criminal proceedings against the accused.

[3] The category "Other *Criminal Code* offences" includes mischief, counterfeiting currency, bail violations, disturbing the peace, offensive weapons offences, prostitution, and other offences not included within the categories of violent and property crime.

[4] The category "Cleared otherwise" includes those incidents where an accused is identified but not charged for one of the following reasons: complainant request, departmental discretion, suicide of accused, death of the accused, death of the complainant, reasons beyond the control of the department, diplomatic immunity, age of accused (less than 12 years old), committal of the accused to a mental hospital, involvement of accused in other incidents, prior sentencing of accused, and admittance into a diversionary program.

5 Includes provincial/territorial courts and federal courts.

6 Data exclude Manitoba, the Northwest Territories, and Nunavut. In cases where there is more than one charge, the cases are classified according to the "most serious offence." All charges are ranked according to an offence seriousness scale which is based on the average length of prison sentence imposed on guilty charges between 1994–95 and 2000–01.

7 Where cases involve more than one type of sanction, cases can be categorized according to the "most serious sentence," meaning cases are ranked from the most to least restrictive sanction.

8 Although British Columbia also has its own parole board, statistics on grant rates are unavailable.

PART TWO
Voices of Actors in the Criminal Justice System

CHAPTER 3
The Role of the Prosecutor

INTRODUCTION

Most people are familiar with the role and function of a defence counsel: to argue the accused's side against the case of the state. This means rebutting evidence against the accused wherever possible and advancing the interests of the accused's right through to the sentencing hearing (in the event of a conviction). At the sentencing hearing, the defence proposes a sentence that would be in the best interests of the accused, and his or her representation of the accused may not stop here if an appeal of the conviction or sentence is launched.

The role of the Crown is less well known. In this chapter, Brian Manarin, an experienced Crown attorney in the province of Ontario, uses his experience to illustrate the role of the Crown or prosecutor. He discusses the various decisions that confront a Crown counsel, such as determining the charge to be laid (including whether it is in the public interest to proceed with a prosecution at all) and the advisability of bail for the accused person, and submitting evidence on sentencing.

Role of the Prosecutor[1]
Brian Manarin, Crown Counsel

The vast majority of criminal misconduct cases in Canada are prosecuted in the lower level provincial division courts. If one pictures an inverted funnel, with the provincial courts representing the wide opening at the bottom and the Supreme Court of Canada representing the narrow spout at the top, one can better appreciate just how busy the provincial courts really are.

Crown attorneys (and any assistant Crown attorneys in their charge) are lawyers responsible for preparing and prosecuting cases for alleged criminal and quasi-criminal offences occurring within the province in which they are employed. Although countless statutes govern allegations of criminal conduct, the preeminent legislation that governs the prosecution of criminal offences in Canada is known simply as the *Criminal Code*.[2] Within this lengthy federal statute is a detailed sketch of what Parliament considers to be acceptable and unacceptable conduct in civilized Canadian society. The *Criminal Code* of Canada can be considered the catalyst behind all criminal prosecutions that take place in the country.

The majority of prosecutors earn their living in the courtroom. Their role focuses on searching for the truth during the trial process. However, many issues that are integral to the administration of justice are dealt with far from the courtroom. Other prosecutorial responsibilities include drafting court documents and providing professional advice to the police, related agencies, and the general public on criminal matters. In addition, prosecutors must possess a thorough knowledge of criminal law and procedure and the rules of evidence, as well as a strong comprehension of the workings of the *Canadian Charter of Rights and Freedoms*,[3] the supreme law landing Canada. Finally, prosecutors must bring superior judgment and a healthy degree of common sense to their workday duties.

What distinguishes prosecutors from any other type of lawyer is their role in the trial process. The parties to any criminal prosecution are Her Majesty the Queen on the one side and those accused of committing the offences on the other (Wijesinha and Young, 1978, p. 1). The prosecution must ensure that the accused receives a fair trial. The end goal is not to register a finding of guilt, but rather, to come to a just result born out of the evidence presented at trial. Without a doubt, the best definition of the role of the Crown can be found in the often-quoted words of Mr. Justice Rand of the Supreme Court of Canada in the case of *Boucher v. R*[4]:

> It cannot be over-emphasized that the purpose of a criminal prosecution is not to obtain a conviction; it is to lay before a jury what the Crown considers to be credible evidence relevant to what is alleged to be a crime. Counsel have a duty to see that all available legal proof of the facts is presented: it should be done firmly and pressed to its legitimate strength, but it must also be done fairly. The role of the prosecutor excludes any notion of winning or losing; his function is a matter of public duty: in civil life there can be none charged with greater personal responsibility. It is to be efficiently performed with an ingrained sense of the dignity, the seriousness, and the justness of judicial proceedings.

The goal of every prosecutor is to meet the high standards that Justice Rand emphasized in his classic statement on the subject. However, prosecutors are human and thus subject to the same foibles and fallibility as any other person in any other walk of life. Putting aside one's passions to make way for moderation and impartiality requires constant effort.[5] Maintaining neutrality does not, however, translate into a lacklustre effort. To the contrary, the Crown counsel, like any other advocate, is entitled to advance his or her position forcefully and effectively.[6]

In contrast, the role of the defence counsel is to be openly partisan toward his or her client. The defence has a duty to protect the client from being found guilty of a criminal offence; and, to that end, the defence may use all the available evidence and defences as long as they are not false or fraudulent. Therefore, the defence is not obligated to assist the prosecution at trial. In fact, the defence is entitled to assume an entirely adversarial role toward the prosecution.[7] Whereas the prosecution must disclose the case in its entirety to the defence, the defence does not need to state in advance what specific defence will be made against the accusation, who the witnesses are, or what they will say on the witness stand. Distilled to its most fundamental, a person accused of committing a crime is presumed to be innocent until the prosecution proves his or her guilt beyond a reasonable doubt. As a result, an accused person has a right to remain silent to avoid the potential for self-incrimination. The burden of proving guilt always rests with the prosecution.

Thus, the prosecution and the defence each have different roles and responsibilities in the trial process. In order to illustrate the typical duties and obligations of a prosecutor practising in the provincial courts, the remainder of this article will describe three sets of tasks that a Crown attorney deals with during a normal week: (1) charge screening and disclosure; (2) bail hearings; and (3) sentencing. The trial process itself will not be dealt with in any direct way.

CHARGE SCREENING AND DISCLOSURE

Although there is always a need for policing in Canadian society, there is not a concurrent need to prosecute all alleged offenders. The decision to continue or terminate a prosecution is among the most difficult Crown counsel must make (*Crown Policy Manual*, 1994, p. 1). At this early stage of the proceedings, prosecutors need to remember the true function of their job:

> A Crown attorney must be ever alert to prevent abuses of the criminal
> process. He [or she] must stand independent between the accused and
> overzealous police. He [or she] must recognize and prevent vexatious or
> multifarious charges being laid or prosecuted. He [or she] must recognize
> unworthy or vindictive complainants and not become wittingly or unwit-
> tingly an instrument of persecution. He [or she] must remain objective,
> exercising his own discretion and judgement, especially in cases that have
> caused public outrage or incensed his community. Cases that have political

overtones, cases that have attained a great deal of publicity, or cases that appeal to prejudices, such as race or religion, must be dealt with in the same fashion (Bynoe, 1968, p. 102).

Screening occurs when the prosecution receives a brief of the allegations from the agency responsible for laying the charge or charges—usually the police or an individual. Screening is an ongoing process and must be completed before a date can be set for a preliminary inquiry or trial. The Crown attorney screens each charge to decide (among other things) the following: (1) whether there is a reasonable prospect of conviction; (2) whether it is in the public interest to discontinue a prosecution even if there is a reasonable prospect of conviction; (3) whether the proper charge has been laid; (4) whether the investigation is complete; and (5) whether an offer of diversion should be made to the accused (*Crown Policy Manual*, 1994:2).[8]

If there is no reasonable prospect of conviction, then the Crown attorney must terminate the prosecution. The test objectively considers the availability and admissibility of evidence, the credibility of witnesses, and the viability of any apparent defences. After considering the issue of reasonable prospect of conviction, the prosecutor must then contemplate the public interest. Although deciding what is in the public interest can be a daunting task even for a seasoned prosecutor (or for the courts as well), the following questions guide the screening process:

- Is the incident in question grave or trivial?
- What are the victim's views?
- What is the age and health, both physical and mental, of an accused or witness?
- Would public confidence in the administration of justice be maintained by the screening decision?
- Are issues of national security or international relations involved?
- What is the degree of culpability for the accused in the grand scheme of the particular offence being alleged?
- Is there a prevalence of this type of offence being committed in the community?
- Would a conviction be unduly harsh or oppressive in relation to this particular accused person?
- Has the accused cooperated in the police investigation, or is he or she willing to do so now?
- How strong is the Crown's case?
- How old are the allegations?
- How long and costly will the prosecution be compared with the likely sentence for the crime?
- Are alternatives to prosecution available? (*Crown Policy Manual*, 1994, pp. 4–5)

Although police officers are required to have a sufficient working knowledge of criminal law to allow them to make arrests and lay charges, Crown counsel must ultimately decide whether the proper charge has in fact been laid or whether another charge should be substituted at the screening stage. Often a changing of charge can result in reducing duplicate charges, since one single action can result in the commission of many criminal offences. In other circumstances, substituting one charge for another can save valuable resources by keeping a case within the jurisdiction of a provincial division judge. Additionally, when prosecutors notice more subtle legal nuances, they can recommend that the police lay a more (or less) serious charge than they originally contemplated.

In addition, neither an accused person nor a prosecutor can truly assess the strengths or weaknesses of a particular case until the police investigation is complete. For this reason, the prosecutor must be satisfied that all avenues of a police investigation have been exhausted before completing the screening process. If not, then Crown counsel must direct the police to complete the areas of the investigation that are incomplete. At this point, the prosecution should invite the defence counsel to point out any other oversights by the police.

Finally, Crown counsel has the opportunity to divert a criminal charge away from the criminal justice system. This means that no prosecution will proceed, and the person accused of the offence will not acquire a criminal record. Historically, a prosecutor has always had the discretion to withdraw a charge or charges against an accused, as described in the *Criminal Code*. Today's prosecutors have the option to use diversion programs devised by the attorneys general, lieutenant-governors in council, or their respective designates in each province, collectively recognized as "alternative measures" by the *Criminal Code*.[9] Generally speaking, if an accused person admits to his or her involvement in the commission of an offence and does not wish a trial, the prosecutor may recommend alternative measures as long as they are not inconsistent with the protection of society. The interests of society and those of the victim are weighed against each other. Similarly, the prosecutor makes efforts to protect the interests of the accused in this process by (1) ensuring that he or she fully and freely consents to the alternative measures, and (2) ensuring that a trial is actually held if that is what the accused desires.

Alternative measure programs may involve the diversion of charges for mentally disordered accused, prostitutes, and their patrons, Aboriginal Canadians, young offenders,[10] as well as minor (and generally first-time) offenders. Each diversion requires the accused to complete a program or act of contrition that satisfies the prosecution's terms and conditions. By offering alternatives, the prosecutor discourages the offender from offending again and prevents a criminal record. Also, the state is spared the necessity of a costly trial.

BAIL HEARINGS

Bail, or *judicial interim release* as it is described in the *Criminal Code,* means the release from custody of accused persons so that they can maintain their liberty while awaiting trial. In certain circumstances, a police officer or a justice of the peace can arrange a person's release (Trotter, 1992). However, this article will concentrate on bail hearings conducted in court where a prosecutor is called upon to make a decision whether an accused person should be detained in custody until trial.

The decision for or against bail is often difficult. Picture, if you will, bail court on a Monday morning where, in addition to the normal volume of weekend arrests, there have been raids on illegal establishments and final "take-downs" of various special police crime prevention projects, resulting in further large-scale arrests. The courtroom this morning is full. As you can imagine, the ability to make intelligent, fair, and informed decisions about the release or detention of each detainee can be an overwhelming task. Digesting the allegations pertinent to each accused person, considering the positions of the police, defence, and complainants, and considering strategy for the bail hearings in such circumstances requires a cool head and a large measure of confidence.

The outcome of a bail hearing is often pivotal to the outcome of the case itself. Statistics show that over 80 percent of all charges dealt with in the provincial division courts result in guilty pleas (Martin, 1993:15). Moreover, experience has shown that persons detained without bail are much more likely to plead guilty so that they may start serving their sentence immediately. Justice through trial seems much less appealing when a person is waiting for his or her "day in court" without a release on bail. As such, it is perhaps at the bail hearing where the prosecutor is under the most intense pressure to be firm but fair.

What are the fundamental concerns at a bail hearing? The court will grant an accused person a form of bail unless the prosecution can show why the detention of the accused person is justified. In fact, law requires that the least onerous form of release be granted to an accused person unless the prosecution can show why a more stringent form of release should be imposed.[11] However, six situations can shift the onus onto the accused to show why his or her detention is *not* justified. Five of these six situations are relevant to a provincial division bail hearing:

1. Has the accused person allegedly committed another indictable offence while on release?
2. Has the accused person allegedly committed an offence involving organized crime for which the maximum punishment is imprisonment for five years or more?
3. Has the accused person allegedly committed an indictable offence and is not ordinarily resident in Canada?

4. Has the accused person allegedly failed to attend court as required on a previous outstanding release or failed to otherwise live up to the terms of the previous release?
5. Has the accused person allegedly committed or conspired to commit an offence involving the production, trafficking, or importation of certain controlled drugs?[12]

Whether the burden is on the accused or prosecution, bail hearings consistently address three different areas of concern: (1) Is the accused person's detention necessary to ensure his or her attendance in court in order to be dealt with according to law? (2) Is the accused person's detention necessary for the protection or safety of the public? (3) Is the detention necessary to maintain confidence in the administration of justice, having regard to all the circumstances, including the apparent strength of the prosecution's case, the gravity of the nature of the offence, the circumstances surrounding its commission, and the potential for a lengthy term of imprisonment?[13]

Although the *Criminal Code* clearly defines when a prosecutor may seek to detain a person in custody until trial, a prosecutor should not apply these criteria automatically. By rigidly following the rules, a Crown counsel can fall short of the standards of fairness that are expected from his or her office. The following three examples illustrate the point.

Example #1
A refugee claimant from Cuba has come to Canada to escape the repressive Castro regime, where he had been a vocal opponent. He has left family and friends behind. Six months into his stay in Canada, he is charged with a street robbery that occurred in an area of Toronto plagued by this type of offence. The identity of the perpetrator of this crime is clearly an issue at trial. No significant injuries were suffered by the victim. Although the accused person has no real roots in the community, he has no criminal record and has two sureties who will guarantee his release on bail and who will, in addition, offer a cash deposit.

Although protection of the public is important, as well as the fact that this type of offence generally commands a lengthy term of imprisonment upon conviction, the foremost concern in this situation tends to be whether this accused will flee if granted bail. With no ties to the community, it would appear that flight from prosecution should be a concern. Should Crown counsel simply point out that because the accused is not normally resident in Canada, he should be detained, and it is up to the accused to show why he should be released? Or do the facts require more detailed consideration?

Although the accused has not yet established himself in Toronto, the prosecution clearly is aware that he has come to Canada to escape his homeland. Why would a person flee to a country where he knows he faces likely persecution? Moreover, there are weaknesses in the Crown's case, because the accused has not been clearly identified as the culprit. The fact that the accused has no criminal record bodes well for his release. For these reasons, the Crown could suggest a form of release without abdicating its duties as a minister of justice.

Example #2
The police are called to a residential dwelling, the scene of an earlier domestic assault by a husband on his wife. The accused had been drinking heavily at the time of the incident but is now sober and remorseful. The accused has no criminal record, and the police discover from family sources that his behaviour was an aberration likely stemming from the loss of his job. Although there are no apparent injuries, the victim is concerned that her husband broke a sacred trust between them, and she fears that he may repeat this conduct if he is granted bail. The victim is financially dependent on her spouse and has two small children to care for. The accused has a surety who will allow him to live at his home, far away from the family abode, while awaiting trial. He will also get the accused some treatment for what appears to be an alcohol problem.

Society's general abhorrence for spousal assault cannot be overstated. What was once considered a problem to be worked out within the family is now understood to be a serious criminal offence that brings with it significant criminal sanctions. Both police and prosecutors realize that an inordinate number of homicides result from domestic violence. However, the truly objective prosecutor must not be influenced by his or her disgust for certain alleged conduct. Although it is understandable that the spouse may fear a repetition of the abuse, all indications reveal that this assault was an isolated incident.

The fact that a strong surety has come forward who can put some physical distance between the abuser and the victim should also alleviate certain concerns. Despite the seriousness of this kind of violence, the Crown counsel really has no choice but to immediately concede that this accused person is a candidate for bail. Although complete protection of the victim can only be achieved in certain situations by denying the abuser any form of release, in this case, a carefully crafted bail order would meet the ends of justice.

Example #3
The accused person is on a police release for communicating for the purpose of engaging in prostitution. One of the terms of his release is that he abide by a curfew that requires him to be in his place of residence between 11:00 p.m. and 6:00 a.m. every day. He is seen by the police staggering down the road at 3:00 a.m. on the day in question, and, upon investigation, it is discovered that he is in violation of his curfew. The accused is clearly guilty of failing to comply with a fundamental condition of his release. Although this is a reverse-onus situation, the accused seeks another bail and can produce a substantial surety to the court. At the time, the accused has no criminal record.

Prosecutors can fall into the habit of rationalizing that since an accused will likely be found guilty at trial, the notion of release pending that foregone conclusion is inappropriate. Certainly, the strength of the prosecution's case is an important consideration when deciding whether bail is a viable option; but in a situation like this one, other factors must be considered. Except for his curfew violation, this accused would be a candidate for the alternative measures program for his prostitution-related offence. As for the curfew violation itself, despite the fact that violating a release condition is a serious offence, it is highly unlikely that the accused would be sentenced to a period of custody. As such, a detention order at the accused's bail hearing would be overly harsh given what he could expect as a just punishment for either or both offences. Sound judgment dictates a further release for this accused person, but with more restrictive conditions.

SENTENCING

Arguably nothing is more vexing for a prosecutor than making submissions on sentence. By definition, the accused now stands guilty as charged as a result of a guilty plea or after being found guilty at trial. In either situation, the accused is at his or her most vulnerable, and so is the Crown counsel. The former is vulnerable because the passing of sentence can result in the loss of liberty as well as the stigmatization of the offender for several years. The latter is vulnerable since the quality of justice is often measured by the submissions of the prosecution on sentence. A lack of impartiality at this most emotional stage of the proceedings can tarnish the entire office of the Crown attorney, not just the reputation of the individual prosecutor. For this reason alone, the role of Crown counsel has been measured on the strength of the following statement: "With the result, as with the verdict at the trial, he is enormously unconcerned" (Humphreys, 1955, p. 748). In other words, prosecutors must remain unemotional in their role without any appearance of desiring a particular outcome.

However, being unconcerned about the outcome of a prosecution is not the same as being apathetic, such as in a situation where the Crown counsel had relinquished his or her responsibility to strive for a just sentence. Thus, historically, the prosecution is expected to display a lack of concern at the end as well as the beginning of the trial process, to acquit itself without feeling in order to dispassionately reach a just conclusion.

The purpose and principles of sentencing are now largely incorporated into the *Criminal Code* of Canada.[14] Entire texts have been written on the subject of sentencing, which makes the topic too complex to discuss in a single article. However, hearings are almost entirely governed by the facts presented, rather than by laws or theories. Therefore, no two proceedings are ever exactly the same, despite efforts to treat like offenders in similar fashions.

One area of sentencing that is worthy of special comment pertains to the *conditional sentence*.[15] Amendments to the *Criminal Code* in 1996 created a new type of sentence in Canada. When a person is convicted of an offence that does not have a minimum term of imprisonment spelled out in the *Criminal Code*, the court may order that the offender serve the sentence in the community. The sentence must be less than two years of imprisonment, and the court must be satisfied that the offender will not be a danger to the community. In addition, the court must be satisfied that serving the sentence in the community would be consistent with the fundamental purpose and principles of sentencing as set out in the *Criminal Code*.

The advent of the conditional sentence means that offenders who traditionally went to jail are now increasingly serving their sentences in the community subject to conditions. But so far, many prosecutors have had difficulty accepting the conditional sentence as a reasonable alternative to traditional incarceration for these two reasons: (1) It is hard to appreciate how the value systems in Canadian society have shifted so dramatically in recent times that Parliament has allowed offenders who would have been jailed before to serve their sentences in the same community whose trust they violated; (2) Due to scarce resources, the administration of criminal justice is ill equipped to monitor or prosecute those offenders who do not live up to the conditions of their sentences in the community. A shortcoming of the conditional sentence is that many judges, defence counsel, and prosecutors view it as a second-class form of punishment. It is bandied about more as a tool for plea-bargaining purposes than as a legitimate form of sentence. Anecdotal evidence suggests that conditional sentences are more often imposed for a guilty plea than they are for a guilty verdict.

How should Crown counsel remedy the misuse of the conditional sentence? The answer is obvious. The prosecution has a positive duty to apply the law as expressed by Parliament and to actively urge conditional sentences upon the court whenever the circumstances dictate. This would be in keeping with the highest traditions of the Crown and entirely consistent with the expected objectivity that goes with the office. To lead by example is to conscientiously discharge the duties of the prosecution.

CONCLUSION

The provincial division courts are the cornerstone of the Canadian criminal justice system. They have been variously described as ungovernable battlefields and as arenas of remarkable cohesion. Regardless, the prosecution plays an essential role in making the busiest of all Canadian courts a functional role model for the administration of justice. By maintaining an objective frame of mind, Crown counsel ensures that the adversarial process works. It is not always an easy task.

DISCUSSION QUESTIONS

1. *As noted in the introduction to this reading, the criminal justice system is attempting to become more sensitive to the needs of crime victims. Some people have suggested that prior to making a plea bargain with an accused, the Crown should seek and obtain the approval of the victim. Do you think this is a good idea?*

2. *As Mr. Manarin notes, the accused in a criminal trial is not obligated to take the stand to testify. But in some cases, it would make the Crown's task easier if the accused were compelled to testify. What is your reaction to changing the rules of evidence to compel the accused to testify if the Crown so desires?*

FURTHER READINGS

Brockman, J., and Rose, G. 1996. *An Introduction to Canadian Criminal Procedure and Evidence.* Toronto: Nelson Canada.

Stenning, P.C. 1994. Current Issues Concerning the Court Process. In Curt T. Griffiths and Simon N. Verdun-Jones (Eds.), *Canadian Criminal Justice,* 2nd ed. Toronto: Harcourt Brace Canada.

REFERENCES

Bynoe, B. 1968. The Role and Function of Crown Counsel. 3 C.R.N.S. 90.
    Crown Policy Manual. 1994. Policy # C.S.-1, Charge Screening, January 15.
Humphreys, C. 1955. The duties and responsibilities of prosecuting counsel. *Criminal Law Review,* 739: 748.
Martin, G. 1993. *Report of the Attorney General's Advisory Committee on Charge Screening, Disclosure, and Resolution Discussions.* Toronto: Queen's Printer for Ontario.
Trotter, G. 1992. *The Law of Bail in Canada.* Toronto: Carswell.
Wijesinha K., and Young, B.J. 1978. *Aids to Criminal Investigation.* Scarborough: Panju Canada Ltd.

ENDNOTES

[1] The comments found herein are solely those of the author, made in his personal capacity.

[2] R.S.C. 1985, c. C-46, as amended.

[3] S. 33, Part I of the *Constitution Act, 1982,* being Schedule B to the *Canada Act 1982* (U.K.), 1982, c. 11.

[4] *Boucher v. R.* (1955), 110 C.C.C. 263 at 270.

[5] *R. v. Bain* (1992), 10 C.R. (4th) 257 at 264 (S.C.C.), wherein Mr. Justice Cory recognizes that passions are not easily stilled, even when considering counsel for the Crown: "[T]hey, like all of us, are subject to human frailties and occasional lapses ... I do not make these observations in

order to be critical of Crown Attorneys. Rather they are made to emphasize the very human frailties that are common to all, no matter what the office held."

6 *R. v. Daly* (1992), 57 O.A.C. 70 at 76, para. 32 (C.A.).

7 *R. v. Stinchcombe* (1991), 68 C.C.C. (3d) 1 at 7 (S.C.C.).

8 Contained therein is a more exhaustive list of considerations that must be addressed by the Crown attorney's office.

9 *Supra* note 1, ss. 716, 717.

10 *Young Offenders Act*, R.S.C. 1985, c. Y-1, s. 4, as amended.

11 *Supra* note 1, s. 515(1).

12 Ibid., s 515(6).

13 Ibid., s. 515(10).

14 Ibid., ss. 718–718.2.

15 Ibid., ss. 742–742.7.

CHAPTER 4
The Role of a Defence Counsel

INTRODUCTION

One of the critical professions in the criminal justice system, and the one with which people may be most familiar from court shows on television, is the defence counsel. Although people know what defence lawyers are, they don't necessarily have a good understanding of their role in the criminal justice system. Moreover, when asked to rate the performance of different criminal justice professionals, Canadians assign relatively poor ratings to members of the defence bar. People appear to overlook the vital role that defence lawyers play in the adversarial system of justice.

In this chapter, Paul Burstein, an experienced criminal defence lawyer practising in Toronto, discusses the professional life of a defence counsel and addresses a question he is frequently posed.

The Role of a Defence Counsel
Paul Burstein of the Ontario Bar

As a criminal defence lawyer, I am often asked by friends and family whether it bothers me to work so hard in the defence of someone who I know is guilty. For reasons that I hope to make clear a little further on, I have never found this to be a very difficult question to answer. However, the other day, my seven-year-old daughter asked me a slightly different question, one that I found myself struggling to answer.[1] She asked me how I could defend bad people. My daughter's question led me to rethink the soundness of the explanations that I had long offered to critics of criminal defence lawyers. Fortunately, after some long periods of thought, I have managed to once again come to terms with this skepticism with respect to the importance of criminal defence work for our society.

In order to emphasize the importance of what criminal defence lawyers do, I think it is necessary to first explain what it is that we do. Simply put, criminal defence lawyers represent people who find themselves accused of crimes. As a result of the proliferation of television legal dramas, most people mistakenly perceive a defence lawyer's job to begin and end with the trial. In fact, most of a criminal defence lawyer's time is spent helping clients long before their cases actually get to trial. Indeed, the vast majority of criminal cases do not ever go to trial. Although the numbers have varied over the past couple of decades, no more than 5 to 10 percent of criminal charges are resolved through trials. If so few criminal cases result in trials, what are all those criminal defence lawyers doing hanging around the courthouses? It may sound trite, but they are trying to help their clients stay out or get out of jail.

THE CLIENT AT THE POLICE STATION

Typically, a criminal defence lawyer's "job" begins long before the client's case even gets to trial. In fact, a criminal defence lawyer often becomes involved in a case even before the client goes to court. In Canada, s. 10(b) of the *Canadian Charter of Rights and Freedoms* provides that:

> 10. Everyone has the right on arrest or detention
>   (b) to retain and instruct counsel without delay and to be informed of
>   that right ...

Canadian courts have interpreted this constitutional right to mean that the police must tell someone who has been arrested that he or she can immediately contact a lawyer for free legal advice.[2] Where a "detainee" (i.e., a person who has been detained) requests to speak to a lawyer, our courts have also held that the police are obliged to help that detainee get in touch with a lawyer right away, such as by providing him or her with a phone and a phone book.[3] For those detainees who call a lawyer from the police station (not all of them do), the defence lawyer will almost always urge the detainee to assert his or her right to remain silent.

Contrary to a popular misconception, even detainees who are not guilty can end up "confessing" to the police while being held in detention. In effect, these "innocent"[4] people provide the police with a false confession. In addition, detainees who are not guilty of the charge sometimes end up providing the police with an account of the events that is confused or mistaken. After all, these people are being held in custody and are being interrogated by very skilled and experienced questioners. More often than not, those police interrogators confront the detainee with overblown claims of a case against the person in the hope of stimulating some sort of incriminating statement. These overblown accusations can frighten an accused into agreeing to a lesser accusation, even if it is untrue. Thus, to prevent the creation of unreliable "confessions," the law guarantees a detainee the right to remain silent upon arrest. The defence lawyer must not only remind the detainee of this right during that first phone call but also help the detainee build the courage to maintain that silence in the face of any subtle or confrontational police questioning. In my experience, the vast majority of police officers, when told by the criminal defence lawyer of the detainee's desire to remain silent, will do the honourable thing and refrain from questioning that detainee any further. To the chagrin of many defence lawyers, certain clients, no matter how many times they come in contact with the criminal justice system, never seem to be able to learn what it means to "shut up"![5]

RELEASE OF THE CLIENT ON BAIL

The other task of a criminal defence lawyer during that first phone call from the police station is to attempt to persuade the police to allow the client-detainee to be released on bail. While the police usually have already made a decision about bail, a defence lawyer's input can help satisfy the arresting officer that it is appropriate to release the detainee directly from the police station. If not, then the defence lawyer will ask where and when the client-detainee will be brought to court for a hearing before a justice of the peace to determine whether or not the client should be released on bail. The *Criminal Code* requires that a person who has been arrested and who has not been released at the scene or at the police station to be brought before a justice of the peace within a day or two of the arrest for a bail hearing. Many lawyers believe that the bail issue is the most important one in the criminal process. Given the long delays that occur between the time of the arrest and the time of trial, some people will have a strong incentive to plead guilty to their charge(s), even when they are not in fact guilty, simply to avoid a lengthy wait in a pretrial remand facility for their trial date.

In preparation for a bail hearing, a defence lawyer will need to help his or her client to find a *surety*—someone who is willing to pledge a sum of money as a guarantee of that person's ability to supervise the detainee if released. In many cases, defence lawyers also must function as social workers or counsellors and help arrange for their clients to obtain treatment, secure employment, or re-enroll in school, since the justice of the peace will want to know that the client isn't sitting at home watching television until the trial date arrives. I cannot tell you how many times I have been in bail court and have heard the expression "the devil finds work for idle hands."

DEFENCES

Win or lose, the bail hearing does not end the case for a person who has been charged with a criminal offence. The next stage in the process involves trying to determine whether the client has a defence to the charge(s) he or she faces.

At the risk of grossly oversimplifying what I do, criminal defences can generally be divided into two categories: *factual defences* and *legal defences*. The factual type of defence involves a challenge to the evidence that the police have gathered in the course of the investigation that resulted in the charge(s) against the client. Perhaps the witness is lying. Maybe he or she implicated the accused in order to benefit himself or herself, such as through a lesser sentence for his or her own charges or for a monetary reward. Maybe the eyewitness is mistaken. As noted elsewhere in this book (see Chapter 19), eyewitness identification is notoriously unreliable.

The other type of defence, the legal kind, focuses on whether or not what the person is accused of doing should be considered "criminal." For example, there may be no dispute that my client shot her husband, but it may have been in self-defence and, thus, is legally justified. In trying to determine what (if any) defence a client has to a criminal charge, the defence lawyer needs to gather information relevant to the case. That information comes from the police reports and witness statements, which the prosecutor is legally obliged to disclose to the defence in advance of the trial,[6] as well as any information the client and other potential witnesses provide. (This practice is known as the Crown providing "disclosure" to the defence.) In addition, the defence lawyer may have to do some research into the law that governs the features of the client's case; for example, whether the police have engaged in an illegal search, whether self-defence includes the defence of one's property, or whether two lovers in a parked car are in a "public place." Once the defence lawyer has determined the nature and extent of the available defences, the lawyer is ready to advise the client how next to proceed.

At this juncture, the defence lawyer presents the client with two options: plead guilty in the hope of obtaining a more lenient sentence from the court as a reward for sparing everyone the time and expense of a trial, or schedule a date for a trial, at which time the client can plead not guilty and contest the prosecutor's case. As noted above, in the vast majority of cases, persons charged with criminal offences opt to have their lawyer try to negotiate a plea bargain with the prosecutor (see Chapter 4).

The term *plea bargain* connotes exactly what it means: in exchange for giving up the right to a full trial, the accused receives the prosecutor's recommendation for a more lenient sentence than would normally be sought in a trial sentencing. This bargaining is often done at the prosecutor's office and is sometimes mediated by a judge. Upon learning the bottom-line offer of the prosecutor, a defence lawyer must always seek the input of the client before accepting or rejecting it. When asked by clients whether I would take the plea bargain if I were in their shoes, I am always left to explain that my risk–benefit analysis of trial versus guilty plea will, by definition, be different from theirs. As I tell them, given the nature of my work, I am quite used to spending my days in jail and am quite comfortable hanging around with criminals. If, on the other hand, the client is one of the minority who decide to reject the plea bargain in favour of a trial, the court will schedule a trial for some time down the road.[7]

PREPARING FOR TRIAL

Preparing a case for trial is very much like producing a film or a play. First, you have to develop the story on which the play will be based. By this, I certainly do not mean that lawyers help clients fabricate stories in order to avoid conviction. I am simply referring to the development of the narrative that takes into account the evidence that the defence lawyer believes will be accepted by the jury (or judge) at the end of the case *and* that is consistent with innocence. That is what a criminal defence lawyer does in representing a client at a trial: develop an "innocence" narrative to compete with the "guilty" narrative constructed by the police. For instance, the police may not have interviewed all of the potential witnesses, some of whom may not only cast doubt on the claim by others that a client is the guilty party but also shed light on the true identity of the perpetrator.

However, the development of a competing narrative is no easy task. By the time a defence lawyer becomes involved in a case, the prosecution narrative has already been constructed. The raw material (i.e., the evidence) is rarely still sitting at the scene waiting to be collected and examined. Nevertheless, a defence lawyer must visit the scene of the crime to discover the competing innocence narrative. Perhaps the one feature of criminal defence work that is fairly reflected on television is the sleuthing that criminal defence lawyers do in the preparation of their clients' cases.

I recall once going to a seedy hotel in downtown Toronto in preparation for a murder case where my client, a young female prostitute, had been charged with stabbing her customer to death. The case was about whether she had acted in self-defence. Thus, her opportunities to escape would play a critically important role in the jury's decision. After waiting for the elevator for 10 minutes down the hall from the room where the stabbing had occurred, I decided to take the stairs back down to the lobby. It was only then, when I saw that the staircase had been locked (apparently to prevent prostitutes from servicing clients in the stairwell and thereby avoiding the $50 room charge) that I better understood why my client would have felt that there was no means of escaping her attacker. This visit provided me with evidence to present at trial.

The next element of the trial drama is the cast of characters, and some are indeed characters. Who are the people who will tell the story to the jury? What is their background? Are they neutral and impartial, or are they motivated by revenge against the client? Do these people have a criminal record or a history of substance abuse? Usually, as part of the disclosure, the defence lawyer receives this sort of information about the proposed witnesses. However, in some cases, a defence lawyer must hire a private investigator to gather information about the witnesses. Unfortunately, even with the assistance of a private investigator, a criminal defence lawyer will never have the investigative resources that were (and are) available to the police and prosecutor. This is one of the principal justifications for insisting that the prosecutor bear the burden of proving guilt beyond a reasonable doubt, rather than asking the accused to prove that he or she is innocent.

With the storyline developed and the cast of characters defined, the defence lawyer must then turn to "directing" the play. In stark contrast to television legal dramas, most criminal defence lawyers do not simply stand up after the prosecutor finishes questioning a witness and begin cross-examination of that witness. Cross-examination must be carefully thought out and planned so that it does not do more harm than good. Moreover, a criminal defence lawyer must also maintain the jury's interest in the case: important points that arise in the middle of a long and meandering cross-examination of a witness will be lost if the jury are day-dreaming. In an effort to maintain the jury's interest, lawyers also use visual aids to illustrate the testimony of the witnesses, such as by diagrams, photographs, or computer simulations. The ultimate efficacy of the "production" in the courtroom depends on the time invested in its planning.

CONSTITUTIONAL ISSUES

While the outcome of the majority of trials depends on the narratives created by the witnesses and the evidence, some trials are not about who did what, where, why, and to whom. Occasionally, a trial instead focuses on the law itself.

One of the most famous Canadian examples is the trial of Dr. Henry Morgentaler. Most Canadians recall that in 1988, the Supreme Court of Canada declared that anti-abortion laws violated s. 7 of the *Canadian Charter of Rights and Freedoms*. What most lay people do not appreciate, however, is that this ruling was made in the context of Dr. Morgentaler's trial on criminal charges for performing abortions. Dr. Morgentaler never denied that he had performed the abortions on the women in contravention of s. 251 of the *Criminal Code*. Instead, his defence focused on the constitutional validity of the law itself. In other words, Dr. Morgentaler's lawyer argued that it did not matter whether or not his client had done what the prosecutor was alleging because even if he had done those things, the *Charter* prohibited the Government of Canada from making it a crime to do those things.

Section 52 of the *Constitution Act, 1982,* known by lawyers as the "supremacy clause" states:

> 52(1) The Constitution of Canada is the supreme law of Canada, and any law that is inconsistent with the provisions of the Constitution is, to the extent of the inconsistency, of no force or effect.

In plain English, this means that the Canadian Government is not entitled to make laws that violate the rights that are set out in the *Canadian Charter of Rights and Freedoms*. Accordingly, a trial judge has the power to strike down a provision of the *Criminal Code* that is inconsistent with the *Charter*, just as the Supreme Court of Canada did when it struck down s. 251 of the *Code* in Dr. Morgentaler's case. This means that a lone criminal defence lawyer, armed with nothing more than a solid legal argument, can make (or, rather, unmake) law, a feat not possible even for the prime minister.

It was not long into my career as a criminal defence lawyer before I started to raise "section 52" challenges to criminal laws that I (and my clients) felt were oppressive and unfair. In 1993, about a year and half after being called to the bar, I launched a challenge to Canada's criminal prohibition on marijuana on behalf of a client who was charged with growing some plants in his house for his own personal use. As a result of a very good plea bargain that quickly followed that challenge, the court was never given the opportunity to decide the issue. However, less than two years later, along with my friend and mentor Professor Alan Young, I became involved in another challenge to Canada's criminal prohibition on marijuana that has since wound its way to the Supreme Court of Canada. Should the Supreme Court of Canada agree with our reasoning that the law violates the rights enshrined in s. 7 of the *Charter*, the Court would declare the law to be "of no force or effect" pursuant to the supremacy clause in s. 52 of the *Constitution*. This would mean that our client would be acquitted of the marijuana offences with which he was charged back in 1995. More importantly, though, it would also mean that no other Canadian could henceforth be convicted of breaking this law because the law itself will be effectively erased from the books.

In some instances, criminal defence lawyers instead challenge only the scope of a particular criminal law, as opposed to the law itself. For example, in the marijuana case, one of the alternative arguments is that the criminal prohibition on cannabis, as it is referred to in the legislation, should be limited to the type of cannabis that can be used by people to get high. While it may sound silly to think that people could be convicted of possessing hemp, the non-intoxicating form of cannabis, the law is unfortunately not so clear. Indeed, the drug analyst who testified at the trial admitted that based on the testing protocol, he would willingly certify a piece of hemp clothing as cannabis, since the clothing would contain all of the elements that the law required for something to be certified as cannabis. Rather than compelling the court to strike down the law, this argument would simply require the court to redefine the law in a way that would produce a more appropriate definition of the "crime" being challenged.

In a similar vein, I was also involved with Alan Young in a challenge to the breadth of the criminal law that prohibited the "Thornhill Dominatrix" from offering her clients sado-masochistic services for hire. She had been charged with operating a common bawdyhouse on the basis that the sado-masochistic services were the equivalent of criminally proscribed sex-for-hire. On the strength of expert evidence concerning its sociological, psychological, and cultural dimensions, we argued that the nature and purpose of S&M activities is not sexual but rather psychological stimulation; namely, the thrill associated with the anticipation and experience of pain (and/or humiliation).[8] Therefore, we argued, the criminal prohibition should not apply as it was properly limited to activities that were specifically aimed at providing sexual stimulation in exchange for money. But despite the inferential support to the argument provided by prior case decisions, the courts reaffirmed their monopoly on being paid to administer punishment and rejected these arguments.

My involvement in these constitutional challenges also highlights another important feature of being a criminal defence lawyer: the need (or opportunity) to study new disciplines beyond the confines of law. For the constitutional challenge concerning marijuana, I had to educate myself on the psychopharmacological, sociological, criminological, botanical, and historical perspectives on the criminal prohibition of marijuana. For the Dominatrix case, I had to become versed in the culture of S&M in order to be able to explain it to the court and, more importantly, to be able to demonstrate why the stereotypical perception of this practice is misguided.

For other cases, I have had to learn about psychiatry, literature, chemistry, toxicology, biology, and even entomology (i.e., the study of bugs). This pursuit of knowledge can be a burden of the criminal defence lawyer's job. Indeed, I recall having to spend all of my Friday evenings, for weeks on end, sitting on a stool in the cramped office of our engineering expert in the "Just Desserts" murder case, in order to learn all about digital image processing in preparation for the case. Then again, this is probably one of the great benefits of being a criminal defence lawyer: the opportunity to learn about things in the world to which I might never otherwise have been exposed.

DEFENDING PEOPLE WHO MAY BE GUILTY

Despite the very long hours, the limited financial rewards, and the general lack of respect from the public, most of the time I love my job. I meet interesting people, learn fascinating new things, and visit places I would otherwise likely never have gone. In many ways, the job of a criminal defence lawyer is exotic and exciting.

Having explained why someone might want to be a criminal defence lawyer and what it is that criminal defence lawyers do, I am left to answer the questions as to how I could defend someone who I "know" is guilty. To begin with, it is important to remember that the Canadian criminal justice system, while good, is far from perfect. One need only pay heed to the increasing number of wrongful convictions that are emerging in Canada (and in the United States as well). Indeed, look back to the media coverage of the arrest of Guy Paul Morin, a man now proved innocent of the murder with which he was charged. But back in 1985, the public "knew" he was guilty. It was not until almost a decade later that the public realized its mistake. Perception is not reality.

The only way to reduce the number of wrongful convictions is to ensure that the system never cuts corners, no matter how heinous the crime. If someone truly is guilty, the system should be able to arrive at that determination in a fair and just manner—that is, by following the usual rules. Everyone must be subject to the same set of rules, no matter who he or she is or what he or she has been accused of doing. Unfortunately, there are many countries where that is not the case. In those places, the rules depend upon who you are or whom you know. These are governments that exist in part because there are no defence lawyers to challenge the arbitrary detention and imprisonment of people these governments label as "criminals." While Canada is a long way off from that paradigm, Canadians must never take for granted their rights and freedoms nor those whose job it is to defend those rights and freedoms. Defending the "guilty" is a necessary part of ensuring that Canadians all continue to enjoy their rights and freedoms.[9] In short, defence lawyers keep the criminal justice system honest.

That still leaves me with my daughter's question of how I can defend "bad" people, as opposed to people who have been accused of doing a bad thing. Why is it that "bad" people should benefit from all of my hard work as a criminal defence lawyer? Why should someone who has a long history of violating other people's rights be entitled to the same rights and freedoms as everyone else? The answer is that for better or for worse, the Canadian criminal justice system is one that seeks only to punish people for what they have done, not for who they are. It has to be that way.

Consider what it would mean to base punishment decisions on whether a person was "good" or "bad." Even in such a system, it would be unfair to punish those who were bad through no fault of their own: for example, those who suffered from fetal alcohol syndrome or those who had grown up being physically abused in group homes after being abandoned by their families. Instead, we would have to punish bad people only after having a trial to determine if they were bad by choice or by circumstances. If we did not care to make that distinction, we would have to be prepared to charge all those who may have contributed to the person's crime of being bad, such as parents, schools, peers, and government. Of course, when I explained all of this to my daughter, she was quick to agree and reminded me that by that logic, I should therefore be the one serving her detention at school, because it is my fault, not hers, that she was bad.

Spoken like the daughter of a criminal defence lawyer.

DISCUSSION QUESTIONS

1. *Consider this chapter in light of the preceding chapter written by a prosecutor. How does the role of a defence counsel differ from that of a prosecutor?*
2. *Some people think that the system is too protective of the rights of the accused. Others believe the opposite, that the state has too much power in prosecuting accused persons. What is your opinion?*

FURTHER READING

Greenspan, E. 1980. The role of the defence counsel in sentencing. In
   B. Grosman (Ed.), *New Directions in Sentencing*. Toronto: Butterworths.

ENDNOTES

1   Being the father of Courtney, age 7, and Nikki, age 4, has taught me more about how to ask and how to answer more "tough" questions than my many other experiences in the criminal law sphere.

2   *R. v. Bartle* (1994), 92 C.C.C.(3d) 289 (S.C.C.).

3   You would be amazed at how many first-time detainees go about choosing the defence lawyer who will represent them by simply going to the section in the yellow pages that lists "criminal lawyers" and starting at the A's. You would, no doubt, be equally amazed at how many criminal defence lawyers were named "AAAAAAAAAASmith" at birth!

4   Whether they are "factually" innocent (i.e., did not do what the police have alleged) or "legally" innocent (i.e., have not done something that actually amounts to a crime).

5   For example, in *R. v. Manninen* (1987) 34 C.C.C.(3d) 385 (S.C.C.), one of the seminal cases on the "right to counsel" in Canada, the accused, a "rounder," is savvy enough to assert his right to speak to a lawyer when arrested on a robbery charge. However, he then proceeds to engage in the following dialogue with the arresting officer:

   Q.   Where is the knife that you had along with this (showing the accused the CO2 gun found in the car) when you ripped off the Mac's Milk on Wilson Avenue?

   A.   He's lying. When I was in the store I only had the gun. The knife was in the tool box in the car.

   Q.   What are these for?

   A.   What the fuck do you think they are for? Are you fucking stupid?

   Q.   You tell me what they are for, and is this yours? (showing the grey sweatshirt)

   A.   Of course it's mine. You fuckers are really stupid. Don't bother me anymore. I'm not saying anything until I see my lawyer. Just fuck off. You fuckers have to prove it.

6   See *R. v. Stinchcombe* (1991), 68 C.C.C.(3d) 1 (S.C.C.).

7   The lag between the "set date" and the trial can range up to a few years. The length of the delay is dependent upon the jurisdiction and upon the nature of the case; more complicated cases require more court time and, thus, are harder to slot into already very busy schedules.

8   Apparently, much like bungee-jumping, skydiving, or white-water rafting.

9   Throughout history, criminal defence lawyers have been accused of being unpatriotic. In one of the most eloquent descriptions of the importance of defence lawyers, Henry Brougham, defending Queen Caroline on charges of adultery before the English House of Lords many centuries ago, said: "An advocate, in the discharge of his duty, knows

but one person in all the world, and that person is his client. To save that client by all means and expedients, and at all hazards and costs to other persons, and, among them, to himself, is his first and only duty; and in performing this duty he must not regard the alarm, the torments, the destruction which he may bring upon others. Separating the duty of a patriot from that of an advocate, he must go on reckless of consequences, though it should be his unhappy fate to involve his country in confusion." (*Trial of Queen Caroline*, by J. Nightingale, Vol. II, The Defence, Part I (1821), at p. 8).

CHAPTER 5
A Day in the Life of a Judge

INTRODUCTION

Many people think that judges simply supervise trials and sentence convicted offenders; but judges have a great deal more to do than that. Judges are required to perform many judicial functions over the course of a typical day. In addition to their in-court activities, they also supervise pretrial conferences, meet with lawyers, see police officers about search and other kinds of warrants, write judgments (quite lengthy at times), and stay current with a large number of areas of the law. The professional life of a judge is not helped by the backlog of cases.

In this reading, a very experienced provincial court judge in one of Ontario's busiest courts describes a typical day in his professional life.

A Day in the Life of a Judge
Judge David P. Cole, Ontario Court of Justice, Toronto

I became a lawyer in 1975, practising exclusively as criminal defence counsel until my appointment as a judge of the Ontario Court of Justice (Provincial Division)[1] in 1991. What follows is a narrative of a typical day in one court at the Metro East (Scarborough) Court facility in Toronto, including its major phases, players, and communications with one another and before the bench. In order to better present what happens in a judge's life, the following explains—from one judge's perspective—daily life in court as court personnel and I go about our duties in dealing with the accused.

When I arrive at the court building each morning, I find on my desk in my office the list of the cases scheduled to be heard that day (the "docket"). On the day that I shall describe (September 1, 1998), I had to deal with the following charges: failing to appear (Mr. Ashbury); impaired driving (Ms. Andrus); breach of probation (Mr. Burns); assault (Mr. Fisher); mischief to private property/prowl by night (Mr. Goode); and two young offenders, K.B. and R.S.[2] On this particular day, Ms. Crisante[3] was the Crown assigned responsibility for prosecuting all the new cases on the trial list. Normally—though, regrettably, by no means always—the trial Crown is given the Crown files ("briefs") for preparation the afternoon before the court hearing.

The paperwork for even the simplest cases is often voluminous. For example, the charge of failing to appear against Mr. Ashbury was legally quite simple: Could the Crown establish to my satisfaction that Mr. Ashbury had an obligation to appear in court and that he had failed to do so? Once the Crown could prove these things, the *Criminal Code* directed that Mr. Ashbury would be found guilty of this offence unless he could establish that he had a lawful excuse for not appearing. However, there is considerable paperwork necessary to prove such a charge; at a minimum, the Crown would need certified copies of the form of the accused's release on bail, a certified copy of the charge that he failed to appear, and a certificate of the court clerk indicating that he had not appeared on the scheduled date. The trial Crown would then have the responsibility for checking to see that the investigating police officer (or, in this case, the accused's probation officer) had included all the necessary documents in the brief. Failure to do so would likely result in an aborted prosecution.

The Crown brief for the impaired driving charges against Ms. Andrus might be several centimetres thick, depending on the facts and issues raised. It would usually contain the statements of police officers and civilian witnesses, a computer printout of the accused's breath readings, reports from a toxicologist explaining the significance of those readings, and a videotape of some of the time she was in the police station. Also likely to be included would be photocopies of precedents from other cases that Crown counsel thinks the defendant might submit in arguing her case.

Unlike some European systems in which the presiding judge is deeply involved in investigating every detail of cases from their outset, the Canadian justice system is designed in such a way that the judge is supposed to know as little as possible about the cases he or she is assigned. Thus, I would not usually see much, if any, of this paperwork prior to the trial. Similarly, fairly elaborate steps are taken to ensure that I would not be assigned to try cases of which I have any previous knowledge.

Before going into court, I normally do not look at the docket of the new cases I am about to try. On this day, the only cases with which I was familiar ahead of time were those concerning the two young offenders, K.B. and R.S. I had already started these cases on prior occasions, and these were the only cases to which Mr. Kerr, the other Crown listed on the court docket, had been assigned. As the day developed, he dealt with some of Ms. Crisante's cases in order to maximize efficient use of court time. She prepared herself to respond to last-minute arguments that defence counsel in Ms. Andrus's impaired driving case (driving with over .80 milligrams of alcohol per millilitre of blood) had announced he was going to raise.

As the first item of business, the Crown usually calls up the cases that defence counsel or the investigating police officer has not spoken to her about in order to determine the status of the cases. When Mr. Burns's case was called, he told me that he had not been able to arrange for a lawyer to represent him on the charge of breaching a probation order because he could not afford the $25 fee to process his application for legal aid. He asked to have his case adjourned. I examined the paperwork, which disclosed that Mr. Burns was charged with not paying the restitution that was part of a previous probation order. It also revealed that he had agreed several months earlier that he would proceed to trial on September 1 regardless whether he had counsel. If I were to find Mr. Burns guilty, he faced the possibility of going to jail (depending on the circumstances of the breach and his previous record). Nevertheless, given his previous indication that he was prepared to proceed to trial without counsel, I ruled that unless there was some extraordinary reason for him to have another chance to get a lawyer, I would not grant a further adjournment.

Mr. Burns then told me that since the charge had been laid, he had paid off the outstanding order for restitution. At this point, Crown counsel intervened, saying that her brief indicated that while partial restitution had been made, a balance of $200 remained outstanding at the time the brief had been prepared, and that unless she received further information, she was not prepared to withdraw the charge. Mr. Burns said, "My old lady took a hundred dollar money order down to my PO [probation officer] last week."

I told the accused that while, in his mind, it might be true that he had "fixed it ... with his PO," could he please explain how he could have done this while $100 apparently remained outstanding? In response, Mr. Burns simply stared at the floor. The Crown explained to the accused that the probation officer had caused the accused to be charged because, in the probation officer's opinion, Mr. Burns had willfully declined to complete paying restitution when he was in a position to do so. I told Mr. Burns that it was up to the Crown, not his probation officer, to decide whether the charge would proceed, but that we should wait for the probation officer to arrive at court (due to pressure of work, they are almost always late) to further update the Crown.

Mr. Burns then told me that he could not wait because he had to go to work and asked what he "would get ... if I cop [plead guilty] to the charge." Such an inquiry by an accused is quite common and raises several difficult issues for the court system. First, while I told Mr. Burns that I would not and could not tell him in advance what I might do if he were to plead guilty, strictly speaking, this was not true. There are many cases in which I am consulted in advance if a plea bargain is contemplated. I did not feel comfortable doing so in this case because Mr. Burns had neither his own counsel nor duty counsel to advise him. For this reason, I sent him off to the duty counsel office in the hope that the standby duty counsel might be able to advise him. Unfortunately, he returned to court a few minutes later, saying that he had been told that the standby duty counsel was busy and would not be available for some time, if at all.

Surprising as it may sound, many accused enter pleas of guilty despite the fact that they may have legal or factual defences to the charge. They decide for their own reasons, which often seem very sensible to them, that they are not interested in presenting a defence. As a judge, I cannot accept a plea unless the accused makes an informed waiver of his or her rights and is prepared to admit to all the elements necessary to support the Crown's case. In this case, had Mr. Burns insisted on pleading guilty, because he was not represented by counsel, I would have conducted what is termed a "plea comprehension inquiry," reviewing with him his understanding of his right to contest the allegations and his willingness to admit to each element of the Crown's case. If he had balked at any stage, I would likely have struck the plea and remanded the case to another trial date. The practical difficulty that arises is that on the next date, the accused may go through the same process, this time pretending that he is making an informed waiver and conceding the elements of the case just so he can get it over with.

Luckily, by this time, Mr. Burns's probation officer arrived. Crown counsel suggested that the case be "held down" to allow the parties the opportunity for some brief discussion. Although I was not privy to discussions among the accused, the probation officer, and Crown counsel, they eventually presented me with a compromise. Mr. Burns's case would be adjourned for 30 days. If he voluntarily performed 25 hours of community service prior to the return date by way of extra punishment for not having done what he was supposed to do, the parties agreed that the criminal charge would be withdrawn on the next appearance.

This case neatly illustrates several of the time allocation dilemmas regularly faced by the criminal justice system (and the extent to which the professionals are driven by the need to use court time as efficiently as possible). Given the relative unimportance of this case compared with the others on the list, the Crown likely had very little interest in prosecuting Mr. Burns that day, particularly since, being unrepresented, his case would probably take about 90 minutes to try. According to the Ministry of the Attorney General's current guidelines, a court day is supposed to consist of eight hours of trial time.[4] After extensive discussion in our court's delay reduction committee, our trial coordinator has been instructed to "load" 14 hours of trial time per day into a court such as this one. This is based on assumptions—well understood by court professionals though not by some accused and the general public—that a substantial number of cases will not proceed to trial despite having been scheduled as if they would be. As will be learned from what follows, Mr. Burns's case was the first of several that day to be diverted away from a trial.

Moreover, by the time the trial date comes up, Mr. Burns's probation term will have expired, thus making the agreement negotiated on the court date virtually unenforceable. If Mr. Burns does not perform the agreed-upon community service, all that can be done when his case next came before the court (on September 30) would be to process the original charge of breaching his probation by failing to make restitution. Once again, Crown counsel assigned to this court on that date, facing another list containing at least 14 hours of cases, would not likely have much interest in prosecuting the charge.

Did Mr. Burns know or guess some or all of this? Did he put off the day of reckoning by luck or by design? I do not know for sure. Ironically, in our adversarial system, the judge in the courtroom is usually the person who least knows the accused. Apart from the brief series of questions I asked in response to his request for an adjournment, I am not supposed to engage in much dialogue with an accused. (And if Mr. Burns had had counsel there to represent him, he would likely have stood mute, leaving it up to his lawyer to speak on his behalf.) Because of this, over the years, I have learned to try as hard as I can to resist the human temptation to speculate and judge without sufficient evidence.

Although this example illustrates an acceptable way of proceeding, problems can and do occur when cases are not completed the same day that they start. This is particularly the case when the evidentiary portion of a trial has to be remanded to another day, as in the case of Ms. Andrus. The accused's lawyer brought a pretrial motion to dismiss the charges on the basis that she had not been given her constitutionally guaranteed right to counsel.[5] Because of the time needed to deal with the cases ahead of hers, her case could not be started until the afternoon (this is quite typical). The defence counsel's evidence on the motion to stop the proceedings (on the basis that her *Charter* rights had been violated) was already completed. In reply, the police testifying had given most of their evidence. Unfortunately, because of insufficient time, I had to defer the remainder of their testimony (including cross-examination by the defence) to March 4, 1999. After taking ten minutes of court time to deal with the trial coordinator's concerns and those of the lawyers, I determined that this was the earliest date that the time required could be matched with the schedules of the witnesses, the lawyers, and me.[6]

In such cases, in addition to taking what I hope are accurate notes of what is said by each witness as he or she gives his or her evidence, as soon as I leave court at the end of the day, I try to make notes immediately of how I am responding to the evidence as it is unfolding (recognizing, of course, that my preliminary impressions may change during the case). This includes such things as whether I think there is an adequate connection between Fact A and Fact B, why certain questions have not been asked (or properly answered), and, most importantly, what I think of the witnesses' credibility. While I try not to make up my mind until I have heard all the evidence and the lawyers' submissions, the reality of the situation is that given these lengthy delays and the danger of wrongly convicting an innocent person, most judges in this position would be more likely to acquit when the case is resumed six months later. This kind of ongoing resource problem is something that all court professionals are well aware of, and that is likely why the Crown seemed resigned or disappointed while the defence seemed quietly elated when the conclusion of the case is put off like this.

Why were more consecutive days not scheduled to avoid such unreasonable delays? This is a constant systemic problem that can be solved if more resources are available. As a result of aggressively pre-trying cases, Scarborough's courts have made significant efforts toward reducing the backlog of case.[7] However, despite repeated requests, no more resources are likely to be made available in the near future. As a result, cases such as this one tend to "slip through" the system.

What happened in Ms. Andrus's case was this: as soon as defence counsel decided that he wished to launch a "right to counsel" constitutional challenge, the court rules required him to serve a formal "Notice of a Constitutional Question" on the Crown and with the court. This notice must be filed at least 15 days prior to the trial date in order to give Crown counsel an opportunity to prepare to respond to the motion. He did not do so, asking that I permit him to proceed with his motion despite his failure to file it on time (which I have the power to do). He claimed that the reason he did not do so was simple inadvertence on his part. Crown counsel responded by saying that this was "too bad. The rules are there for a purpose. I am sick and tired of defence counsel going about their business as if the rules don't exist."

While I appreciated the defence counsel's apparent candour, how did this help me in deciding whether to allow him to argue the motion? Although I have not seen him for many years, the defence counsel was known to me as someone whose word could be accepted. Was he subtly reminding me, as an ex-defence counsel, that I, too, might have made such a slip and that I should not show him up in front of his client? Was he signalling me that he wasn't really serious about the motion and was just going through the motions of presenting a defence? (After all, "right to counsel" issues are probably the most frequently argued motions under the *Charter*. A counsel as experienced as he surely would have noticed the issue earlier. From what I know of the case to date, that should have been easy.) Or was he signalling perhaps that his client was not paying him as quickly as he would have liked and that he was "playing hardball" with her, refusing to file the motion until she had completed paying his retainer?

And how should I have responded to the Crown's position? Should she, as soon as she realized that the defence had filed a motion, have filed a written application to dismiss it as being beyond the time frame allotted by the rules of procedure? That is doubtful unless this was an extremely serious case; and apart from the clerk in the office making sure that the motion was put in the Crown brief, no one in the Crown's office would have looked at the motion until late on August 31. What if the motion ultimately turned out to be valid, and the charges were dismissed for a breach of the accused's constitutional rights? Should I have refused to hear it simply because it was not filed on time?

What have I learned about this for the future? Should I be more careful with this particular lawyer if I see him in the future? Should I modify my practice in such cases to penalize counsel for sloppy conduct by saying that I will hear only out-of-time motions if they agree to pay for a complete transcript if the case has to be remanded to another date? Or might that only penalize the poor? Should I have ordered a transcript so that I am not forced to rely on my substantive notes of the evidence when the case is resumed?

The court clerk occupies a very important position. In addition to ensuring that all the various court documents are located and brought to court each day by the scheduled start time, he or she ensures that each time I make an order, it is accurately reflected in the court records. This may be as simple as ordering that a case be remanded to another date, or it may be very complicated, such as ensuring that varying terms of imprisonment or probation are properly apportioned to each charge. As I write this, the newspapers have reported an apparently appalling case in which an accused wrongly spent a week in jail. This took place despite several supposedly fail-safe procedures designed to protect against this very kind of miscarriage of justice. Apparently, someone had ticked off the wrong box on a court form designed to record judicial orders. Instead of recording that the accused had been given a year to pay his fine of $1,000, it was recorded that the accused had been sentenced to jail for a year. No one, including the justice of the peace who made the order, noticed the mistake.

In order to protect against this very type of error, many of the orders that I make—particularly penalties of various forms—are presented to me at least twice for signature: once when the court clerk writes up what I have said, and again when the formal order has been typed. On a very busy day, I might be asked to sign upward of 50 orders. Although I suppose I could refuse to sign them until I have an opportunity to check them against my notes, the reality is that if I do that, everything will be delayed. If I delay signing remand papers for incarcerated accused, the jail will refuse to accept them, which means that the backlog of incoming prisoners to the jail at the end of the day will be extensive. If I decline to sign probation orders immediately, those placed on probation may tire of waiting and leave the court, not knowing when and where they are supposed to report next. Because I have realized that it causes all kinds of problems if I stop to read each paper in detail, like many other judges, I have tacitly condoned the practice of agreeing to sign them as they are prepared. The result is that I am constantly having such papers thrust at me throughout the day, even when I am on the bench trying to concentrate on the proceedings. In practice, this means that the judge relies heavily on the court clerk and the support staff who type the orders to ensure their accuracy.

The problem does not end there. Despite the best efforts of the court personnel, errors occur because the staff are simply not trained to pick up some types of errors. This week, our court probation officer saw me about a case from some months ago. She pointed out that I had clearly made an error by imposing a period of probation in circumstances in which I had no power to do so. I did not spot the error at any stage (the day had been a particularly busy one), nor did the lawyers (who had urged this disposition on me). What is even sadder is that the accused, a man of limited intelligence, was clearly in no position to realize that he had been improperly dealt with.

According to ministry statistics, in 1997, I dealt (however briefly) with some 2,400 cases. Like other judges, I often worry about cases in which I may have made mechanical errors (such as errors writing the warrant), which may have resulted in an improper process being applied (or not applied[8]) against an accused.

As I have previously mentioned, the trial coordinator has been instructed to put more cases onto a trial list than can actually be dealt with. What happened with the rest of the cases is a good illustration of how this kind of daily gamble works.[9]

While Ms. Crisante was outside the courtroom "brokering" Mr. Burns's case, as usually occurs, she was also able to plea-bargain or divert all but Ms. Andrus's case. Some of the cases were relatively simple for her to deal with. In Mr. Fisher's case, the alleged assault victim (complainant) did not turn up at court, which happens in about 40 percent of cases. There may be many reasons for this: the complainant may have moved since the charge was laid on December 30, 1997, and may not have received the mailed subpoena; or the complainant may simply have decided that, having called in the police to intervene, he or she is not interested in proceeding with the charge.[10]

Even when complainants do come to court, as occurred in Mr. Goode's case, they may tell the Crown that they would be satisfied with a reduced charge. In that case, Mr. Goode, the accused, while drunk[11] and despondent about breaking up with his girlfriend, had hung around her townhouse one night intending to persuade her to resume their relationship. When she spurned his advances, he smashed the windshield of what he assumed was her new lover's car. In fact, the vehicle belonged to, as I was told, "her religious advisor."[12] What the ex-girlfriend wanted was an order for the accused to stay away from her. What the male complainant wanted was the cost of repairing his car. After verifying that the accused had lived up to the term of his bail order that required him not to communicate with his ex-girlfriend, Crown and defence counsel jointly proposed that I order the accused to post a "peace bond." In exchange for having the charge withdrawn, the accused would promise to keep the peace and be on good behaviour for one year. If he did not live up to the conditions of the order (staying away from the two complainants and making restitution for the windshield), he would stand to lose $500 (the amount of the peace bond) and would be liable to be prosecuted for being in breach of the bond. All parties left the courtroom content.

Mr. Ashbury's case raised different issues. Given the carnage on our roads, police forces tend to be very intolerant of suspected drunk drivers. Even where there are few signs of impairment and the accused's breath reading is just over the limit (as happened here), police are under instructions to lay charges rather than sending the accused home in a cab. Because of aggressive lobbying by groups such as MADD (Mothers Against Drunk Driving), for many years, Crown counsel have been under a directive to prosecute vigorously all drinking and driving charges. In part because of their lobbying, the severity of the mandatory minimum penalties has been increased considerably.

Unlike most other criminal charges, large numbers of middle-class people are charged with drinking and driving offences. As they wish neither the inconvenience of being without a licence (up to a year for a first offender) nor the stigma of a criminal record, they are often prepared to invest considerable resources in defending themselves against these charges. Thus, in most cities, there are specialist defence counsel who devote much of their practices to defending impaired drivers.[13] They frequently employ expert toxicologists whose role is to uncover technical flaws in the Crown's case.

Once again, Crown counsel was faced with a dilemma that day. As only one other court had offered help (by now it was about noon), she could not send out Mr. Ashbury's case (or that of Ms. Andrus) to another court. Thus, she was virtually forced to enter into a plea bargain with Mr. Ashbury's very skilled defence counsel. Although I was not present during the plea bargaining (which all happened in Crown counsel's office), having done it myself for some 16 years, I can imagine that the conversation went something like this (salty language deleted):

Crown: If I agree to drop the charge of failing to appear, will your client plead to the over .80?

Defence: Forget it, I've got my tox [expert toxicologist] on standby, and he'll be able to provide "evidence to the contrary."

Crown: Well, in that case, I'll proceed on both, one at a time. Even if I lose one, if we don't finish today, you'll just have to come back. I've got to get something out of this.

Defence: You might lose both. You know these charges have been going since '92, and they might get thrown out for undue delay.

Crown: Yeah, but that's only because your client disappeared and wasn't re-arrested until '97. Besides, you haven't filed a motion under the new rules, so you can't argue it anyway.

Defence: Judge Cole will let me abridge the time. You know these ex-defence counsel....

Investigating Officer: Look, I've got better things to do than watch you two try to out-macho one another. I've been talking to the accused outside. He isn't a bad guy. He's got no other driving record that I know of and the [breath] readings were pretty low. I'm not interested in blood. I'll be content as long as he gets a big fine.

Crown: All right, with this reading, the new directive allows me to let him plead to careless driving under the provincial *Highway Traffic Act*. But he'll have to plead to the fail to appear.

Defence: Sounds good to me. At least, this way, he'll keep his licence. Give me ten minutes to talk to him.[14]

The bargain ultimately proposed was as follows: the Crown would allow the accused to plead guilty to the lesser charge of careless driving. Both parties would agree that the accused should be fined $1,000. The accused would plead guilty to failing to appear; in exchange, Crown counsel would agree not to ask for jail but would join in asking for a fine of $300. The accused would be given six months to pay.

According to the rules that are expected to guide me, I may depart from plea bargains if I find them offensive; but in order for all parties to know what to expect, I normally go along with them. I was entirely content to do so in this case. On the basis of what I was told (unlike some other cases, the first I heard of the contents of the plea bargain was in open court), the proposed disposition seemed entirely sensible, having been made by experienced counsel well aware of the strengths and weaknesses of their case.

During the time that Ms. Crisante had been negotiating outside court, Crown counsel Mr. Kerr was speaking to the continuing cases of the two young offenders (R.S. and K.B.) assigned to me. I describe these two cases in some detail not because young offenders are generally more violent (that is a myth unfortunately perpetuated by those who seek to make political hay through scaremongering), but because they illustrate the range of cases with which I deal on a daily basis.

In February 1997, I found R.S. guilty of armed robbery and aggravated assault. The accused had begun to demonstrate a variety of disturbed behaviours from about age ten. He was hospitalized from time to time, complaining that he had visual hallucinations and that demons were controlling him. He identified his parents as persecutors and from time to time had little to do with them, withdrawing to his room for days on end. One night in June 1996, just after his fourteenth birthday, he told his father he was going to the neighbourhood convenience store. He concealed a knife in his jacket, which he brandished at the proprietor. The accused fled the store, having taken 50 cents that happened to be sitting on the counter top. He was pursued by a friend of the proprietor. As they reached the other side of the road, R.S. was tackled to the ground. He stabbed his pursuer several times, necessitating some 40 stitches. Some of the victim's scarring was permanent.

The accused was arrested a few minutes later. When he was taken to the police station, he gave some coherent responses to questions asked by the officers. Sometimes, however, he spontaneously broke into monologues, claiming, "Kurt Cobain told me that the guy in the store was the Devil, and that I had to kill him or I would go to hell forever."

At first, there were questions about whether the accused was fit to stand trial. After some period of assessment in a psychiatric facility, during which he was assessed as suffering from a severe form of schizophrenic disorder, he was stabilized on medication so that he was deemed fit to stand trial. As the doctors who assessed him considered that he had been insane at the time he committed the offences, he raised the defence of insanity at his trial. I rejected that defence[15] and sentenced him to two and a half years.

The *Young Offenders Act*[16] provides that an accused in these circumstances has the right to have his status reviewed every six months. R.S. has insisted on availing himself of that right (I suspect because it gives him a day out of the facility he is being held in) despite the fact that, for many months, he refused to take the medication that he so obviously needed. In his untreated state, he was prone to assaulting other prisoners and staff, which of course meant that he could not put together any release plan that had any hope of success. According to a report that was forwarded to me as part of his review, progress seemed to have been made. He was now taking a medication that agreed with him (many schizophrenia medications have unpleasant side effects), and the social workers reported that he had become much easier to manage. Through his counsel, he agreed that his case should be remanded for another six months. I assumed that if his counsel felt that R.S.'s progress was sufficient, he would request a substantial hearing, at which time I could be asked to release him on probation.

The second young offender I dealt with that day was K.B. She was born in another country, and her father died in an accident when she was a few months old. Because her mother objected to that society's deeply rooted custom that women should not remarry, she elected to come to Canada, leaving the six-month-old K.B. in her grandparents' care. Although K.B. saw her mother every year for a few weeks, she did not live with her until she was six years old. Both agreed that, as unfortunately happens so frequently in these situations, mother and daughter did not bond well. This was compounded by the fact that soon after they began to live together, the mother became involved with a man she ultimately married.

Sometime after K.B. started high school, she began to go through teenage rebellion, albeit in a very moderate form. Her parents objected to the fact that she began to go out with J.C., a boy from a different culture. They told her that she could not continue the relationship. There were fights, often of a physical nature, between mother, stepfather, and daughter.

In April 1998, the parents told K.B. that she would be grounded until she stopped seeing J.C. The young couple met secretly and persuaded one another that the only way out was for them to murder her parents and get their money so that they could flee to the United States, where they "could live happily ever after."[17] After discussing this for a few days, K.B. let J.C. into her house in the middle of the night. By pre-arrangement, he had a mask and was armed with a large knife that he had taken from home. He crept into the parents' bedroom and started to slash at them while they were sleeping. He nearly severed the mother's thumb and stabbed both parents numerous times, fortunately not fatally. All the while, K.B. remained outside the room, listening to what was going on. After J.C. escaped, the police were called.

Since the parents were initially unclear as to whom their assailant was, K.B. was asked by the police to provide a description of the intruder. She told them that it was a "black youth with a Jamaican accent."[18] On the basis of her description, the police conducted an investigation. As the case had attracted some public attention, they issued a public warning containing this description and handed out fliers to neighbours warning them to be vigilant. Two days later, K.B. was questioned again, and this time she admitted that she had lied. J.C. was arrested and charged with attempted murder. (Ironically, he had confessed to his parents, who had assisted him in disposing of the knife and mask. They, too, were arrested and charged with obstructing justice.)

As this was an important case, one Crown counsel was immediately assigned to all three cases. The Crown applied to have J.C. transferred to be tried as an adult (he was fifteen); that hearing would take place before another judge at Scarborough court.[19]

Crown counsel Mr. Kerr realized from the outset that he had considerable legal hurdles in the prosecution of K.B. The only evidence against her on potential charges related to the attempted murder of her parents was her own confession to the police. Because the officers dealing with the case had not been fully trained in taking statements from young offenders, they had taken the incriminating statement from her as though she had been an adult. Unbeknown to these officers, the Supreme Court of Canada had recently insisted on very high standards of informed waiver before a statement taken from a young person could be admitted into evidence. It did not take long for Mr. Kerr to realize that he could not use K.B.'s statement to convict her.

The only other way the Crown could hope to convict K.B. would be to call J.C. as a witness against her. This could be very risky for the Crown. If J.C. was called without the Crown's knowing what he might say on the stand (he would likely refuse to cooperate with the Crown unless he got some benefit from it), he could say anything, some of which might hurt the Crown's case against K.B. If he was to be a cooperative witness, the Crown would likely secure his cooperation only by agreeing to some reduced charge against him, which it was not prepared to do given the circumstances and the severity of the injuries caused. For these reasons, Crown counsel proposed (and defence counsel was only too happy to accept) to proceed only on a charge of public mischief (lying to the police) against K.B.

Although I was not the scheduled pretrial judge on the day the parties came to their proposed plea bargain, they asked to see me in chambers. This happens regularly at the Scarborough court. The lawyers "judge shop" as part of their plea bargain, seeking to find a judge who will agree in advance to commit him- or herself to a range of sentence.[20] They told me that the Crown would ask for a sentence of 12 to 18 months, but that I should make some allowance for the amount of pretrial custody that the accused would have served by the time I ultimately sentenced her. The defence would ask for probation, arguing that the amount of pretrial custody was equivalent to some ten months,[21] and that was sufficient given her age and Parliament's view of the seriousness of the offence, as expressed by the maximum possible penalty of two years. I agreed that counsel's suggestions were in the range, and that so long as mental health assessments (which I would order as soon as she pleaded guilty) were not devastating, I would not exceed the sentence sought by the Crown.

The accused entered her plea of guilty that same day, and the case was remanded so that mental health assessments and a predisposition report (a social history of the accused prepared by a youth probation officer) could be obtained. On September 1, the parties made their formal submissions based on the facts and what was disclosed in the various reports. Having heard what they said, I told the lawyers that I needed time to think about what they had said and put the case over until after my next chambers day on September 4.[22]

During the sentencing hearing, a joint victim impact statement was filed on behalf of both parents. I accepted it because both parties agreed that it should be filed. As I thought more about the case, I wondered if I should have done so. The report documented the devastating impact their daughter's behaviour has had on the parents' lives. They are both physically and mentally unable to work; it appears that because they cannot pay their mortgage, they will lose their home, their only form of substantial saving. However, because of the accused's guilty plea, I was not, strictly speaking, sentencing her for her part in causing harm to her parents. I concluded that what happened on that awful night only provided the backdrop for the lies that she told the police. As a result, I decided that I should factor in the victim impact statements only to the extent that they would give me some sort of clue to the accused's likelihood of reoffending (the psychiatric report concluded that it was low) and only because they told me that her parents were not prepared to offer her any support at this time.

On September 10, I gave oral reasons, sentencing the accused to 10 months of open custody, followed by 12 months' probation. The lengths of the various terms were tailored around the accused's schooling (school is a real strength for her). Like R.S., she could come back to ask me to review her status after six months of open custody.

This, then, is part of a day in the life of a busy court. It is usually intense, sometimes tragic, always human, and endlessly fascinating. It may even be socially useful.

DISCUSSION QUESTIONS

1. *In this chapter, Judge Cole discusses the issue of plea bargaining, a common practice in the Canadian criminal justice system. Some people argue that this*

practice should be abolished since it undermines public confidence in the jus-tice system. What is your opinion?

2. *Judge Cole notes that the law generally prohibits the publication of the name of a young person facing a charge in youth court. The news media often argue that they should be free to routinely publish the names of young persons appearing youth court. Do you agree or disagree with their position?*

ENDNOTES

1. At the time of writing, the Provincial Division of the Ontario Court of Justice comprises about 260 judges, about 180 of whom preside over 95 percent of the criminal cases in the province.

2. Initials are used because the *Young Offenders Act* provides that no young offender's name may be published.

3. As of the date of writing, this particular Crown's office employs almost 50 percent women, up from about 30 percent when I started as a judge in Scarborough in 1991. This reflects the general trend in the Ontario bar, where now over 50 percent of recent graduates are women. Currently in Ontario, the percentage of Provincial Division women judges is still less than one-third, and even fewer in the Superior Court.

4. I have no idea where the bureaucrats come up with this notional figure. To allow for the movement of prisoners from remand centres to the court (some may be transported as much as 40 km through rush-hour traffic), experience demonstrates that it is almost impossible to start a trial court before 10:00 a.m. Because it is very difficult for court reporters to be able to concentrate for longer than about 90 minutes at a time, on the best of days, morning court goes from 10:00 a.m. to 1:00 p.m. with a 15- to 20-minute break. Court normally resumes at 2:00 p.m., again with an afternoon break. Court usually recesses at 4:30 p.m. to allow court staff to finish their paperwork and prisoners to be returned to their remand centres.

5. Section 10(b) of the *Canadian Charter of Rights and Freedoms* provides: "Everyone has the right on arrest or detention to retain and instruct counsel without delay and to be informed of that right." The Supreme Court of Canada has generally interpreted this to mean that an accused should have the right to telephone a lawyer as soon as practicable fol-lowing arrest or detention. Police forces have responded to this by pro-viding private access to duty counsel or a private lawyer by telephone from the police station.

6. The reason that this cumbersome process took place on the record in open court was that, in fact, there were some earlier dates available. Knowing that the case was already on the verge of being dismissed for taking too long to come to trial, everyone (including myself in an oblique way) felt the need to protect his or her position by saying that, while he or she could be available, it was the other party's "fault" that they could

not take advantage of those dates. Some of the final compromises were interesting. The police officer had to telephone his staff sergeant to get approval to come to court on a date he was scheduled to be away, thereby being eligible to "pick up a court card," entitling him to be paid at double the normal shift rate. He was obviously delighted. Defence counsel and the accused were also content because they could defer the potential day of reckoning by another six months (if convicted, Ms. Andrus stood, at the very least, to lose her licence for a year). Crown counsel, who is currently working part-time, seemed mostly concerned to adjourn this to a date when her child-care needs could be accommodated (so that another Crown attorney would not be forced to take over the case). For myself, March 4 was a scheduled "chambers day," a regularly scheduled time during which I am supposed to read the approximately 500 pages of case law, legislative updates, and other items of interest that cross my desk each week, or to write judgments or articles (such as this one). One of my concerns was whether the trial coordinator could find me another chambers day.

7   Since January 1996, as a result of the police, the Crowns, the Legal Aid Plan, and the judges finding new resources or diverting existing staff, we have cut our backlog by 32.5 percent. However, because we have done so well, the bureaucrats have deemed that we are no longer on the chronic list of courts experiencing extreme delays, and it has been difficult for us to argue that our Crown and judicial complement should be maintained. As a result, both complements have been somewhat cut back, and we are beginning to slip again, as this delay signifies.

8   An example of this arose here. As I was typing this article, I realized that in the case of Mr. Ashbury's charge of failing to appear, I should have at least considered whether to impose a 15 percent victim surcharge to his $300 fine under the *Criminal Code*. These surcharges are to be applied to raise money for various forms of victim support services. Neither the Crown nor the clerk drew this to my attention, and I simply neglected to raise the issue.

9   I leave it to the reader to consider whether this fits the definition of a "working" criminal justice system. Some observers have questioned whether it is "a system" at all.

10 This seems particularly to be the case in charges of wife assault. Consistent with data from other jurisdictions, recent Toronto figures suggest that about 40 percent of complainants do not appear for trial. (Anecdotal evidence from Crowns who prosecute such cases puts the figure even higher.) This is the case despite police and prosecutorial directives mandating "no-tolerance" responses to such incidents.

11 There is some consensus among criminal justice professionals that alcohol or drugs figure in about 75 percent of criminal offences.

12 What he was doing there at 11:00 p.m. on a Saturday night was not made clear to me. Sometimes criminal court offers wonderful opportunities for

creating fantastic fiction à la Marquez or for reciting Shakespearian verse à la Rumpole!

13 The going rate in Toronto for some of the top counsel at the time of writing is about $5,000 per case, not including the costs of various experts. It may even be higher in areas of the country where there is no public transit. Accused people willingly pay this fee because of the economic and social costs of doing without a licence.

14 Variants of this type of conversation occur every day. Depending on the exhaustion level of the lawyers, more bargaining (some would call it haggling) can take place over the amount of the proposed fine. Interestingly, the lawyers would be unlikely to bargain about the length of time the accused should have to pay the fine. For his part, the accused might be less concerned about the amount of the fine; he would likely be more concerned about how long he would have to pay it. This illustrates one of the fundamental differences between lawyers and accused. The former tend to be more concerned about form, while the latter tend to be more concerned with substance.

15 Insanity pleas are quite rare. This is the only one I have had since my appointment. On the other hand, dispositions of "not criminally responsible" (another type of mental impairment defence) are relatively frequent. I probably hear one (usually on consent of both parties) about once every two months.

16 On April 1, 2003, the *Young Offenders Act* was replaced by the *Youth Criminal Justice Act*. The processes here remain the same under the new law.

17 K.B. later told the police that one of her other motivations for the offence was that her stepfather had sexually assaulted her on several occasions. She refused to provide the police with any further information and indicated that she did not wish to have her stepfather charged.

18 The racial stereotyping is particularly troubling.

19 Obviously, that judge and I refrain from talking with one another about our respective cases. Given the seriousness of the matters, each of us might have to solicit the advice of our colleagues who, as always, are generous with their advice. We have agreed to handle this by leaving the lunchroom whenever the other wishes to discuss the case with another colleague.

20 Appellate courts across the country have been very clear that, because plea bargains so obviously give the impression that what happens in open court merely rubber-stamps what has been worked out in advance (the very term "plea bargain" is frowned on by the appellate courts, and judges usually prefer to use such neutral phrases as "pretrial discussions"), the judge should decline to agree to any particular sentence and agree only, if at all, to a particular range or type of sentence. Frankly, this is observed daily in the breach in busy provincial courts. Many of us consider that if we do not agree to precise plea bargains, our lists will likely be even more backlogged. Luckily, in this case, the parties came to me with a range of sentence rather than a precise sentence proposal.

21   Although, as a matter of law, I do not have to make any allowance for pre-trial custody in the sentence ultimately imposed, the Supreme Court of Canada has ruled that an allowance should normally be made, usually on a "two-for-one basis." In other words, for each day spent in pretrial custody, two days should be taken off the normally appropriate sentence.

22   In fact, in addition to my chambers day, I spent a lot of time reading and thinking about this case throughout the Labour Day weekend. The judicial life may seem "cushy" to outsiders (our salaries are good, our pensions are excellent, we get 8 weeks of holidays and up to 36 chamber days per year, and we cannot be fired except in the most extreme circumstances). However, most judges I know spend much of their weekends and some of their holidays preparing for upcoming cases.

CHAPTER 6
The Probation Officer's Report

INTRODUCTION

When most members of the public think about the criminal justice professionals who run the justice system, lawyers, judges, and police officers come most readily to mind. Probation officers have a lower public profile than these other professions; yet in many respects, their role in the criminal justice system is critical because most offenders are sentenced to community-based sanctions. As Karen Middlecoat, an experienced probation officer in Ontario, describes in this chapter, members of the probation service supervise offenders on probation, offenders serving conditional sentences of imprisonment in the community, and provincial parolees.

Supervising offenders is a challenging task. Although the probation officer must ensure that the court-ordered conditions of the probation order or conditional sentence order are observed, offenders also need assistance in taking steps toward rehabilitation. When a condition of a probation order or conditional sentence order appears to have been violated, the probation officer must decide whether to return the offender to court. This is a difficult decision, since it may well result (particularly if the offender is serving a conditional sentence) in the imprisonment of the offender.

The Probation Officer's Report
Karen Middlecoat, Probation Officers' Association of Ontario

Several years ago, a distinguished justice at the Superior Court of Ontario was invited to be a guest speaker at a professional development day for probation and parole officers. He praised us for helping troubled individuals in times of dwindling social resources and expressed almost bewildered admiration for us. In fact, he confessed, "To be honest with you, when judges don't know what to do with someone, we put them on probation." The feelings of relief and validation in the room were practically palpable: finally, a judge was acknowledging what we had known all our professional lives.

CASELOAD OF A PROBATION OFFICER

In Ontario, approximately 1,000 probation officers supervise approximately 75,000 individuals, comprising about 20,000 young persons and 55,000 adults. Young persons (aged 12 to 17) are actively supervised as alternative measures cases, probation cases, and open custody residents. Adults (aged 18 and older) are probationers, conditional sentence cases, and provincial parolees. Probation officer caseloads vary significantly from small towns to major cities, and the duties of probation officers vary widely across the province. In parts of northern Ontario, probation officers have smaller caseloads but are required to fly into remote areas to see clients. In Toronto, probation officers have adult caseloads that average approximately 120 clients. Young person probation officers may have fewer clients, but their responsibilities are more extensive, since they must maintain ongoing contact with parents, schools, and counselling agencies.

Generally, most probation officers supervise adult offenders, who are defined as persons 18 years of age or over on the date of their offence. Adults report to probation officers for several reasons, but most are supervised on a *probation order*. A probation order is a legal document requiring the offender to comply with certain probation conditions for a specific period of time. An adult probation order cannot exceed three years, although some offenders can be on probation continuously for several years, if judges continue to place them on probation each time they are sentenced. Probation orders have four standard conditions:

1. The offender shall keep the peace and be of good behaviour;
2. The offender shall appear before the court when required to do so by the court;
3. The offender shall notify the probation officer before any change of name or address; and
4. The offender shall notify the probation officer before any change of education or employment.

In addition, judges can impose other conditions designed to respond to the specific needs of the particular offender. For example, a court can order an offender to reimburse the victim or perform unpaid work for the community. Probationers may also be ordered not to go to certain locations. An example of this type of condition would be one prohibiting the offender from entering certain premises where the offence occurred. Someone found guilty of shoplifting could be forbidden from entering the store where the offence was committed;

a man convicted of assaulting his wife could be prohibited from returning to the marital home; or a woman convicted of Communicating for the Purpose of Prostitution could be barred from entering a part of the city after the judge's specifying the perimeter of the prohibited area.

Ensuring That the Conditions of Probation Are Observed

Despite the obvious intent of the probation conditions to assist offenders while deterring them from committing further offences, these same conditions are fraught with enforcement difficulties. The enforcement of probation conditions is an important part of a probation officer's job. According to the *Criminal Code* of Canada, an adult has breached probation when he or she has failed or refused to comply with a probation condition "without reasonable excuse." Therefore, not every violation of probation results in the offender's return to court; and probation officers must make the final decision whether or not to charge an individual with breaching a probation order.

Discretion is often exercised regarding the reporting condition (the obligation to report to a probation officer) of a probation order, as it is the most common optional condition and therefore the most often violated. Probation officers will rarely charge a client who has missed one or two appointments, even if the reason is one of simple forgetfulness. However, if the offender establishes a pattern of missing scheduled appointments after having repeatedly been cautioned, a probation officer will pursue a charge, since this is clearly unreasonable. In the case of high-risk offenders, the probation officer would not wait for a pattern to be established because the safety of a victim or the general public would be of paramount concern. Conversely, if there are extenuating circumstances, a probation officer may choose not to charge an individual even if the reporting condition has been violated.

Difficulties can arise in some circumstances when the offender has mental health problems and doesn't understand the importance of keeping appointments. In these cases, a "reasonable excuse" is somewhat evident, but the probation officer will not take the risk of leaving such an individual in the community without some sort of ongoing supervision. Instead, the probation officer will override the reasonable excuse rule, err on the side of caution, and lay a breach of probation charge in order to protect the individual and the community, especially if medication or the lack thereof was of particular concern.

The case of Benjamin illustrates this issue. Benjamin was a 30-year-old who suffered from a bipolar affective disorder and refused to take medication. He was also in a wheelchair due to the amputation of both his legs following a suicide attempt at a subway station. He was on a two-year probation order for Fraud Accommodation and Assault, resulting from a hotel stay for which he refused to pay and spat on one of the employees. Benjamin was ordered to report to a probation officer as often as directed, but he had no fixed address and could not be contacted. The probation officer made contact with Benjamin's parents and left messages for Benjamin, since he would phone his parents occasionally to ask for money. Benjamin called his probation officer twice and flatly stated that he had no intention of reporting. The probation officer decided to charge him for not reporting and issued a warrant for his arrest.

Approximately three months after the warrant was issued, Benjamin was arrested again in a hotel room for damaging furniture and smashing mirrors. He was sentenced in court several months later and received more probation with a condition to attend for psychiatric counselling. Unfortunately, he never reported and within two months had committed suicide. In this case, the probation officer had realized that Benjamin, given his medical condition, would probably never report or attend psychiatric counselling, regardless of how many probation orders he was given or how many times he was charged with breaching probation. Yet the probation officer still charged him in an attempt to protect Benjamin from himself and to fulfill probation services' responsibility to the community and to the justice system. Unfortunately, doing all the right things did not ultimately help Benjamin.

Community service work, which requires the offender to perform volunteer work, can cause problems if the offender has full-time employment as well as other responsibilities that limit his or her ability to complete the hours ordered. Occasionally, community service work has been ordered on offenders who are long-distance truck drivers, construction workers who work twelve-hour shifts, single mothers with full-time jobs, and young offenders in school with homework and part-time jobs. Individuals in these categories have difficulty in performing the work ordered by the court.

Even more problematic is community service work that is imposed on individuals, such as sex offenders and persons with disabilities, who are difficult to place in a community service work agency. Community service is equally imposed on individuals who are capable of performing the hours but who choose not to perform the prescribed hours. When community service becomes problematic, the probation officer must consider all the facts and decide whether or not to charge the offender, keeping in mind that the *Criminal Code* states that a breach of probation has been committed when the offender has failed or refused to comply with probation "without reasonable excuse."

The different situations of Charlene and David illustrate the discretion that a probation officer must exercise regarding community service work enforcement. Charlene was a 36-year-old single mother of a six-year-old girl. She had been convicted of shoplifting and ordered to perform 100 hours of community service work at a rate of 10 hours per month during a one-year probation order. However, because she had a full-time job, Charlene had only limited time on weekends to perform community service at the food bank to which she had been assigned. She managed to perform community service every month but never completed the prescribed monthly rate of 10 hours. At the expiration of her probation, Charlene had completed only 68 of the 100 hours ordered; yet her probation officer decided to exercise her discretion not to return her to court. Given Charlene's circumstances, she had made a reasonable effort towards complete her community service work.

In contrast, David was a 20-year-old, convicted of possession of stolen property. He lived with his parents, who were aware of his offence and his probation term with its requirement to perform 100 hours of community service work at a rate of 10 hours per month during a one-year probation order. For the community service, David was placed at a church that provided hot meals and beds to homeless people. David was not in school and worked sporadically for a friend's roofing business when work was available. David failed to perform any hours for the first three months, citing forgetfulness, work opportunities, and vague references to insufficient time. He was cautioned that if he failed to begin his hours he would be returned to court and charged with failing to perform community service work at the monthly rate.

During the third quarter of probation, David performed a total of 22 hours; and in the final three months, he completed another 15 hours, for a total of 37 hours. He was returned to court, found guilty of not completing community service work, and given another year's probation with a condition to perform a fresh set of 100 hours of community service work. One may assume that the judge's intention was to let David know that he could not avoid the imposition of community service work; certainly, David knew now that he had a second conviction on his criminal record. During his second probation order, David performed 53 hours, but his employment situation had not changed and his reasons for incompletion remained vague and unsubstantiated. He was again returned to court and fined $400 with no more probation or community service work.

Restitution

The court's intention when imposing a restitution condition is more straightforward; yet the "reasonable excuse" clause raises much more complex issues. When the amount of money is relatively small and the offender's ability to make restitution is established, then restitution is usually paid and no enforcement is necessary. However, if the amount is considerable and the offender is unable to pay the entire amount, then he or she is practically set up for failure and subsequent enforcement.

Although the probation officer could exercise discretion and not breach the individual if the "reasonable excuse" clause is applicable, all restitution cases have victims, unlike community service work, and the recipients are persons who have no recourse to reclaim their money except via the courts. In these cases, probation officers are very reluctant to deny the victims their entitlement to see the offender held accountable for non-payment. For this reason the offender will be brought back to court, and a judge will decide what the appropriate response to non-payment should be.

The case of Edward is a good example of the way in which a court's best intentions can miscarry, creating a dilemma for the probation officer. Edward was a 46-year-old man convicted of defrauding his landlord of approximately $30,000. Edward was sentenced to the maximum of three years' probation to allow him as much time as possible to repay the victim. However, the court's restitution condition read as follows:

> ... to pay restitution at a monthly rate until the restitution is paid in full. A monthly amount will not be specified but a payment must be made each and every month until probation expires.

Unfortunately, the order did not stipulate that the full amount of restitution was to be paid by the end of the probation period; and as no monthly rate was given, the offender made a monthly payment, by money order, of one cent. In an attached letter that accompanied his first payment, the offender made it clear that he was not breaching the restitution condition in any way and even acknowledged that, although he had to pay four dollars every month to purchase a money order, he would still pay only one cent monthly to the victim.

Although the probation officer had the option to return the case to the original judge and request a variation in the payment schedule, the effort may not have gained the desired result; and the offender, or his attorney, could express an objection to a more onerous payment system. Nevertheless, the probation officer was able to advise the victim that financial recovery was available to him through a civil court action. The victim agreed to pursue this remedy but expressed great frustration at the expense of time and money to regain his own money.

Another example of an unsuccessful restitution case is that of Frank, a 33-year-old convicted of Mischief to Private Property. Following an argument in a bar, Frank left the establishment and vandalized his opponent's truck. He was convicted and ordered to pay $1,800 restitution over a two-year probation period. Frank lived in the basement apartment of his parents' home but had very little interaction with them, since his parents were aware that Frank sold drugs while receiving disability income. However, they felt somewhat protective of Frank as he had developed some brain damage from years of drug use and could not maintain regular employment. Over the two years of probation, Frank reported regularly but insisted that the victim would just keep the $1,800, as his insurance company would cover the cost of the repairs. Frank was advised repeatedly that he had still been held responsible by the court for damages and had a legal requirement to compensate the victim.

While on probation for Mischief, Frank was arrested and convicted of cocaine possession and sentenced to two weeks imprisonment and one year probation. Upon expiration of his first probation order, Frank had paid only $350 of the total restitution and was returned to court for breaching probation. At the time of his trial Frank stated that he could not afford to pay the stipulated amount due to his limited income on disability, but had done the best he could. He was acquitted of the charge of breach of probation.

Cases such as Edward's and Frank's reinforce probation services' ongoing desire not to be utilized as collection agencies by the courts; however, when restitution is successful, it communicates a worthwhile lesson for the offender and provides the victim with a sense of closure rarely experienced by other victims in the justice system.

Enforcing Conditions That Restrict an Offender's Lifestyle

Ironically, the easiest violations of probation to prove are also the most difficult on which to obtain convictions; these are the "lifestyle" conditions. Such conditions include requiring the offender to abstain from alcohol or drugs, or to see a mental health professional on a regular basis. Violations of these abstinence- or treatment-related conditions are often discovered by the police, who apprehend the individual in an intoxicated state, or by the probation officer, who can determine a client's compliance with psychiatric treatment though a phone call to the relevant mental health professional.

Although the offender's noncompliance can be clearly established, determining that the offender breached the condition "without reasonable excuse" is very difficult, as some judges may consider substance abuse and mental illness medical conditions over which an individual has little control. As a result, a court that imposes a probation condition prohibiting the offender from consuming alcohol or non-prescription drugs can unintentionally bring the offender back into the system. Furthermore, requiring the offender to seek treatment for substance abuse, psychological difficulties, or even spousal abuse does not guarantee that the offender will comply with the condition, and a return to court for a breach of the treatment condition may hold the offender accountable without addressing the underlying problem that gave rise to the offending.

The most common cases are those like George's, involving substance abuse. George was a 48-year-old convicted of assault. After consuming alcohol, George slapped and pushed his wife, who called police. He was found guilty and placed on probation for 18 months with a condition to attend counselling for partner assault. However, the court acknowledged that alcohol was a factor in the assault and added a condition on the probation order that instructed the offender "to consume alcohol moderately." Unfortunately, no one advised the court that George was in fact an alcoholic, and that by his standards, moderation in alcohol consumption

was not in all likelihood the standard that the court intended. The probation officer could not send George to alcohol counselling as only partner
abuse counselling had been ordered, and George expressed no interest in
going voluntarily. Therefore, although the probation officer arranged
partner abuse counselling and cautioned George that failure to complete
the program would result in a breach, his inherent problem of alcohol
abuse remained untreated.

Probation orders that require the offender to "abstain absolutely from the
purchase, possession, or consumption of alcohol" also cause enforcement difficulties for probation officers. Monitoring these conditions is simply not possible, and violations are rarely discovered unless the offender is in public and
arrested by police. Interesting exceptions, however, are cases like Harry, an
admitted alcoholic, who was found guilty of impaired driving. He was fined
$1,200, placed on probation for one year, required to attend a program, and
prohibited from drinking for one year. Harry was self-employed in his own
well-established renovations company and stated that he could not attend
any residential program but agreed to attend weekly AA meetings held at the
probation office.

Within a few months, Harry's wife notified the probation officer that
Harry had been violating his abstinence condition. As she was the only person
who could testify that Harry had been drinking, she was advised that she
would be required to attend court as the sole witness. Immediately she stated
that she would not go to court to testify against her husband. When the probation officer indicated that the incidents would be discussed with Harry at
his next appointment, she begged the officer not to say anything to Harry as
he would know she had informed the probation officer of his violations. In
these cases, probation officers are placed in difficult positions between con-
fronting the offender and violating his wife's request for secrecy; and should
the probation officer have returned Harry to court to hold him accountable
for violating his abstinence condition, the case still risked a withdrawal if the
sole witness, Harry's wife, failed to testify. Furthermore, once Harry's probation order expired, he would be able to resume drinking and cease attending
AA meetings, and one could only hope that the program would have had a
sufficiently positive effect on him to encourage him to seek out meetings in
the community voluntarily.

Treatment and counselling conditions raise similar concerns, and no
offence is a better example than domestic assault. Ian was a 32-year-old convicted of assaulting his wife. He was prohibited from returning home until he
had completed a program for partner assault and had obtained written permission from his wife allowing him to return home. Ian attended two sessions of
the 16-week program then stopped, stating that he had no time to go. He was
charged by the probation officer, returned to court, found guilty, and ordered
to attend the program again. Again he failed to complete the sessions and began
harassing his wife with phone calls and unscheduled visits. She called police,
and again, Ian was returned to court. He was sentenced to thirty days in jail and

probation for one year, with a condition, for the third time, to attend counselling. He failed to attend the program and within weeks had seriously assaulted his wife, breaking her arm and nose. He was incarcerated for eight months; but despite three probation orders, counselling conditions and custodial sentences, Ian believed that his right to see his wife superseded any legal authority that stipulated otherwise. Cases like Ian's are common in the justice system, and despite the thorough work of police, probation officers, and the courts, Ian's wife and women like her continue to live in fear.

Indeed, all cases that involve high-risk offenders, high-need offenders, or persons with serious charges require more intensive supervision from the probation officer. Within the past five years, procedures regarding the supervision of sex offenders, domestic assault offenders, and mental health and substance abuse cases have become more complex and stringent, stressing ongoing contact with the offenders, victims, and treatment agencies. Although probation officers recognize the necessity of these standards, the resulting escalation in workload has detracted from their time spent with lower-risk clients, some of whom form a bond with their probation officers and grow to rely on them for support and guidance. Many probation officers choose their profession because they enjoy human interaction and genuinely want to "help people." Ironically, the ones they may be able to help the most are the ones with whom they can't spend enough time, due to ever-increasing workloads and the court's reliance on community supervision as the most frequently used sentencing option.

CONDITIONAL SENTENCE OFFENDERS

Probation officers also supervise offenders serving conditional sentences of imprisonment. Conditional sentences were introduced in 1996 as an additional sentencing option to fill the void between probation and incarceration. Conditional sentence offenders have committed a crime that warrants imprisonment, but because the court does not consider them a threat to the community, they are allowed to serve the sentence at home. Some examples are offenders who have committed serious frauds or violent offences, but who may have full-time jobs and families to support.

The conditions of probation orders are also standard on conditional sentences, but the reporting condition that is optional on probation orders becomes a mandatory condition for a conditional sentence. Notably, the only additional mandatory condition on conditional sentences prohibits the offender from leaving the province without written permission from the probation officer. One major difference between probation orders and conditional sentence orders is that the latter will often include a condition of house arrest that confines the offender to his or her home, except for court-authorized exceptions. Unfortunately, when judges list exceptions beyond work, religious services, and medical emergencies, house arrest loses much of its perceived effectiveness. The recent case of John illustrates this problem.

John was given a one-year conditional sentence for aggravated assault and assault causing bodily harm against an ex-girlfriend and her new boyfriend. He was placed under house arrest but among the exceptions to confinement was permission to shop for groceries. This exception gave John free rein to be in the community, since he would have a ready explanation for any absence from home. Conditions with exceptions of this kind create problems for the probation officer and do not enforce the intended restrictions.

Theoretically, the enforcement of conditional sentences is intended to be a much swifter process than probation enforcement; but in practice this is generally not the case. Unlike an alleged breach of probation, which is an entirely new criminal charge, an alleged breach of a conditional sentence simply results in a court hearing, during which the onus is upon the offender to prove he or she did not violate the conditional sentence. If a breach is deemed to have occurred, the presiding justice has four options:

1. Take no action;
2. Change the optional conditions;
3. Suspend the conditional sentence and direct that the offender serve a portion of the unexpired sentence in custody with the balance to resume upon release; or
4. Terminate the conditional sentence and direct that the offender serve the full balance of the conditional sentence in custody.

Unfortunately, the conditional sentencing process is in its legal infancy, and the implications of conditional sentence conditions are still being discovered. An example is the case of Lloyd, who received a one-year conditional sentence for assaulting his wife for the second time in three years. Lloyd was ordered to attend partner abuse counselling and to complete it by the end of his conditional sentence. Due to an extensive waiting list and some delays on Lloyd's part, he began the program nine months after the conditional sentence started. Lloyd attended every session until his conditional sentence expired, at which point four sessions remained outstanding. Lloyd refused to complete the program but could not be breached by the probation officer because no balance remained on the order that could be converted to custody.

YOUNG PERSONS

Probation for young persons offers many of the options available to adults; however, the maximum period for young person probation is two years, rather than the three years for adults. Although the same issues exist for monitoring and enforcing young person orders, a notable distinction is the influence of peer groups, an effect seen regularly among young persons whose offences involve co-accused who occasionally are fellow gang members.

Mark was a 17-year-old found guilty of theft over $5,000 and possession over $5,000. He had stolen his parents' car; and when police found him in a parking lot with two friends hours after the car had been reported stolen, all three were charged, although Mark's two co-accused eventually had their charges dropped. One of Mark's conditions prohibited him from having any contact with his two friends; however, information from the police indicated that Mark had stolen the car as part of his initiation into a gang and had met his friends to show successful completion of his task. Mark denied any connection to a gang during interviews with his probation officer, and the requisite loyalty to his group overrode any court-imposed non-association condition or any threat of enforcement that his probation officer could make.

Generally, the courts impose as few conditions as possible on young persons, favouring the restorative and rehabilitative aspects of probation as they relate to the offence. However, some conditions become onerous and present the probation officer with clear challenges.

Nagenthan was a 17-year-old found guilty of theft under $5,000 as a result of shoplifting a portable CD player from an electronics store. He was placed on probation for one year and prohibited from entering the electronics store. Nagenthan was also ordered to take classes in English as a Second Language. Although he was 17 at the time of the offence, he had turned 18 by the time of sentencing and had already graduated from Grade 12, with plans to attend college the coming September. Because the ESL condition had no relevance to his offence and conflicted with his college schedule and part-time job at a local restaurant, the probation officer exercised his discretion and advised Nagenthan that the ESL condition would be set aside providing that the youth continue his education and employment.

Another notable difference between adult and young person supervision is the involvement of parents. The probation officer must establish contact with the parents or guardians to ensure that information is being exchanged regularly. However, some parents have the misplaced belief that once their child has been through the justice system and now has a probation officer to whom he or she must report and legal requirements with which to comply, discipline issues and behavioural problems at home will be corrected. Sadly, this is not the case. Probation officers explain to parents that, as agents of the court, they can only enforce the conditions of probation and offer the youth some guidance, not guarantee improvements in the youth's behaviour. Probation officers often receive calls from parents complaining that their child is out late, not doing house chores, or not telling them where he is going or with whom he is socializing. Indeed, a parent once called her son's probation officer and complained that he was still leaving dirty dishes in the kitchen sink and not cleaning his room, despite being on probation!

Obviously, the probation officer has no authority over the young person in these circumstances, although some parents believe that probation officers could fix problems in one year that had developed over the previous sixteen. Conversely, some probation orders will require the youth to "be amenable to the routine and discipline of the family home," and in many cases this stipulation will bring some sort of clear expectations into the household, especially if the probation officer meets with the youth and his parents and writes a contract that all parties sign.

Regrettably, this well-intentioned condition may not achieve its desired results, as in the case of Paula, a 16-year-old found guilty of assaulting her mother for refusing to give Paula money. Paula was placed on probation for 18 months and required to report to a probation officer, write a letter of apology to her mother, reside at home and be amenable to the routine and discipline of the home. The probation officer met with Paula and her mother and wrote out a contract with four rules regarding curfew, chores, phone privileges and respectful behaviour.

Approximately five months later, Paula's mother advised the probation officer that the home situation was deteriorating and rules were not being followed. At the next probation appointment, Paula admitted that she was breaking rules but that her mother was becoming too unreasonable. The probation officer suggested family counselling but Paula refused. The probation officer then arranged for Paula and her mother to attend the next appointment together; however, Paula's mother called the officer within a few weeks and advised that money and jewelry were missing and that Paula's whereabouts were unknown.

Clearly the probation officer's difficult decision was whether to wait and hope that Paula would resurface, thus avoiding her reinvolvement in the court system with more criminal charges, or to issue a warrant for her arrest and have police actively look for her and prevent her from any harm she could encounter on city streets. By the next week, Paula's mother called the officer. She'd heard from friends of her daughter's that Paula was staying with various acquaintances and had no intention of returning home. Paula's mother was becoming extremely anxious about her daughter's safety and questionable companions, and the officer decided to issue the warrant. Paula's mother was advised and encouraged to tell Paula's friends of the warrant with the hopes that Paula would contact the probation officer. True enough, Paula called her officer to question the existence of the warrant but refused to go to the local police station to address the outstanding charge and stated unequivocally that she had no intention of returning home.

Months later, Paula was arrested for shoplifting, and the outstanding warrant came to light. Paula was found guilty of both offences and despite her mother's statement that she would accept Paula back home, Paula told the court she did not plan to return home. She was given another year's probation, instructed to report as required, and live at a residence approved by her probation officer. Since Paula had had no approved residence since her mother's, any friend's house or city shelter became an approved residence because the alternative was the street. Paula continued to report satisfactorily and was advised that the probation officer would be calling the residences she provided to confirm her housing. However, by the expiration of probation, Paula was 18 with no fixed address, no employment, and no family support, despite the best intentions and efforts of probation services.

SUCCESSES

Fortunately, not all cases end as bleakly as Paula's; and when an individual does appear to have benefited from probation supervision, the officer feels a rare sense of success, as in the case of Rick. Rick was a 25-year-old factory worker convicted of assault, arising from a fight outside a bar. He was placed on probation for one year, with conditions to report as directed, to maintain employment, and not to be on the premises where the offence had been committed. Rick reported regularly and complied with conditions, but the probation officer suspected that Rick had an alcohol problem, among other issues. However, she could not engage him in meaningful conversation. At the third appointment, the probation officer asked Rick about his activities and interests, and he expressed surprise that the probation officer would care about subjects that did not relate to probation supervision. She responded that he seemed somewhat troubled and unhappy, and she was willing to listen if he felt like talking. He again expressed surprise but offered little response. However, over the next few appointments, he spoke about his estrangement from his family, with the exception of his only sister who lived in British Columbia, and even spoke fondly about his cat, Sully. He mentioned AA meetings that he'd attended in the past but had not found helpful and that he wasn't interested in resuming them.

The probation officer's next contact with Rick was a phone call. He was in a phone booth and admitted he'd been drinking. He planned to withdraw all his money from his bank account, buy alcohol, rent a motel room, and commit suicide. The probation officer asked what had happened, but Rick simply stated that he was fed up with life. As the probation officer continued to talk to him, she waved down a colleague passing in the hallway and wrote a note explaining the ongoing emergency. Rick's probation officer managed to learn Rick was in a phone booth near his bank, the bank's location, and even what he was wearing. At one point, Rick stated, "I know what you're trying to do, but it won't work." The probation officer reminded him that his life mattered, to his family, his sister, and even his cat, which would be abandoned and neglected without him.

In the meantime, the probation officer's colleague had relayed Rick's description and whereabouts to police, and eventually, officers located Rick in the phone booth and transported him to hospital. Rick remained there for a few days and, upon his release, reported to his probation officer. He could not verbalize any event that had led to his suicidal thoughts, but had felt a general depression that became exacerbated by his alcohol consumption. Nevertheless, he thanked his probation officer for helping him that day and revealed that, after he returned home from hospital, he phoned his sister in British Columbia and resumed contact. As Rick's probation came to an end, he decided that he was going to use his banked savings to move to British Columbia to be near his sister, who was happily expecting him. A few months after Rick's probation terminated, his probation officer received a postcard. Rick was living with his sister temporarily, working at a landscaping company, and had attended two AA meetings. He ended the note by thanking the probation officer again for caring. She heard from him only one more time: he sent her a Christmas card that year, enclosing a photograph of him and Sully.

Although cases like Rick's are somewhat outnumbered by less successful ones, these are the cases that make the probation profession worthwhile, and the opportunities to make a difference, and the challenges therein, never cease. Many cases are never resolved the way the courts intend and probation officers wish, but the desire to help individuals who've made mistakes to move beyond them and get their lives back in order remains. Like the judge at the professional development day, probation officers may not always initially know what to do with their offenders either, considering the challenges of each case and the complexity of the probation officer's roles. We are responsible for ensuring that the offenders comply with their conditions; for returning them to court when those conditions are violated; for providing support, counselling, and direction to assist in rehabilitation, thereby reducing recidivism; and to keep the victims and general public protected at all times to the best of our abilities. As long as probation officers continue to accomplish these goals, they continue to derive satisfaction from knowing they are doing the right thing.

DISCUSSION QUESTIONS

1. *After reading this chapter, what in your view is the hardest part of the job of being a probation officer?*
2. *In your opinion, do probation officers have too much discretion, not enough discretion, or about the right amount of discretion in terms of dealing with offenders?*

FURTHER READINGS

Abadinsky, H. 1997. *Probation and Parole: Theory and Practice*. Upper Saddle River, N.J.: Prentice Hall.

Bottomley, K. 1990. Parole in transition: A comparative study of origins, developments, and prospects for the 1990s. In M. Tonry and N. Morris (Eds.), *Crime and Justice: A Review of Research*, 12. Chicago: University of Chicago Press.

Petersilia, J. 1998. Probation and parole. In M. Tonry (Ed.), *Oxford Handbook on Crime and Punishment*. Oxford: Oxford University Press.

CHAPTER 7

The Professional Life of a Federal Parole Officer

INTRODUCTION

Most prisoners serving time in Canada's prisons leave prison before their sentence has expired to spend the rest of the sentence in the community under supervision. The most well known form of "early release" is *parole*. Most inmates can apply for release on full parole after having served one-third of their sentence in prison. Once in the community, these individuals are supervised by parole officers. But the professional activities of a parole officer are probably less well known to the general public than are those of other professionals involved in the criminal justice system, such as defence lawyers. In this chapter, a federal parole officer with over a decade of professional experience describes his role in the criminal justice system.

The Professional Life of a Federal Parole Officer

Sheldon Schwartz, Correctional Service of Canada

Few Canadians understand the roles and duties of a Parole Officer (PO). The average person seems to know that a PO deals with offenders and monitors their behaviour. This is true and represents a good start. However, it is also very general. I have been a Federal Parole Officer with the Correctional Service of Canada (CSC) for ten years. The federal correctional system deals mainly with individuals who are serving sentences of two years or more. Offenders serving sentences of less than two years fall under the jurisdiction of the provinces. There is one exception: in parts of Canada where there is no provincial correctional system in place, all offenders sentenced to a term of incarceration end up in the federal system.

In dealing with offenders serving two years or more, federal POs work with every type of offender up to and including those serving sentences of life imprisonment. I should also mention that I am a community-based PO. Whereas some parole officers are assigned to prisons, I supervise only prisoners who have been released to the community. For example, a significant number of offenders who are serving life sentences have now been paroled. Assuming that they remain in the community (they may be returned to prison for a violation of their release conditions), POs will supervise them until their death.

The title *parole officer* is a universal term in western societies. In Canada, however, it may be somewhat misleading. The Canadian correctional system has both *day parole* and *full parole* releases of federal offenders. An individual released on day parole is required to reside in a community residential centre or a community correctional centre (better known as *halfway houses*). A full parole release is a conditional release to the community with the offender residing in a location he or she has chosen and which the National Parole Board has approved.

In Canada, there is also a form of release referred to as *statutory release* (SR). Where an offender has not applied for or been denied release on day parole or full parole, he or she will usually be released on SR at the two-thirds mark of his or her sentence. The release is also a conditional release to the community. It is a legislative right of an offender and only rarely is it denied. If a prisoner is believed to represent a risk to the community, he or she may be detained[1] in prison until the end of the sentence. My experience has been that few people know about statutory release and assume that any prisoner serving a portion of his or her custodial sentence in the community must have earned release on parole. However, for several reasons,[2] many offenders do not even apply for parole. Instead, they wait for their statutory release date. Generally speaking, offenders released on statutory release pose more of a risk than the average offender released on parole because the higher-risk inmates are either denied parole or don't bother applying for parole.

I work with the Team Supervision Unit (TSU) in Toronto. This unit deals only with the highest-risk offenders. Almost all the individuals whom we supervise left prison on statutory release. As a result of the recommendations of a number of inquests in the early 1990s, the TSU was developed to focus on the higher-risk offenders and to provide more intensive supervision of these individuals. While a stable federal offender who is supervised by a regular parole unit may be required to meet with his or her PO only once a month (or even once every three months in some cases), offenders in the TSU program are seen by their Parole Officers at least twice a week. In addition, the PO's conduct unannounced curfew checks at night, showing up at the individual's residence to verify that he or she is in fact at home as required by the conditions of the release.

Another public misconception is that the CSC and the National Parole Board (NPB) are the same organization. In fact, these agencies are separate. The NPB is composed of appointed members who decide which inmates are to be granted release on parole and determines the conditions of parole. In contrast, the CSC provides assessment reports about each prisoner applying for parole. These reports usually contain recommendations regarding whether or not the prisoner should be granted parole. However, the NPB is not bound by CSC recommendations. While usually agreeing with the CSC recommendation, the NPB may vote against a CSC recommended course of action. CSC also has the power to temporarily reincarcerate a released offender (i.e., suspend a release). However, the NPB has the final say on the suspension.

CSC is the agency responsible for managing and enforcing an offender's sentence of imprisonment. In the community, the parole officer enforces the conditions of release and the offender's adherence to a correctional plan. The development of the offender's correctional plan commences soon after the offender is sentenced. By the time the offender is released, the plan represents a finely tuned blueprint of what is required for an offender's risk to be considered manageable in the community and what he or she needs to do to reintegrate successfully both during the sentence and in the long term. The principal duties of a PO include monitoring an offender's behaviour, performing ongoing risk assessments, and taking timely and effective action when necessary.

CSC in the Toronto community is multidimensional. Front-line Parole Officers managing and working with released offenders also work with a Programs department, a Psychology department, a contracted Psychiatrist, and a Chaplaincy section. Additionally, CSC works closely with the main mental health and substance abuse agency in Toronto, other contracted psychologists, a contracted employment service, and various social services and agencies. It also works in partnership with local, provincial, and federal police services and other law enforcement agencies such as the immigration service. In particular, there is an ongoing dialogue (including meetings and training) between parole officers and specialized police units, such as the robbery squad, the sex crimes unit, the gangs and guns unit, and the outlaw biker unit.

The cases of offenders in PO caseloads, all of which are serving sentences of two years or more, are multifaceted. While we do categorize offenders (sex offenders, organized criminals, street gang members, property offenders, and so forth), within each category, no two cases are alike. I have supervised every type of offender from one who had consumed a human body part to offenders who had sexually abused their own children to property offenders who could not walk a city block without being tempted to steal something. Many offenders fall into more than one category.

Parole officers must get to know the individuals they supervise by being aware of all significant areas of an offender's life. People may wonder what a property offender's relationship with his girlfriend has to do with his risk of reoffending. However, there is considerable evidence that risk is affected by interpersonal relationships. Individuals in stable relationships are less likely to relapse into the kinds of habits that give rise to offending. In addition, offenders with meaningful relationships have more to lose if their parole status is cancelled and they are recalled to prison. I have rarely had a problem overcoming the objections of an offender about needing to know about significant areas of his or her life, once I explain the relevant rationale.

What does a parole officer do? In order to supervise their caseloads effectively a parole officer must consider many issues: For example, the effects of medications, medical diagnoses, physical and mental diseases and disorders, legal requirements and legislation (corporate, offender, family, etc.), law enforcement, psychology, and financial accounting. Legally, POs are peace officers who enforce the conditions of an offender's release. To a large degree, the PO is also a broker who refers the offender to relevant resources in the community and/or engages other professionals to assist with case management. Whether these other professionals realize it or not, they become an extension of the case management team. For instance, if an offender is on a program of methadone (a legal medication that helps an offender overcome heroin addiction), the relevant methadone doctor is an essential resource not only for the offender but also as a consultant for the PO. In many instances, that doctor will learn before the PO does if an offender has breached his drug abstinence condition.

Parole officers meet with offenders both at and away from the office. While it is easiest to meet with offenders in the office, it is also important to observe the offender in other environments, particularly at home and at his or her place of employment. It is also useful to communicate with *collateral contacts* in the community in order to get other perspectives on an offender's performance. Examples of these collateral contacts include police officers, employers, family members, friends and acquaintances, program delivery officers, psychologists, and landlords. Collateral contacts have varying degrees of reliability for gathering accurate information on the offender and his other activities; however, the greater the range of collateral contacts, the more accurate the overall picture will be. Of course, contradictory information will lead the PO to further investigate the relevant matter for clarification.

The main objective of a parole officer is to protect the community. Ideally, this is achieved through the successful reintegration of offenders back into the community. In such cases, everyone is a winner, and this is the best long-term investment for society. However, sometimes protecting the community is achieved by taking measures of varying degrees of severity, up to and including removal of an offender from the community. Partnerships with other law enforcement agencies, such as the police and immigration officers, are ever evolving and being improved. All these professionals ultimately have the same objective, and thus timely sharing of information, improved communication mechanisms, and awareness of all our roles in the offender justice system help make everyone's work more successful.

In order to meet the objective to protect the community and perform the duties of his or her job, a PO must meet Standard Operating Practices (SOPs). These formally documented SOPs have been developed over the years and are continually being refined and amended, based on experiences with cases and "best practices" models.

Most POs would agree that one of the main challenges of the job is to balance time management with meeting professional standards. If a PO ever says, "I'm all caught up," there is a problem. I can honestly say that I have never been "all caught up." While a PO may have reached certain standards for that week and may have met relevant deadlines, I can guarantee that there are more file reviews, collateral contacts, and case conferences that need to be done. So time management is a key skill, as is prioritization of job-related duties, all of which come with experience of the job. The Government of Canada screens applicants for time-management skills using the "in-basket" test. This test gives applicants a list of outstanding matters that need to be resolved. Applicants must prioritize these matters and indicate the actions they would take as well as how much time they would spend on each. Such screening helps ensure that new POs have good time-management skills.

As with any other job, a PO has a daily/weekly/monthly agenda. However, each day can be full of surprises—in this environment, not generally positive ones. Learning that the offender has failed a drug test, receiving a phone call from a spouse claiming she was assaulted by an offender, being contacted by the police who are investigating an offender for new charges, and not being able to locate an offender are just some examples of typical surprises. Depending on the type of new information, an entire day or more may end up being dedicated to one situation, and the original agenda goes out the window.

A PAROLE OFFICER'S CASELOAD

In a regular supervision unit, a PO supervises caseloads averaging 20 to 25 cases. These offenders are required to report to their parole officer anywhere from eight times per month to once every three months. This frequency of contact is determined in a structured manner and depends on the rating of a case, the level of risk, and the needs of an offender. However, in the high-risk offender TSU where I work, each PO has a maximum of ten cases. Each PO has two or three face-to-face interviews per week with each offender. Additionally, the POs must make numerous collateral contacts in order to gain accurate perspective and observation on the offender's community functioning.

SAFETY AND SECURITY CONCERNS

I am regularly asked about the dangers of the job and whether I carry a gun. (I do not.) It would be naive to not recognize that the job of a PO involves potential danger and risk. The safety and security of POs are always under discussion and examination. Within the prisons, security systems and safety processes have greater structure and foundation; but in the community such systems are still evolving. For example, in my TSU, curfew checks are only performed with POs in partnered pairs. Indeed, all community-based contact with an offender where there is concern of risk is usually conducted by POs in pairs, and in some cases, this pairing is mandatory. At the office, parole officers must follow safety policies and know how to use emergency equipment, such as personal alarms.

On October 6, 2004, Parole Officer Louise Pargeter became the first Federal Parole Officer to be murdered in the community by an offender under supervision. The offender had previously been convicted of manslaughter. Since PO Pargeter's murder, safety and security systems and policies have been further amended and refined. This process continues to evolve. A parole officer should be extremely prudent, not only while on duty but when off duty as well. POs deal with individuals whose behaviour cannot always be predicted. For example, I go out of my way to protect my personal information. As well, even when walking through a mall on my own time I try to be aware of what's going on around me at all times.

Sometimes, dangerous situations stem from the most unlikely sources. For example, one evening during June 2004, my partner and I had just completed a curfew check on an offender in a high-rise apartment building. We left the apartment unit; as we were waiting for the elevator, doors at both ends of the hallway simultaneously burst open and two police officers from each end ran toward us with guns drawn screaming "Get down, face down!" I thought this was some kind of joke, but it didn't take long to realize that the officers were deadly serious. We hit the floor. They seemed somewhat nervous themselves; within seconds, my partner and I had four semi-automatics pointed at our heads at close range. On the way down to the floor, my partner was able to get out the words: "We're parole officers." Once we were lying flat, one officer asked for ID. I said that I had this in my pocket. He told me to get it. As I placed my hand in my pocket, I was praying that the officers on the other side of the hallway had heard their colleague tell me to reach into my pocket. I took out my badge and slid it to the officer as instructed. They immediately apologized, there was some chuckling by all, and the officers were quickly on their way. My partner and I then had to descend 18 stories on foot since the elevators had been shut down. We later learned that there was a report of an individual pointing a gun at others in the building.

PROFESSIONAL INSTINCTS

Instincts play a large role in supervising offenders. Parole supervision is a "people" business; thus, the individuals interested in working as a PO are "people persons" and have good instincts. Good instincts help a PO anticipate an offender's behaviour. Effective supervision often involves staying one step ahead of the offender. This trait can assist a PO in gathering, processing, and assessing information, and possibly predicting what is about to happen, possibly even preventing further crime. It is one thing to take action after a crime has occurred or when an event is known to have happened, but it is better to prevent such an event. A PO's action (such as re-incarcerating the offender) is often taken based upon an assessment of the offender's deteriorating behaviour before an actual negative event has occurred. In such cases, the PO may never know what actions he or she prevented. However, the probability is that it was something undesirable.

However, instincts cannot be defined easily and certainly cannot form the basis of an action taken or a recommendation on a case. A PO's actions and recommendations must be based on facts and credible information. In some cases, the action/recommendation is glaringly obvious; in other less obvious circumstances, the PO must make a case to support an opinion. The case management team forms opinions and recommendations that represent several perspectives. Where there is dissenting opinion, the PO and his or her supervisor have the final recommendation, since the supervisors are responsible and accountable for the enforcement of the release conditions and management of risk. When the PO and Parole Supervisor (PS) disagree, the PS has the final say.

Supervising offenders also involves managing some basic instincts. A PO may want to believe what an offender is saying; however, experience dictates that much of what offenders say must be verified. Years ago, I worked in public auditing. There was an audit principle employed that was referred to as *reasonable scepticism*—that you should always exercise a reasonable degree of scepticism in the workplace. I still apply this principle in my work as a parole officer. Most offenders sit in front of me, especially at the commencement of their release, and tell me about all the plans they have for life after release from prison. In the TSU where I work, many of these plans fail to materialize. I often tell the offender: "Every offender sitting across from my desk tells me the same thing. Why should I believe you?" This will also set the ground for an offender understanding why a PO has to keep on verifying information the offender is providing. In time, an offender's word becomes credible after a pattern of honesty and openness has been established. However, this level of trust takes time.

THE BALANCING ACT

Parole officers have numerous roles to perform, although some are more significant than others. The role a PO plays in supervising and managing a case is to a large degree determined by the offender. Part of my initial interview with a newly released offender is to convey this message to him. I tell the offender that my role and style of interaction depend on his or her performance and response to supervision. I explain that his or her case presents positive signals or negative ones. An experienced PO learns to balance the good with the bad, and will know what role to play and when. Supervising a case without the right balance can upset the case and raise the risk to the community. Thus, the PO must learn about the offender and become aware of his or her reactions to certain structures, interventions, and communication styles. In the end, the offender is responsible for his or her own behaviour. However, case management can help create a positive outcome when the PO's style and interventions complement an offender's positive behaviours and are able to monitor and take timely action in response to an offender's negative behaviours.

In addition, decision making in a case can be quite complex. The complexity of decision making explains why there is a Case Management Team. Here is an example of a very common situation that can present a difficult decision-making process:

A parole officer is supervising an offender, 25 years of age, who is serving time for multiple robberies. The offender has no drug addiction history, and the robberies were committed strictly for financial gain. Correctional planning has identified that the offender's attitude is a matter of considerable concern because he tends to make impulsive and antisocial decisions when he is under financial pressure. Another area of considerable concern is employment. The offender has never held a job for any significant period and has very few marketable skills. During his community release, he has secured employment as a landscaper. An employer has taken him under his wing and is teaching the offender landscaping skills and the skills of operating a small business. The landscaping job requires workers to work long hours in the spring, summer, and fall. The workday often extends well into the evenings. The employer has made it clear that he requires the offender for all of these hours, as his right-hand man.

In planning the offender's release, the strategy for his return to the community has placed the offender on a waiting list for a CSC program that teaches offenders about changing their values to more prosocial ones by thinking about and avoiding situations that can lead to undesirable consequences. Several weeks into the offender's employment (which was going very well), the PO receives a call from CSC programming saying that the program the offender is waitlisted for is about to commence. The program will run 3 evenings per week for 12 weeks beginning at 6:00 p.m. The offender would have to leave work by 4:00 p.m. on these days in order to get to the program on time. However, the employer cannot accept this schedule; thus, the offender would have to quit his job to participate in this program. What should the PO do?

Should the PO have the offender terminate his employment for the sake of the program, or should the PO endorse the employment contrary to a component of the offender's correctional plan? Obviously, there is a choice to be made, since the offender cannot do both. Which plan stands to benefit society more in the long run? Quitting work to attend the program will likely cause a great deal of frustration for the offender. However, a decision by the PO to maintain the employment and not force the offender to participate in the program may become be a source of disagreement among the parole officer, the programs department, and management. What would the PO do? If it were me, I would stress that the development of work ethic, marketable skills, and business acumen would form more of a solid foundation and a better long-term investment than a program would. However, this assessment is subjective.

Another complex task for a PO can arise if and when disclosure about the nature of an offender's offences needs to be made in order to protect the community. The criterion used is *foreseeability of risk*. When a team assesses an offender and determines that his or her release meets this criterion, disclosure regarding the nature of the relevant offences needs to be made. Disclosure may need to be made to a potential girlfriend, an employer, a relative, or a landlord. When it has been determined that disclosure needs to be made in order for risk to be managed, I usually allow offenders a short period of time to make the disclosure themselves. However, I tell them that I will be confirming what they told the relevant party and that I will fill in any gaps if I need to, in order to ensure the individual has an adequate level of awareness to make an informed decision. Here is a practical example of such a situation.

An offender with an extensive property theft history lands a job with a computer business, which carries an extensive inventory of computer products. Such a situation presents a foreseeable risk, and the employer would have to be informed accordingly. However, there is also a significant chance that the employer will not want to hire the offender after being notified of his situation. While there is the duty to make notification to the employer, is there a way to do so that would be less likely to jeopardize the offender's employment? In this scenario, the PO may offer to meet the employer together with the offender so that, in addition to being notified about the offender's history, there may be a level of assurance conveyed to the employer that the offender is under supervision. Plenty of employers are willing to give a known offender a chance, as long as they are reassured that community supervision is in place.

In some such situations, the employer may decide to terminate the offender's employment. Obviously, this can have a very negative effect on the offender's confidence and attitude. However, the bottom line is that the community must be protected. There are many other situations where difficult decisions have to be made. Allowing an offender to leave his jurisdiction for a family event, waiving a curfew for employment purposes, and allowing an offender with a domestic violence history to date a woman (a degree of disclosure would have to be made to the woman) all represent situations where there may be a perceived conflict between flexibility in allowing an offender the opportunity to reintegrate successfully into the community and potential risk to the community.

DOCUMENTATION AND REPORT WRITING

In addition to travelling, meeting with offenders and collateral contacts, attending staff and professional meetings, investigating incidents, and receiving training, a significant amount of time must be spent on documentation and report writing. Each relevant contact (including telephone contacts) and/or meaningful discussion about a case must be recorded. Additionally, at regular intervals POs have to complete reports and applications regarding the offender's progress or regarding other significant developments to the NPB. There are time frames and deadlines for all of these, everyday case notes included (there is a five-day deadline for a case note to be documented from the time an event has occurred). The PO job and the correctional environment in general are very documentation oriented. The premise is that any event could become relevant in a future court case or other legal proceeding. Thus, documentation must be accurate and precise, including all dates and times.

For example, consider this possible scenario. A PO has a scheduled appointment for an offender to report to him at the PO's office. The offender phones him in advance of the appointment time and complains that the transit system is currently slow and that he may be a few minutes late. In the background, the PO can hear the sound of subway trains. However, the PO doesn't write down the phone call and therefore doesn't record its time. The offender shows up at the PO's office on time. The PO records the details regarding the meeting. The next day, the Hold-Up Squad contacts the PO and reports that the offender is a suspect in a bank robbery that occurred the previous day during a period just prior to the offender's meeting with the PO. The PO has the precise time of his meeting with the offender. He also recalls the phone call before the meeting, but does not have the precise time. Obviously, this time could be critical information to the police investigation. Could the robbery have occurred between the offender's phone call to the PO and the meeting? Maybe the phone call was planned this way to provide an alibi for the offender. How should the PO respond to questioning by the police regarding the time of the phone call?

In my opinion, the worst thing the PO could do in this scenario is to guess about the time of the phone call and provide it as fact. This could actually provide an alibi for the offender that would be based on the PO's estimate. In responding to the police investigation, any estimate of time should be qualified as such. It is better to say, "I don't know for sure, I inadvertently forgot to record it," than to state something as factual when it is not.

While a PO renders opinions and is sometimes called upon to predict future behaviour, if an element of current and past dynamics hasn't been verified as factual, then it can't be recorded as a fact. Words such as "apparently" and "seemingly" are very important to use when conveying unverified information such as rendering an opinion. An offender's self-disclosure is not always taken at face value, for obvious reasons. It is a good idea to complete documentation with the attitude that it could make its way to court. While this may seem somewhat overprotective on the surface, it is prudent conduct for a PO. I believe there is a healthy concept that I refer to as "reasonable paranoia" for a parole officer, whereby a PO will function, not with undue fear, but with enough pressure on him- or herself to prudently cover his or her backside as much as is reasonably possible when documenting.

WORKING WITH VICTIMS OF CRIME

In recent years, CSC and the NPB have been placing an increasingly greater emphasis on communicating with victims, providing relevant information about offenders, and listening to victims' concerns. Victims may formally register as victims, so that they can receive information about offenders and their locations and supervision and ensure their own safety. Victims or potential victims who are not formally registered can contact relevant parole officers to express concerns and ask questions. While respecting the privacy rights of the offender, the PO can discuss what he or she is allowed to discuss and can take effective and timely action when necessary. The main objective is to protect the community. Parole officers are trained to be mindful of victims, both past and future.

CONCLUSION

The job of a Federal Parole Officer is challenging, stressful, and at times thankless. However, it is also rewarding and fulfilling. Most POs would say that there are no two days alike in this job. My colleagues would also tell you that they are clock watchers; but unlike the clock watchers who want time to go more quickly, the POs I know want it to slow down. When they see it is 2 p.m., they wish it were still noon. It sounds strange, but I believe it speaks to the challenge of time management, always being busy, and finding the job challenging and interesting.

DISCUSSION QUESTIONS

1. *The author describes two release programs: parole and statutory release. Prisoners have to apply for the first, but the second is granted almost as a right. Do you think all prisoners should have to apply for release from prison?*
2. *Having read this chapter, you now have a much clearer idea of the job done by federal parole officers. What in your view is the most challenging task that they face?*

FURTHER READING

The Correctional Service of Canada website at http://www.csc-scc.gc.ca is comprehensive and includes relevant legislation, policies, standards, and a list of publications.

ENDNOTES

[1] In order detain an offender to the end of his or her sentence, correctional authorities must have reasonable grounds to believe that the offender is likely to commit one of the following crimes before the expiration of their sentence: a sexual offence involving a child, an offence causing death or serious harm to another person, or a serious drug offence.

[2] Some prisoners may not wish to go through the steps to apply for parole or may believe their chances of getting released on parole are slim. Instead, they will just wait until the two-thirds mark, and then leave prison on statutory release, as they are entitled to by law (unless correctional authorities deem and can establish that the prisoner represents a danger to the community if released).

CHAPTER 8
A Life Prisoner's Story

INTRODUCTION

In a snapshot profile of the federal prison population, lifers accounted for almost one out of every five inmates. This chapter tells the story of one female life prisoner in her own words. Gayle was 43 when she was sentenced to life imprisonment with no possibility of parole until she had served 10 years. The chapter contains extracts from two interviews with Gayle. The first was conducted while she was still in prison (in 1990), the second was conducted in the community after she had been released on parole (in 2001). A life sentence never ends; although most prisoners sentenced to life will eventually be released on parole, they will be on parole for the rest of their natural lives.

A Life Prisoner's Story
Gayle

Life sentences are cruel. I mean, they give you a sort of mandatory [sentence of life imprisonment]. You serve a certain amount of time, but that doesn't mean anything. The hoops you have to jump through ... Even a National Parole Board member told me, "If you ask me to tell you what I did ten years ago, I wouldn't be able to tell you, so I find it hard to ask somebody if they have remorse over something they did ten years ago." And that's ten years. Can you imagine what the life-25 guys [life imprisonment with no parole until 25 years have been served in prison] are like? It's beyond reality. Before the death penalty was abolished, second-degree was seven years instead of ten, so after five years you were eligible for day parole; three years, you're out on passes. Now that is fairly logical; a reasonable amount of time. Before the death penalty was abolished, the number of first-degree and second-degree convictions, as a percentage of all homicides, was only in the twenties—27 percent or something. The rest were manslaughter convictions. And right after the death penalty was abolished, the total numbers turned around. As a matter of fact, manslaughter convictions were only 19 percent of all homicide convictions; the rest were first- and second-degree.

I think every case has to be taken individually. In my case, I don't see how putting me in prison is justified at all. I have to say that, honestly, because I'm not a threat to society, number one. I'm a totally productive person, and, I mean, you could force me to work for the government for 20 years. That would be penalty enough. You know, I mean, I could be productive. You could say to me, "Okay, for 10 years 50 percent of your salary has to be donated to this family you offended." I could be productive. Why lock me up and tell me to behave like a seven-year-old kid and take away every kind of value that I have? Or try and take it away? All it does is make me bitter. I have no respect for any authority in this system.

What society has to understand is that people don't go out and say, "I'm going to go out and kill somebody tonight." That is not the reality. Four out of five murders are murders that are committed on people they know—family or close friends. All the research has been done. They already know all that. And the murder during the commission of a crime, say an armed robbery or something, well, I really don't know; I don't know if prison is really the answer there either. Because why does that person want to take money and stick a gun in somebody's face? But nobody cares about why. Putting people in prison isn't going to change that kind of attitude, especially because they are desensitized persons in the first place. They don't give a fuck. They go out and they couldn't care less how you're feeling at all about what they're going to do. So putting them in prison and not caring about them is not going to teach them how to care. It doesn't make sense.

The only people who should be in prison in my estimation are people who cannot control themselves from one moment to the next and sexual offenders who need intensive therapy. And an institutionalized environment is the only place they're going to actually be able to get it, where you can control them and make sure they're going to do it. What's wrong is wrong; but how can I compensate? I cannot bring the person back, so the only thing I can do is try and be as productive a person as I can.

[This second interview with Gayle took place at her home in the Lower Mainland in the spring of 2001.]

To help prepare for my parole application, I knew I needed to do a couple of things. The authorities agreed to call in a woman psychologist, and I saw her for three years, so that was great. The other thing is I knew I needed to have some kind of pass experience behind me before I could go up for day parole. I finally got a pass to go to Simon Fraser University to pick up my certificate in Liberal Arts. That was my first pass. Other than that, there was not a lot done that I did: it was my sisters who campaigned feverishly among friends and family to get letters written. I had about 65 letters to the parole board. I had a tremendous amount of support. Plus, I had to find a halfway house. Since I was federal, that was the big dilemma. I didn't want to go to the only one available for women, because it was under provincial jurisdiction. When different halfway house people would come in, I would talk to them to see if they would accept a woman. Seven Steps was the only one. I knew some people that were there and they had lifers there. They were willing to take me for a three-year duration, so everything was sort of set for me to be successful at my first parole hearing. What happened was they granted me an unescorted temporary absence for 30 days. During that time, I applied for parole right from Seven Steps, and I was granted day parole based on the 30-day performance.

A friend of mine went with me to be there as support at the parole board hearing. Des Turner is a retired gentleman who became interested in prison and parole issues after my sister had spoken to him about my case. Because you're a lifer, you have to have three board members there. Naturally, they ask you questions about whether or not you have remorse and what your feelings are about everything, and so on and so on. They felt that I was quite aggressive at the time. I tried to be as calm as I could, but of course I was quite anxious. That hearing versus the hearing later on when I went to get my full parole after I had served three years on day parole—I went to the board then and they commented on how calm I was and what a change had come over me and they felt that I was really showing signs of being rehabilitated. I basically said, "Well, I'm not inside, that's why I'm calm." It's so simple and it's so obvious, but it's not obvious to people who don't know what it's like to serve time.

I had to see a parole officer, originally once a week and then once every two weeks, and then once a month for two years. In the third, year it was every second month. Now I see her every three months. I've been very fortunate. I had an excellent parole officer the first time around, and I had him for two years. He was really good, very supportive, and didn't seem to be overly suspicious—he took me at my word. Then I had another gal and she was pretty good. I have another woman now, and she's very good. As far as making suggestions, they really didn't have to make a lot of suggestions with me because I already had my family support and jobs lined up. I was already working towards things. I basically reported to them on what I was doing. Things were still there for me. I had my family and friends there. Everybody sort of welcomed me back. I had a car. I got a job within four months. I wanted to finish my degree so I did that first at SFU.

But I didn't feel like I was back. I didn't feel like I belonged. I thought that ... it was amazing to me that if I felt like that after having a full life, a full career, a family, and everything before, what would happen with people that have nothing? I always said it was a little bit harder for me in some respects to go inside because I was leaving so much behind, whereas other people were leaving very little. But returning after a certain period of time (for me it was seven years), I found myself quite paranoid, which is something that most lifers talk about. I didn't feel that I belonged. My son had to remind me to buy new clothes, to change, to get in step with things. I couldn't have cared less because I got used to wearing the same thing every day. As long as it was clean, I didn't care. I'm still like that. Basically, my family is still saying, "Why don't you get dressed up?" So that's something that I lost that was actually, in my opinion, a good thing to lose because it was so superficial. In effect, the real world is like that. The real world wants to see you keep up with the fashion and look a certain way.

Then driving, I found it very strange because the things that I had left behind weren't there. A lot of the buildings were gone and the streets had changed. Some were one way. There were new highways, new bridges. I had a difficult time in the beginning to find my way around—I'd get turned around very easily. If there was an accident or if I saw a policeman pull somebody over, I would just start shaking. I was terrified of being pulled over and sent back, even though I had no reason, I wasn't doing anything, but I had that great fear. So that part of me, it took me about two years before I felt that I belonged here. Up until then, I didn't feel I belonged. It's a hard thing to describe what I mean by that. I don't really know how to describe it other than I didn't feel safe; I didn't feel a part of this world anymore; I was still inside. In some respects, part of me always will be inside.

There's a saying: "You may be out of prison but the prison is never out of you." What happened was I just sort of went back to being who I was in a way: getting into business, getting back into the industry that I was in before, rushing around, having family dinners, shopping—a regular sort of life. But part of me still was involved with what was going on because I felt so indebted, and I still feel indebted, to people inside who helped me through that time. We shared an existence that was akin to what people share in the trenches during wartime.

One of the things that is vitally important for me occurred when I was in Kingston at the Prison for Women (P4W). Prior to going inside, I worked in an industry that was male-dominated. I had male children, was married, had a lot of friends who were men—I wasn't really trustful of women. I realized, through speaking with the psychologist and so on, that I had quite a bit of suspicion and resentment towards women. One of the reasons was being part of one race and part of another, I was rejected quite a bit. I only had certain friends who accepted me at that time. This is a historical thing; things aren't like that any longer, but they were like that then. If I'd be called names, racial slurs, it would be mainly by other girls, because that's who your peer group is. When I went to Kingston, I learned very quickly—it was like a thunderbolt that struck me—how women were so wonderful to one another. All of these women who had come from terribly abusive homes and conditions of extreme poverty, who were illiterate, a lot of them, who didn't have families who were supportive of them, who really had nothing and no chances, were like sisters to one another, were like mothers to one another, took care of each other, found time to do the most incredible, creative things and give everything they had to each other. When somebody was in trouble, for instance, this one young woman, Corine, who is dead now, when she slashed we would hide her so she wouldn't be taken to the hole. We'd try and bandage her up and keep her quiet. The one time this same young woman, when the guards came to take her to the hole, everybody in the top tier came out. That's 25 women who came out and stood outside their cells and said, "No, you're not taking her." That kind of solidarity, that kind of concern, willing to stick your neck out, literally, because they could bring in the storm troopers, was such an example of love for one another. I gained so much respect for women that I never had before I went inside. They cared a great deal for me and so fasted when I was fasting, alongside me, to support my efforts to get back to B.C.

When I went to Matsqui institution, we still wrote to one another. I still contributed articles to the *Tight Wire,* the prison newspaper there, and the articles, as I read them now, were full of a huge amount of rage and anger. Then when I got to Matsqui, there were a few guys who weren't happy to have a woman there. Part of them was threatened, I guess, part of them thought that I had privileges because I could wear my own clothes, even though I didn't have access to a lot of the things that they had access to, but they didn't see it like that. The majority of guys were extremely good to me, treated me like a sister, very protective. I was probably the safest woman in Canada at the time. There were a lot of fellows who needed someone to talk to and they couldn't talk to a guy about problems they were having with their wife or girlfriend because they'd be considered wimps and cry-babies, but they'd talk to me. We'd talk for long periods of time about what was going on, so I got very close. When things were happening to me, when they tried to ship me out and served me with an involuntary notice, the lifers group signed a petition to try to keep me there.

They tried to ship me to Burnaby Correctional Centre when they just opened it. I didn't want to go to the provincial prison because, number one, the conditions were terrible there compared to what I had. I had open visiting privileges, all the programs, the hobby shop. I would have had nothing. Also, I knew that my chances of parole and getting in a halfway house were a lot better if I stayed in the federal system versus going to provincial. So, I certainly didn't want to go. They served me with an involuntary transfer notice to say, "No, you're going, whether you want to or not." The lifers group signed a petition, the student union guys signed petitions to show their support for me at Matsqui. That was amazing. They didn't have to do that. It wasn't my suggestion—they just did it on their own. I was part of the student council at that time and part of the lifers group. I was on the board of the lifers group. I had been nominated for the prisoners' committee as hospital rep even though I was denied the opportunity to run by the warden. The guys showed me a tremendous amount of respect. We had a lot of solidarity between us. Their issues I understood very well, particularly the lifers. Because there were so many of them, we could really do a lot of things and share opinions about things. It broadened my view on the whole prison system. I saw the differences in the men's systems versus the women's. I saw the differences in the way the staff treated men versus the way the staff treated women. I was quite amazed that guys could basically swear a lot of times and not get charged, whereas a woman, all she had to do was give somebody a dirty look and she could be charged with threatening.

I was in the hospital unit at Matsqui, so I saw a lot of the prisoners being brought in for medical treatment. They came in from all the different prisons in the region. In particular, there was one fellow who had a tremendous number of headaches. He was an Aboriginal fellow, one of their best carvers. What happened was he was diagnosed with an inoperable brain tumour. He was in a tremendous amount of pain. Before that, he was only getting Tylenol. If you were not a prisoner, you would have gone to a regular doctor, probably had a CAT scan. After a certain period of time, they would have discovered that and you would certainly have been relieved of your pain. So he suffered a tremendous amount until they finally agreed, and this was after two or three tests, that he did have a brain tumour. I was with him right until he died. I'd go into his room, which was next to mine, and clean his room for him just because he couldn't stand to have guards around. Seeing the differences between what happened to him and what would happen to other people outside, it was so obvious that it wasn't right.

There was Craig Hill, who was in a wheelchair. Claire Culhane [a prisoners' rights advocate] was instrumental in finally getting him out on Royal Prerogative of Mercy. He was a young man who couldn't do much for himself since he was very debilitated, dependent on his wheelchair, and couldn't stand alone without leaning against the wheelchair; nevertheless, the parole board said that since he could still stand he was still a danger to society and had denied him again. I was charged with disobeying a direct order because I had gone into a prisoner's bedroom when I heard him fall, to pick him up. That was another thing, in a regular situation you would naturally go to help your neighbour who had fallen, and you knew they were very sick. I think there were four or five fellows who died during the time I lived in the hospital. So, as soon as you are a prisoner, you're treated differently. I was amazed that it went right through the so-called health care as well. I saw the same thing with the women in Kingston; if they slashed, they went to the hole first, not to the hospital to get fixed.

Do I see the prison system as having improved over the years? One step forward, two steps back. If I look at myself, I was so naïve that I thought as soon as you walked inside the door the most important thing would be to be productive, to work on everything you could do to make yourself a better person so that when your time came to walk out the door you would be better prepared, whether it was addressing some physical problem you had, or an emotional or a mental instability, or whether or not it was gaining training or going to school, or learning something concrete that you could use in the outside world. But no. As a matter of fact, anybody who achieves anything inside does it despite the system, not because of the system. Especially now, they have all these programs that are six weeks long, and they shuffle people through. They are just numbers to prove that they are taking all these so-called programs. Cognitive skills: how to think properly, anger management.

To give you an idea, I remember in Kingston they brought this anger management course in. They decided that I was one of the people that needed to take this. There were seven of us in the class. After the first class of anger management, because you're naturally bringing up a lot of issues that make you angry, you've got nobody to deal with the issues, so within 24 hours, I was the only one who wasn't charged with having a fit of temper or whatever.

Along with anger management, there should be assertiveness training. There are two sides of the coin. How do you deal with issues that are beyond your control? How do you sort out which are beyond your control and which you can do something about, maybe not immediately but step by step, and then you can achieve some kind of relief from the frustrations that you're feeling? The way that it's taught was basically point the finger: it's all your fault, so you're the one who needs to control things and realize that you're wrong. I used to tell women: "You have a right to be angry, you have a reason to be angry." There are times when anger is a totally normal human response. I guess this is the problem with the prison system. Once you're a prisoner, you're a prisoner. You're not a person anymore.

When Lucie McClung [the commissioner of Correctional Service Canada at the time] says the Canadian prison system is the best system in the world, it means, obviously, that the prison systems around the world are really brutal and terrible. We already know that. To say that the Canadian system is best in the world is a crock. They may have one part of it that may be a good idea but they don't expand it enough. In other words, in the women's system, they decide to build all these regional facilities, and they were going to have all these beds for women to have children with them. Well, they now have more segregation beds than they have ever had; in fact, they have about ten times more beds in maximum security than they do for women with children. So they've downplayed, cut back that whole program in favour of having more and more maximum-security beds. They're continually going towards a more controlled model. Even the healing lodge, which was originally a great concept—it was supposed to be an Aboriginal healing lodge with Aboriginal staff, and everything went around treatment or healing concepts—now it's moved towards a control model. The staff is gradually being replaced with CSC staff.

There's one healing lodge: Maple Creek, Saskatchewan—the Okimaw Ohci Healing Lodge. That's right, that was where Yvonne Johnson was and where Rudy Wiebe went to visit her when they were working on her book *Stolen Life, The Journey of a Cree Woman*. To give you an idea, she was doing quite well there. I have a lot of respect for Yvonne, she's been through a lot. She wanted to address some of the problems about being abused as a child. She went through tremendous abuse. The elders there now didn't feel that the healing lodge was the appropriate place to deal with it. Well, where else for God's sake if not the healing lodge? It's supposed to be a place for healing. So what do they do? She agreed to go to Sask Pen, to the women's unit to deal with some issues. She gets there ... I got a letter from her a couple of weeks ago. She gets there, no programs, she's now being warehoused. She can't get back to the healing house so she's in a men's penitentiary right now.

I wasn't invited to the closing of P4W [The Prison for Women, which housed federal female offenders]. Correctional Service Canada (CSC) wouldn't pay for any travel expenses to the people who were invited. They were supposed to invite all the original task force members to be there but they weren't going to pay for their travel, which I thought was interesting. So it ended up being mostly CSC people with the big celebration for closing P4W. Meanwhile, now the women actually have it worse in some respects. They're separated into small groups in four different regions, and there are so many staff there, and there is a coercive kind of tactics going on. Women are afraid to speak out. They tell me that they can't even write a letter without a guard over their shoulder saying, "Well, I don't think you should write that." They don't know what their rights are; they don't know how to access them. Right now, they are always threatened that they'll be sent to a men's SHU (Special Handling Unit) if they step out of line. Unfortunately, I think there are 13 women in the SHU in Prince Albert, and they call it a women's unit. I think, out of the 13, 11 are Aboriginal women. All the women from P4W should have gone to the regional facilities. Number one, there's no reason for any of the women to be in maximum security in men's facilities. They have enough beds in the regional facilities. What they need to do is move the minimum-security women out of the regional facilities and into the community.

There's a huge amount of money being spent in corrections, as everybody knows, over one and a half billion dollars a year now. Most of it is in salaries. If you look at the people that are doing the so-called programs, they're all guards, basically. Not many of them have any real qualifications. I know that they say they like to have somebody with a year's university, but that really doesn't say anything about training, does it? So there are no programs going on inside except for the ones CSC calls programs. Unfortunately, the people who are taking those so-called courses aren't learning anything that they can use in the outside world. In other words, their certificate in living skills or anger management doesn't help them get a job, it doesn't train you to get a job. It gives you no education. The university program was really the only thing that people serving long sentences could do and continue on and increase their learning and their knowledge versus other programs. If you're finished in six weeks and you're doing a life sentence, what good is a six-week program? By the time you're ready to move along, you'd have to retake the program.

Meanwhile, you have to take all of these things; otherwise, they won't recommend you to parole. People are forced into taking things that they know aren't helping them a damn bit and there's no continuity to anything on the outside, so it's a dead end. They go to the board, and they've got all these tick marks opposite their name, but it hasn't increased their ability to function in the outside world in the slightest. There are some parts of the programs, I'm sure, that are good; but overall they're costly and don't really help the person to reintegrate and become a better member of society.

What they need is real training for people. If they have a vocational program, such as the machine shop, it should be identical to the one outside. So when people go through the program, they have an actual certificate that is equivalent to something they would achieve outside. So they can go out and get a job and make enough money to keep their families relatively well or at least get some place. At this point in time, it is very difficult to get a job. It was even difficult for me. The only reason I was able to was because I had some friends who were able to get me on. It was not an easy thing—and I had a lot of training. If I had been able to get new training, I would have gone into a new area, but I wasn't able to get anything like that.

People coming out of prison can totally appreciate how scary it must be for people who've never been to a prison, never talked to anybody who has been in prison. They think that all prisoners are dangerous or all former prisoners are dangerous. Prisoners need to come out into the community and speak at community centres and volunteer their time and have some kind of normalization period so that both the public and the prisoner can get used to one another again. The fact is that everybody's going to get out of prison—we all know that. You need to have halfway houses because they have structure there. They have hours that you have to be in and hours that you can be out. There need to be more services, though, transportation and so on for people coming out so they know how to get along and get around. People who live in communities that don't want prisoners as a group might consider having transition houses where they have a mix of people. There are lots of street people and battered wives, for instance, who have a lot in common with women coming out of prison. They've all had a lot of the same experiences. Transition houses could accommodate some, but there needs to be more safe housing, period. You want the neighbourhood to be safe, too. It's a matter of screening the people that come into the halfway house. That's very important. I can appreciate people not wanting to have a serial criminal in their midst; I can totally appreciate that. But people who have been incarcerated one time in their life, there's no reason to think that they can't make it on the outside and can't contribute to a better society again. It's an irrational fear that the public has about what a criminal is.

I had never been to prison before; I didn't know anybody in prison. I was busy with my life, working and raising my family, and I thought that anybody who is in prison must have done something wrong and that's why they were there, and assuredly they'd be there learning some kind of a trade or getting more education, and learning how to become better people and when they got out they would be able to get jobs and get on with their lives. If they didn't want to work and they wanted to have it easy, which is my idea of what people were trying to do that ended up in prison, then they'd go back and that's what they deserved. That's how naïve I was. I honestly thought that people went inside and learned how to become better people. I thought that's what they were doing in there. In fact, that's so far from the truth that it's very, very sad and depressing. All that money is wasted. Instead of somebody going inside to try and increase his or her knowledge, go to school, do a trade, all that happens is you learn how to exist and survive in prison. That means you learn how to cope with the constant pressure to put on a face that is acceptable to the administration and to get along with other people that you might have never met in your whole life but who are also in prison.

You're caught up with trying to stay in touch with the real world outside, which is your family and friends and community, and living in the world of prisons that is a totally unreal world. Nobody in the outside world could imagine what it is like never to feel safe in your own shower, never to feel safe or be able to sleep through a night. A lot of the people who are inside are there because they have never been able to communicate or build relationships. One of the reasons is because they're illiterate. They are full of fear all the time, they're fearful of not being able to do something correctly, they never build any confidence and just do what they need to do to survive. The money that is being spent—you could hire teachers to go in and teach. Never mind guards to teach. Guards should just be doing what they're trained to do and that's guarding. All the rest of the people inside could be going to classes, could be researching, and going back to when they were kids and trying to figure out what it is that they wanted to do with their lives.

I'm a lot calmer now, mainly because I don't have the stressors any more. I don't have to worry about the door slamming in my face. I feel very sad about what's happened to people who I know inside, people who are still there. It forces me to maintain contact because I feel that a lot of those people helped me to get through the time. I want to try and be there for them, even in a limited way. I belong to a group called Strength in Sisterhood Society. It's a group of former prisoners and prison advocates and supporters that try to provide a voice for women. We attend different conferences and we do a lot of speaking engagements, write letters to Parliament. We network with other women's organizations and justice groups across the country. I still go to West Coast Prison Justice Society, which is another non-profit society that was formed while I was still inside at Matsqui. They provide legal information to prisoners and produce a newsletter that talks about current cases. I've done radio shows; for example, we did the Prison Justice Day special on August 10th on CBC. I've also done quite a few newspaper interviews and comments, things like that.

The other side concerns my own family and what their needs are, and trying to be there for them as well. Without a doubt, I'm a better person because of the prison experience. I'm a lot more compassionate and understanding, less judgmental. I think with 16 percent of the female federal prison population serving sentences for life and 15 percent of the men, you've got a population that is growing, aging, and that could be contributing in so many ways; but instead they're being used primarily to keep the prisons calm. I think it's so necessary for lifers to keep in touch with one another, to see what's going on in each region, to see what's available when they do get out, just to find out what everybody's doing.

Lifers are a very close-knit group of people. As soon as you meet somebody else who is doing life, you know what it means, and you want to know that they're safe and hopefully that they are doing okay. I know that the women I've gone in to see when I was in Kingston were so happy that I'm doing well. It gives them a great incentive to know that they can get out and they can do it.

DISCUSSION QUESTIONS

1. *Does anything in this chapter change the perceptions that you have of offenders sentenced to prison for life?*
2. *In your view, is there enough emphasis on rehabilitation in Canada's prisons?*

FURTHER READINGS

Melnitzer, J. 1995. *Maximum, Medium, Minimum.* Toronto: Key Porter Books.
Murphy, P., Johnsen, L., and Murphy, J. 2002. *Paroled for Life. Interviews with Parolees Serving Life Sentences.* Vancouver: New Star Books.
Murphy, P., and Johnsen, L. 1997. *Life-25: Interviews with Prisoners Serving Life Sentences.* Vancouver: New Star Books.

PART THREE
Current Issues in Criminal Justice

CHAPTER 9

Community Policing in Canada: The Broad Blue Line

INTRODUCTION

Community policing represents one of the most important developments in policing in Canada and elsewhere. The community policing approach reemerged in recent years in response to a certain degree of disenchantment with traditional policing. At the heart of the community policing movement is a desire to produce a closer connection between the police and the communities they serve. As well, community policing reflects a broader approach toward responding to crime. In the past, the emphasis was on individual offenders, and the response of the police stressed "solving crimes," which meant apprehending and charging suspects. That has changed with the advent of community policing. However, the so-called community policing revolution has not occurred overnight, and elements of the old-style policing still remain. There is also a certain lack of clarity about some aspects of the new style of policing. In this article, Barry Leighton explores the nature and function of community policing.

Community Policing in Canada: The Broad Blue Line
Barry N. Leighton, Carleton University

The idea of community and police working together to solve local crime and disorder problems is an old idea: public policing was originally conceived by Sir Robert Peel in 1829, when he established modern public policing in

London, England. When working in partnership with the community they serve, police can form a "broad blue line" to solve local crime and disorder problems.

This metaphor of the "broad blue line" is an adaptation of the "thin red line" imagery used to describe the defeat of a Russian cavalry charge on British forces during the 1854 Battle of Balaklava in the Crimea (also made famous in Tennyson's poem, "The Charge of the Light Brigade"). When there were too few troops available to cover the line against the Russian cavalry, Sir Colin Campbell commanded the 93rd Regiment of Argyll and Sutherland Highlanders to stand fast in ranks two-deep rather than the customary four-deep. The "thin red line" strategy succeeded, thereby dispelling the military wisdom of the day that infantry could not withstand a mounted horse charge. This romantic picture of a beleaguered few, defying the odds and overcoming them, has since been used many times in descriptions of military as well as policing confrontations. The "us against them" strategy using a small number of uniformed police, all spread thinly against much larger opposing numbers, has worked well for the traditional approach to policing. However, the alliance between police and the community they serve—as in a community policing approach—transforms the thin blue line of uniformed police into a "broad blue line."

To better explain the police-community alliance, this chapter discusses the following questions: What is a useful definition of community policing, and what are its main strategies? What is the broader context of community policing? How does community policing contrast with traditional policing? What theories support this approach? How is community policing practiced in Canada? What is the empirical evidence showing that community policing works? Finally, what does the future hold for community policing?

DEFINITION AND CORE STRATEGIES

The term *community policing* has also been labeled *community-oriented policing*, *community-based policing*, and *problem-oriented policing*. Differences between the meanings of these terms are slight, and all bear a family resemblance to each other. So while the meaning of *community policing* may to some extent be in the eye of the beholder, the broad concept is so compelling that it is now the most widely-recognized approach to public policing in western industrialized countries. Community policing may be defined as "a philosophical, organizational, and operational approach to urban policing which emphasizes a police-community partnership to solve local crime and disorder problems" (Leighton, 1991). The two core strategies of community policing are problem solving and community partnerships.

Problem solving means addressing identified local crime and disorder problems by finding patterns among similar incidents (Goldstein, 1979; Murphy, 1991). Rather than responding to each call from the public as a separate case, the police take appropriate crime reduction and prevention steps to solve the common, underlying causes. For example, these actions may involve "target hardening" (e.g., installing better locks and lighting) and other prevention tactics prescribed by the *environmental design approach*, whose main strategy is to reduce opportunities for crime. Reducing crime opportunities may also include arranging for more intensive policing around crime places at higher risk of hosting criminal events. These troublesome places are sometimes called crime *hot spots*, or *hot places* at *hot times*. Police routinely play the lead role in reducing opportunities for crime in such situations.

At the same time, community policing uses longer-term steps to reduce the motivations of offenders or potential offenders for committing crime (especially teenagers and young adult males). Solutions may involve crime prevention through social development activities in partnership with other community and government agencies to reduce or remove the underlying social causes of criminality, such as poverty. Other steps may be directed towards victims and vulnerable groups (especially, women, children, and the elderly), including encouraging them to reduce their exposure to high-risk circumstances, such as walking alone at night in rough neighbourhoods. Where the appropriate solution involves addressing the underlying social causes of crime, the police contribute in a supportive way to the partnership. The police alert their partner organizations to the need for certain types of response that can only be provided from outside the criminal justice system.

The second core strategy of community policing is a broad *community partnership* between the police and the community they serve. This partnership usually takes the form of public participation and consultation. Partnership activities provide the focal point for identifying local crime and disorder problems, setting priorities for the problems, and developing solutions. Problems are viewed as shared problems with shared solutions, which are provided by the police and other criminal justice agencies in partnership with social service agencies and other resources in the community. This partnership in identifying and ameliorating local crime and disorder problems makes them "co-producers" of order and civility (Wilson and Kelling, 1982; Murphy and Muir, 1984) and "co-reproducers of order" (Ericson, 1982). As suggested at the outset, the police and their community become allies as a "broad blue line" to reduce crime at the local level.

These two core strategies originated in Peel's principles. One such principle asserts that the police are just members of the community serving full-time in that role; another suggests that the police are volunteers who help the community, rather than the community being volunteers who help the police. These principles were developed by Rowan and Mayne, the first two commissioners appointed in 1829 by Sir Robert Peel to head the new metropolitan police force of London (Reith, 1975). Like many other British innovations, such as a draft Criminal Code, it was quickly adopted in Canada without much debate. Similarly, the Royal Irish Constabulary, another Peel invention, became the model for the North West Mounted Police, which later became the Royal Canadian Mounted Police.

While the two strategies of problem solving and community partnerships are conceptually joined, one core strategy can exist without the other. For example, police may undertake problem solving on their own without community involvement. This is known simply as "problem-oriented policing," as championed by Herman Goldstein (Goldstein, 1979). On the other hand, community participation may exist without problem solving, an approach known as "community relations." But both strategies are necessary in order to support authentic community policing.

These two strategies also have a number of organizational prerequisites, including organizational arrangements, human resources, financial resources, and other management strategies (Leighton, 1991). In particular, decentralized police management and resource deployment empower police officers to work with their community to use whatever tactics are appropriate to the neighbourhood and its specific crime problems. New management approaches found elsewhere in the public and private sectors, such as continuous quality improvement, customer orientation, client satisfaction, shared decision making, workplace democracy, empowerment of the front line, decentralization, and accountability, have influenced the structure of community policing.

In addition, community policing uses a variety of *tactics* within the context of the two core strategies. For a particular crime problem in a particular community, tactics may include the following: police mini stations or storefronts; neighbourhood patrol by car, foot, bicycle, or even by boat or horseback; dedicated beats or zones; differential response; interagency partnerships; and consultative committees. Not all are appropriate for all communities; for example, foot patrol may not be very effective in low-density, spread-out suburbs. But because the objective of these tactics is to facilitate greater police-citizen contact, the right tactics must be chosen to reduce particular crime problems, and they must be appropriate for the community's circumstances.

In addition, when talking about community policing, we need to define and clarify two key terms. The first is the word *community*. Widespread confusion over the meaning of this word can render the notion of *community policing* almost meaningless. This is because most traditional definitions of *community* focus on geographical space, such as neighbourhoods. But in a highly mobile society that is increasingly more connected electronically than it is geographically, this definition is outmoded. Many people only sleep in the suburbs while working and playing elsewhere. Adopting a traditional definition transforms community policing into a romantic fiction of old-fashioned self-policed communities with little crime. Modern definitions of *community* replace geography with *social networks*. These new definitions allow community policing to embrace both local (homes) and non-local (professional, business, and recreational) types of communities (Leighton, 1988). We can then apply "community as network" to a whole range of different community types other than neighbourhoods, including the electronic "global village" connected by the Internet. The notion of the networked community is also helpful in understanding how different types of non-local crime problems operate, such as transnational organized crime and terrorism.

In addition to the term *community*, the term *partnerships* requires closer scrutiny. This term opens up a number of questions that are too complex to discuss here. However, Mintzberg (1996) has developed a useful typology of the roles in civil society that form the foundation of partnerships in community policing. First, Canadians are *citizens* who are entitled to a certain minimum level of police services (such as that established by a national standard of some sort). Some of these same people can be *clients* who, because of recognized special needs (those at high risk of victimization under certain circumstances, such as women, children, and elderly), are provided with additional policing services. Others can also be considered *customers* who decide to purchase additional services from the public police or, more commonly, from private police. Finally, all citizens are also *subjects* with duties and responsibilities. For community policing, this means taking reasonable measures, within the limits of the law, to protect ourselves, our families, and our communities. These responsibilities range from locking our doors at night to assisting the police and volunteering in other ways through our various communities.

COMMUNITY POLICING IN CONTEXT

Community policing can also be defined by contrasting it with other policing approaches. All approaches to policing belong within the broader social science concept of *social control*. During the last century, sociologists theorized that when the informal mechanisms of family, religion, school and community failed to socialize people with the appropriate norms and values of the dominant society to create internalized control, then "leakage" would occur and formal controls would take over. In one sense, our culture would move from having a "policeman in our heads" to having a "policeman at our elbows" to control any criminal tendencies. Because of the weakening of traditional societal institutions, maintaining order in society now rests within a slightly shorter spectrum of formal social control mechanisms.

At one end of this spectrum, private police or *para-police* serve the security needs of individuals and corporations, largely for the protection of property, although high-profile politicians, business leaders, and celebrities also employ security guards for their physical safety. Public policing is organized along jurisdictional grounds that reflect consitutional responsibilities. First, the police at the local level serve a muncipal function, then regionally as a provincial function, then finally nationally as a federal function However, while these three levels are distinctive, their operations are often closely linked, such as when the federal police combat organized crime where it has roots in local communities. The national end of the policing spectrum, with its mandate including the fight against terrorism, transnational organized crime, and other threats to national security, more clearly shows that the police act as agents of the state. This "higher" level of protecting Canada's national security has been called *high policing*, in contrast to the *low policing* in local communities (Brodeur, 1983). However, these terms are confusing, since those who are dedicated to community policing likely consider the pursuit of community safety and security to be the "higher" form of policing

Public policing has its roots in history. The "technology of order maintenance" has changed dramatically since the days when troops were regularly called out to reestablish order in communities (for example, the Twenty-sixth Cameronian Rifles quelling the "Gavazzi Riots" in Montreal during the summer of 1853)(Atherton, 1914). Between community-based watch systems and formal troops with fixed bayonets, there were few options available to civil powers. But calling in the army was a very costly exercise, both in terms of expenses and lives lost. The subsequent development in Canada of Peel's style of the public policing solved this problem, as well as helping to reduce the cost of private policing. Foot patrol of neighbourhoods quickly became the core strategy, eventually aided by the technological advance of police telephones on street corners so they could ask for help when needed. With the advent of police patrol cars, a rapid response to crimes in progress became the watchword for motorized patrol. The downside of this invention was that it distanced police from the communities they served. Wireless two-way radios fostered more rapid response, while on-board computers allowed police to check information on suspects. But it took the invention of global positioning systems (GPS) and personal digital assistants (PDAs) to free police from the patrol car, allowing them to keep in touch electronically while patrolling neighborhoods on foot or bicycle. However, some technologies tend to counter this renewed image of the friendly community police officer, particularly the bulky bullet-proof vest and other pieces of equipment previously used only by tactical or emergency response units. Moreover, in addition to carrying a firearm, police officers on foot now carry a variety of other tools on their belts, all of which project a different image than what Peel had originally envisioned: that of a member of the community who just happened to be in uniform. The combination of these two contrasting images—the community police officer and the tactical squad member in full battle dress—invite further exploration.

TWO MODELS OF POLICING

Community policing differs from other approaches to public policing, especially from the professional (or bureaucratic or traditional) model of policing. Under the professional policing model, crime is the exclusive "property" of the police, who use a technology-driven, rapid-response strategy combined with random motorized patrol, assuming all of this has a deterrent effect on potential criminal events (Kelling and Moore, 1988). Usually associated with the crime control approach under which the police "own" crime problems and exercise a monopoly on the response to it, the professional police are seen as forming a "thin blue line" against crime. However, with crime as their exclusive professional domain, these police unfortunately also end up forming a thin blue line against the community. In contrast, community policing forms a "broad blue line" or coalition against local crime and disorder problems, because the police-community partnership unleashes new or underutilized community resources (Leighton, 1991).

The difference between the community policing model and the professional model can be illustrated with a health care analogy. Professional policing corresponds to a police force that works like a hospital operating exclusively as an emergency ward. Most of the time the staff would be patiently waiting for a 911 call for an ambulance to make a rapid response to a life-threatening incident, even though these incidents are relatively few in number compared with most hospital visits. Doctors would randomly cruise the streets in ambulances as a deterrent for accident-prone, high-risk people who are driving unsafely or under the influence of alcohol or illegal drugs. On vary rare occasions, perhaps when cruising accident *hot spots*, they might come across an accident in progress and then be readily available for assistance. Consequently, most patients would arrive only by an emergency-response ambulance, regular wards would be used only for follow-up care, and the underlying causes of health problems would remain unaddressed.

In contrast, community policing is closer to preventive medicine, with an ambulance making an emergency response in only a small proportion of calls for health care. The focus of treatment and response (or the *unit of analysis*) is the individual, rather then the event or incident. This holistic approach to health care promotes and maintains good health through exercise and a balanced diet in much the same way that building a healthy community results in a safer community with a lower risk of crime and disorder problems. As a result, the police business costs less, is more affordable for communities, and is less of a burden on society in the long run. In short, community policing is sustainable policing.

COMMUNITY POLICING IN THEORY AND PRACTICE

Community Policing in Theory

While a comprehensive theory of community policing has yet to be developed, the *broken windows* argument advanced by Wilson and Kelling (1982) has popular support and academic credibility (Kelling and Coles, 1996; Sparrow, Moore and Kennedy, 1990). The broken windows argument mirrors the notion of the self-fulfilling prophecy, as developed by sociologist W.I. Thomas: if a situation is defined as being real, then it will be real in its consequences.

The broken windows theory proposes that when potential offenders perceive neighbourhood decay and deterioration (such as broken windows, derelict cars, or graffiti), then they will likely conclude that the neighbourhood has few defences against crime and is "ripe for the picking." However, when the visible signs of crime and urban decay are removed, then the neighbourhood is more likely to be perceived as being low in crime because it is well defended, resulting in an actual reduction in crime. That is, when changes in perceptions and attitudes result in changes in reality, then crime is actually reduced, thereby making streets and homes safer.

But the idea that a neighbourhood in decay will inevitably lead to disorder and then to crime has been challenged (Greene and Mastrofski, 1988). Critics argue that it "explains too much" and might better serve as simply an explanation for neighbourhood disorder and order maintenance, rather than overextending itself to cover crime as well. On the other hand, compelling research (Skogan and Hartnett, 1997) demonstrates an empirical link between disorder and crime, thereby providing strong support for this theory.

Another theory supporting community policing is the hypothesis that its effectiveness is directly related to the degree of community involvement in solving crime and disorder problems with its local police. However, this idea has been criticized by those who are suspicious of police being involved in the community beyond what is necessary to respond directly to crime. Under the *minimalist policing* or *fire hall model* of policing, police are trusted only enough to wait in the police station until called out in emergencies. Under a *maximalist policing* or *penetration model*, the police are seen as the Big Brother who exploits the community policing ruse to spy on and place tighter handcuffs on the community (Gordon, 1987). In a similar argument, some critics attack community corrections programs, claiming that they lead to a widening of the net of government control over the community, rather than recognizing them as genuine alternatives to incarceration. If we look at police involvement with the community through a more positive lens (Duffee, 1990), we can recognize that the old professional model of policing reflects a minimalist policing approach, while community policing reflects a maximalist approach.

However, the theory of police-community partnerships requires further development. What has yet to emerge is a comprehensive theory of community policing that encompasses the underlying causes of crime, such as offender motivation or structured inequalities. Such a theory would also have to encompass several broad areas: it would have to address the nature of the police response to crime; explain why community policing has emerged and whose interests it serves (Reiner, 1992); address broader perspectives, such as an analysis of risk (Ericson and Haggerty, 1997); locate the police role in the context of social control generally; incorporate policing into a model of the state; and answer questions about both the role of the community in policing and the role of police in the community.

Community Policing in Practice

Despite much rhetoric in the media, the reality of community policing practices in the closing decades of the 20th century did not live up to its own advertising. But community policing was originally introduced as an add-on program, a sideline on the organization chart along with public relations, victim services, and crime prevention units. The impact of this approach was to marginalize and render it ineffective. For example, the first police mini-stations and storefront offices were not authorized to take calls for service from the public or do problem-solving projects (Walker and Walker, 1989). Instead, they ended up being no more than stationary "grin and wave squads" or public relations outposts handing out crime prevention brochures, making school visits, or sending police out on foot patrol and bicycle patrols. It is not surprising, therefore, that community policing was mistakenly identified with highly visible but marginal add-on programs to "real policing."

However, since then, and after a decade of experimentation with add-on programs, community policing has improved. Police organizations recognized the distinction between *strategies* and *tactics,* as described above. They also acknowledged that the specific tactics and police services delivered by the police depend on the needs of a particular neighbourhood, on the local crime and disorder problem being addressed, and on the solutions jointly developed by the police and the community. Consequently, there is no standard template or model for community policing. The appeal of community policing is its flexibility to deliver its two core strategies through a variety of tactics that differ from community to community and from problem to problem. In effect, "designer policing" tailors its tactics and services to the particular client community.

An overview of the current state of community policing in Canada suggests that community policing is well supported. First, it reflects the rhetoric and official positions of the majority of Canadian police chiefs and police boards. Second, in 1990, it was officially endorsed by Public Safety and Emergency Preparedness Canada (the federal department known then as Solicitor General Canada) as the preferred approach to modern urban policing (Normandeau and Leighton, 1990). Third, many provincial governments have made it official policy. The province of Ontario went even further by formalizing its community policing policy in legislation (the *Ontario Police Services Act*). Fourth, Canada's national police service, the Royal Canadian Mounted Police, along with provincial and municipal services, have formally adopted community policing as their policing approach.

Anecdotal evidence shows that the core strategy of problem solving is working well, with Canadian community police officers often winning top awards at international conferences. The partnership strategy is also popular, evident through the widespread use of community consultative committees. Some of these successes have been published through police- or government-sponsored reports. Good examples include reports on community policing in Edmonton (Koller, 1990) and in Montreal (Laudrum, 1998). However, there are still very few independently conducted research studies (Leighton, 1994) and the lack of empirical research in Canada is lamentable.

DOES COMMUNITY POLICING WORK?

Whether or not community policing is effective in reducing and preventing crime is a key question (Rosenbaum, 1994). Some critics claim there is very little proof that community policing works or, if there is such proof, community policing is just making people "feel good" by simply changing their attitudes and levels of fear of being personally victimized, instead of reducing or preventing crime.

A well-known experiment in New York City provides some insight on the effectiveness of community policing. During the 1990s, William Bratton, the commissioner of the New York Police Department, claimed that reductions in crime during that decade were due to the effectiveness of community policing. Bratton had just taken over the NYPD after significantly reducing crime on the New York subway by applying the broken windows strategy of cleaning up the signs of crime, especially graffiti. Beginning in 1983, his department produced daily crime statistics for each precinct and then compared them in weekly meetings (called "compstats") in order to provide feedback to precinct commanders on the relative success or failure of their problem solving and other community policing exercises. These statistics helped the commanders make decisions about reallocating resources to new crime hot spots at different times and places once previous ones were sucessfully handled (Silverman, 1999).

However, critics have suggested that the NYPD emphasis on comparing statistics merely encouraged precinct commanders to reduce at almost any cost the number of crime incidents reported to the police by the public. Hence, the celebrated *compstat factor* may reflect the manipulation of crime and clearance rates as much as it does the success of problem solving and related tactics. As well, there did not seem to be much evidence of the second community policing strategy—stronger police-community partnerships.

To further muddy the waters, official rates for serious and violent crime declined for five years in a row across the United States during this period, not just in New York City. Consequently, it is difficult to untangle all the factors that may have contributed to a decline in crime. Some of the other factors include more affluent economic conditions, which reduce the motivations for engaging in criminality, as well as an aging society in which there are fewer young, at-risk males. These factors may have as much to do with official crime levels as tougher laws, law enforcement, and sentencing. So the jury is still out as to how much the decline in crime in New York City can be credited to community policing, and how much can be attributed to broad social trends.

Rather than focusing mainly on reducing crime rates, Canadian community policing has sought a balance between crime reduction and crime prevention through the police-community partnership. Only four major Canadian evaluations of the effectiveness of community-based policing programs are currently available. One described the history and development of the Metro Toronto Police mini-stations and found them to be well received by local residents (Murphy and de Verteuil, 1986; Murphy, 1988). Another study evaluated community police stations in Victoria. It found that a majority of the residents were aware of neighbourhood community stations, and a significant proportion had also contacted their local community station (Walker and Walker, 1989). A series of five studies of the Windsor Police Service's use of evaluation evidence found that community policing did have an impact on crime trends, despite little support by its member officers and an attitude spilt among management (Schneider, Pilon, Horrobin and Sideris, 2000).

Perhaps one of the most rigorous evaluations of a community policing program conducted anywhere is that of the Edmonton Police Service's Neighbourhood Foot Patrol Project, where 21 constables worked on foot based in mini-stations strategically located in selected neighbourhoods (Hornick et al. 1990; 1991). The study reported that the project (1) significantly reduced the number of repeat calls for service in the beat neighbourhoods with foot patrol, (2) improved user satisfaction with police services, (3) improved constables' job satisfaction, and (4) increased constables' knowledge of the neighbourhoods and their problems. This pilot project led to the department-wide implementation of community policing.

Thus, research on community policing in Canada suggests that (1) it is now the "official" approach to policing in most Canadian police services; (2) it is well beyond the stage of experimentation and demonstration; and (3) it is integrated into the daily operations of policing. On the other hand, we still find many police services where (1) community policing remains marooned as an add-on program with highly visible tactics; (2) the two core strategies of community policing are disconnected; (3) the tailoring of a specific package of tactics to specific community needs is not yet widespread; and (4) there is a little support for community policing at the working level.

CONCLUSION: THE FUTURE OF COMMUNITY POLICING

In light of terrorist events during the first decade of the 21st century, it is reasonable to ask whether community policing has a future and, if so, what that future might be. In the last edition of this book, this chapter suggested the police might have resisted the community policing model, retrenching into the professional model in the wake of 9/11 terrorist incidents in New York, Pennsylvania, and Washington in 2001. Today, there are clear signs that this traditional policing approach is once again on the rise. Indeed, as Murphy (2005) notes, Canadian police are rapidly becoming "securitized."

Police organizations now place greater emphasis on combatting terrorism and other "hard crimes," such as organized crime and mass murders involving automatic weapons. For example, the Ottawa Police Service has recently purchased assault weapons for many of its patrol officers, apparently because it takes too long for the tactical unit to respond to large-scale events, such as the mass murder at Columbine High School. Moreover, our borders are hardened with more security features, including more rigorous document and physical screening.

It remains to be seen whether community policing survives the recent trend back to old-style policing, and, if so, whether it has been eclipsed. But it may once again return to greater visibility should the police preoccupation with terrorism and organized crime fade. Accordingly, the future of community policing is not clear—or perhaps, as with many other phenomena, its popularity is just going through another drop in the cycle and we can expect it to return to predominance in the decades to follow. When this happens, Sir Robert Peel's vision of community policing may once again be manifest in our streets.

DISCUSSION QUESTIONS

1. *How would you characterize the nature of police presence in your community? Does it correspond to the community policing model outlined by Leighton, or does it more resemble the old-style kind of professional policing?*
2. *Building partnerships with communities is clearly at the heart of community policing. Would you say that in your community, a good relationship exists between the police and the public that they are supposed to serve and protect?*

FURTHER READINGS

Kelling, G., and Coles, C. 1996. *Fixing Broken Windows*. New York: Free Press.
Leighton, B. 1991. Visions of community policing: Rhetoric and reality in Canada. *Canadian Journal of Criminology* 33: 485–522.
Rosenbaum, R. (Ed.). 1994. *The Challenge of Community Policing: Testing the Promises*. Thousand Oaks, CA: Sage Publications.

REFERENCES

Argyll and Sutherland Highlanders, Museum. 2005. *"The Thin Red Line" Balaklava*, 1854. Accessed online 23 May 2005: http://www.aboutscotland.com/argylls/93bala.html
Atherton, W. 1914. Montreal, 1534–1914. *Under British Rule, 1760–1914*, Vol. II. Montreal: S. J. Clarke.
Brodeur, J.P. 1983. High policing and low policing: Remarks about the policing of political activities. *Social Problems*, 30: 507–520.
Duffee, D. 1990. *Explaining Criminal Justice: Community Theory and Criminal Justice Reform*. Prospect Heights, IL: Waveland Press.
Ericson, R. 1982. *Reproducing Order: A Study of Police Patrol Work*. Toronto: University of Toronto Press.
Ericson, R., and Haggerty, K. 1997. *Policing the Risk Society*. Toronto: University of Toronto Press.
Goldstein, H. 1979. Improving policing: A problem-oriented approach. *Crime and Delinquency*, 25: 236–258.
Gordon, P. 1987. Community policing: Towards the local police state. In Scraton, P. (Ed.), *Law, Order and the Authoritarian State*, (pp. 121–144). Milton Keynes: Open University Press.

Greene, J.R., and Mastrofski, S. (Eds.). 1988. *Community Policing: Rhetoric or Reality*. New York: Praeger.

Guth, D. 1987. *The Common Law Powers of Police: The Anglo-Canadian Tradition*. Paper presented at the Canadian Law in History Conference, Carleton University, Ottawa, 8–10 June.

Hornick, J., Burrows, B., Tjosvold, I., and Phillips, D. 1990. *An Evaluation of the Neighbourhood Foot Patrol Program of the Edmonton Police Service*. User Report No. 1990-09. Ottawa: Ministry of the Solicitor General of Canada.

Hornick, J., Burrows, B., Phillips, D., and Leighton, B. 1991. An impact evaluation of the Edmonton neighbourhood foot patrol program. *Canadian Journal of Program Evaluation*, 6: 47–70.

Kelling, G., and Coles, C. 1996. *Fixing Broken Windows*. New York: Free Press.

Kelling, G., and Moore, M. 1988. From political to reform to community: The evolving strategy of police. In J.R. Greene and S.D. Mastrofski (Eds.), *Community Policing: Rhetoric or Reality*. New York: Praeger.

Koller, K. 1990. *Working the Beat: The Edmonton Neighborhood Foot Patrol*. Edmonton: Edmonton Police Service.

Laudrum, K. 1998. Measuring the results of community policing. *Canadian Police Chief Magazine*, July, 10–20.

Leighton, B. 1988. The concept of community in Criminology: Toward a social network approach. *Journal of Research in Crime and Delinquency*, 25: 351–374.

———. 1991. Visions of community policing: Rhetoric and reality in Canada. *Canadian Journal of Criminology*, 33: 485–522.

———. 1994. Community policing in Canada: An overview of experience and evaluations. In D. Rosenbaum (Ed.), *The Challenge of Community Policing: Testing the Promises*. Thousand Oaks, CA: Sage Publications.

Leighton, B., and Mitzak, M. (Eds.). 1991. *Community Policing: Shaping the Future*. Ottawa and Toronto: Solicitor General Canada and Solicitor General Ontario.

Loree, D. 1988. Innovation and change in a regional police force. *Canadian Police College Journal*, 12: 205–239.

Mintzberg, H. 1996. Managing government, governing management. *Harvard Business Review*, May–June, 75–83.

Murphy, C. 1988. Community problems, problem communities and community policing in Toronto. *Journal of Research in Crime and Delinquency*, 25: 392–410.

———. 1991. *Problem-Oriented Policing*. Federal-Ontario Community Policing Report Series. Ottawa: Ministry of the Solicitor General of Canada.

———. 2005. Securitizing community policing: Towards a Canadian public policing model. *Canadian Review of Policing Research*. Issue 1, 2005. Online at: http://crpr.icaap.org/issues/issue2.html

Murphy, C., and de Verteuil, J. 1986. *Metropolitan Toronto Community Policing Survey*. Ottawa: Ministry of the Solicitor General of Canada.

Murphy, C., and Muir, G. 1984. *Community-Based Policing: A Review of the Critical Issues*. Ottawa: Ministry of the Solicitor General of Canada.

Normandeau, A., and Leighton, B. 1990. *The Future of Policing in Canada*. Discussion Paper. Ottawa: Ministry of the Solicitor General of Canada.

Reiner, R. 1992. *The Politics of the Police*. Toronto: University of Toronto Press.

Reith, C. 1975. *The Blind Eye of History: A Study of the Origins of the Present Police Era*. New Jersey: Patterson Smith.

Rosenbaum, R. (Ed.). 1994. *The Challenge of Community Policing: Testing the Promises*. Thousand Oaks, CA: Sage Publications.

Schneider, F., Pilon, P., Horrobin, B., and Sideris, M. 2000. Contributions of evaluation research to the development of community policing in a Canadian city. *Canadian Journal of Program Evaluation*, 15: 101–129.

Silverman, E. 1999. *NYPD Battles Crime*. Boston: Northeastern University Press.

Skogan, W. 1990. *Disorder and Decline: Crime and the Spiral of Decay in American Neighborhoods*. New York: Free Press.

Skogan, W., and Hartnett, S. 1997. *Community Policing Chicago Style*. New York: Oxford University Press.

Sparrow, M., Moore, M., and Kennedy, D. 1990. *Beyond 911: A New Era for Policing*. New York: Basic Books.

Walker, C., and Walker, G. 1989. *The Victoria Community Police Stations: An Exercise in Innovation*. Ottawa: Canadian Police College.

Wilson, J., and Kelling, G. 1982. Broken windows. *Atlantic Monthly*, March: 29–38.

CHAPTER 10
Plea Bargaining

INTRODUCTION

Judges are frequently criticized for imposing lenient sentences, particularly for crimes of violence (although the news media do not always give the full story). Another important source of public dissatisfaction concerns the practice known as *plea bargaining*. Many people were outraged when Karla Homolka was sentenced to only 12 years in prison for her role in the Bernardo murders. That sentence, which was universally denounced as too lenient, came about as a result of a plea bargain. Polls have shown that people have a very negative perception of plea bargaining (Cohen and Doob, 1989). As with sentencing, however, public perceptions of this phenomenon may well be at odds with reality. We should not let individual examples of plea bargaining that led to unpalatable consequences determine our reaction to all instances in which discussions take place between the Crown and the counsel for the accused.

As the following reading makes clear, plea bargaining consists of more than a simple exchange in which the offender receives a lenient sentence for having agreed to plead guilty. The public has the perception that plea bargaining always works to the offender's advantage at a cost to the state or the victim. However, systematic research into plea bargaining suggests that this perception is not necessarily accurate.

Plea Bargaining
Simon Verdun-Jones, Simon Fraser University

In countries such as Canada, Australia, and the United States, up to 90 percent of criminal cases are resolved through the entry of a guilty plea (Canadian

Sentencing Commission, 1987; Seifman and Freidberg, 2001; Verdun-Jones and Tijerino, 2005). Although it is not possible to be precise, a significant percentage of these guilty pleas are entered following a so-called *plea bargain* between the prosecuting and defence lawyers.

For many years, plea bargaining has been one of the most controversial—and, perhaps, least understood—practices in the Canadian criminal justice system (Griffiths and Verdun-Jones, 1994, p. 317). For criminal justice researchers, plea bargaining is a compendious term that describes a broad range of behaviours that may occur among actors in the criminal court system (Verdun-Jones and Hatch, 1988, p. 1). The police, Crown counsel (prosecuting lawyers), and defence counsel may engage in conduct that ranges from simple *discussions*—through to *negotiations*—and on to concrete *agreements*, all of which are perceived to be binding on the parties. Of course, discussions and negotiations may not ultimately lead to any form of agreement between the parties; nevertheless, these activities have generally been considered by researchers to constitute components of the practice of plea bargaining (Griffiths and Verdun-Jones, 1994, p. 318). However, in order to provide a clear focus for discussion, this chapter focuses on the concept of a *plea agreement,* which constitutes the outcome of a successful process of negotiation between the Crown (prosecution) and defence counsel.

One of the most useful definitions of *plea agreement* was furnished by the Law Reform Commission of Canada (1989, p. 3–4), which stated that a plea agreement is "an agreement by the accused to plead guilty in return for the prosecutor's agreeing to take or refrain from taking a particular course of action" (see also Cohen and Doob, 1990, p. 85). The term *plea agreement* is more appropriate than *plea bargain* because, in Canada, there is no guarantee that any agreement will ultimately be carried into effect by the sentencing judge, who is not bound by any promises made by the Crown to the defence.[1]

Furthermore, some researchers have questioned whether the term *plea negotiations* is appropriate, given the so-called "realities" of the criminal justice process. For example, Ericson and Baranek (1982) asserted that the word *negotiate* is not meaningful in light of the stark imbalance of power between the police and the Crown on the one hand, and the defendant on the other. These researchers argued that it is more realistic to view the accused's decisions within the criminal justice system as being "coerced" or "manipulated" and that, therefore, the accused will scarcely perceive any accommodation with the Crown as constituting a genuine "bargain" (see also McCoy, 2005).

However, assuming that it is feasible for the Crown and the defence counsel to enter into a *plea agreement,* what may the Crown offer in order to persuade the defendant to plead guilty? Broadly speaking, the promises that may be made by Crown counsel fall into three overlapping categories: (1) promises relating to the nature of the charges to be laid (*charge bargaining*); (2) those relating to the ultimate sentence that may be meted out by the court (*sentence bargaining*); and (3) those relating to the facts that the Crown may bring to the attention of the trial judge (*fact bargaining*).

These three categories of plea bargaining encompass a considerable variety of promises that the Crown may offer to the accused. For example, Verdun-Jones and Hatch (1987, pp. 74–75) set out the following list of possible promises and agreements:

---

1. *Charge Bargaining*

   (a) Reduction of the charge to a lesser included offence;
   (b) Withdrawal or stay of other charges or the promise not to proceed with other charges;
   (c) Promise not to charge friends or family of the defendant; or
   (d) Promise to withdraw a charge in return for the defendant's undertaking to enter into a peace bond.[2]

2. *Sentence Bargaining*

   (a) Promise to proceed summarily rather than by way of indictment;
   (b) Promise to make a specific sentence recommendation;
   (c) Promise not to oppose defence counsel's sentence recommendation;
   (d) Promise to submit a joint sentencing submission;
   (e) Promise not to appeal against sentence imposed at trial;
   (f) Promise not to apply for a more severe penalty (for example, by not giving notice to seek a higher range of sentence based on the accused's previous conviction based on s. 727 of the *Criminal Code*);
   (g) Promise not to apply to the trial court for a finding that the accused is a dangerous offender (s. 753 of the *Criminal Code*) or a long-term offender (s. 753.1 of the *Criminal Code*);
   (h) Promise to make a representation as to the place of imprisonment, type of treatment, etc.; or
   (i) Promise to arrange the sentence hearing before a particular judge.

3. *Fact Bargaining*

   (a) Promise not to "volunteer" information detrimental to the accused during the sentencing hearing;
   (b) Promise not to mention a circumstance of the offence that may be interpreted by the judge as an aggravating factor (see, for example, the aggravating factors listed in s. 718.2(a) of the *Criminal Code*).

THE RESPONSE OF CANADIAN JUDGES TO PLEA NEGOTIATIONS

Over the past 30 years, the extent to which the courts have been willing to accept plea bargaining as a legitimate component of the system of criminal justice in Canada has changed tremendously (Griffiths and Verdun-Jones, 1994, pp. 319–322; Verdun-Jones and Tijerino, 2001, 2004, and 2005). Until the final quarter of the 20th century, plea bargaining was routinely "frowned upon" and most criminal justice personnel were loath to admit that it took place at all (Verdun-Jones and Cousineau, 1979). As recently as 1975, the Law Reform Commission of Canada (1975) scornfully proclaimed that plea bargaining was "something for which a decent criminal justice system has no place" (p. 14). Significantly, this derisive attitude toward the practice was subsequently echoed by Chief Justice Dickson of the Supreme Court of Canada in his judgment in the *Lyons* case (1987), where he quoted from the very same Law Reform Commission Working Paper: "justice should not be, and should not be seen to be, something that can be purchased at the bargaining table" (para. 103). However, by 1989, the Law Reform Commission had undergone a remarkable change; after boldly asserting that "plea negotiation is not an inherently shameful practice," it even recommended that the practice become more open and accountable (Law Reform Commission of Canada, 1989, p. 8). At the same time, the Canadian Sentencing Commission (1987) also recommended that plea bargaining be recognized as a legitimate practice subject to judicial scrutiny and control (p. 428).

Most significantly, in 1995, the Supreme Court of Canada roundly endorsed the view that plea bargaining was indispensable to the functioning of the Canadian criminal justice system. Indeed, in *R. v. Burlingham* (1995, p. 400), Justice Iacobucci stated that:

> To the extent that the plea bargain is an integral element of the Canadian criminal process, the Crown and its officers engaged in the plea bargaining process must act honourably and forthrightly.

There is little doubt that the tolerant stance adopted by the Supreme Court of Canada toward the practice of plea negotiations has been firmly embraced by the appellate and trial courts of the various Canadian provinces and territories. For example, in 2001, the B.C. Court of Appeal placed its seal of approval on plea negotiations and sent a clear signal to the trial courts that, since plea bargaining is vital to the efficient operation of the criminal justice process, trial courts should generally endorse the contents of plea agreements entered into by Crown and defence counsel. Indeed, in *R. v. Bezdan* (2001, para. 15), Madam Justice Prowse stated:

> It is apparent that the administration of criminal justice requires cooperation between counsel and that the court should not be too quick to look behind a plea bargain struck between competent counsel unless there is good reason

to do so. In those instances in which the sentencing judge is not prepared to give effect to the proposal, I also agree that it would be appropriate for that judge to give his or her reasons for departing from the "bargain."

Why have the courts been willing in more recent years to accept the legitimacy of so-called plea bargaining in spite of its somewhat tarnished public image? The major reason seems to be pragmatic: namely, there is a perception among many judges and prosecutors that without a steady stream of guilty pleas, the criminal court system would collapse under the weight of a massive backlog of delayed trials (Di Luca, 2005; Lafontaine and Rondinelli, 2005).

The perception that plea negotiations are necessary was strongly reinforced by the report of the Martin Task Force (Ontario, Attorney General, 1993), which was established to devise remedies for what was considered to be a serious crisis situation in the Ontario court system in the early 1990s. The task force recommended that, where appropriate, defendants should be routinely encouraged to plead guilty through the offer of sentence discounts (Roach, 1999, pp. 98–99). To this end, trial judges were exhorted to participate in pretrial conferences that would facilitate plea bargaining—primarily by giving an indication of the perceived appropriateness of any recommended sentence. Therefore, Roach (1999) concluded that the report of the Martin Task Force constitutes powerful evidence that plea bargaining in Ontario "was no longer a 'dirty secret' hidden in the corridors of the courtroom but was now openly facilitated in the judge's office" (p. 99).

It is significant that in the same year as the Martin Task Force report, the Crown in Ontario made a plea bargain that attracted a considerable degree of public criticism (McGillivray, 1998). In the notorious case of Karla Homolka (1993), the Crown accepted a plea from Homolka to a charge of manslaughter and advanced a joint sentencing submission to the effect that the accused should be sentenced to a term of imprisonment of 12 years. The Crown took the view that it was necessary to offer this plea bargain to Homolka, who was considered a willing accomplice to the killings of Kristen French and Leslie Mahaffy by her husband, Paul Bernardo. At the time when the bargain was made, Crown counsel was apparently convinced that without Homolka's testimony against her husband, it would not have been possible to convict Bernardo of the murders. In response to the public expressions of anger at the perceived lenience of Homolka's sentence, an independent inquiry was established to investigate the circumstances underlying the Homolka plea bargain. Ultimately, the inquiry found that given its knowledge of the circumstances at the time, the Crown had absolutely no choice but to enter into the plea agreement with Homolka's counsel if it wished to ensure the conviction of Paul Bernardo (Galligan, 1996, pp. 215–218).[3] Although there was widespread criticism of the sentence that was jointly recommended by the Crown and defence, the *Homolka* case nevertheless shows the extent to which plea bargaining has been accepted as a necessary—albeit somewhat unattractive—element in the administration of justice in Canada. The increasing degree of acceptance of plea bargaining in Ontario is best demonstrated by *Boudreau v. Benaiah* (2000). In this case, the Ontario Court of Appeal upheld a trial court's ruling that an accused person was entitled to receive substantial damages from his counsel because the latter failed to properly communicate with him the contents of a proposed plea agreement with the Crown.

The extent to which Canadian courts have accepted the reality of plea negotiations is also demonstrated by their willingness to accept joint sentencing submissions advanced by both the Crown and defence counsel (Manson, 2001, pp. 204–205). It is significant that joint sentencing submissions are generally predicated on the acceptance of a plea agreement by the accused. In *R. v. G.W.C.* (2000), the Alberta Court of Appeal forcefully articulated the view that trial courts should be reluctant to undermine the plea negotiations process by rejecting a joint sentencing submission that has been agreed upon by both Crown and defence counsel. Indeed, Justice Berger stated (para. 17):

> The obligation of a trial judge to give serious consideration to a joint sentencing submission stems from an attempt to maintain a proper balance between respect for the plea bargain and the sentencing court's role in the administration of justice. The certainty that is required to induce accused persons to waive their rights to a trial can only be achieved in an atmosphere where the courts do not lightly interfere with a negotiated disposition that falls within or is very close to the appropriate range for a given offence.

THE LACK OF A FORMAL PROCESS FOR REGULATING PLEA NEGOTIATIONS IN CANADA

Undoubtedly, members of the Canadian judiciary have now accepted the fact that plea negotiations play a significant role in the efficient administration of justice and have sustained it by embracing sentencing policies that largely give effect to the agreements negotiated by Crown and defence counsel. However, despite the recommendations of the Canadian Sentencing Commission (1987) and the Law Reform Commission of Canada (1989), there is still no formal process by means of which Canadian courts are required to scrutinize the contents of a plea bargain and to ensure that there is adequate protection for the rights and interests of all of the affected parties—the Crown, the accused, the victim(s) and members of society in general (Verdun-Jones and Tijerino, 2005).

In contrast, in the federal and state courts of the United States, trial judges are required to scrutinize plea agreements between the prosecuting and defence attorneys and have the power to accept or reject them (Herman, 2004; Pan and Kaiser, 2001). In this process, judges are expected to examine the basic facts surrounding the charges laid against the accused and to consider the interests of all of the affected parties, including society in general, the justice system, the accused, and the victim(s) of the offences (Verdun-Jones and Tijerino, 2001 and 2004). In many American jurisdictions, the victim of an offence is entitled to provide input to the court during a plea agreement hearing, although in no jurisdiction is the victim given a right of veto over a proposed agreement (U.S. Department of Justice, 2002). Judges do not involve themselves in the process of negotiation, since their power is limited to accepting or rejecting the proposed plea agreement. The major advantage of this procedure is its transparency, since the existence of the plea agreement is openly acknowledged and is usually examined in open court. Furthermore, plea agreements are, by law, regulated by the judiciary.

In Canada, the *Criminal Code* (R.S.C. 1985, c. C-46) does make provision for the holding of formal pretrial hearings before a judge in order "to consider the matters that, to promote a fair and expeditious hearing, would be better decided before the start of the proceedings, and other similar matters, and to make arrangements for decisions on those matters" (section 625.1). However, these pretrial hearings are not held for the specific purpose of examining a proposed plea agreement. Indeed, the *Criminal Code* does not require that the existence of a plea agreement be made known to the court in the course of such hearings; nor does the *Code* impose a duty on trial judges to investigate the circumstances underlying a plea agreement, if it comes to their attention that an agreement has, in fact, been reached between Crown and defence counsel.

Since 1992, the *Criminal Code* has required that a trial judge take steps to ensure that an accused person who pleads guilty is doing so voluntarily. More specifically, section 606 (1.1) requires that before accepting a plea of guilty, the trial judge must first be satisfied that the accused person is pleading guilty voluntarily and that he or she "understands that the plea is an admission of the essential elements of the offence, the nature, and consequences of the plea, and that the court is not bound by any agreement made between the accused and the prosecutor." Clearly, section 606 (1.1) only provides protection for the rights of the accused person. Unlike American judges, the Canadian trial judge is under no duty to scrutinize the facts underlying a plea agreement and is not required to hear evidence as to whether or not it serves the best interests of the various stakeholders concerned (including the victim(s) and the community at large).

THE ROLE OF VICTIMS IN RELATION TO THE PLEA NEGOTIATIONS PROCESS

Since there is no formal judicial procedure for scrutinizing plea agreements in Canada, there is no opportunity for the victims of crime to express their views to a trial judge concerning the contents of a proposed plea agreement. However, victims may have a role to play at an earlier stage of the pretrial process.

Most Canadian provinces and territories have enacted legislation that entitles victims of crime to receive information concerning the status of the investigation and prosecution of "their" cases (Roach, 1999; Verdun-Jones and Tijerino, 2001, 2004 and 2005). However, at present, the only Canadian jurisdictions that have enacted legislation that explicitly deals with the role of victims in the plea negotiation process are Manitoba and Ontario. The Ontario legislation merely requires that victims "should have access to information" about "any pretrial arrangements that relate to a plea that may be entered by the accused at trial" (*Victims' Bill of Rights*, S.O.1995, c. 6, s. 2(x)). It is significant that the Martin Task Force Report (Ontario, Attorney General, 1993), which was published two years before the enactment of the Ontario *Victims' Bill of Rights*, had recognized that victims should be consulted about plea bargains "where appropriate and feasible." However, as Roach (1999) points out, the recommendations of the Martin Task Force were not designed to enhance the level of direct victim participation in the criminal justice process in Ontario, and it made clear that victims should not be given the right to veto an agreement of which they disapproved (p. 99). According to Roach, the report assumed that the exercise of power in plea bargaining should remain squarely in the hands of the criminal justice professionals, and the primary goal of the Task Force in recommending more widespread acceptance of plea bargaining was not that of victim empowerment but rather that of enhancing the efficiency of a court system that would collapse if most defendants decided to exercise their right to a full trial (p. 99).

Moreover, in 2000, the province of Manitoba implemented part of a new *Victims' Bill of Rights* (C.C.S.M. c. V55), which created a right for victims to be *consulted* (as opposed to merely being *informed*) about various aspects of the prosecution of "their" cases. Unfortunately, even when provincial legislation grants rights to victims in relation to proposed plea agreements, these rights may not be enforceable in the courts. For example, in *Vanscoy v. Ontario* (1999), a judge of the Ontario Superior Court of Justice held that the Ontario *Victims' Bill of Rights* did not create any substantive rights. In this case, the complainants asserted that their right to be informed about plea negotiations had been violated when the Crown had failed to inform them that a plea agreement had been reached with defence counsel. Justice Day ruled (para. 22) that the Ontario legislation did not create enforceable *rights* but rather articulates certain *principles*:

> I conclude that the legislature did not intend for s. 2(1) of the *Victims Bill of Rights* to provide rights to the victims of crime. The Act is a statement of principle and social policy, beguilingly clothed in the language of legislation. It does not establish any statutory rights for the victims of crime.

It is noteworthy that the *Victims' Bill of Rights* in Manitoba is a trailblazing statute insofar as it creates an administrative mechanism designed to hold criminal justice officials to account if they fail to perform their statutory duties to provide information to—and consult with—victims of crime. Disgruntled victims may take their complaints to the Director of Victims' Support Services and may also seek the assistance of the provincial Ombudsperson, who must appoint a Crime Victim Investigator to deal with such complaints (Verdun-Jones and Tijerino, 2005, p. 196).

RESEARCH INTO PLEA NEGOTIATIONS IN CANADA

Although plea negotiations constitute a significant element in the criminal justice system in Canada, there is a surprising paucity of empirical research into the phenomenon. Some evidence suggests that police officers and prosecutors are willing to admit that plea negotiations occur with frequency. For example, a study by Jonah et al. (1999) examined the practices, perceptions, and attitudes of 1,545 police officers across Canada in relation to the enforcement of impaired driving laws. About two-thirds of the police officers surveyed indicated that plea bargaining had occurred in impaired driving cases in which they were concerned (28.2 percent indicated it occurred in at least some cases, and 36.7 percent responded that it occurred frequently). The major reason cited for plea bargaining was to "speed up the court process" (59.2 percent). Similarly, in a study of decision making by Crown counsel in relation to dangerous offender applications in British Columbia and Ontario, Bonta, Harris, Zinger, and Carriere (1996) found that 71 percent of Crown counsel indicated that "they would consider plea bargaining as a viable option if evidentiary problems existed" (p. 39).

The most comprehensive Canadian study of plea negotiations was conducted some 25 years ago. A group of researchers at the University of Toronto's Centre of Criminology conducted a major study of discretionary decision making in the criminal justice process. The study employed several research methods, including direct observation of the plea bargaining process. One hundred and one accused persons were tracked through the criminal justice system from arrest to sentence. The data from this study were reported in several sources, the most comprehensive of which is a book by Ericson and Baranek (1982).

To create a detailed picture of plea negotiation processes in one county in Ontario, this study kept verbatim transcripts of interviews with the accused and interviews with lawyers. It also made recordings of conversations in the Crown attorney's office. Researchers also observed the court appearances of the defendants in the sample. As a result, the study became the first Canadian study in which researchers were able to document the complex dynamics involved in the process of plea bargaining.

Ericson and Baranek (1982, p. 117) employed the term *plea discussions* rather than *plea bargaining*, because the former expression makes clear that discussions may be entered into without an agreement ever being reached. They concluded that "plea discussions were a widespread and integral part of the order out of court" (p. 121). In this respect, they found that lawyers for as many as 57 of the 80 accused said that they had entered into plea discussions (p. 117–18). Furthermore, they discovered that participation in plea discussions was not confined to Crown and defence counsel; indeed, the police were frequently involved at various stages in the plea discussion process (p. 121).

Ericson and Baranek suggested that the existence of multiple charges appears to constitute a major element in the circumstances that lead to plea discussions taking place. Of the 23 accused whose lawyers did *not* engage in such discussions, 17 had only one charge laid against them (compared with only 9 of the 57 accused whose lawyers were involved in plea discussions). The authors believed that multiple charging is a vital component of the plea discussion process in Canada; and that without the existence of multiple charges, the defence would not be able to negotiate for the withdrawal of some charge(s) in return for the entry of a guilty plea to others. Lawyers who engaged in discussions with the Crown reported that withdrawal of charges was the major topic of conversation in plea discussions (Ericson and Baranek, 1982, p. 119).

Given the finding that there was widespread involvement of lawyers in plea discussions, what was the most likely outcome of these encounters? Ericson and Baranek (1982) discovered that although many of the lawyers engaged in plea discussions, only about a quarter of them stated that they had reached an agreement that could be considered a bargain (p. 143). For this group of lawyers, the most frequently mentioned agreement was one that included a sentence concession. Of the remaining lawyers who entered plea discussions, 12 percent stated that they had not reached an agreement, while lawyers for the remaining 88 percent claimed that the agreement reached brought no real advantage for the accused. More than half of the lawyers (representing 23 accused) thought that an agreement had brought no tangible benefit because the charges that were withdrawn or reduced in their cases did not represent a genuine concession, but were merely the result of overcharging by the police in the first place (Ericson and Baranek, 1982, p. 145).

Solomon (1983) also analyzed the data from this study and concluded that plea negotiations "did not result in important concessions for the accused." In the Provincial Court, almost 80 percent of the criminal cases that were not withdrawn by the Crown terminated with guilty pleas, and 60 percent of these cases involved plea discussions. It appears that the discussions between defence counsel and the Crown and/or police usually focused on the charges to which the accused would plead guilty, rather than on the sentence (although there was some discussion of the approach that the Crown would adopt at the sentencing stage).

Plea agreements resulted in the dropping of charges (which were often not justified in the first place) and at least a tacit agreement about the Crown's recommendation as to sentence. However, Solomon (1983) pointed out that there was no clear relationship between the charges to which the accused ultimately pleaded guilty and the sentence handed down by the court (p. 37). Furthermore, the sentencing recommendations made by the Crown had no direct impact on the sentence actually handed down by the court. In these circumstances, an accused person who entered into a plea arrangement with the Crown had no guarantee that his or her guilty plea would make any difference whatsoever to the ultimate outcome of the case.

This pioneering study by the University of Toronto criminologists provided a valuable snapshot of plea negotiations that took place almost a quarter of a century ago. Circumstances have undoubtedly changed considerably since then and, as noted above, the courts are now considerably more willing to accept joint sentencing submissions from Crown and defence counsel. Therefore, it would be unwise to assume that the findings by Ericson and Baranek (1982) and the analysis by Solomon (1983) reflect the nature and scope of contemporary plea negotiations practices either in Ontario or in other parts of Canada. Clearly, there is a need for a similar type of study to be conducted in contemporary circumstances.

More recent research has identified a powerful reason for accused persons to seek a plea agreement with the Crown. Indeed, a recent study by Kellough and Wortley (2002) concludes that the detention of an accused person in custody prior to trial is a significant factor in persuading him or her to enter into plea negotiations with the Crown. In a study of more than 1,800 criminal court cases that came before two Toronto bail courts in the six-month period (between October 1993 and April 1994), Kellough and Wortley found that accused persons who had been held in custody were more likely to plead guilty than their out-of-custody counterparts. When an accused person had been held in custody, the Crown usually refused to drop any of the original charges until he or she pleaded guilty to other charges. However, if an accused person had been released on bail into the community, he or she was less willing to plead guilty to any of the charges, thereby making the Crown's task of obtaining a conviction more difficult. In this respect, Kellough and Wortley (2002, p. 204) concluded:

> An out-of-custody accused is more likely to have all of the charges dropped but a detained accused who resists pleading guilty is more likely to spend more time in custody. In the majority of cases, being in custody prior to trial eventually means being persuaded of the wisdom of entering into plea negotiations with the Crown.

A study by Simon Fraser University researchers, Viljoen, Klaver, and Roesch (2005) indicates that another reason that may influence accused persons to enter into plea negotiations with prosecutors is their perception of the strength of the case against them. A study of legal decision making by youths detained in a Washington State pretrial facility was found that adolescents (aged 15–17) were more likely to plead guilty and enter into a plea agreement if they perceived that the evidence against them was strong.

CONCLUSIONS

Plea negotiations are a well-established feature of contemporary criminal justice in Canada. The courts have accepted the legitimacy of this practice and have encouraged it by demonstrating their willingness to accept joint sentencing submissions by Crown and defence counsel. Plea negotiations are accepted as a necessary evil in a criminal justice system in which the Crown has finite resources with which to prosecute cases. Since the Crown does not have the ability to take the majority of criminal cases to a full trial, it needs to provide an incentive to criminal defendants to plead guilty to at least some criminal charges (Bjerk, 2005; Roberts, 2000). The strongest incentive for a guilty plea is the offer of a less severe sentence. There is no doubt that defence counsel enter into negotiations with Crown counsel in the belief that a plea agreement will make provision for a sentence that is more lenient than the sentence that is likely to be imposed should the accused person be convicted of the original charges following a full trial (Ericson and Baranek, 1982; Solomon, 1983, p. 41).

While plea negotiations have acquired a certain degree of acceptance and grudging respectability, they are still not subject to a formal process of regulation by the judiciary, as is the case in American criminal courts. As McGillivray (1997–98) has aptly commented: "plea bargaining is a closed-door and often hasty process, unmediated by the judiciary" (para. 20). If plea negotiations are indeed an "integral element of the Canadian criminal process" (to quote the Supreme Court of Canada), it would surely constitute sound public policy for the Parliament of Canada to amend the *Criminal Code* with a view to establishing the necessary machinery for their regulation by the courts. Furthermore, there is a need to open the process of plea negotiations to public scrutiny and to create an opportunity for victims to have their views heard concerning proposed plea agreements. Finally, the other Canadian provinces and territories should follow the lead of Manitoba and require prosecutors to consult with victims before entering into plea agreements with defence counsel.

Plea negotiations have certainly come of age in the 21st century. However, the criminal justice system has been excruciatingly slow in developing mechanisms to regulate plea negotiations and has failed to ensure that plea agreements serve not only the traditional interests of prosecutors, offenders, and the court bureaucracies, but also the compelling interests of the victims of crime and of Canadian society as a whole.

DISCUSSION QUESTIONS

1. *The large volume of criminal cases being processed by the system and the high percentage (approximately 90 percent) of accuseds who plead guilty means that abolishing plea bargaining would swamp the courts with additional trials. Abolition of this practice is therefore unlikely. Even if it were possible, however, would it necessarily be a good thing?*

2. *Victims are sometimes shocked to learn that the Crown has accepted a plea to a lesser, included offence rather than proceed to trial on a more serious charge, with the accused pleading not guilty. Victims are seldom consulted or kept apprised of developments in negotiations with the accused. Should individual victims have a greater say in plea negotiations? Should they be given the power to overrule any plea arrangement?*

FURTHER READINGS

Ericson, R., and Baranek, P. 1982. *The Ordering of Justice: A Study of Accused Persons as Dependants in the Criminal Process*. Toronto: University of Toronto Press.

Law Reform Commission of Canada. 1989. *Plea Discussions and Agreements*. Working Paper No. 60. Ottawa: Law Reform Commission of Canada.

Verdun-Jones, S., and Hatch, A. 1985. *Plea Bargaining and Sentencing Guidelines*. Ottawa: Department of Justice Canada.

REFERENCES

Bala, N. 1999. Legal responses to domestic violence in Canada and the role of health care professionals. *Syrtash Collection of Family Law Articles* (SFLRP/2000-004). Online at Quicklaw.

Bjerk, D. 2005. *On the Role of Plea Bargaining and the Distribution of Sentences in the Absence of Judicial System Frictions*. Hamilton, Ontario: McMaster University, Department of Economics. Online at: http://socserv.mcmaster.ca/bjerk/pleabargain1.pdf

Bonta, J., Harris, A., Zinger, I., and Carriere, D. 1996. *The Crown Files Research Project: A Study of Dangerous Offenders*. Ottawa: Public Safety and Emergency Preparedness Canada. Online at: http://ww2.psepc-sppcc.gc.ca/publications/corrections/pdf/199601_e.pdf

Cohen, S., and Doob, A. 1989. Public attitudes towards plea bargaining. *Criminal Law Quarterly*, 32: 85–109.

Cousineau, D., and Verdun-Jones, S. 1979. Evaluating research into plea bargaining in Canada and the United States: Pitfalls facing the policymakers. *Canadian Journal of Criminology*, 21: 293–309.

Di Luca, J. 2005. Expedient McJustice or principled alternative dispute resolution? A review of plea bargaining in Canada. *Criminal Law Quarterly*, 50: 14–66.

Ericson, R.V., and Baranek, P. 1982. *The Ordering of Justice: A Study of Accused Persons as Dependants in the Criminal Process*. Toronto: University of Toronto Press.

Etherington, B. 1994. *Review of Multiculturalism and Justice Issues: A Framework for Addressing Reform. Rapport sur les questions relatives au multiculturalisme et à la justice: projet de reforme*. Ottawa: Department of Justice (WD1994-8e/8f). Online at: http://www.justice.gc.ca/en/ps/rs/rep/1994/wd94-8a.pdf

Galligan, P.T. 1996. *Report to the Attorney General of Ontario on Certain Matters Relating to Karla Homolka*. Toronto: ADR Chambers.

Gillis, C. 2005. Karla Homolka: Girl next door. *Macleans*, March 15, 2005. Online at: http://www.macleans.ca/topstories/justice/article.jsp?content=20050321_102168_102168

Griffiths, C.T., and Verdun-Jones, S.N. 1994. *Canadian Criminal Justice*, 2nd ed. Toronto: Harcourt, Brace and Jovanovich, Canada.

Herman, G.N. 2004. *Plea Bargaining*, 2nd ed. Charlottesville, VA: LexisNexis.

Jonah, B. et al. 1999. Front-line police officers' practices, perceptions and attitudes about the enforcement of impaired driving laws in Canada. *Accident Analysis and Prevention*, 31: 421–443.

Kellough, G., and Wortley, S. 2002. Remand for plea. Bail decisions and plea bargaining as commensurate decisions. *The British Journal of Criminology*, 42: 186–210.

Lafontaine, G., and Rondinelli, V. 2005. Plea bargaining and the modern criminal defence lawyer: Negotiating guilt and the economics of the 21st century criminal justice. *Criminal Law Quarterly*, 50: 108–127.

Law Reform Commission of Canada. 1975. *Criminal Procedure: Control of the Process*. Working Paper No. 15. Ottawa: Information Canada.

———. 1984. *Disclosure by the Prosecution*. Report No. 22. Ottawa: Ministry of Supply and Services.

———. 1989. *Plea Discussions and Agreements*. Working Paper No. 60. Ottawa: Law Reform Commission of Canada.

Manson, A. 2001. *The Law of Sentencing*. Toronto: Irwin Law.

McCoy, C. 2005. Plea bargaining as coercion: The trial penalty and plea bargaining reform. *Criminal Law Quarterly*, 50: 67–107.

McGillivray, A. 1997–98. *R. v. Bauder*: Seductive children, safe rapists, and other justice tales. *Manitoba Law Journal*, 25: 359–383.

McGillivray, A. 1998. "A moral vacuity in her which is difficult if not impossible to explain": Law, Psychiatry and the Remaking of Karla Homolka. *International Journal of the Legal Profession*, 5: 255–288.

Ontario, Attorney General. 1993. *Report of the Attorney General's Advisory Committee on Charge Screening, Disclosure and Resolutions Discussions*. Toronto: Queen's Printer.

Pan, J., and Kaiser, M.G. 2001. Thirtieth annual review of criminal procedure: Guilty pleas. *Georgetown Law Journal*, 89: 384–437.

Roach, K. 1999. *Due Process and Victims' Rights: The New Law and Politics of Criminal Justice*. Toronto: University of Toronto Press.

Roberts, J. 2000. *Plea Bargaining with Budgetary Constraints and Deterrence*. Working Papers from University of Toronto, Department of Economics. Toronto: University of Toronto. Online at: http://www.chass.utoronto.ca/ecipa/archive/UT-ECIPA-JOROB-00-01.pdf

Seifman, R.D., and Freidberg, A. 2001. Plea bargaining in Victoria: The role of counsel. *Criminal Law Journal*, 2: 64–74.

Solomon, P. 1983. *Criminal Justice Policy, From Research to Reform*. Toronto: Butterworths.

U.S. Department of Justice. 2002. *Office for Victims of Crime, Legal Series Bulletin # 7: Victim Input into Plea Agreements* (Washington, DC: Office for Victims of Crime). Online at: http://www.ojp.usdoj.gov/ovc/publications/bulletins/legalseries/bulletin7/welcome.html

Verdun-Jones, S.N., and Hatch, A. 1985. *Plea Bargaining and Sentencing Guidelines*. Ottawa: Department of Justice Canada.

Verdun-Jones, S.N., and Tijerino, A.A. 2001. *Victim Participation in the Plea Negotiation Process in Canada: A Review of the Literature and Four Models of Law Reform.* Ottawa: Department of Justice Canada.

——. 2004. Four models of victim involvement during plea negotiations: Bridging the gap between legal reforms and current legal practice. *Canadian Journal of Criminology and Criminal Justice,* 46: 471–500.

——. 2005. Victim participation in the plea negotiation process: An idea whose time has come? *Criminal Law Quarterly,* 50: 190–212.

Viljoen J.L., Klaver J., and Roesch, R. 2005. Legal decisions of preadolescent and adolescent defendants: Predictors of confessions, pleas, communication with attorneys, and appeals. *Law and Human Behavior,* 29: 253–77.

CASES CITED

Boudreau v. Benaiah (2000), 142 C.C.C. (3rd) 97 (Ont. C.A.).

R. v. Bezdan, [2001] B.C.J. No. 808 (C.A.)(QL).

R. v. Burlingham, [1995] 2 S.C.R. 206.

R. v. G.W.C., (2000) 150 C.C.C. (3d) 513 (Alta. C.A.), Supplementary Reasons, [2001] 5 W.W.R. 240 (Alta. C.A.).

R. v. Lyons, [1987] 2 S.C.R. 309.

R. v. Neale, [2000] B.C.J. No. 668 (C.A.)(QL).

Vanscoy v. Ontario, [1999] O.J. No. 1661 (Ont. S.C.)(QL).

ENDNOTES

1 The principle that courts are in no way bound by a plea agreement is illustrated by the most unfortunate case of *R. v. Neale* (2000). Neale had agreed to plea guilty to a charge of robbery in exchange for the Crown's undertaking to make a submission in support of a five-year sentence, less the time already spent in custody. Unfortunately, counsel neglected to inform the trial judge that this plea agreement had been reached. Subsequently, the trial judge sentenced Neale to seven years in prison. Even though Neale did not receive the sentence recommended by the Crown (and even though the trial judge was never informed that a plea bargain had been struck), the Court of Appeal nevertheless dismissed the appeal against the sentence. Justice Lambert noted (para. 14) that, in his opinion, "no injustice is being done to the appellant in this particular case through the processes before the sentencing judge." He stated that "the sentence is a fit one with the appropriate range and the circumstances of the sentencing were not such as to create any injustice...."

2 Peace bonds may be imposed under sections 810, 810.01, 810.1, and 810.2 of the *Criminal Code.* Under a peace bond, an accused person enters into a "recognizance" (a binding promise) to be of "good conduct" for a period up to 12 months. Breach of this recognizance is a criminal offence (s. 811 of the *Criminal Code*). This procedure is followed where there is a

reasonable fear that the accused person will commit a serious offence; for example, a sexual assault against a child or a crime of domestic violence (see Bala, 1999).

[3] Homolka eventually served the entire 12 years of her sentence in prison. She was not granted parole or statutory release (see Gillis, 2005).

CHAPTER 11
Preventing Gun Crime

INTRODUCTION

If asked to identify the number one crime problem in their country, many Canadians would cite gun-related crimes, particularly if they live in or near Toronto. Canada's largest city has witnessed a number of high profile shooting incidents in recent years, culminating in the tragic shooting on Yonge Street in December 2005, which resulted in the death of a young woman. How should the justice system respond to a crime problem of this nature? Are exceptional measures appropriate or necessary? Other jurisdictions have adopted a wide range of solutions, from providing police officers with additional powers to search suspect's residences through to tough mandatory sentencing laws for offenders convicted of gun-related crimes. In the Spring of 2006, the federal government introduced reform legislation to address the sentencing in cases of gun crime. In this chapter, Tom Gabor reviews the policy options for preventing gun violence.

Preventing Gun Crime
Thomas Gabor, University of Ottawa

In 2005, a series of events catapulted the issue of firearms onto the front pages of the nation's newspapers. Unlike Canada's neighbour to the south, concerns about crime and justice have been a low priority relative to health care, education, and economic concerns (Goff, 2004, p. 100). Occasionally, however, due to the inherently dramatic nature of certain crimes, these issues seize the media's and public's attention, at least momentarily. This was certainly the case following the 1989 massacre of 14 women by Marc Lepine at the University of Montreal. That event mobilized interest groups and a large number of Canadians, made gun control a major part of the Liberal Party's program in 1993, and culminated in the Firearms Act of 1995 under a Liberal government. That Act increased penalties for the use of firearms in 10 major crimes and introduced a national registry for long guns (a registry for handguns had already existed from the 1930s). This article describes the context in which the firearms issue has seized the spotlight in Canada. It presents some trends and patterns in firearm mortality and assesses existing gun control strategies and suggestions for preventing gun violence in Canada.

RECENT HIGH-PROFILE GUN CRIMES

As with the mass killing of women in Montreal, high-profile incidents have once again raised the level of awareness of the issue of gun violence among Canadians and their leaders. On March 3, 2005, Canada experienced the worst single incident involving police casualties, as four Royal Canadian Mounted Police (RCMP) officers were gunned down in Mayerthorpe, Alberta, as they were raiding a farm alleged to be the scene of various illegal activities (Walton and Harding, 2006). These four deaths exceeded the average number of police officers killed on duty in an entire year across the entire country. For example, in 2003, no police officers were murdered in Canada; and in 2002, only one officer was murdered on the job (Dauvergne, 2004; Savoie, 2003). Another high-profile killing of a police officer occurred on December 14, 2005, when a 25-year-old female officer was gunned down in the Montreal area.

It was Toronto, however, that was most consistently at the centre of gun-related carnage in 2005. A total of 300 people were shot that year in Canada's largest city, including 52 fatalities—a record for the city. The issue of guns and gangs has surfaced on and off for more than a decade in Toronto. Discussions of this issue have been sensitive, as they have frequently revolved around the issue of race, because both the perpetrators and victims of many of these shootings have been young black men (Fowlie, 2004).

Especially disconcerting was that the Toronto shootings occurred in public places, with little regard for bystanders. In July 2005, four men were gunned down within a week, attracting considerable coverage from the international media. On November 18, 2005, 18-year-old Amon Beckles was attending the funeral of a friend whose killing he had witnessed. He was confronted by three men in the church's lobby. One of the men shot and killed Beckles with a semi-automatic weapon, while 300 attendees ducked for cover. Bill Blair, Toronto's Chief of Police, was appalled by the shooting: "The public nature of this violence demonstrates the callousness … some of these gang members have and the total disrespect they have for their community and for public institutions, like churches" (CTV.ca, 2005).

However, it was on Boxing Day 2005 that the issue of gun crimes came to a head in Toronto. Boxing Day is one of the busiest shopping days of the year, and the downtown area along Yonge Street was congested with shoppers. Gunfire erupted during the day, killing 15-year-old Jane Creba and wounding six others. Jane had been out shopping with her mother when she was caught in the crossfire between two groups of young men (CBC.ca, 2005). This incident, combined with the many brutal and public killings earlier in the year, left the city reeling and instantly transformed firearms into a major election issue during the federal campaign of January, 2006. The rival political parties scrambled to develop policies to deal with the problem.

Two-thirds of the homicides in Toronto, during 2005, were committed with guns, far in excess of the national average, which tends to range between 25 and 30 percent. Overall, Toronto's homicide rate was lower than that of many other Canadian cities; but the more frequent use of firearms (usually handguns), the public settings of many Toronto homicides, and the racial dimension, as well as the city's status as the hub of Canadian commerce and media, accounted for the high profile of Toronto's gun violence issue.

The national situation is very different from that of Toronto, creating dilemmas for those responsible for setting policy in this area. In Canada, the federal government is responsible for making criminal law. The challenge is that overly restrictive gun control measures may be perceived as excessive in much of the country, even if they are embraced by Torontonians. Indeed, nationally, there are signs that the use of firearms in various violent crimes, such as homicide and robbery, has been declining for more than a decade. The rate of firearm homicides has declined steadily from 1991, and the proportion of homicides involving firearms has also declined. In 2002, this figure was 26 percent, the lowest recorded since records were first collected on gun homicide in 1961 (Dauvergne, 2004; Savoie, 2003). In addition, from 1991 to 2004, the firearm robbery rate in Canada declined by 63 percent (Sauve, 2005). Further reinforcing the point that gun-related crime is not epidemic throughout Canada are the results of the most recent General Social Survey undertaken by Statistics Canada (Gannon and Mihorean, 2005). This large national victimization survey found that just 3 percent of those experiencing a violent offence in 2004 had been attacked or threatened with a gun.

However, balancing such reassuring figures are two developments that are more of a concern. First, handguns have displaced long guns as the weapons of choice in Canadian homicides whenever firearms are used. Currently, about two-thirds of all firearm homicides involve handguns (Dauvergne, 2004). This development suggests that handguns may have become more accessible in Canada, although the data on this matter are soft, since many firearms are smuggled into the country and are unregistered. A second development is that street gang activity in Canada appears to have intensified over the last 10 to 15 years. One indication is that gang-related homicides have quadrupled during that period (Dauvergne, 2004).

Thus, there is no nationwide epidemic of gun violence in Canada. The gun-related violence that has gained the public's attention appears to be an urban phenomenon that is often linked to gang activity. Unregistered handguns brought illicitly into Canada are an immediate concern.

FIREARM OWNERSHIP AND MORTALITY LEVELS IN CANADA

While there is some variation across surveys, there are between 7 and 11 million legally-owned firearms in Canada, and approximately 25 percent of Canadian households own at least one firearm (Canadian Firearms Centre, 2000). Long guns (shotguns and rifles) outnumber handguns by a ratio of between 6:1 and 9:1 (Gabor, 1997; Gabor, 1994; Hung, 2000). Most firearms are owned by residents of small communities, and the primary motive for gun ownership in Canada is for hunting (Gabor, 1994). Other reasons offered for gun ownership are target shooting, gun collecting, and self-defence. Self-defence is rarely considered a legitimate reason for ownership in Canada; but in national surveys, about 1 to 5 percent mention this as a reason for ownership (Gabor, 1997).

Each year, about one thousand Canadians die as a result of gunshot wounds (Hung, 2000). Roughly 80 percent of these deaths are suicides, another 15 to 20 percent are homicides, and a small number are unintentional (accidental) deaths. Historically, most firearm homicides were committed with long guns rather than handguns, a situation which was consistent with the much greater volume of long guns. In the last 10 years, this situation has reversed itself, as handguns are used in about two-thirds of firearm homicides (Dauvergne, 2004). In 1989, about two-thirds of gun homicides were committed with long guns. At first glance, this dramatic change in the proportion of homicides involving handguns appears to lend support to elevated concerns regarding handgun violence. But in fact, the national rates of homicide with handguns have not increased; rather, the rates of homicide involving long guns have declined. Thus, handgun homicides have not increased in absolute terms: they have only increased relative to long-gun homicides.

The decline in homicides committed with shotguns and rifles has been interpreted as evidence of the effectiveness of a number of controls imposed upon long guns through legislation passed in 1991 and 1995 (Coalition for Gun Control, 2005). Collectively, these two packages of legislation regulated the storage of firearms, increased the minimum penalties for the use of firearms in ten serious crimes—this provision applies to all firearms—and established a national registry for long guns. A registry for handguns had already existed from the 1930s.

APPROACHES TO PREVENTING GUN VIOLENCE

The previous sections indicate that gun violence is neither epidemic nor even increasing across Canada. Nevertheless, gun violence is a legitimate concern, particularly in various urban settings, given the escalation of gang violence and the brazenness of many shootings. There are three broad strategies available to reduce the level of gun violence:

1. legislation;
2. crime prevention through social development; and
3. situational prevention strategies.

These three groups of strategies are not mutually exclusive.

LEGISLATION

The most common approach to combating gun violence has involved legislative reforms. Often referred to as "gun control," these measures are quite diverse:

- Controlling Gun Use: These measures require people to have permits to carry firearms, and they limit the use of guns to certain activities (e.g., hunting and target shooting).
- Requiring Safe Storage: Owners may be required to store guns in certain places, to keep them locked up, and to store ammunition separately.
- Educating Owners: Owners may be required to take courses on the safe use and storage of firearms.
- Enhanced Sentences: These measures often take the form of mandatory minimum sentences for using a gun in the commission of a crime.
- Licensing Owners: Owners may be required to apply for a license, and high-risk users may be prohibited from owning guns.
- Waiting Periods: Establishing waiting periods for purchases means that there is a cooling-off period for those wishing to buy a gun for the specific purpose of committing a crime or suicide. Such a waiting period also allows for the screening of prospective owners by law enforcement agencies.
- Disrupting the Supply of Prohibited Weapons: Law enforcement and customs agencies may attempt to interrupt or reduce the illegal flow of firearms into a country.
- Reducing the Lethality of Firearms: Certain models of firearms and types of ammunition may be banned. Permitted barrel length and magazine size may be reduced. Police may require protective clothing in dangerous encounters.
- Reducing Firearm Availability: Banning and restricting firearms, controlling imports, and establishing gun amnesty programs or buyback schemes can reduce the inventory of firearms in a society.

There has been a lively debate over the success of some of these measures (Gabor, 1994; Kleck, 1997). Some scholars even suggest that many gun control measures are counterproductive, since restricting access to firearms denies citizens a potentially useful means of deterring crime (Lott, 1998). The firearms literature contains a great deal of rhetoric since relatively few of these strategies has been subject to a thorough, non-partisan evaluation

(Kleck, 1997, p. 377). Nevertheless, certain strategies have been shown to be effective in relation to certain forms of crime or self-injury:

- Licensing and permit laws that involve background checks;
- Bans on gun possession for ex-offenders and mentally ill persons;
- Mandatory penalties for unlicensed gun carrying; and,
- Enhanced penalties for committing a crime with a firearm (Kleck, 1997, p. 377).

In Canada, legislation regarding licensing, firearms prohibition orders, and enhanced penalties is quite stringent. For example, the licensing of owners and the registration of all firearms are obligatory. As well, individuals can be prohibited from owning firearms for lengthy periods, and mandatory minimum prison sentences of up to four years exist for the use of guns in crime.

While firearm crimes have been declining with the passage of increasingly stringent gun laws during the 1990s, it is difficult to establish the impact of these laws relative to other developments over the same 10 to 15 years. Canada's population has been aging, and its economy has been growing (Ouimet, 2002). Thus, social and economic factors may have also played a role in declining gun crime. One American study examined the relative influence on state firearm deaths of the presence or absence of restrictions on gun use and of various socioeconomic variables, such as the poverty level, unemployment rate, and alcohol consumption level. These socioeconomic variables were found to play a more significant role on gun deaths than did the legislation (Kwon et al., 1997). Thus, the second strategy, preventing crime through social development, deserves our attention.

CRIME PREVENTION THROUGH SOCIAL DEVELOPMENT

Crime prevention through social development (CPSD) involves an amalgam of measures aiming to improve social conditions, in order to combat the "root causes" of crime. In addition, these measures are designed to assist at-risk individuals and groups. CPSD does not address gun-related crime in particular, but rather crime and violence more generally. Educational and vocational training programs, family-oriented programs (e.g., home visitation, parenting skills, daycare), preschool and school-based programs, and programs designed to build neighbourhood cohesion (e.g., the Chicago Area Project) are some examples of initiatives that can potentially reduce crime and violence in the short or long term.

More specifically, home visitation and parenting skills programs have been found to be effective in dealing with aggressive behaviour in children (Welsh et al., 2002, p. 21). The Michigan-based Perry Preschool Program, which was introduced in the 1960s, has been a resounding success in providing disadvantaged children with high-quality learning for a two-year period. Follow-up studies to the age of 27 revealed that program participants had half the arrests of a control group (Schweihart, 1993). In Montreal, hyperactive and aggressive boys were given school-based training to boost their social skills, and their parents were trained in the use of non-punitive and consistent discipline. Follow-ups of the boys into their teens indicated that they were less aggressive than a control group. As another example, programs such as the Chicago Area Project try to improve community cohesion by working with local gangs and including them in neighbourhood improvement efforts (Lab, 1988). While the impact of this project remains unclear, its goal is to reduce the sense of exclusion that may have played a role in the reckless shootouts in Toronto during 2005.

SITUATIONAL CRIME PREVENTION

Situational crime prevention involves measures that increase the risk or effort required to commit a crime, reduce the payoffs from crime, or induce guilt or shame for committing crime. With respect to firearm-related crime, the police, private security officers, merchants, or private citizens can make it more difficult to access firearms, can raise the risks of arrest or personal injury for those using guns, or can create disincentives by making it more difficult for armed individuals to achieve their goals. In addition, technology can be used to prevent armed individuals from gaining access to events or places in which they can cause casualties and create disorder. In New York City, the introduction of an aggressive "zero tolerance" style of policing in the 1990s appeared to play a major role in dramatic reductions in violent crimes, including gun homicides and robberies (Kelling and Bratton, 1998). Homicides overall dropped by 60 percent and robberies by 48 percent between 1993 and 1997. Officers were instructed to stop and search individuals for the most minor infractions (e.g., drinking or urinating in public), yielding many concealed weapons and other contraband. A similar program in Kansas City in 1994 targeting guns in crime hot spots was credited with reducing the rate of gun crimes in the targeted areas by 49 percent (Sherman et al., 1994).

A robbery prevention program introduced in the 1970s in Southland Corporation's 7-Eleven convenience stores has served as the prototype for commercial robbery prevention programs for more than 25 years. This program, developed with the aid of career armed robbers, has been shown to reduce the number of robberies (whether gun or other robberies), as well as losses per robbery (Gabor et al., 1987). Employees of retail establishments in this program have to follow seven steps, including surveying the store more accurately, improving lighting around stores, increasing the visibility of cash registers from the street, and limiting the cash circulating in stores. Subsequent research has added to the program some features that might lower an establishment's risk of being robbed (Hunter and Jeffery, 1992).

While the evidence across jurisdictions has been mixed, the experience in a number of American and British cities suggests that improving street lighting can reduce gun-related as well as other crime (Farrington and Welsh, 2002). Many experts believe that the installation of fixed and "pop-up" video screens has reduced the number of bank robberies in Australia and post office hold-ups in England (Ekblom, 1992). Closed-circuit television monitors (CCTV) have been found to reduce muggings on the London underground (Mayhew et al., 1979). The introduction of passenger and baggage screening produced a dramatic decline in airline hijackings in the 1970s (Wilkinson, 1986). Following the attacks of September 11, 2001, refinements of such screening have been introduced to detect weapons and explosives. In addition, detection systems and screening for weapons by security personnel are now being used in other environments, from public schools and buildings to the Super Bowl.

CONCLUSION

What is Canada to do about gun violence? The situation in Canada is complex, since concerns about gun violence are confined for the most part to a limited number of urban centres. The use of guns in Toronto is especially a concern, and given the city's status as the economic and cultural centre of Canada, all levels of government ought to do what they can to prevent a descent into chaos and disorder. Since criminal law is the responsibility of the federal government, that level of government must play a key role with regard to legislation. The enactment of new criminal statutes or penalties, however, must be undertaken in a circumspect manner, as these laws will be applicable to all of Canada's regions.

Three broad strategies are available to combat gun violence—legislative reform, crime prevention through social development, and situational prevention. Elements of all three strategies ought to be adopted. With regard to legislation, Canada already has some of the most strict gun control measures in the world, including four-year mandatory penalties for using guns in major crimes and a national registry for all firearms.

At the time of writing, the new Conservative Government is considering the dismantlement of the registry for long guns but proposes to strengthen the mandatory minimum penalties. Increasing the mandatory penalties may be counterproductive, since experience indicates that prosecutors often are reluctant to lay charges in cases where the penalties that already exist are viewed as disproportionate (Gabor and Crutcher, 2001). When penalties are seen as excessive, their implementation tends to be less consistent. Hence, the certainty of punishment, arguably more important as a deterrent than its severity, is compromised.

I would recommend the introduction of a mandatory penalty of, say, one year in prison for the illegal carriage of a concealed firearm in a public place. While the concern related to illegal carriage varies across jurisdictions, such conduct poses a threat to public safety. In any event, such a law would be enforced aggressively only in those jurisdictions in which gun crime is a priority. Jurisdictions in which gun violence is not a major concern would focus their resources on other issues. In Toronto, there is strong public will to deal with this issue, and actors within the justice system—the police, prosecutors, and judges—need to be mobilized to strictly enforce this measure. Toronto may need to place more officers on the street and deploy additional patrols in the heart of the city and in high-risk neighbourhoods. The police require the support of the entire city, as well as the communities that will be especially affected. There is every indication that those communities that have been terrorized by street gangs will cooperate.

However, the deployment of additional police personnel in vulnerable areas is, in itself, insufficient. As in New York City's successful application of "zero tolerance" policing, the unlawful carrying of weapons can only be uncovered through an aggressive posture on the part of officers. In New York, even minor traffic violations were used as opportunities to search individuals and their vehicles. Torontonians must decide whether they have the stomach for such aggressive tactics. They must decide between a strategy in which the police merely respond to incidents, such as the Boxing Day shootings, and a more proactive policy.

Following the many brazen incidents in 2005, there is every indication that the city as a whole, including many prominent leaders within minority communities, is ready for a more assertive approach. If the city adopts a crackdown on the unlawful carriage of firearms, this initiative should be accompanied by a high-profile media publicity campaign, because such campaigns enhance any deterrent effect. The use of video surveillance, through the installation of cameras in Toronto's core and its subway system, may serve as a deterrent to attacks and may aid in the investigation of crimes. Such surveillance has been used effectively in a number of contexts (Poyner, 1992). Critics of a "get-tough" approach will argue that violence cannot be addressed effectively without dealing with its "root causes." While the underlying causes of Toronto's current problems can be debated, I regard social development approaches as complementing the more aggressive law enforcement approach. Family issues, social disadvantage, and feelings of exclusion experienced by some of those involved in the gun violence can be addressed through an array of programs. They are, however, mostly medium and long-term solutions, requiring financial commitments of sufficient duration by the different levels of government.

DISCUSSION QUESTIONS

1. *In your view, what is the single most effective response to gun-related crime?*
2. *One radical suggestion to reduce the incidence of gun crime is to enforce a curfew on certain age groups. Is this an appropriate response to the problem?*

FURTHER READINGS

Gabor, T. 1994. *The Impact of the Availability of Firearms on Violent Crime, Suicide and Accidental Death.* Ottawa: Department of Justice Canada.
Hemenway, D. 2004. *Private Guns, Public Health.* Ann Arbor: University of Michigan Press.
Kleck, G. 1997. *Targeting Guns.* New York: Aldine de Gruyter.

REFERENCES

Canadian Firearms Centre. 2000. Overview, Analysis and Development of a Baseline Model (Internal document). (Available from the author of this chapter.)

CBC.ca. 2005. *Toronto Police Release Name, Details of Shooting Victim.* December 28.

Coalition for Gun Control. 2005. *Myths and Facts about Gun Control.*

CTV.ca. 2005. *Man Shot to Death during Toronto Funeral.* November 18.

Dauvergne, M. 2004. Homicide in Canada, 2003. *Juristat,* 24.

Ekblom, P. 1992. Preventing post office robberies in London: Effects and side effects. In R.V. Clarke (Ed.), *Situational Crime Prevention: Successful Case Studies.* New York: Harrow and Heston.

Farrington, D., and Welsh, B. 2002. *Effects of Improved Street Lighting on Crime: A Systematic Review.* London: Home Office.

Fowlie, J. 2004. Toronto crime figures reveal racial disparity. *Globe and Mail,* January 7, A8.

Gabor, T. Baril, M., Cusson, M., Elie, D., Leblanc, M., and Normandeau, A. 1987. *Armed Robbery: Cops, Robbers, and Victims.* Springfield, IL: Charles C Thomas.

Gabor, T., and Crutcher, N. 2001. *Mandatory Minimum Sentences: Their Effects on Crime, Sentencing Disparities, and Criminal Justice Expenditures.* Ottawa: Department of Justice Canada.

Gabor, T. 1997. *Firearms and Self-Defence: A Comparison of Canada and the United States.* Ottawa: Canadian Firearms Centre.

Gabor, T. 1994. *The Impact of the Availability of Firearms on Violent Crime, Suicide, and Accidental Death.* Ottawa: Department of Justice Canada.

Gannon, M., and Mihorean, K. 2005. Criminal victimization in Canada, 2004. *Juristat,* 25.

Goff, C. 2004. *Criminal Justice in Canada,* 3rd ed. Scarborough: Nelson.

Hung, K. 2000. *Firearm Statistics.* Ottawa: Department of Justice Canada.

Hunter, R., and Jeffery, C. 1992. Preventing convenience store robbery through environmental design. In R. Clarke (Ed.), *Situational Crime Prevention: Successful Case Studies.* New York: Harrow and Heston.

Kelling, G., and Bratton, W. 1998. Declining crime rates: Insiders' views of the New York City story. *Journal of Criminal Law and Criminology,* 88: 1217–1231.

Kleck, G. 1997. *Targeting Guns.* New York: Aldine de Gruyter.

Kwon, I., Scott, B., Safranski, S., and Bae, M. 1997. The effectiveness of gun control laws: Multivariate Statistical Analysis. *American Journal of Economics and Sociology,* 56: 41–50.

Lab, S. 1988. *Crime Prevention: Approaches, Practices, and Evaluations.* Cincinnati: Anderson.

Lott, J. 1998. *More Guns, Less Crime.* Chicago: University of Chicago Press.

Mayhew, P., Clarke, R.V., Burrows, J.N., Hough, J.M., and Winchester, S. 1979. *Crime in Public View*. London: Home Office.

Ouimet, M. 2002. Explaining the American and Canadian crime "drop" in the 1990s. *Canadian Journal of Criminology*, 44: 33–50.

Poyner, B. 1992. Video cameras and bus vandalism. In R. Clarke (Ed.), *Situational Crime Prevention: Successful Case Studies*. New York: Harrow and Heston.

Sauve, J. 2005. Crime statistics in Canada, 2004. *Juristat*, 25.

Savoie, J. 2003. Homicide in Canada, 2002. *Juristat*, 23.

Schweihart, L., Barnes, H., and Weikart, D. 1993. *The High/Scope Perry Preschool Study Through Age 27*. Ypsilanti MI.: High/Scope Press.

Sherman, L., Rogan, D., and Shaw, J. 1994. The Kansas City gun experiment— NIJ Update. *Research in Brief*. Washington: National Institute of Justice.

Walton, D., and Harding, K. 2006. Mayerthorpe: What have the Mounties learned from a tragedy? *Globeandmail.com*, February 27.

Welsh, B., Farrington, D., Sherman, L., and MacKenzie, D. 2002. What do we know about crime prevention? *International Annals of Criminology*, 40: 11–31.

Wilkinson, P. 1986. *Terrorism and the Liberal State*, 2nd ed. New York: New York University Press.

CHAPTER 12
Serving Time at Home

INTRODUCTION

Most criminal justice systems allow certain offenders to serve their sentences of imprisonment at home, provided they comply with a number of conditions. If these conditions are violated, the offender is required to appear in court and may be ordered to serve the remainder of the sentence in prison. The *conditional sentence* of imprisonment in Canada is an example of a sentence of custody that is served at home. One of the most often discussed conditions imposed on offenders serving a conditional sentence of imprisonment is the curfew or house arrest.

What is it like to live under house arrest? This chapter reports findings from interviews with offenders who are serving a sentence of imprisonment— at home. This research also explores the experiences and perceptions of people who live with offenders serving these sentences. Their views are important for two reasons: first, because they share many of the restrictions imposed on offenders; and second, because they play an important role in ensuring that the offender complies with the conditions imposed by the court.

Serving Time at Home
Julian V. Roberts, University of Ottawa

The views of offenders were not often considered in studies of the criminal justice system. There appears to be a certain unspoken agreement that having been sentenced ... the views of the individual so dealt with are irrelevant. (Mair and Nee, 1990, p. 52).

In 1996, Canada's Parliament added a new sentence to the range of options used by the courts. The phrase *conditional sentence of imprisonment* is in a sense a paradox: it is a term of custody that the offender serves at home. If a judge believes that no sentence other than imprisonment is appropriate, he or she must then decide whether the offender may serve the sentence at home or be committed to a prison. Certain criteria must be met before the offender is allowed to serve the sentence at home. For example, if the offence carries a mandatory term of imprisonment, then the offender is not eligible. If the offender is ordered to serve his or her sentence at home, the court imposes a number of conditions. The offender may have to obey a curfew or strict house arrest. This means being confined to home except for court-authorized absences: for example, to go to work or attend school. In addition, the court may order the offender to follow a treatment program and perform service for the community. The offender will also be supervised by a probation officer. In the event that the offender violates the court-imposed conditions without a reasonable excuse, the offender will be brought back to court and may be ordered to serve the remainder of the sentence in an institution.

PUBLIC STEREOTYPES OF SENTENCING

Misperceptions about prison life can lead people to dismiss a sentence of years in prison as "a slap on the wrist," one that the offender can do "standing on his head." For this reason, it's not surprising that there are misperceptions about home confinement. One public stereotype of the conditional sentence of imprisonment is that offenders serving sentences at home enjoy all the benefits of home life, and the conditions they must obey (such as going to work or school and attending medical appointments) are simply those duties that any law-abiding citizen must do on a daily basis. This somewhat naive (and cynical) view of a conditional sentence accounts in part for the widespread public opposition to the use of home confinement for offenders convicted of crimes of violence. For violent crimes, the public expects a severe response from the courts. To most of the public, being confined to one's home is not severe enough to represent an adequate response to violent crime.

At one time, this perception may have been fairly accurate. In the early days of the conditional sentence regime, offenders on whom this sentence was imposed had few conditions to follow. House arrest, for example, was practically unheard of (Roberts, Antonowicz, and Sanders, 2000). Curfews were rare and many were very flexible (for example, requiring the offender to be home only after 10:00 p.m. and until 7:00 a.m.). In some respects, the sanction was little different from a term of probation. However, since then, conditional sentence orders have become tougher: house arrest is more frequent, and curfews tend to be more restrictive, beginning shortly after the offender has finished work for the day (Roberts, 2002). An accurate picture of the true impact of any sanction can only be gained from understanding the perspective of the people who experience it. What do offenders think about a sentence of imprisonment served at home?

OFFENDER ATTITUDES ABOUT SERVING TIME AT HOME

It is like being with the people that I love, and doing my time with them, but it's not easy. Actually, I think it's tougher than being in jail.[1]

Institutional versus Community Imprisonment

Many people may be surprised to learn that some offenders prefer to go to prison rather than serve a tough community-based sanction. This reaction reflects the perception that prison is always more punitive than its alternatives. In addition, research examining the impact of conditions such as electronic monitoring and home confinement reveals that there are important parallels between prison and home confinement: many (but by no means all) of the "pains of imprisonment" can be reproduced in the home. Payne and Gainey (1998) compare the experience of prison to life on electronic monitoring. They point out that many of the aversive features of imprisonment, including loss of personal autonomy and deprivation of liberty, are endured by people on electronic monitoring.

Several individuals serving sentences at home have commented that while community imprisonment was clearly preferable to prison, it was not necessarily easier; living on a conditional sentence created challenges and difficulties not encountered in prison. In one sense, prison was the easier sanction, because offenders simply had to "wait out" the sentence: "I didn't like being behind bars, but being out is harder than being in jail." Another offender described life on a conditional sentence in the following words: "You have to think about what you are doing." Some individuals expressed pride at having lived through house arrest. One said: "It's been a long haul but I'm proud of what I've done." Such statements are seldom heard from people leaving prison or those ending a period on parole.

Perceptions of Active versus Passive Sentencing

In jail, you know what you got. What you're doing. You may as well sit there for six months.

Prison creates a passive environment: prisoners react and respond to instructions from the institutional authority. In contrast, a conditional sentence is a far more active disposition: the offender can (and should) take steps toward rehabilitation and restoration. Some judges impose obligations on offenders to actively change their lives. This contrast between the two forms of imprisonment was brought home by one offender who said: "I've been in jail and there's nothing to do, you just eat. If you don't want to eat, you sleep. You stay the whole day sitting down. Being outside is preferable because I can prove to myself that I'm not that kind of person. I can prove to [other] people that I'm not that kind of person." This illustrates the positive potential of serving a sentence at home rather than in prison.

Daily Life in the Virtual Prison

> I was working in the kitchen while in remand, that was the only thing worthwhile in prison ... the community is the better way to go. It's also a lot harder, it teaches you [to make] a lot of sacrifices.
>
> I have a bit of a problem sitting at home on a beautiful day when the 7-Eleven is five steps away.
>
> The hardest part would be dealing with your friends and family, explaining why you couldn't go out.
>
> The hardest for me was absolute house arrest, it's hard when ... you've gotta do something, and you can't. For example, our lease is up ... and I got to go find another place, and I can't do it.

What is it like to live under a tight set of court-ordered conditions, including house arrest or a strict curfew? Many offenders in Canada and elsewhere report that living under home confinement conditions was harder and the conditions more intrusive than they had anticipated (see Church and Dunstan, 1997). The conditions that are hardest to respect are likely to account for the most breaches. The one issue on which all the Canadian offenders agreed was that the most difficult part of serving a conditional sentence was complying with house arrest or a very restrictive curfew. This result is consistent with Petersilia and Deschenes' (1994) research, wherein offenders were asked to rate the perceived difficulty of a number of community correctional conditions: house arrest with electronic monitoring was rated as the most difficult condition imposed on them.

Many of the offenders interviewed had been sentenced to absolute (i.e., 24-hour) house arrest. The consequences of this condition included preventing offenders from participating in social activities, interfering with family outings and special occasions, and creating stigma when other people realized that the offender was serving a sentence. For one offender, the hardest condition was performing community service on top of his job. Nevertheless, he found it a rewarding experience: "When you're working 50 hours a week, it makes for some very long days. But it wasn't just a punishing experience, it was a rewarding experience."

Impact of Conditional Sentence on Children of the Offender

An important consideration in imposing a community sentence rather than prison is the presence of a family. There is an additional incentive for courts to avoid incarcerating the offender if he or she has dependents, and many of the offenders who spoke to us about the experience of home confinement often had families and young children. The most punitive element for these offenders was the impact that the sentence had on their children, whose interactions with their parents and daily lives were affected for the duration of the sentence. One offender noted that the sentence was "especially hard on the kids … because we used to go out, especially in the summer. Every time they ask me, I say I can't."

A female offender discussed the house arrest condition in the context of other conditions imposed: "The absolute curfew is the hardest thing. I can't go anywhere without telling my PO [probation officer]. Absolute curfew is like house arrest. My daughter wants to go the park, but I can't take her." She added that it put a lot of strain on her when she had to try and explain why they couldn't go to the park: "Sometimes I'd say, 'Oh, I'm tired,' or 'We just can't do that today.' It's hard because I don't know what to say. [pause] I have to make excuses." However, she added that staying home was easier than going to jail. She preferred staying home with her children and believed that if not for the children, she would have been sent to jail.

Effect on Interpersonal Relationships

One must be wary of generalizations about the effect of home detention on issues such as relationships. Close confinement for long periods has different effects depending on the personalities of the individuals involved, the nature of the relationship, and the home environment. Although not yet formally tested, an *intensification* effect may exist: home environments characterized by conflict and tension are likely to become worse as a result of the enforced confinement of the offender. Walters (2002) found that offenders on curfew orders in England and Wales reported that the curfew placed a strain on their relationships because it was hard to "walk away from arguments" (p. 32). It is worth noting that these offenders were on curfew orders for a relatively short period: fully 70 percent of those interviewed in that study were serving curfew orders of less than four months. Facing a curfew order of two years—as is possible in Canada—would be a far more daunting proposition, which might create even more stress on relationships.

Partners are also affected by the sentence. One offender said:

> [It has] been very hard on my girlfriend. She felt strapped down. She couldn't go nowhere, I couldn't drive her anywhere … it was also hard for her because she didn't want to tell her friends that I was on a conditional sentence … My girlfriend often tells me how it affects [their relationship]. All we can do is cook some supper if I get groceries on Sunday. All we can do is watch movies if she goes and gets them. I don't have problem with [the other conditions imposed] but the 24 hours at home are too much.

On the other hand, home detention in generally positive environments may enhance human relationships. There is certainly evidence from the Canadian research that young adult offenders confined to homes with loving parents reported that the sentence had been a positive experience. The restrictions on the offender's movements can help rupture antisocial contacts and prevent individuals from being drawn into life patterns that can lead to further offending.

Feeling Pressure to Lie to Others about the Sentence

Few members of the public stop to think about the impact of a conditional sentence on the ways people react to an offender. However, these reactions can amplify the stigma associated with the sentence. Offenders talked about the stigma that they felt when they had told their co-workers about the court order and its associated restrictions.[2] Some individuals expressed concern about potential "whistle-blowers," people who might call the police if they believed that the offender was violating some condition of his or her order. This reaction underlines the important reality that surveillance is not the exclusive domain of probation officers. If it were, ensuring compliance would be impossible, since probation officers simply have too many clients to adequately monitor their behaviour. The negative reaction of friends and co-workers appears to create pressure on conditional sentence offenders to passively hide their status or actively deceive other people.

Offenders sentenced to a conditional sentence and obliged to wear an electronic monitor often have to explain their status to people with whom they have some kind of relationship. In Canada, few offenders are subject to electronic monitoring, since the equipment is not currently available in most provincial correctional systems. However, the restrictions on their movements mean that most offenders have to confront the question of how much to disclose to other people. Fearful of the consequences, many offenders elected to hide their status, particularly with respect to the workplace. In the case of employers, some offenders said nothing rather than explain the true state of affairs. As one individual noted, "I think I'll get fired if I tell my employer." In some cases, however, it was impossible to hide the fact of the sentence, since there were occasions when they were expected to stay after work.

Having to explain the court order to other people, particularly to children, was a source of considerable anxiety for many offenders. In the case of relatively young children, some offenders resorted to deception or simply said (in response to requests to go out) that they "couldn't go out right now." Other offenders explained matters more fully: "My son is fourteen. I sat down with him this summer and I told him what I did and what had happened. The main reason I told him is because he's approaching that age. I told him I don't want him to follow in my footsteps."

LOSS OF SPONTANEITY

Serving a term of imprisonment at home means that daily life has to be planned far more carefully. Offenders have to consider whether particular acts will constitute a breach of the court order, and they have to contact their sentence supervisors in order to apply for permission to attend particular events. For older offenders, making an application to a younger probation officer was a "humbling" experience, as one such individual remarked. In order to join people for coffee after one of his group therapy meetings, he had to obtain the permission of his probation officer; otherwise, he would have been in breach, as the order required him to return directly home once the meeting had ended.

Most (but by no means all) offenders seemed concerned about the consequences of breaching the order by returning home late. One individual noted: "I never actually ran out of time [returning home after a court-authorized shopping trip], but I was always worried about running out of time." Time pressures were a source of considerable stress for these offenders. For the general public, the worst consequence of dawdling while shopping is missing the bus home; for conditional sentence offenders, being late home may result in arrest and, ultimately, committal to custody (for breaching the conditions of the sentence).

EXPERIENCES AND PERCEPTIONS OF FAMILY MEMBERS AND OTHER SPONSORS

> I don't think the judges understand when they hand down this sentence
> that they're handing down the same sentence to the family.

There are important reasons for needing to hear from co-residents of offenders serving sentences of custody at home. First, their lives are dramatically affected when their loved ones are placed under a condition such as house arrest or a strict curfew. Imprisonment affects the lives of people other than the offender. When an offender is sentenced to serve time at home, many of the conditions imposed also affect his or her family members. This is particularly true when electronic monitoring is used. Electronic monitoring creates a zone of surveillance, which encompasses the offender's co-residents. Aungles noted this effect in her study of the prison and the home in Australia: "The surveillance of the prisoner in the home must inevitably be control and punishment shared by both the prisoner and his wife [sic] or parent" (1994, p. 69).

Second, family members and partners play a vital role in ensuring that the offender complies with his or her conditions. In most jurisdictions, probation caseloads do not permit more than perfunctory monitoring of most conditional sentence offenders, except for the higher-risk cases. Whether an offender respects conditions like an absolute curfew, a non-association order, or a prohibition against alcohol consumption depends on the support of his or her family or partner. If the conditional sentence is successful, its success will be more a consequence of the vigilance and support of family members than of even the most draconian threats from the court or the most intrusive surveillance by probation officers. This explains why detainees in New South Wales identified family and social support as the most important contributors to successful completion of the home detention order (Heggie, 1999).

Family members and partners of conditional sentence offenders in Canada and elsewhere were acutely aware of the effect of the sentence. One family member noted: "We felt like we were kind of being judged too." King and Gibbs (2003) report the same reaction from sponsors of offenders on home detention in New Zealand. This effect on families is one of the costs of this form of sentence.

Moreover, family members resented that the court had seemed unaware that a sentence would affect the entire family, not just the offender. This lack of consultation resulted in the parents of young offenders feeling left out of the process. They were passive bystanders at the sentencing hearing as the court imposed a sentence that would change their lives for up to the next two years. One man attending the sentencing of his son said that while the judge was reading each of the conditions, he had been wondering how they would affect his family: "[After] each condition, I'm thinking, okay, how am I going to do this, how am I going to do that? I certainly felt that I walked out of there with a bigger burden."

Offenders, too, were well aware of the impact of their sentence on the people with whom they lived (see also Payne and Gainey, 1998, who found that almost two-thirds of their sample of electronically monitored offenders described negative effects upon their families). "My parents feel like they're the ones being punished; they feel like they're on a sentence," one offender remarked, typical of the comments of others in the study. He added that in his view, his parents had been turned into "his jailers." Another said: "It's been hard on my family, very hard, since I have missed family gatherings, religious ceremonies, and other important family events."

In addition to the anxiety of knowing that a family member may be sent to prison for violating conditions, parents carry the responsibility of assisting the offender in complying with those conditions. What should a parent or spouse do if they see that their son or husband has violated a condition? Call his attention to the fact and, if that fails, report him to the probation authorities? Gibbs and King (2003b) report the same phenomenon with the sponsors of home detainees in New Zealand. Sponsors and other family members "felt the weight of expectation placed upon them by Prison Board members and probation officers: to supervise detainees informally and let probation officers know if things were not working out" (p. 206).

In some jurisdictions, prior to the imposition of a conditional sentence, the court orders an inquiry into the question of the impact of such a sentence on third parties, namely those sharing the residence in which the offender will reside. This includes a consultation with family members. In Canada, a conditional sentence of imprisonment is imposed without any such consultation. The pre-sentence report (prepared prior to sentencing) may address the suitability of the offender for a conditional sentence, but it does not explore the reactions of and consequences for family members. Nor does it solicit any input with respect to the kinds of conditions that might (or might not) promote the purpose they are designed to serve.[3] Thus, family members and partners are expected to play an important role in the administration of the sentence (by encouraging compliance) yet are given no input into the way that sentence is constructed.

Until their son or daughter was sentenced, the parents who were interviewed knew almost nothing about conditional sentences. Many underestimated the intrusiveness of the restrictions that would be placed on the offender's (and their) freedom of action. This was true in Manitoba in 2003 and also in British Columbia a decade earlier (Doherty, 1995). One co-resident noted: "They don't give you much opportunity to speak up." Another commented: "We didn't have any say. You just were told what they were going to do." The exclusion of parents in particular seems curious in light of their obvious importance in helping to assure the offender's compliance with the court-ordered conditions.

The primary response of the relatives interviewed encapsulated two emotions: relief that their family member had not been sent to prison, and anxiety that he or she may nevertheless end up in custody through noncompliance with conditions. A general finding of the research literature is that families and partners welcomed the sentence because it spared the offender from being imprisoned (see Walters, 2002; Church and Dunstan, 1997). It was clear to the parents who were interviewed that in light of the offence (and criminal record) of the offender, committal to custody had been a very real possibility. Accordingly, they were most appreciative of the fact that their son or daughter had been able to come home (most had been in remand at the time of sentencing) rather than being sent to prison. Thus, one family member described the imposition of the conditional sentence as "the best thing that ever happened."

Most of the family members interviewed were parents of young adult offenders. Family members had been told nothing by the judge or any other criminal justice professional, such as the defence or Crown counsel. They were therefore spectators rather than sponsors. Family members expressed great apprehension of the likelihood of committal to custody upon failure to follow the sentence conditions; they did not seem to realize that the offender would have an opportunity to explain to the court why he or she had failed to comply with a condition. One said: "I just feel dread. What happens if she misses her bus? Are they going to throw her back? I dread this all the time." Nor did they seem aware that committal to custody for the duration of the order was only one of several options for the judge at a breach hearing. Some conditions of a conditional sentence order have great potential to create conflict in the family unit. Curfews, for example, generate anxiety among family members that the offender will be late returning home and thereby trigger his arrest: "The six o'clock curfew is important. If I don't take it seriously, he won't take it seriously."

Several parents made statements that illustrate the positive elements of a conditional sentence. For example, some of the conditions that had been imposed, notably abstinence and non-association orders regarding certain individuals, had proved very beneficial and had succeeded in rupturing destructive links between their sons and other offenders. In this respect, it was clear that court-ordered conditions had achieved something that had proved beyond the power of the offender's parents. One family noted that one of the conditions imposed on their son was to avoid all contact with a co-defendant, and that this had proved "a godsend." Over time, the offender had come to realize what a bad influence the individual had been on his life. The parent seemed unsure whether the son would have come to this realization had he not been ordered to avoid contact as part of the conditional sentence, or had he been sentenced to prison.

These family relationships illustrate the complementary relationship that exists between the judicial sentence and the offender's social milieu, notably his or her family. Both elements play a critical role in ensuring compliance with conditions and promoting the offender's rehabilitation. One family member in Canada summed up his experience in the following way: "It was very difficult at first, but it has turned out to be very rewarding. Or at least, a lot of good has come of it."

Another parent couple stated that although they had found the sentence difficult, it also had had a very positive impact on their son. Because of the conditions attached to the order, these parents had acquired more influence over the course of their son's life. This couple needed no convincing of the advantage of a conditional sentence over a term of imprisonment. The families who were interviewed offered clear evidence that some of the conditions imposed as part of the court order, as well as the fact that the offender had been spared an institutional prison term, had contributed to reestablishing relationships among family members. To some degree, this positive effect was also acknowledged by the offenders themselves; one young adult recognized that his relationship with his mother had improved during the time that he had served on the order.

CONCLUSION

The portrait of community custody that emerges from this research is quite different from the image projected by the news media. Offenders serving their prison sentences at home are subject to numerous constraints that change their life in a dramatic manner. As well, there is little discussion in the media about the impact on third parties, or the role that family members play in helping to "administer" the sentence of the court. One of the strengths of this sanction is that it draws upon the resources of the community—the social networks of the offender—to achieve some of its objectives. This strategy, however, comes at a cost: the effect of the sentence is amplified through these networks, and other peoples' lives are affected in significant ways. Of course, this is true of imprisonment as well. When an offender is committed to custody, his partner and his family suffer the loss of their loved one and have to accustom themselves to the inconveniences of visiting hours. The isolation of a prison sentence, however, has a destructive effect on social relations; this is why such a high percentage of relationships fail to survive a lengthy term of incarceration. A conditional sentence may actually strengthen the links between people.

Families and partners of offenders sentenced to conditional sentence have an onerous task thrust upon them, and in most jurisdictions, no institutional support or backup. Yet despite the negatives, there is ample evidence in the research that offenders and their families see a positive element to conditional sentences, and not simply because the sanction spares them the experience of prison. Although on occasion home detention may cause or heighten tension among family members or between partners, for most offenders, the increased time at home appears to have a positive effect on relationships. Many offenders recognize that serving a conditional sentence creates opportunities to change their lifestyle and to preserve social relations that otherwise would be threatened or ruptured by incarceration. In this sense, offenders perceive the sanction as a novel form of custody. Whatever other people may feel about this new form of custody, offenders seem well aware of the potential of the sanction.

DISCUSSION QUESTIONS

1. *Some people argue that serving time at home is never going to be as harsh as spending the same amount of time in prison? What is your view?*
2. *Should the other people sharing the offender's home have to agree before a sentence of home custody is imposed?*

FURTHER READINGS

Gibbs, A. and King, D. 2003. Home detention with electronic monitoring: The New Zealand experience. *Criminal Justice,* 3: 199–211.

Roberts, J.V. 2004. *The Virtual Prison.* Cambridge: Cambridge University Press.

Roberts, J.V., Maloney, L., and Vallis, R. 2003. *Coming Home to Prison. A Study of Offender Experiences of Conditional Sentencing.* Ottawa: Department of Justice Canada.

REFERENCES

Aungles, A. 1994. *The Prison and the Home.* Sydney, Australia: Institute of Criminology Monograph No. 5.

Church, A., and Dunstan, S. 1997. *Home detention: the evaluation of the Home Detention Pilot Programme 1995–1997.* Wellington: New Zealand Ministry of Justice. Online at: http://www.justice.govt.nz/pubs/reports/1997/homedetention/Default.htm.

Doherty, D. 1995. Impressions of the impact of the electronic monitoring program on the family. In K. Schulz (Ed.), *Electronic Monitoring and Corrections: The Policy, the Operation, the Research.* Burnaby, BC: Simon Fraser University.

Gibbs, A., and King, D. 2003. Home detention with electronic monitoring: The New Zealand experience. *Criminal Justice,* 3: 199–211.

Heggie, K. 1999. Review of the NSW Home Detention Scheme. *Research Publication* No. 41. Sydney, NSW: NSW Department of Corrective Services.

King, D. and Gibbs, A. 2003. Is home detention in New Zealand disadvantaging women and children? *Probation Journal*, 50: 115–126.

Mair, G. and Nee, C. 1990. *Electronic Monitoring: The Trials and Their Results.* Home Office Research Study No. 120. London: H.M.S.O.

Payne, B. and Gainey, R. 1998. A qualitative assessment of the pains experienced on electronic monitoring. *International Journal of Offender Therapy and Comparative Criminology*, 42: 149–163.

Petersilia, J., and Piper Deschenes, E. 1994. Perceptions of punishment: Inmates and staff rank the severity of prison versus intermediate sanctions. *The Prison Journal*, 74: 306–328.

Roberts, J.V. 2002. The evolution of conditional sentencing in Canada. *Criminal Reports*, 3 (6th Series): 268–282.

Roberts, J.V., Antonowicz, D., and Sanders, T. 2000. Conditional sentences of imprisonment: An empirical analysis of conditions. *Criminal Reports*, 30: 113–125.

Walters, I. 2002. *Evaluation of the National Roll-out of Curfew Orders.* Home Office On-line Report 15/02. London: Home Office: Research, Development and Statistics Directorate.

ENDNOTES

[1] Unless otherwise indicated, all offender quotes in this chapter come from focus groups and interviews with conditional sentence offenders and their co-residents, conducted in Canada (see Roberts, Maloney and Vallis, 2003).

[2] Of course, prison carries a great deal of stigma too; but an offender who spends three months in prison can easily explain his absence from the community by saying that he was away. In this sense, imprisonment at home is a more public punishment and may carry even more stigma than imprisonment. This is especially true in small communities.

[3] According to s. 742.3(2)(f) of the *Criminal Code*, the optional conditions of this sanction in Canada should secure "the good conduct of the offender" and prevent " a repetition by the offender of the same offence or the commission of other offences."

CHAPTER 13
The Treatment of Prisoners in Canada

INTRODUCTION

Imprisonment is generally reserved for offenders convicted of the most serious crimes. As noted in Chapter 2, offenders sentenced to the longer periods of custody—two years or more—serve their time in a federal penitentiary. The federal correctional system thus houses the most serious offenders in the criminal justice system. How should these offenders be treated? Should they be deprived of many of the rights that law-abiding Canadians enjoy? For example, should prisoners serving time have the right to vote?

In this chapter, Shereen Miller discusses the issue of prisoners' rights. The chapter reviews the rights that prisoners have and identifies the reasons why these rights should exist, even in a prison housing offenders convicted of some of the worst crimes.

How Should We Treat Prisoners?

Shereen H. Benzvy Miller, Member of the Ontario Bar

The *Criminal Code* of Canada defines hundreds of activities as crimes because they have offended public values. Offenders convicted of the most serious offences can be and sometimes are sentenced to long periods of custody. So what kind of treatment can an offender expect if sentenced to imprisonment? Do or should offenders lose all their rights? Should they lose any rights—for example the right to hold citizenship or to vote in elections? Why should we care about people who have hurt others and offended against our values?

Winston Churchill once said: "The mood and temper of the public in regard to the treatment of crime and criminals is one of the most unfailing tests of the civilisation of any country. A calm, dispassionate recognition of the rights of the accused, and even of the convicted criminal ... measure[s] the stored-up strength of a nation and [is] sign and proof of the living virtue in it." Thus, protecting the rights of individual members of our society is at the core of Canada's constitutional and legal frameworks. And sentenced or not, offenders remain members of the society to which they will return having served their time. The criminal justice system and corrections specifically must balance the rights of the individuals involved and public safety concerns.

HAVEN'T OFFENDERS FORFEITED THEIR RIGHTS?

Canada's commitment to various international human rights agreements[1] has set certain standards and enshrined many of these obligations in legislation and the *Charter of Rights and Freedoms*. The rights of Canadians are set out in and protected by the Constitution and the *Canadian Charter of Rights and Freedoms*. We retain these rights whether we are hospitalized, serving a sentence of imprisonment, or simply enjoying life (when we are most likely to take them for granted). You may not think much about your right to practice the religion of your choice, the right to freedom of expression, freedom of peaceful assembly and association, the right to legal counsel, the right to a fair hearing, the presumption of innocence, the freedom from arbitrary detention and imprisonment, the right not to be subjected to cruel and unusual treatment and punishment, and the right not to be subjected to unreasonable search or seizure. However, these rights are fundamental to the quality of life in Canada and we should not take them for granted.

Offenders retain the rights and privileges of all members of society, except those that are necessarily removed or restricted as a consequence of the sentence of the court. Statutes such as the *Corrections and Conditional Release Act (CCRA)* protect the fundamental right to life and security, health care, fair and just treatment, and protection from discrimination and mistreatment. Other domestic legislation protects the rights of all Canadians, including offenders, such as the *Canadian Human Rights Act*; the *Privacy Act*; the *Access to Information Act*; the *Official Languages Act*; and the *Transfer of Offenders Act*. By their very nature, the principles of administrative law in Canada protect individuals who enter the criminal justice system. The duty to act fairly, due process, and strictly defined powers and delegations of authority limit what actors may do in the name of the state, be they police, prosecutors, judges, or corrections officials.

You might ask: "But what does this really mean? After all, prison should be a painful and punitive experience, and offenders should have thought about the rights they would lose before committing the crime." If we examine the fundamental rights listed above, it is difficult to find more than one or two that people actually agree should be removed. The argument goes something like this: If we want the world to be a safer place, we need to remove criminals from amongst us. But all offenders except the ones who have committed the most heinous offences will be released back into the community at some point. Thus, if our goal is to maximize the safety of communities and if those who have committed crimes will at some point be back living in society, then we must act responsibly towards them during their period of incarceration. This means that although offenders lose the right to liberty, they do not forfeit entitlement to be treated with dignity and humanity. But what of the right to liberty? Why not incarcerate all offenders for life?

WHY NOT SIMPLY "LOCK 'EM UP AND THROW AWAY THE KEY"?

Locking up offenders and throwing away the key might have been the strategy of some penal systems in the past and may still be how some Canadians might prefer sentences were administered. But we should consider the purpose and principles of incarceration when considering locking people up. Sending offenders to prison can serve any or all of five purposes: it can be a) a form of *retribution* or *punishment* for the misdeed; b) a way of *incapacitating* the individual and preventing them from committing further crimes in the community, at least during the period of detention; c) a way of expressing societal disapproval of the individual and *denouncing* the criminal conduct; d) a means of deterring the offender and other potential offenders from further offending; e) an opportunity to provide treatment and rehabilitative programming to ensure safe *reintegration* of the offender back into the community when the sentence of imprisonment ends.

The last purpose of imprisonment is the most difficult to accomplish and also the most important. For this reason, Parliament defined the purpose of incarceration[2] in Canada in section 3 of the *Corrections and Conditional Release Act* (CCRA) as follows:

The purpose of the federal correctional system is to contribute to the maintenance of a just, peaceful, and safe society by

(a) carrying out sentences imposed by courts through the safe and humane custody and supervision of offenders; and

(b) assisting the rehabilitation of offenders and their reintegration into the community as law-abiding citizens through the provision of programs in penitentiaries and in the community.[3]

Having a stated purpose and a Mission Statement is important in ensuring direction for an organization, but respecting and applying the underlying values is a monumental task when one considers the correctional system's responsibilities in supervising the sentences of 22,000 people on any given day, 13,000 of whom are incarcerated and 9,000 of whom are supervised in the community.

The Correctional Service of Canada (CSC) manages 54 penitentiaries of different security levels (including treatment centres and annexes within penitentiaries), 17 community correctional centres, and 71 parole offices.[4] In addition to federally operated facilities, CSC partners with community-based, nongovernmental organizations that run approximately 200 community-based residential facilities across the country (i.e., half-way houses). A fundamental value of CSC's work is the respect for the dignity of individuals, the rights of all members of society, and the potential for human growth and development. CSC assumes that people have the potential to live as law-abiding citizens. These are important assumptions if the goal is safer communities.

Incarceration is expensive, both in fiscal terms and in human terms. Moreover, it is disruptive to families and communities and should only be used when all other options are exhausted or deemed unsafe. Courts therefore do not incarcerate all offenders into perpetuity because it is unnecessary and even counterproductive to promoting the safety of the community. Moreover, it would be dangerous to staff to try to manage people devoid of hope and with nothing to lose because the keys to the cell have been thrown away! The rehabilitation and reintegration of offenders is therefore a top priority. Penitentiaries are not "warehouses" for offenders, but rather institutions in which a prisoner can receive treatment and participate in education and employment programs. These programs are designed to address factors identified as contributing to their criminal behaviour and help in ultimately controlling and reducing the risk that these people will present in the future.

WHY LET PRISONERS OUT BEFORE THE ENTIRE SENTENCE IS OVER?

Most prison systems around the world have programs that permit prisoners to serve part of their sentences of imprisonment in the community. *Parole* is the best-known example of such an early release program. Prisoners apply for conditional release from prison, meaning that they serve the last part of the sentence in the community, subject to conditions imposed by the parole authorities. The purpose of conditional release supervision is to protect society by helping offenders become law-abiding citizens by providing them with assistance and programs. Conditional release is also intended to improve public safety over the long run. Released offenders must adhere to certain standard conditions set out in the release certificate. The releasing provisions in the CCRA allow the parole board to set individually crafted conditions to minimize the risk of reoffending and to increase the likelihood of success in the community. Canada and CSC have invested heavily in research in order to understand the individual needs of offenders. Good correctional practice guides the specific conditions that are imposed in order to help the offender make the adjustment back into society.

For example, offenders must travel directly to their homes or to a residential facility upon release and must report regularly to their parole supervisor. The parole board may also impose additional conditions. These conditions can include curfews, restrictions on movement, prohibitions on drinking, and prohibitions on associating with certain people (such as children and former victims). CSC parole officers can take action if they believe the offender is violating release conditions or is planning to commit another crime. They can suspend the release and return the offender directly to prison until the risk is reassessed. Some of these offenders may remain in prison. Others may be released again, but under more severe restrictions and only after more supervision or community support services are in place.

In essence, research has shown interventions and supervision are the best way of promoting successful community reintegration. One example of a community intervention for accountability for offenders serving sentences for sexual assault is the Circles of Support and Accountability initiative.

Circles of Support and Accountability (COSA) initiatives

The vast majority of sexual offenders receive determinate sentences and eventually return to the community. Experience has clearly demonstrated the need for a coordinated approach to sexual offender reintegration; but shortfalls in both service provision and offender accountability have remained.

The *Circles of Support and Accountability* initiative had its roots in the public's response to a single incident: the release into the community from a federal penitentiary of a high-risk, repeat, child sexual abuser. This event triggered picketing, angry calls for political intervention, heightened media attention, and 24-hour police surveillance. In response to the offender's pleas for assistance, a Mennonite pastor gathered a group of congregants to offer both humane support and create a realistic accountability framework. Following a similar intervention with another offender a few months later, the Mennonite Central Committee of Ontario (MCCO) agreed to sponsor a pilot project called the Community Reintegration Project. From this project, the Circles of Support and Accountability (COSA) movement was born.

COSA has had a profound effect on all stakeholders: offenders, community volunteers, affiliated professionals, and the community-at-large. Ninety percent of parolees reported that in the absence of COSA, they would have had difficulties adjusting to the community, and two-thirds report that they likely would have returned to crime. COSA volunteers said they believed the community became safer as a result of the initiative.

Professionals and agencies involved in COSA included police officers and social services professionals. They report that COSA increased offender responsibility and accountability, and that community safety and support are the focus of the project. Results from a survey of the community-at-large showed that 68 percent of respondents reported they would feel safer if they found out that a high-risk sexual offender in their community belonged to a Circle.

Reoffending among COSA group members occurs at a much lower rate than their matched counterparts, even though COSA participants have a higher risk profile. In each of the three instances of sexual recidivism in the COSA group, the new offence was less severe than the offence for which they had most recently served sentence. The recidivism results compiled in evaluating the COSA pilot project are very encouraging. Sexual recidivism by COSA participants is 70 percent lower than that of the matched comparison sample and is less than one-quarter of projected sexual recidivism rates. It is interesting to note that a risk assessment completed upon the release of the first two parolees to participate in COSA indicated a 100 percent chance of reoffending within seven years. But by the time of the COSA evaluation in 2002, both men had reached their 11th anniversary of crime-free life in the community.

SO HOW DOES CANADA ENSURE THAT THE FOCUS ON HUMAN RIGHTS REMAINS SHARP?

Everything we do is about human interaction, about respect and about modeling ethical behaviour. Compliance with the laws of Canada is all about respecting human rights. No amount of policy, legislation or oversight mechanisms can ever ensure, in and of themselves, respect for the rule of law and for human decency. That responsibility rests with each of us individually.[5]

Being incarcerated in a federal institution means that many decisions affecting the prisoner's life are relegated to someone else's authority, such as Correctional Officers, Parole Officers, Program Managers or Institutional Heads. A former inmate of Beaver Creek Institution, a minimum-security facility in Ontario, marvelled at the CSC's power to affect a prisoner's freedom and what he called "CSC's license to trample human rights" (Melnitzer, 2003, p. 83). Hearing such a statement makes one wonder what mechanisms exist to protect inmates from the immense power of the CSC and its 15,000 employees. The CSC is accountable to the public for its performance.

CSC's operations are monitored by external bodies that hold it accountable for its operations. As a federal government agency, CSC is responsible to the Parliament of Canada, which upholds the rights and freedoms of all Canadians. The Auditor General monitors the proper conduct of government business and audits CSC's financial accounts. The Information Commissioner investigates complaints from people who believe they have been denied rights under the *Access to Information Act*, which is Canada's freedom of information legislation. Like all Canadian citizens, offenders can exercise their right to submit complaints to the Information Commissioner. Another mechanism for external oversight is the Office of the Privacy Commissioner, which advocates for the privacy rights of Canadians. The Canadian Human Rights Commission administers the *Canadian Human Rights Act* and ensures that the principles of equal opportunity and nondiscrimination are followed in all areas of federal jurisdiction, including and especially in the criminal justice system.

One of the most active external oversight bodies for CSC is the Office of the Correctional Investigator (OCI). The *Corrections and Conditional Release Act*[6] mandates that the Correctional Investigator act as the Ombudsman for federal offenders. The primary function of the Office is to investigate and resolve individual offender complaints. As well, the OCI reviews and makes recommendations on the CSC's policies and procedures associated with the areas addressed in inmates' complaints. The Office of the Correctional Investigator publishes an annual report detailing the CSC's application or nonapplication of the recommendations made by the OCI. It records incidents of failure to comply with its governing legislation, policies, and directives, and reports annually to Parliament.

The CSC is not without other critics and watchdogs. In 1994, an *Inquiry into Certain Events at the Prison for Women in Kingston* was commissioned on the recommendation of the Solicitor General. In her report, the Honourable Justice Louise Arbour wrote that the CSC does not understand or respect the rule of law. This report led to a complete reassessment of how the CSC provides for women offenders, as well as a great deal of soul searching to ensure that all CSC decisions were governed by the rule of law. In 2002, Michael Jackson wrote a book called *Justice Behind the Walls*[7] about CSC's failure to respect basic human rights in Canada's prisons. In December 2003, the Canadian Human Rights Commission (CHRC) produced a systemic review of human rights in Correctional Services for the federally sentenced.

The CHRC is important to inmates because it administers the *Canadian Human Rights Act* to ensure that the principles of nondiscrimination are followed in all areas of federal jurisdiction. The CHRC's job is to resolve complaints of discrimination filed against employers, unions, and service providers under the federal government, but this process includes offenders as well. Offenders therefore have access to the CHRC's complaint process. If it cannot resolve a complaint, the Commission may investigate the case further, and may ultimately request that the Canadian Human Rights Tribunal hear the case.

In 2004, in a special report entitled *Protecting Their Rights: A Systemic Review of Human Rights in Correctional Services for Federally Sentenced Women*, the Canadian Human Rights Commission wrote that female prisoners[8] continued to face systemic human rights problems in the federal correctional system. The CHRC recommended that the correctional system needs to be tailored to the unique needs of, and lower security risks posed by female offenders. Specifically, they agreed that the correctional system should take a more gender-based approach to custody, programming, and reintegration for women offenders. Nineteen recommendations for action were included to ensure that the treatment of federally sentenced women became consistent with human rights laws.

Some people argue that the media constitute an accountability mechanism because they report on successes and failures throughout the criminal justice system. But the media are not a systemic mechanism for reporting results. The media require a sound bite or an image, and much of CSC's operations cannot be reduced to a brief report. As a result, media coverage has often distorted or sensationalized events taking place in Canada's prisons. For example, the video clip of a tragic 1999 incident where an inmate died from a seizure in the basement of an isolated institution was played repeatedly on television. The media coverage implied that ominous events were occurring in the institution. Not one reporter asked the more interesting question: How did the video come to exist? No tourist standing on a balcony could have filmed this incident. The answer is that CSC films all "use of force" interventions and strip searches to ensure that these difficult situations can be reviewed later. Instead of hiding this library in a vault under the Commissioner's desk, every tape is sent to the Correctional Investigator for review. In this case, the copy of this video was shared with the Coroner who conducted the inquest into the death.

In addition, CSC has an Offender Redress system,[9] which is a formal internal mechanism that addresses complaints by individual prisoners or groups of inmates. The system is designed to provide offenders with access to a fair and effective redress mechanism and to recommend corrective action in cases where there is mistreatment or injustice. The Offender Redress mechanism helps ensure that offenders' problems and expectations are brought to the attention of personnel across the Service by providing grievance-based information on trends and specific issues. There are four levels of appeals in the Service, the final level being the Commissioner or his designate at National Headquarters (NHQ). In 2005/06, Offender Redress at NHQ processed 1,333 Offender Grievances from a total of 19,129 Offender Complaints (and grievances) at all levels of the process. CSC serves many functions that are handled by a myriad of agencies and infrastructures in the outside world, from food service and mail delivery to transportation of people and personal effects around the country. If decisions are being made about all aspects of running these small cities, some people will be unhappy with them.[10] As Winston Churchill said: "Criticism may not be agreeable, but it is necessary. It fulfils the same function as pain in the human body. It calls attention to an unhealthy state of things." Critics or oversight bodies are critical to the good health of an organization and help ensure respect for rights.

HOW WOULD A DECISION MAKER CONSIDER THE 'SPIRIT' OF LAW?

The values underlying the *Corrections and Conditional Release Act* were captured in a statement of principles in section 4. These principles assist decision makers in exercising their discretion properly. The most relevant principle includes the following:

(d) that the Service will use the least restrictive measures consistent with the protection of the public, staff members, and offenders;

(e) that the offenders retain the rights and privileges of all members of society, except those rights that are necessarily removed or restricted as a consequence of the sentence; and

(g) that correctional decisions be made in a forthright and fair manner, with access by the offender to an effective grievance procedure.

For day-to-day operations, a set of Commissioner's Directives (or policies) outline the rules and practices that CSC employees are expected to follow. These directives act as an operational guide for procedures and decision making. What would constitute a least restrictive measure? Here is a practical example.

Inmates who are in segregation are often required to wear restraint equipment in the form of handcuffs when leaving their cells or the segregation area. The intention of the policy on the Use of Restraint Equipment is to ensure the safety of staff, inmates, and the public. It specifies how, when and why restraints should be used. Restraint equipment should only be used as a temporary control measure. Paragraph 12 states:

Following an individual risk assessment, restraint equipment may be authorized by the Institutional Head or his/her delegate to protect staff, inmates, and the public in the following circumstances:

(a) to escort inmates within the institution, including:
  (i) escorting to segregation,
  (ii) escorting from segregation,
  (iii) escorting a high-risk inmate,
  (iv) movement within the Special Handling Unit;
(b) as a precautionary measure against escape or as necessary for controlling inmates under escort outside the institution for any purpose other than work, including:
  (i) transfers,
  (ii) court appearances,
  (iii) medical and dental appointments,

        (iv) hospitalization,

        (v) interviews,

        (vi) other escorted temporary absences as approved; and

    (c) to prevent self-mutilation, injury to others, or property damage, when all other reasonable methods of control have been tried and have failed, or are not the safest and most reasonable intervention given the situational factors.

If the objective of restraints is to protect people, and if a person in segregation is neither violent nor dangerous, should restraint equipment be used? Would it be needed? Would it be lawful to use, knowing that it is not the least restrictive measure and that using it under these circumstances would not be consistent with the intention of the very policy that defines its use? These are some of the questions that decision makers have to consider.

WHAT KINDS OF COMPLAINTS DO INMATES HAVE, AND HOW DOES CSC RESPOND?

Imagine institutions as small, self-contained cities. They are places where food is prepared, clothes are washed, leisure time is spent, work is done, skills are learnt, waste is disposed of, etc. Ideally, all the parties involved resolve their issues in appropriate and expeditious ways. Since prisoners are parties in this system, they cannot be penalized for using the grievance system.

Typical prisoners' grievances include involuntary transfers between institutions, denial or limitation of visits, use of force, and harassment or discrimination. A large number of grievances relate to Claims against the Crown for lost or damaged property. Inmates may have up to $1,500 worth of personal effects in their cells. Moreover, to the extent that they remain in control of these items, they are responsible for their safekeeping. But when the CSC accepts responsibility for these effects (for example, when offenders are removed from their cells and sent to segregation or when they are being transferred), the CSC may then be liable for the cost of these effects if they are lost or damaged.

DOES THE SYSTEM VIOLATE PRISONERS' RIGHTS?

Rights are not absolute: my right to swing my fist stops at the end of your nose. The Canadian correctional system has a vast of array of law and policy as well as oversight mechanisms and complaint systems aimed at preventing the needless (or malicious) limitation of rights. But as in any "people business," much depends on the exercise of judgment by individual actors in a variety of situations. Good training and supervision, strong accountability mechanisms, and a culture that emphasizes discretion are important for assuring that rights are respected. Some stakeholders believe that systemic problems need attention. They raise these concerns in a variety of ways, such as through the annual Correctional Investigator (CI's) Report to Parliament.

CSC submits its response to this report, along with the CI's Report, to the Minister of Public Safety and Emergency Preparedness, who tables both reports together. Special commissions, internal audit systems, the Auditor General's audits, and internal investigations help highlight other problems. Moreover, the access to information legislation exposes any document produced by the CSC. In a typical year, approximately 500 access to information requests occur within the corrections system.

WHY SHOULD CANADIANS CARE?

Canadians should value and protect the rights of all citizens all the time, not only because it is the moral thing to do, but because it is also good public policy. Respecting rights helps ensure that offenders have the best chance of rehabilitating themselves, which in turn makes the country a safer place. How civilized are Canadians compared to the standards in Churchill's quotation, cited earlier? The answer depends on how well the spirit and letter of the law is followed. A culture of respect for the rule of law is essential to ensuring that every Canadian is safe, wherever we find ourselves in whatever circumstances.

DISCUSSION QUESTIONS

1. *One of the prisoner rights that has been hotly contested in recent years is the right to vote. Some people think that prisoners should not be allowed to vote in federal and provincial elections. What is your view?*
2. *The author says that the news media tend to focus on "events" rather than on the day-to-day running of institutions. This means that the public hear about dramatic "bad news" stories but not about the daily success stories. Do you think the media have a responsibility to describe the successful working of the system?*

FURTHER READINGS

Jackson, M. 2002. *Justice Behind the Walls. Human Rights in Canadian Prisons.* Vancouver: Douglas and McIntyre.

Melnitzer, J. 1995. *Maximum, Medium, Minimum.* Toronto: Key Porter Books.

Zinger, I. (Ed.) 2006. *Prison Oversight and Human Rights.* Special Issue of the *Canadian Journal of Criminology and Criminal Justice,* 48 (2).

REFERENCES

Melnitzer, J. 2003. Prisoners' Rights. In J.V. Roberts and M. Grossman (Eds.), *Criminal Justice in Canada,* 2nd ed. Toronto: Thompson Nelson.

Wilson, R., Picheca, J., and Prinzo, M. 2002. *Circles of Support and Accountability: An Evaluation of the Pilot Project in South-Central Ontario.* Ottawa: Correctional Service of Canada 2005 N° R-168. May, 2002.

ENDNOTES

1 These international instruments include the United Nations Charter, Universal Declaration of Human Rights, Convention on the Rights of the Child, International Covenant on Civil and Political Rights, International Convention of the Elimination of All Forms of Racial Discrimination, Convention Against Torture and Other Cruel, Inhumane or Degrading Treatment of Punishment, and the Standard Minimum Rules for the Treatment of Prisoners.

2 The *Corrections and Conditional Release Act* applies to offenders who are sentenced to two years or more in a federal penitentiary and supervised on conditional release in the community by the Correctional Service of Canada.

3 This statement of purpose was derived from the Mission document CSC developed in 1989 which reads: "The Correctional Service of Canada (CSC), as part of the criminal justice system and respecting the rule of the law, contributes to the protection of society by actively encouraging and assisting offenders to become law-abiding citizens, while exercising reasonable, safe, secure and humane control."

4 CSC also manages an addictions research centre, five regional headquarters and staff colleges, a correctional management learning centre, and a national headquarters.

5 Commissioner Lucie McClung, cited in *Let's Talk,* Vol. 29, No. 2.

6 See Part 3 of the *Corrections and Conditional Release Act.*

7 The book can be accessed on the Internet: www.justicebehindthewalls.net.

8 Female offenders are particularly affected by the experience of imprisonment. They are often the primary caregiver for children, and they have high rates of mental and physical disability, self-destructive behaviour (such as slashing and cutting), depression, and suicide attempts. Eighty percent report prior abuse. They experience significant poverty and have higher unemployment rates than their male counterparts and Canadian women as a whole.

9 Sections 90 and 91 of the CCRA read as follows:

90. The procedure for fairly and expeditiously resolving offenders' grievances on matters within the jurisdiction of the Commissioner and the procedure shall operate in accordance with the regulations made under paragraph 96(u).

91. Every offender shall have complete access to the offender grievance procedure without negative consequences.

10 These external and internal oversight mechanisms are crucial so that CSC and its employees are accountable to the public, the government, and to offenders. Some of the other mechanisms include Citizens Advisory Committees, Inmate committees, prisoners' rights and advocacy groups, internal disclosure, government accountability documents, and *Access to Information and Privacy Act* (ATIP) mechanisms.

CHAPTER 14
Inhuman Rights

INTRODUCTION

Prisoners should not lose all their rights once they are admitted to custody. Lawyer and inmate Julius Melnitzer has spent time in correctional institutions at all security levels. In 1995, he wrote a memoir about his experiences. That book, entitled *Maximum, Minimum, Medium*, provides a fascinating look at Canada's correctional system from the inside. As a lawyer with a great deal of experience in the criminal justice system, the author's analysis of life in Canada's prisons is unique. Drawn from his book, this chapter examines the issue of prisoners' rights from the perspective of an actual prisoner, and one with a great deal of knowledge of the law.

INHUMAN RIGHTS
Julius Melnitzer

> *Freedom is not divisible; it disappears from a society as soon as it is denied to any member of that society.* —Dr. Gabor Maté

After more than 18 years as a trial lawyer in Ontario, including a decade as a criminal lawyer who served for a time as a Provincial Director of the Ontario Criminal Lawyers Association, I went to jail, a criminal serving a nine-year sentence for fraud. As a criminal lawyer, I always believed my job ended with my client's acquittal or sentencing. But two-and-a-half years in maximum, medium, and minimum security federal institutions in Ontario taught me that criminal lawyers who abandon their incarcerated clients as spent briefs should rethink their commitment to their profession and their role in society. Here's why.

The civil rights of prisoners are the lowest common denominator of democracy. In jail, correctional supervisors are the judges in internal disciplinary courts, where their foot soldiers are the prosecutors (one CS [correctional supervisor] convicted a prisoner in the absence of witnesses because "no guard would take the trouble to write out a charge unless it was true"); permission to telephone a lawyer during business hours hangs on the whim of employees of the State; prisoners do not have access to Bell information or telephone books on their ranges; calls are collect only unless written permission is obtained; and telephone discussions with lawyers transpire in a public place or in a CO's (classification officer's) office in the presence of CSC (Correctional Service Canada) staff.

The apathy of all but a few criminal lawyers as well as the Canadian Civil Liberties Association; the reluctance of a cash-starved Legal Aid system to spend its budget on the convicted; the low levels of education and high levels of illiteracy in the system; and CSC's ignorance and disregard of basic procedural fairness in its day-to-day operations all ensure a trampling of prisoners' rights. Ironically, until a recent court case forced authorities to change the practice, CSC forbade the use of the Inmate Welfare Fund, inmates' money, for legal assistance.

The protection of our democratic core lies in the hands of a few committed activists such as the late Order of Canada recipient Claire Culhane and her legacy, the Vancouver-based Prisoners' Rights Group; Ruth Morris from Toronto; Ontario Provincial Court Judges David Cole and Bob Bigelow; prison law practitioners in the Kingston, Ontario, bar; and Queen's University's Faculty of Law's Correctional Law Project, until recently headed by Professor Ron Price, who is now practising correctional law in the private sector.

This is not a commentary on the rights prisoners should have: that is for the voters and their elected representatives to decide. Nor is it a denial of the relatively humane conditions under which we warehouse the convicted; rather, it speaks to the disregard of due process that pervades our penal system. As sentences get lengthier, paroles become rarer, and more people spend more time in jail, the prevailing attitude seems to be, "Let's feed them and keep them out of the cold." In a democracy, that will not do; so long as society sees fit to give rights to prisoners, it must protect its values even among its exiles. Our failure to do so says much about our penal system's rehabilitative delinquencies.

CSC's response to the public outcry resulting from my tennis partner, convicted murderer Philippe Clement's assault on a Gravenhurst woman after his escape from minimum-security Beaver Creek was perhaps my starkest experience with civil rights sacrificed on the altar of public opinion and media hype. In the six months following the public outcry, CSC set out to purge the Creek of violent offenders, many of whom were sent to Warkworth, and some of whom opened their files to me. I was appalled at the haste and lack of justification for the majority of the transfers; in no instance was there an immediate threat of escape or violence, yet none of these inmates were given a chance to contact their lawyers before transfer.

My apprehensions about the panic that had set in with Les Judson [a former warden at Beaver Creek] and his superiors were confirmed orally by some Warkworth COs who were now stuck with these men. One CO put her findings in writing:

> On December 23, 1992, the subject was transferred to higher security
> (Warkworth Institution) as the staff at Beaver Creek had information that
> the subject, along with other perpetrators, had broken into the inmate can-
> teen and stole $3,200 worth of merchandise ...

These suspicions were never confirmed. No charges, either institutional or street, were laid against the subject. There is no evidence tying the subject to this offence. Therefore, there is no valid reason why the security classification on the subject should change. He is still classified as minimum security.

"The subject" was unusually lucky. He was back in minimum within six months. Had his CO been unsympathetic, it would have taken him from 12 to 18 months to have his grievance processed. And likely, "the subject," who was barely literate, would have had to do it on his own: Legal Aid refused his application, and for three months, his collect calls to lawyers went unanswered.

Apart from "the subject," not a single one of the men summarily ejected from Beaver Creek in the fall of 1992 had made it back to minimum one year later. Even those with lawyers were stymied by the delaying tactics of the Crown in Federal Court and the sluggishness of that court's process.

The greatest price of this arbitrary conduct, apart from the diminution in democratic values, is the cost to society. Many of the transferred cons were the system's successes, the most likely candidates for rehabilitation, men who had spent many years fighting institutionalization and their criminal backgrounds and who had been adjudged, step by grudging step, to have the best potential for a productive return to society.

Wade, a very young-looking, intelligent, and self-educated 40-year-old, with two daughters in their twenties and a son in his teens, had fought his way back from tragic alcoholism and drug abuse that led to conviction for two sexual assaults and a 12-year sentence. He had been a model for other prisoners, a star in every therapeutic program he had taken for seven years. At the Creek, he continued his exemplary ways, working in the kitchen, tutoring other inmates, and minding his own business.

Even in the aftermath of the Clement escape, the Parole Board was sufficiently impressed by Wade's record to grant him unescorted three-day passes to a halfway house in Toronto. On his first pass, he dutifully attended the Clarke Institute of Psychiatry for a psychological assessment; there he told the examining psychologist that he had taken one drink almost a year previous, on New Year's Eve.

Wade's honesty was just the excuse Beaver Creek needed to rid itself of another bothersome high-profile case. Wade was summarily advised that the Administration had been "informed"—by parties unmentionable, of course—of "derogatory remarks" Wade had made about the deputy warden. Lacking knowledge of his accusers and without access to counsel, Wade had no opportunity to defend himself and was promptly transferred to Warkworth, where he remained until his statutory release in February 1994. CSC's extraordinary powers made a strong impression on me when I reported for transportation to a Kingston hospital for medical testing. The escorting officers politely told me to undress.

"Am I under suspicion for anything?" I asked.

"No," was the quick reply.

My question was deliberate. I had researched the new prison legislation as it related to searches and discovered that "routine" strip-searches were unlawful in the absence of individualized suspicion, except for some carefully circumscribed exceptions that did not apply here.

"Then you've got no right to search me," I asserted.

The officers resolved their confusion by phoning the security office.

"You can't go if you refuse a search," the senior guard told me as he got off the phone.

"Fine," I replied, "I'll go back to my Block." Visions of medical lawsuits and grievances for damages danced in my head.

"The IPSO [internal preventative security officer] says we have to search you anyway."

"You mean that I'm now under suspicion because I insisted on my rights."

"I don't know," said the guard abashedly, "you're the lawyer. I just do what the keeper tells me."

"What are my choices?"

"Go to the hole. They'll strip-search you there." Previous personal experience told me that a request to call my lawyer would not be well received, serving only to heighten suspicion about my refusal to be strip-searched.

I was in a quandary. If I refused, I'd be in the hole. I tried to imagine the write-up on this incident: by the time the IPSO finished, I would doubtlessly be labelled as "under suspicion," CSC's favourite phrase, of trafficking in something or other. I complied, wondering how many thousands of inmates would be searched in ignorance of their rights.

The "cavity search," a fishing expedition through body orifices, is distinguished from assault only by the mandated presence of a doctor and is a more sublime form of intrusion than a strip-search. If a tactile proctological examination doesn't reveal anything, the doctor may use an instrument best described as an anal crank to have a better look through a larger opening.

Refusal to submit to a cavity search is, in a system where random urinalysis testing is common, a virtual admission to drug trafficking. Being labelled as a trafficker is, in turn, an invitation to unremitting harassment, restrictions on visits, and a practical bar to early parole.

Cavity searches are, however, expensive, time-consuming, and embarrassing when fruitless. CSC prefers the "dry cell," where the toilet can't be flushed by the inmate. In Kingston Penitentiary, the nine-by-four windowless cell contains a bed, an eating surface, a steel toilet, and a sink. The lights are on all day, and at night, a bulb strong enough to read by intrudes on sleep, but no books are allowed. The cell is video-monitored 24 hours daily, and patrolling guards have an unobstructed vista through a plastic plate on the ceiling. The cell design allows the guards to watch the prisoner's excretions, which remain with him in the uncovered toilet, until the guards find time to come around and secure the evidence.

Just how far down the human rights scale prisoners have fallen can be demonstrated by comparing the dry cell experience with recent court decisions prohibiting police from detaining suspects until they have a bowel movement, enabling authorities to search stool samples for drugs.

Random urinalysis, recently declared constitutional by the courts, is slowly replacing the cavity search and the dry cell, but the tests are no less intrusive, if somewhat more humane.

To those law-and-order aficionados who cheered their way through the last few paragraphs, I merely point out that these methods are designed to prove guilt. Until and if the shit hits the fan, so to speak, the innocent must pay the price with the guilty. The innocent have no recourse if the suspicions against them prove groundless. The irony is that they therefore have far more incentive than the guilty to submit to these barbaric intrusions.

Occasionally, an activist Inmate Committee chairman tries to help inmates assert their rights. The Inmate Committee exists at the discretion of an institution's warden, but now that CSC is legally required to consult with inmates on all matters affecting them other than security, the Inmate Committee is a handy funnel to the population.

The inmate chairman is elected by the population every six months and appoints his own executive. The chairman's capacity to represent the inmates is severely limited, however, because the chairman is himself a prisoner, whose fate hinges on the whims of his keepers.

While politicization is creeping into institutional politics, wardens tend to deal swiftly and severely with chairmen whom they see as rabble-rousers. Shortly before I got to Warkworth, Greg, a 50-year-old first-timer serving a 14-year-sentence for the attempted murder of his wife, was elected chairman. Greying, fatherly, and somehow tweedy in his prison greens, Greg was educated and clever, with a knack for organization.

Greg set out to enforce the Supreme Court of Canada's declaration, in a precedent-setting decision giving prisoners the right to vote, that inmates were entitled to all civil rights other than those that necessarily accompanied the loss of freedom.

To that end, he first presented the Administration with a scheme for effective inmate representation at the grass-roots level. Censorship was his next target: I helped him draw up a grievance against the Administration's refusal to allow the popular Sharon Stone movie *Basic Instinct* into Warkworth; after months of enduring explicitly violent martial arts movies on prison video, I laughed at the exclusion. Simultaneously, Greg hotly protested against the Administration's control and occasional misuse of the Inmate Welfare Fund. The powers-that-be were most unhappy with him.

"They're going to get me, Julius. They don't want a chairman who does anything," Greg told me.

As the tension rose, Greg desperately tried to get in touch with a lawyer; he wrote both to the Ontario Provincial Criminal Lawyers Association, which continued its historical disregard of those who had already paid their bills, and the Canadian Civil Liberties Association, which must have had more popular fish to fry and didn't bother to answer. I finally called my lawyer, Bob Bigelow, who agreed to see Greg on his next visit to Warkworth.

Before Bob could see Greg, the Administration pounced, blaming him for irregularities in the canteen; without explanation, he was hauled out of a visit with his wife and sent to the hole. Soon afterward, Greg resigned and became a non-presence in short order.

Inmate Committee chairmen are not the only targets of the kind of intimidation Greg experienced. Grant, convicted by an internal disciplinary court of possession of a joint after eight offence-free years in the pen, objected to the severity of the penalties for his minor offence. On the street, he would have been fined lightly, at worst; in prison, he lost his single cell in Warkworth's model non-smoking unit, was transferred back to double-bunked Reception, had his pay cut by four levels, lost his job, and spent a week in the hole awaiting Disciplinary Court.

With the law clerk's certificate he had earned in prison from the American Trial Lawyers Association in hand, and with some guidance from me, Grant filed a claim in the Federal Court challenging the severity and multiplicity of his punishments. The attorney general applied to quash Grant's claim but failed in its summary motion. Grant, who worked in the kitchen, thanked me for my help with a plate of delicately cooked fresh crabmeat that a friendly guard had smuggled in for him.

For a few months I heard nothing more about his case, attributing Grant's silence to the long delays in Federal Court.

"I shut it down," he said six months later, in a hush, averting his eyes.

"Why?" I was sincerely dismayed.

"I've got to do what's right for me. My wife wants me out of here, or at least in camp. I'm on a life beef—they call the shots."

Not yet dislodged from the insulated naïveté of my street days, I had no idea what Grant was talking about.

"They called me in, the unit manager," he went on. "He told me that even if I win, I lose. If I forget it, maybe I get to camp soon."

The threat was not an idle one. And if the unit manager chose to forget his promise once Grant dropped his claim, [the unit manager] could always find new facts to support his change of heart; CSC's power to affect the man's freedom would be as useful in the breaking of the promise as it was in its making.

As I chafed at the injustices, the feelings that drove me as a criminal lawyer came back in spades. In January 1993, I wrote to prison activist Claire Culhane, whose books I had been reading, offering to help in her cause of prisoners' rights. Though my ability to assist was limited by the inaccessibility of research materials, our correspondence continued throughout my incarceration.

CSC's licence to trample human rights stems from its lack of accountability. Politically, the human rights of convicts is hardly an issue with which to blaze to power; an unsympathetic media and public ensure that accountability, where it exists, operates only to inmates' detriment.

Wardens have some discretion in granting passes, escorted and unescorted, as well as work releases. Release in serious cases, the ones in the headlines, are the province of the National Parole Board. Through its case management teams and therapeutic staff, CSC makes highly influential recommendations to the board. Wisdom and insight into the human psyche spout from the mouths of 23-year-old COs barely out of community college, secretarial school graduates who have won the CSC promotion competition, or M.A. students suddenly become "therapists." Their power is frightening and unchecked, often subjective and arbitrary; if quality control or any serious effort at consistency in release decisions and recommendations existed, I couldn't find it in the files I reviewed.

There is little risk for CSC in urging the Parole Board to detain an inmate, but a wrong call for release can have disastrous public relations fallout; thus, it is not surprising that case management teams lean against release. As Jeremiah's CO told him, "Personally, I don't think you should be in here, but I don't want to be the one kicking my lunch bucket down the street." Reid, who had spent 17 years in prison, observed, "When I got in the system, COs tried to help you. Now, they try to find obstacles to keep you in so they can cover their ass."

CSC's materials are essentially unchallengeable before the Parole Board, a body that the late Chief Justice of Canada's Supreme Court, Bora Laskin, called "draconian." The hearings consist of a presentation by the CO, followed by 30 minutes to 5 hours of untrammeled inmate grilling by at least a 2-member board, many of whom are trained only in the fruits of political loyalty and start with the assumption that credibility is not in a criminal's repertoire.

Anything in a CSC report passes for evidence: fact, opinion, hearsay, innuendo, and suspicion—even philosophical musings. Reports are in writing; there is no in-person evidence and no opportunity to cross-examine in the quest for liberty. The inmate's lawyer is reduced to an "assistant," usually sitting by without objection, involved only in procedural matters and ten minutes of final arguments. Where evidence favouring release exists, the Parole Board is notorious for capriciously ignoring it, going so far as to reject, without reasons, recommendations from CSC's own professionals. Homespun psychology is regularly expounded as definitive gospel by politically appointed board members, many of them part time, with little experience and less training: "The offender's response to our questions shows that he has not fully appreciated the consequences of his actions and is not ready for release" are the board's favourite buzzwords.

Always, the spectre of public opinion hangs over the proceedings, twisting the issue of "risk to society"—the fundamental question the Parole Board is empowered to decide—into considerations of "How will it look?" Thus, by ignoring the law, the Parole Board assumes the role of lawmaker, affecting a demagogic juggernaut that tramples on concepts of fundamental justice. These concepts are democracy's triggers of accountability, ever so slight a curtsy to an inalienable right—not to freedom, but to the right to fight for it on even ground.

DISCUSSION QUESTIONS

1. *What is meant by the term "due process," and how does it apply to prisoners?*
2. *Is random urinalysis testing acceptable in prison?*

FURTHER READINGS

Jackson, M. 2002. *Justice behind the Walls: Human Rights in Canadian Prisons.* Vancouver: Douglas and McIntyre.

Melnitzer, J. 1995. *Maximum, Minimum, Medium.* Toronto: Key Porter Books.

CHAPTER 15
Racial Discrimination in the Ontario Criminal Justice System

INTRODUCTION

No issue arouses quite as much concern among criminal justice policy-makers and members of the public as discrimination. A justice system that treats different categories of offenders in different ways is no justice system at all. Conducting research on the treatment of racial minorities in the criminal justice system is very challenging, in large measure because an individual's ethnicity is not generally recorded in most criminal justice statistics.

In this chapter, Scot Wortley and Andrea McCalla review the research exploring the Ontario criminal justice system's treatment of suspects, accused persons, and offenders who are black. The authors place this work in an international context, for the problem of discrimination confronts the justice systems of all western nations.

Racial Discrimination in the Ontario Criminal Justice System
Scot Wortley and Andrea McCalla, University of Toronto

Statistics on race and crime are rarely collected and disseminated in Canada. However, the information available suggests that black people are greatly overrepresented in the criminal justice system. For example, although black people make up only 2 percent of the Canadian population, they represent 6 percent of those held in federal penitentiaries (see Wortley, 1999). The federal incarceration rate for black Canadians (146 per 100,000) is almost five times higher than the rate for whites (31 per 100,000). This overrepresentation is even greater in Ontario. Although blacks constitute only 3 percent of the province's population, statistics reveal that they represent 12 percent of all admissions to federal prisons in the region (Solicitor General of Canada 1997) and 15 percent of all admissions to provincial correctional facilities. The Ontario incarceration rate for blacks is a striking 3,686 per 100,000 population, compared to only 706 per 100,000 for whites (Commission on Systemic Racism, 1995, p. 89). Although Canada often prides itself on being a more racially tolerant country than our neighbour to the south, the racial disparities revealed by these Canadian incarceration statistics are very similar to those found in American prison data (Tonry, 1995; Mauer, 1999).

Why are black people overrepresented in Canadian prison statistics? One possible explanation is that the Canadian criminal justice system is biased against black people. Indeed, community activists, defence lawyers, and academics have frequently argued that both the police and the courts discriminate against blacks and other visible minorities (see Foster, 1996; Henry, 1994). Criminal justice representatives, on the other hand, vehemently deny charges of racism and claim that the system is colour-blind. The Chief of the Toronto Police Service recently expressed this opinion when he stated: "There is no racism ... We don't look at, nor do we consider the race or ethnicity, or any of that, as factors of how we dispose of cases, or individuals, or how we treat individuals" (*Toronto Star*, 2002, p. A14). Similar denials are often expressed by Ontario criminal court judges and prosecutors (Commission on Systemic Racism 1995). Proponents of this "no racism" opinion frequently claim that blacks are overrepresented in prison statistics because they simply commit much more crime than individuals from other racial groups (see Worthington, 2002; Goldstein, 2002; Wilbanks, 1987). The heated debate between the advocates of these two competing explanations erupted once again after the *Toronto Star* released a series of articles alleging police bias against blacks (Rankin et al., 2002a; 2002b) at almost the same time the city was suffering from a rash of violent homicides involving young black offenders and victims (Blizzard, 2002; Goldstein, 2002).

The purpose of this chapter is to provide a brief review of recent research documenting discrimination against black people at all stages of the Ontario criminal justice system. We conclude with a discussion of the various strategies that might reduce racism in the justice system and highlight the need for additional research on this important and very controversial topic.

PERCEPTIONS OF CRIMINAL INJUSTICE

During the 1980s, allegations that the criminal justice system was racially biased were easily dismissed by governmental officials as representing the unfounded opinions of radical black activists. They argued that the vast majority of black and other visible minority citizens had complete confidence in the police and criminal courts. However, subsequent research has shown that perceptions of racial discrimination are quite widespread. In 1994, the Commission on Systemic Racism in the Ontario Criminal Justice System conducted a survey of over 1,200 Toronto adults (18 years of age or older) who identified themselves as either black, Chinese, or white. Over 400 respondents were randomly selected from each racial group. The survey results indicate that three out of every four black Torontonians (76 percent) believe that the police treat members of their racial group worse than they treat white people. Furthermore, 60 percent of the black respondents also felt that members of their racial group are treated worse by the criminal courts. Interestingly, the findings also indicate that perceptions of racial bias are not isolated within the black community. Indeed, over half of the white respondents (56 percent) reported that they think black people are treated worse by the police, and a third (35 percent) think blacks are treated worse by the courts (see Wortley, 1996).

Additional research suggests that a high proportion of black youth also perceive that the criminal justice system is discriminatory. For example, a 1995 survey of 1,870 Toronto high school students found that over half of the black respondents (52 percent) felt that the police treat members of their racial group much worse than the members of other racial groups. By contrast, only 22 percent of South Asians, 15 percent of Asians, and 4 percent of whites felt that they were subject to discriminatory treatment (Ruck and Wortley, 2002). Similarly, another high school survey, conducted in 2000, found that 74 percent of black students believe that members of their racial group are more likely to be unfairly stopped and questioned by the police than the members of other racial groups. This opinion was shared by only 31 percent of South Asians, 27 percent of Asians, and 13 percent of whites (see Wortley and Tanner, 2003). It should be noted that in all three of the studies discussed above, racial differences in perceptions of criminal injustice could not be explained by racial differences in social class or other demographic factors.

Findings such as these have caused some government and criminal justice representatives to admit that the perception of discrimination exists in Ontario and that, at the very least, the criminal justice system suffers from a serious public relations problem. These reports have also motivated various police organizations to implement programs designed to improve relationships with various minority communities (see Stenning, 2003). However, there is still considerable debate about the cause of these perceptions of racial bias. Critics of the justice system feel that perceptions of discrimination reflect reality. On the other hand, the opposing view is that perceptions of injustice are inaccurate and have been created by other factors, such as peer socialization and exposure to stories about racism in the American media. One popular explanation is that most black people in Canada are immigrants who come from countries, such as Jamaica or Nigeria, where the criminal justice system is corrupt, brutal, and oppressive. As a result, many black people have based their opinion about the police and the courts on their experiences in their home country. The hypothesis is that second- and third-generation blacks who have been raised in Canada will have a much better opinion of the Canadian justice system. Research, however, suggests that the opposite is true. Recent immigrants, in fact, perceive much less discrimination in the Canadian justice system than immigrants who have been in Canada for a long period of time. Indeed, blacks who were born in Canada tend to have far worse perceptions of the police and the criminal courts (see Ruck and Wortley, 2002; Wortley and Tanner, 2003; Wortley et al., 1997). How can we explain this finding? Are perceptions of discrimination based on personal and/or group experiences? To answer this question we must turn to the empirical data.

RACIAL PROFILING

Canada's black community has long argued that they are frequently the victim of racial profiling (see Tator and Henry, 2006). With respect to the issue of discrimination within the criminal justice system, racial profiling can be said to exist when members of a particular racial or ethnic group become subject to much greater levels of criminal justice and/or security surveillance than the average or typical citizen. Thus, in the academic literature, racial profiling is commonly defined using these determinants: 1) significant racial differences in police stop and search practices (i.e., driving while black); 2) significant racial differences in Customs search and interrogation practices; and 3) particular undercover or sting operations which target specific racial/ethnic communities (see Wortley and Tanner, 2003; 2005; 2004a; Harris, 2002). It should be stressed that racial profiling is said to exist when race itself—not criminal or other illegal behaviour—is a significant factor in the making of surveillance decisions. In other words, at a societal level, racial profiling exists when racial differences in law enforcement surveillance activities cannot be explained by individual differences in criminal or other illegal activity.

Cecil Foster, in his book documenting the experiences of Caribbean immigrants to Canada, maintains that the police frequently stop, question, and search people of West Indian descent for DWBs—driving while being black violations (Foster, 1996, p. 5). Foster's words reflect the belief, widespread among Canada's black population, that law enforcement and Customs officials needlessly interrogate and harass black people solely because of their racial background. Are black people more likely to be stopped, questioned, and searched by the police than people from other racial backgrounds? Numerous studies conducted in the United States and Great Britain and Canada—using a wide variety of research methodologies (i.e., field observations, qualitative interviews, general population surveys, and official statistics)— have demonstrated that black people are more likely to be stopped, questioned, and searched by the police than are whites (see reviews in Tanovich, 2006; Wortley and Tanner, 2004a; Wortley and Tanner, 2004b; Wortley, 2004; Ontario Human Rights Commission, 2003; Bowling and Phillips, 2002; Harris, 2002). Importantly, in *R. v. Brown*, the Ontario Court of

Appeal acknowledged the existence of racial profiling within the policing community. Nonetheless, numerous police leaders, police unions, and academics continue to question the validity of racial profiling research and deny the existence of racial profiling among law enforcement agencies (see Melchers, 2003; Gabor, 2004).

Unlike police in England and the United States, police in Canada are not required to record the race or ethnicity of the people they stop and/or search. Thus, with one exception (discussed below), official police statistics cannot be used to investigate the presence or absence of racial profiling in this country. However, other forms of investigation have uncovered evidence that racial profiling may exist. For example, James (1998) conducted intensive interviews with over fifty black youth from six different cities in Ontario. Many of these youths reported that being stopped by the police was a common occurrence for them. There was also an almost universal belief that skin colour, not style of dress, was the primary determinant of attracting police attention. James (1998) concludes that the adversarial nature of these police stops contributes strongly to black youths' hostility towards the police (p. 173). Neugebauer's (2000) informal interviews with 63 black and white teenagers from Metropolitan Toronto produced very similar results. Although the author found that teenagers from all racial backgrounds often complain about being hassled by the police, both white and black youth agree that black males are much more likely to be stopped, questioned, and searched by the police than youths from other racial backgrounds. More recently, the Ontario Human Rights Commission (OHRC) (2003) gathered detailed testimonials from over 800 people in Ontario who felt that they had been the victims of racial profiling.

Such qualitative studies are extremely valuable in describing racial profiling incidents and chronicling the extreme pain and frustration that they cause. However, critics have frequently dismissed such studies as anecdotal, since they are typically based on small, non-random samples. Furthermore, although the recent OHRC (2003) report gathered information from a relatively large sample of respondents, it did not systematically compare the experiences of racial minorities with the experiences of white people. Critics have charged, therefore, that the OHRC study provides little proof that racial minorities are actually more likely to be stopped and searched by the police than whites. Thus, although qualitative methodologies have been extremely effective at documenting the lived experience of racial minorities, any thorough exploration of the racial profiling phenomena has to include an analysis of quantitative data. Two types of quantitative study—survey research and official data—have been used to explore the racial profiling issue.

EXPLORING RACIAL PROFILING WITH SURVEY DATA

Survey research has three distinct advantages over qualitative data for investigating racial profiling. First, since surveys are based on large, random samples, research results can be more easily generalized to the total population.

Secondly, surveys permit direct comparisons between people who report that they have been stopped and searched by the police and people who have not been stopped. Thus, we are able to determine if people who are frequently stopped by the police differ from those with little or no contact. Finally, in addition to documenting specific experiences with the police, surveys can be used to investigate the psychological impact that perceived racial profiling incidents have on targeted populations.

To date, two large surveys, both conducted in Toronto, have attempted to document whether racial minorities are more likely to be stopped by the police than white people. The first, a 1994 survey of over 1,200 Toronto residents, conducted on behalf of the Commission on Racism in the Ontario Criminal Justice System, found that black people, particularly black males, are much more likely to report involuntary police contact than either whites or Asians. For example, almost half (44 percent) of the black males in the sample reported that they had been stopped and questioned by the police at least once in the past two years. In fact, one-third (30 percent) reported that they had been stopped on two or more occasions. By contrast, only 12 percent of white males and 7 percent of Asian males reported multiple police stops. Multivariate analyses reveals that these racial differences in police contact cannot be explained by racial differences in social class, education, or other demographic variables. In fact, two factors that seem to protect white males from police contact—age and social class—do not protect blacks. Whites with high incomes and education, for example, are much less likely to be stopped by the police than whites who score low on social class measures. By contrast, blacks with high incomes and education are actually more likely to be stopped than lower class blacks. Black professionals, in fact, often attribute the attention they receive from the police to their relative affluence. As one black respondent stated: "If you are black and you drive something good, the police will pull you over and ask about drugs" (see Wortley and Tanner, 2003; Wortley and Kellough, 2004).

A second study, conducted in 2001, surveyed approximately 3,400 Toronto high school students about their recent experiences with the police (Wortley and Tanner, 2005). The results of this study further suggest that blacks are much more likely than people from other racial backgrounds to be subjected to random street interrogations. For example, over 50 percent of the black students report that they have been stopped and searched by the police on two or more occasions in the past two years, compared to only 23 percent of whites, 11 percent of Asians, and 8 percent of South Asians. Similarly, over 40 percent of black students claim that they have been physically searched by the police in the past two years, compared to only 17 percent of their white and 11 percent of their Asian counterparts.

However, the data also reveal that students who engage in crime and deviance are much more likely to receive police attention than students who do not break the law. For example, 81 percent of the drug dealers in this sample (defined as those who sold drugs on 10 or more occasions in the past year) report that they have been searched by the police, compared to only 16 percent of those students who did not sell drugs. This finding is consistent with the argument that the police focus exclusively on suspicious or criminal activity when deciding to make a stop, not the personal characteristics of citizens. The data further reveal that students who spend most of their leisure time in public spaces (i.e., malls, public parks, nightclubs, etc.) are much more likely to be stopped by the police than students who spend their time in private spaces or in the company of their parents. This leads to the million-dollar question: Do black students receive more police attention because they are more involved in crime and more likely to be involved in leisure activities in public spaces?

While our data reveal that white students have much higher rates of both alcohol consumption and illicit drug use, black students report higher rates of both minor property crime and violence. Furthermore, both black and white students report higher rates of participation in public leisure activities than do students from all other racial backgrounds. These racial differences, however, do not come close to explaining why black youth are much more vulnerable to police contact. Multivariate analysis reveals that after statistically controlling for criminal activity, drug use, gang membership, and leisure activities, the relationship between race and police stops actually gets stronger. Why? Further analysis reveals that racial differences in police stop and search practices are actually greatest among students with low levels of criminal behaviour. For example, 34 percent of the black students who have not engaged in any type of criminal activity still report that they have been stopped by the police on two or more occasions in the past two years, compared to only 4 percent of white students in the same behavioural category. Similarly, 23 percent of black students with no deviant behaviour report that they have been searched by the police, compared to only 5 percent of whites who report no deviance (Wortley and Tanner, 2005). Thus, while the first survey reveals that age and social class do not protect blacks from police stops and searches, this second study suggests that good behaviour also does not shelter blacks from unwanted police attention.

These findings have two major implications. Firstly, because the black community is subject to much greater police surveillance, they are also much more likely to be caught when they break the law than white people who engage in the same forms of criminal activity. For example, 65 percent of the black drug dealers in the above high school study report that they have been arrested at some time in their life, compared to only 35 percent of the white drug dealers.

Imagine that 10,000 people live in a high-density community in downtown Toronto. Imagine further that half of the residents of this community are black and the other half are white. Let us also assume that an equal number of the black and white residents (250 from each group) sell illicit drugs on a regular basis. If black residents are more likely to be stopped and searched by the police because of racial profiling, black drug dealers in this neighbourhood will be more likely to be detected and subsequently arrested than white offenders. For example, if 50 percent of the black residents are randomly searched, compared to only 10 percent of the white residents, this searching practice should yield 125 black arrests and only 25 white arrests. Interestingly, the race-crime statistics (125 black arrests compared to only 25 white arrests) produced by such biased search practices would probably be used to justify the use of racial profiling (i.e., we found more black than white offenders therefore our profiling strategy must be correct). Racial profiling can become a self-fulfilling prophecy. This example helps illustrate how arrest statistics may have more to do with law enforcement surveillance practices than actual racial differences in criminal behaviour. In sum, racial profiling may help explain the overrepresentation of minorities in arrest statistics.

The research discussed above also suggests that the police almost never arrest citizens who are not involved in some form of criminal activity (Wortley and Tanner, 2005). This may create the impression that racial profiling is harmless: if you don't break the law, you will not be arrested. However, the second major consequence of racial profiling is that it serves to further alienate black people from mainstream Canadian society and reinforces perceptions of discrimination and racial injustice. Indeed, research strongly suggests that black people who are frequently stopped and questioned by the police perceive much higher levels of discrimination in the Canadian criminal justice system than do blacks who have not been stopped. Interestingly, being stopped by the police does not appear to increase perceptions of injustice for whites or Asians (Wortley et al., 1997). Being stopped and searched by the police, therefore, seems to be experienced by black people as evidence that race still matters in Canadian society, that no matter how well you behave, how hard you try, being black means that you will always be considered one of the usual suspects. American research further suggests that racialized experiences—including incidents of racial profiling—directly contribute to the stress levels and subsequent mental health of African Americans (see reviews in American Psychological Association, 2001; Amnesty International, 2004).

EXPLORING RACIAL PROFILING WITH POLICE DATA: THE KINGSTON PILOT PROJECT

A second research strategy for examining racial profiling involves the collection of data by the police themselves. In such a strategy, police officers are mandated to record the racial background of all people they decide to stop and/or search. Along with race, police officers should also be required to record the civilian's gender, age, and home address, as well as the reason, time, and location of the stop, and the final disposition of the case (i.e., did the stop result in a search of the person or their vehicle, an arrest, a traffic ticket, a warning, etc.?). Some advocates suggest that, as a validity check, a copy of the stop information (often referred to as a *contact card*) should be given to the civilian, as is common practice in Great Britain. A potential advantage of official data collection programs is that they theoretically capture all of the police stops that took place over a given study period. Unlike surveys, official data are not based on random samples. Therefore, there are no worries about sampling error or potential problems with respondent recall. However, the integrity of all official data collection projects is completely dependent on the willingness of individual police officers to accurately record information on the people they stop. If officers refuse to record information on all of the stops that they conduct, or if they record the required information incorrectly, the quality of the data produced by the project will be negligible and efforts to investigate racial profiling thwarted.

In both the United States and Great Britain, police services are often mandated to collect their own data on the racial background of all people stopped and searched by police officers. In contrast, police forces in Canada are not required to record the race or ethnicity of the civilians they stop and/or search. Thus, official police statistics typically cannot be used to investigate the presence or absence of racial profiling in this country.

Kingston, Ontario, is the only exception. Beginning in the late 1990s, the Kingston Police Service received a number of complaints about racial profiling from the city's relatively small black community. Rather than ignore these allegations, Kingston Police Chief Bill Closs, with the support of the Kingston Police Services Board, decided to engage in a groundbreaking data collection project. Despite strong resistance from police associations across the country, this pilot project went into the field in October 2003. For the next twelve months, the Kingston police were ordered to record the age, gender, race, and home address of all people that they stopped and questioned, along with the time and location of the stop, the reason for the stop, and the final outcome of the interaction (i.e., arrest, ticket, warning, etc.). Information was ultimately recorded for over 16,500 police stops conducted over a one-year period (Wortley and Marshall, 2005).

The results of the Kingston Pilot Project mirror the results of racial profiling studies conducted in the United States and England. During the study period, the black residents of Kingston were three times more likely than their white counterparts to be stopped at least once by the police. Overall, the individual stop rate for black residents was 150 stops per 1,000, compared to only 51 per 1,000 for whites. The results further indicate the individual stop rate is highest for black male residents (213 per 1,000), followed by black females (75 per 1,000), white males (74 per 1,000) and white females (29 per 1,000). Interestingly, racial differences in police stops are most pronounced for young people. For example, the black residents of Kingston aged 15 to 24 years had a stop rate of 410 per 1,000, compared to 109 per 1,000 for similarly aged whites. Nonetheless, significant, though smaller, racial differences in the police stop rate also exist for all other age categories (Wortley and Marshall, 2005).

Most American racial profiling studies that utilize official police data have only focused on traffic stops. This is important because many police officers claim that due to factors like vehicle speed, tinted windows, observing vehicles from behind, etc., they frequently do not know the racial background of the drivers they decide to pull over. One advantage of the Kingston study, therefore, is that it gathered information on both traffic and pedestrian stops. Indeed, over 40 percent of the 16,000 stops conducted during the study period were performed on pedestrians. Thus, if racial profiling does exist, we might expect that blacks would be more overrepresented in pedestrian stops than traffic stops, since the racial background of pedestrians should be more apparent to officers than the race of drivers. This is exactly what the results of the Kingston study revealed. While black people are still greatly overrepresented in traffic stops (2.7 times), they are even more overrepresented in pedestrian stops (3.7 times).

Further analysis indicates that the racial differences in Kingston police stops cannot be explained by racial differences in age, gender, the location of the stop, or the reason for stop. Interestingly, neither racial differences in observed or suspected criminal activity, nor racial differences in observed traffic violations could explain the higher stop rate for blacks (see Wortley and Marshall, 2005). Indeed, only a small proportion of all stops involving the black residents of Kingston involved criminal activity (7 percent), suspected criminal activity (6 percent), or illegal drug use (2 percent).

It is extremely important to note that these racial differences in police stop activity emerged despite the fact that the study was extremely well publicized (even before it went into the field) and that the Kingston police knew beforehand that they were being monitored for possible racial profiling activity. This foreknowledge had led many to argue that the magnitude of the racial differences documented by the Kingston pilot project is quite conservative. In other words, the observed racial differences in police stops could have been much greater if the police had not known they were being monitored.

This brings us to a discussion of the potential benefits of establishing a system in which the police must record the race of the people that they stop and/or search on the street. Besides providing data for researchers, such a monitoring system may actually reduce the incidence of racial profiling. Indeed, police officers will be less likely to engage in illegitimate, racially biased fishing expeditions when they know that they must record and justify their actions. In our opinion, such a monitoring system may also improve the relationship between the police and racial minority communities. Such a system demonstrates that the police are serious about identifying and eliminating racial profiling. The transparency also demonstrates that the police have nothing to hide, and this alone may help build trust.

Unfortunately, despite the Kingston example, other police services in Canada have thus far refused to monitor racial profiling through internal data collection procedures. Indeed, some have attacked the Kingston study for being imperfect and not considering all the sophisticated benchmarking techniques that might have explained racial differences in police stops. We agree that the Kingston study, as the first pilot project of its kind in Canada, could be improved. However, this does not mean that the findings are meaningless.

Indeed, the fact that the results of this study are consistent with other studies—and with community allegations of racial bias—should be used to justify more, better funded, and more ambitious studies. Unfortunately, the political will to spearhead such research and monitoring efforts has yet to emerge.

POLICE USE OF FORCE

Highly publicized American cases of police violence against black people (e.g., Rodney King) serve to reinforce the perception that North American police officers are biased against members of the black community. However, high-profile cases of police brutality involving black victims are not limited to the United States. The names Albert Johnson, Lester Donaldson, Wade Lawson, Marcellus Francois, and Sophia Cook are frequently used to illustrate that police use of force is a problem faced by blacks in Canada as well (see Pedicelli, 1998). Unfortunately, allegations of racial bias in the police use of force are extremely difficult to examine. Official documentation regarding citizens killed or injured by the police is simply unavailable to Canadian researchers (Goff, 2001). However, an examination of news stories suggests that blacks are indeed highly overrepresented among those killed or injured by the police in Ontario (see Pedicelli, 1998, for a detailed review of selected cases from both Montreal and Toronto). For example, between 1978 and 2000, we were able to identify through media coverage 34 separate shootings in which citizens were either killed or severely injured by the police. Nineteen of these cases (59 percent) involved black victims, 10 (29 percent) involved whites, and 5 (16 percent) involved people from other racial backgrounds. Additional analysis reveals that 13 of the 23 people (57 percent) who were shot and killed by the police during this period were black. Although overall numbers are low, the fact that black citizens represent over half of those killed or injured by the police is disturbing, particularly since they make up only 6 percent of Toronto's total population. However, to many observers, these findings still do not constitute proof that the Toronto police are racially biased in their use of force. Indeed, the fact that these cases resulted in few criminal charges (and no convictions) against the police could be seen as evidence that these shootings were justified. This interpretation is consistent with American research (see Fyfe, 1988), which suggests that once situational factors (i.e., whether the suspect had a gun or was in the process of committing a violent felony) have been taken into account, racial differences in the police use of force are dramatically reduced. Nonetheless, until such detailed research is conducted within Canada, questions about the possible relationship between race and police violence will remain.

THE ARREST SITUATION

Early studies of police arrest practices suggested that racial minorities were much more likely to be arrested for minor crimes (drug use, minor assault, vagrancy, etc.) than whites. Compared to whites, that research also found that racial minorities were more likely to be arrested in cases where there was only limited evidence that a crime had occurred (for a review see Bowling and Phillips, 2002). However, recent evidence suggests that racial bias in police arrest decisions may be declining. For example, contemporary observational studies of police-citizen encounters conducted in the United States suggest that after controlling for the seriousness of criminal conduct, race is unrelated to the police decision to arrest (see Delisi and Regoli, 1999; Klinger, 1997). In other words, regardless of their race, the police rarely arrest citizens unless there is strong evidence that a crime has been committed.

Nonetheless, a number of recent American studies suggest that it is the race of the victim—not the race of the offender—that impacts the arrest decision. In other words, there is considerable evidence to suggest that the police are more likely to make arrests in cases involving white victims than minority victims (see Parker et al., 2005). Further analysis suggests that after controlling for other legally relevant factors (including the strength of the case), crimes involving minority offenders and white victims are particularly likely to result in an arrest. For example, Smith et al. (1984) analysed 5,688 police-citizen encounters in 24 police departments and found that police officers were more likely to arrest when the victim was white and the offender was African American. They also found that the police were more likely to comply with a white victim's request that a suspect be arrested. Similarly, Stolzenberg et al. (2004) conducted a multi-level analysis of 145,255 violent crimes reported to the police in 182 American cities during 2000. The authors found that the category of crime most likely to result in arrest involved black offenders and white victims. By contrast, crimes involving black victims (regardless of the race of the offender) were least likely to result in arrest (see also Parker et al., 2005; D'Alessio and Stolzenberg, 2003). Some advocates have argued that this is direct evidence that the police put a higher value on white than minority victims and thus devote more effort and resources to solving such crimes (see Mann, 1993). These findings are also consistent with the racial threat hypothesis, which suggests that the police will treat interracial crimes involving minority offenders and white victims as particularly heinous.

Unfortunately, studies that examine the impact of both offender and victim race on arrest decisions have not yet been conducted in Canada. However, recent Canadian evidence does suggest that race may influence police behaviour once an arrest has been made. An analysis of over 10,000 Toronto arrests between 1996 and 2001 for simple drug possession reveals that black suspects (38 percent) were much more likely than whites (23 percent) to be taken to the police station for processing. White accused, on the other hand, were more likely to be released at the scene. Once at the police station, black accused are held overnight for a bail hearing at twice the rate of whites. These racial disparities in police treatment remain after other relevant factors, including age, criminal history, employment, immigration status, and home address status, have been taken into statistical account (Rankin et al., 2002a). Studies that have examined the treatment of young offenders in Ontario have yielded very similar results (Commission on Systemic Racism, 1995).

PRETRIAL DETENTION

The bail decision is recognized as one of the most important stages of the criminal court process. Not only does pretrial detention represent a fundamental denial of freedom for individuals who have not yet been proven guilty of a crime, it has also been shown to produce a number of subsequent legal consequences. After controlling for factors such as type of charge and criminal record, research suggests that offenders who are denied bail are much more likely to be convicted and sentenced to prison than their counterparts who have been released (see Walker et al., 2004; Reaves and Perez, 1992; Friedland, 1965). Thus, racial disparities in pretrial outcomes could have a direct impact on the overrepresentation of racial minorities in American and Canadian correctional statistics.

American research has demonstrated that non-whites are more likely to be held in pretrial detention than whites. A similar situation seems to exist in Canada. An examination of 1,653 cases from the Toronto courts, conducted on behalf of the Commission on Systemic Racism in the Ontario Criminal Justice System, revealed that blacks are less likely to be released by the police at the scene and more likely to be detained following a show-cause hearing. This disparity is particularly pronounced for those charged with drug offences. Indeed, the study found that almost a third of black offenders charged with a drug offence (31 percent) were held in detention before their trial, compared to only 10 percent of whites charged with a similar offence. This profound racial difference remains after statistically controlling for other relevant factors, including criminal history (Roberts and Doob, 1997).

A second Toronto-area study provides additional evidence of racial bias in pretrial decision-making (Kellough and Wortley, 2002). This research project tracked over 1,800 criminal cases appearing in two Toronto bail courts over a six-month period in 1994. Overall, the results suggest that 36 percent of black accused are detained before trial, compared to only 23 percent of accused from other racial backgrounds. Race remains a significant predictor of pretrial detention after statistically controlling for factors associated with both flight risk (i.e., employment status, home address, previous charges for failure to appear, etc.) and danger to the public (i.e., seriousness of current charges, length of criminal record, etc.). Additional analysis, however, suggests that black accused are more likely to be detained because they tend to receive much more negative moral assessments from arresting officers. *Moral assessments* refer to the subjective personality descriptions that the police frequently attach to show-cause documents. The data suggest that on average, police officers spend more time justifying the detention of black accused than they do white accused. Clearly, this is evidence that police discretion extends from the street and into the courtroom—at least at the pretrial level. Finally, the results of this study suggest that rather than managing risky populations, pretrial detention is a resource that the prosecution uses (along with over-charging) to encourage (or coerce) guilty pleas from accused persons. By contrast, those accused who are not held in pretrial custody are much more likely to have all of their charges withdrawn.

RACE AND SENTENCING

American and British research on race and sentencing has revealed mixed findings. Some studies have found that black and other minority defendants are treated more harshly (Mauer, 1999; Hudson, 1989; Shallice and Gordon, 1990; Hood, 1992), some have found that they are treated more leniently (Wilbanks, 1987), and others have found no evidence of racial differences in sentencing outcomes (Lauristen and Sampson, 1998; Bowling and Phillips, 2002; Walker et al., 2004). Relatively little Canadian research has focused on the sentencing outcomes of blacks or other racial minorities. The Commission on Systemic Racism in the Ontario Criminal Justice System compared the sentencing outcomes of white and black offenders convicted in Toronto courts during the early 1990s. This comparison revealed that black offenders convicted of drug offences were more likely than non-white offenders to be sentenced to prison. This racial difference remained after other important factors—including offence seriousness, criminal history, age and employment—have been taken into statistical account. However, Roberts and Doob (1997) found that the effect of race was statistically weaker at the sentencing stage than at earlier stages of the justice process.

Race and Corrections

As with other stages of the criminal justice system, very little Canadian research has examined the treatment of racial minorities within corrections. However, consistent with studies on the police and the criminal courts, the research that has been conducted suggests that some forms of racial bias exist behind prison walls. For example, the Commission on Systemic Racism in the Ontario Criminal Justice System found that while racist language and attitudes plague the environments of many Ontario prisons, and racial segregation is often used as a strategy for maintaining order, correctional officials do not acknowledge that racism is a significant management problem (Commission on Systemic Racism, 1994). Commission researchers also found evidence of racial bias in the application of prison discipline. Black inmates are significantly overrepresented among prisoners charged with misconducts, particularly the types of misconducts in which correctional officers exercise greater discretionary judgment. This fact is important, because a correctional record for such misconducts is often used to deny parole and limit access to temporary release programs. Indeed, exploratory research suggests that after controlling for other relevant factors, black and other racial minority inmates are somewhat more likely to be denied early prison release (Mann, 1993; Commission on Systemic Racism, 1995). Unfortunately, Canadian research has yet to explore possible racial discrimination in parole decisions within federal correctional facilities.

Finally, Commission researchers highlighted the fact that current rehabilitation programs do not meet the cultural and linguistic needs of many racial minority inmates (Commission on Systemic Racism, 1994; 1995). The current correctional system, it is argued, caters to white, Euro-Canadian norms. The treatment needs of black and other racial minority prisoners are either unacknowledged or ignored. Ultimately, inadequate or inappropriate rehabilitation services for minority inmates may translate into higher recidivism rates for non-white offenders—a fact that may further contribute to their overrepresentation in the Canadian correctional system.

CONCLUSION

Empirical evidence suggests that perceptions of racial bias in the Ontario criminal justice system are not unfounded. With the possible exception of policing, racial disparities at any one stage of the criminal justice process are not huge; however, in our opinion, the cumulative effect of discrimination throughout the system has a major impact on the black community. Clearly, research to date strongly suggests that racial discrimination, along with higher rates of criminal offending, can help explain the overrepresentation of blacks in correctional statistics.

Most Canadian criminologists acknowledge that much more research is needed. For example, more studies incorporating both official and unofficial data are needed to explore racial differences in police stop and search practices, police use of force, arrest decisions, and complaints against the police. Larger studies, especially those focusing on a wider array of criminal offences, are needed to explore racial differences in pre-trail detention, conviction rates, and sentencing. Additional correctional research, particularly at the federal level, is also needed to examine racial differences in parole decisions and access to suitable rehabilitation programming. Finally, good evaluation research is required if we are to properly explore the impact of programs that have been designed to reduce racism within the Canadian justice system. For example, numerous strategies, including community policing initiatives, cultural sensitivity training, formal anti-racism regulations, and campaigns to recruit officers from racial minority communities, have been implemented by police forces across the country. However, these programs have not been evaluated in a scientific manner by external researchers (see Stenning, 2003). How do we know if these programs are working or if they are simply window-dressing designed to convince the public that issues of racism are being addressed?

Future research on racism in Canada is greatly hindered by the current ban on the collection and dissemination of race-crime statistics (see Wortley, 1999). The primary justification for the ban is that information on the racial background of criminal offenders might be used to reinforce racial stereotypes and justify discrimination within all sectors of Canadian society. Unfortunately, there is very little evidence that the ban actually prevents people from drawing connections between race and criminality. Indeed, a recent survey found that almost two-thirds of Ontario residents believe that black people are responsible for a disproportionate amount of crime (Roberts, 2002). These beliefs are likely based more on media coverage of crime (from both Canada and the United States) than on exposure to official crime data. Indeed, recent Canadian studies suggest that the vast majority of news coverage involving blacks is related to criminal activity (see Wortley, 2003; Henry and Tator, 2000). Furthermore, race-crime statistics from other countries are available to those who want to put forth racist theories of crime causation (Rushton, 1988). In sum, we feel that while the current ban on race-crime statistics has little impact on public beliefs about the relationship between race and criminal behaviour, it has served to prevent a more effective investigation of possible racist practices within the Canadian criminal justice system.

Recently, conservative critics have charged that research which documents racism within the justice system does more harm than good. The argument is that publicly discussing evidence of racism creates distrust, damages relationships with specific minority communities, and lowers morale among criminal justice personnel (*Toronto Star*, 2002, p. A14). However, this perspective fails to recognize that good, objective social research does not create social problems: it merely documents them. Research has not caused the problems that exist between racial minorities in Canada and the justice system: it has only documented a situation which already exists. In sum, the discomfort of having to talk about racism and then dealing with it in the policy arena should not be used as an excuse to prevent further research in this area.

DISCUSSION QUESTIONS

1. *The authors argue that routinely collecting criminal justice statistics that include the race of the individual would be a good idea. What do you think?*
2. *If systemic discrimination against black people exists in the criminal justice system of Ontario, what, in your opinion, should be done about the problem? Which remedies are worth considering?*

FURTHER READINGS

Commission on Systemic Racism in the Ontario Criminal Justice System. 1995. *Report of the Commission on Systemic Racism in the Ontario Criminal Justice System*. Toronto: Queen's Printer for Ontario.

Wortley, S. 1996. Justice for all? Race and perceptions of bias in the Ontario criminal justice system—A Toronto survey. *Canadian Journal of Criminology* 38: 439–467.

Wortley, S., Macmillan, R., and Hagan, J. 1997. Just des(s)erts? The racial polarization of perceptions of criminal injustice. *Law and Society Review*, 31: 637–676.

REFERENCES

American Psychological Association. 2001. *Letter to U.S. House in Support of the End of Racial Profiling Act, H.R. 2074*. American Psychological Association: Online at: @URL:http://www.apa.org/ppo/issues/pracialprof.html.

Amnesty International. 2004. *Threat and Humiliation: Racial Profiling, Domestic Security and Human Rights in the United States*. New York: Amnesty International USA.

Blizzard, C. 2002. A crisis of their own choosing: Black leaders insist it's racial profiling, not black-on-black violence. *Toronto Sun*. November 1: 16.

Bowling, B., and Phillips, C. 2002. *Racism, Crime and Justice*. Britain: Pearson Education Ltd.

Commission on Systemic Racism in the Ontario Criminal Justice System. 1995. *Report of the Commission on Systemic Racism in the Ontario Criminal Justice System*. Toronto: Queen's Printer for Ontario.

Commission on Systemic Racism in the Ontario Criminal Justice System. 1994. *Racism Behind Bars: The Treatment of Black and other Racial Minority Prisoners in Ontario Prisons B Interim Report of the Commission on Systemic Racism in the Ontario Criminal Justice System*. Toronto: Queen's Printer for Ontario.

D'Alessio, S., and Stolzenberg, L. 2003. Race and probability of arrest. *Social Forces*, 81: 1383–1399.

Delisi, M., and Regoli, B. 1999. Race, conventional crime and criminal justice: The declining importance of race. *Journal of Criminal Justice*, 27: 549–557.

Foster, C. 1996. *A Place Called Heaven: The Meaning of Being Black in Canada*. Toronto: HarperCollins.

Friedland, M. L. 1965. *Detention Before Trial: A Study of Criminal Cases Tried in the Toronto Magistrate's Court*. Toronto: University of Toronto Press.

Fyfe, J.J. 1988. Police use of deadly force: Research and reform. *Justice Quarterly*, 5: 165–205.

Gabor, T. 2004. Inflammatory rhetoric on racial profiling can undermine police services. *Canadian Journal of Criminology and Criminal Justice*, 46: 457–466.

Goff, C. 2001. *Criminal Justice in Canada*, 2nd ed. Scarborough: Nelson Thomson Learning.

Goldstein, L. 2002. It's not racist to fight violent crime. *Toronto Sun*. October 29: 16.

Harris, D. 2002. *Profiles in Injustice: Why Racial Profiling Cannot Work*. New York: New Press.

Henry, F. 1994. *The Caribbean Diaspora in Toronto: Learning to Live With Racism*. Toronto: University of Toronto Press.

Henry, F., and Tator, C. 2000. *Racist Discourse in Canada's English Print Media*. Toronto: Canadian Race Relations Foundation.

Hood, R. 1992. *Race and Sentencing: A Study in the Crown Court.* Oxford: Clarendon Press.

Hudson, B. 1989. Discrimination and disparity: The influence of race on sentencing. *New Community* 16: 23–34.

James, C. 1998. "Up to no good:" Black on the streets and encountering police. In V. Satzewich (Ed.), *Racism and Social Inequality in Canada: Concepts, Controversies and Strategies of Resistance.* Toronto: Thompson.

Kellough, G., and Wortley, S. 2002. Remand for plea: The impact of race, pretrial detention and over-charging on plea bargaining decisions. *British Journal of Criminology,* 42: 186–210.

Kellough, G., and Wortley, S. (in press). Risk, moral assessment and the application of bail conditions in Canadian criminal courts. *British Journal of Criminology.*

Klinger, D. 1997. Negotiating order in patrol work: An ecological theory of police response to deviance. *Criminology,* 35: 277–306.

Lafree, G. 1980. The effect of sexual stratification by race on official reactions to rape. *American Sociological Review,* 45: 842–854.

Lauristen, J., and Sampson, R. 1998. Minorities, crime, and criminal justice. In M. Tonry (Ed.), *The Handbook of Crime and Punishment.* New York: Oxford University Press.

Mann, C. R. 1993. *Unequal Justice: A Question of Color.* Bloomington: Indiana University Press.

Mauer, M. 1999. *Race to Incarcerate.* New York: The New Press.

Melchers, R. 2003. Do Toronto police engage in racial profiling? *Canadian Journal of Criminology and Criminal Justice,* 45: 347–366.

Neugebauer, R. 2000. Kids, cops, and colour: The social organization of police-minority youth relations. In R. Neugebauer (Ed.), *Criminal Injustice: Racism in the Criminal Justice System.* Toronto: Canadian Scholars Press.

Ontario Human Rights Commission. 2003. *Paying the Price: The Human Cost of Racial Profiling.* Toronto: Ontario Human Rights Commission. Online at: www.ohrc.on.ca.

Parker, K., Stults, B., and Rice, S. 2005. Racial threat, concentrated disadvantage and social control: Considering macro-level sources of variation in arrests. *Criminology,* 43: 1111–1134.

Pedicelli, G. 1998. *When Police Kill: Police Use of Force in Montreal and Toronto.* Montreal: Vehicule Press.

R. v Brown. 2003. *64 O. R. (3d)* 161 at 165.

Rankin, J. et al. 2002a. Singled out: An investigation into race and crime. *Toronto Star.* October 19: A1.

Rankin, J. et al. 2002b. Police target black drivers. *Toronto Star.* October 20: A1

Reaves, B., and Perez, J. 1992. *Pre-trial Release of Felony Defendants.* Washington, DC: U.S. Department of Justice.

Roberts, J.V. 2002. Racism and the collection of statistics relating to race and ethnicity. In W. Chan and K. Mirchandini (Eds.), *Crimes of Colour.* Peterborough: Broadview Press.

Roberts, J.V. and Doob, A. 1997. Race, ethnicity, and criminal justice in Canada. In M. Tonry, (Ed.), *Ethnicity, Crime, and Immigration: Comparative and Cross-National Perspectives,* 21. Chicago: University of Chicago Press.

Ruck, M., and Wortley, S. 2002. Racial and ethnic minority high school students' perceptions of school disciplinary practices: A look at some Canadian findings. *Journal of Youth and Adolescence,* 31: 185–195.

Rushton, P. 1988. Race Differences in sexuality and their correlates: Another look at psychological models. *Journal of Research in Personality,* 23: 35–54.

Shallice, A., and Gordon, P. 1990. *Black People, White Justice? Race and the Criminal Justice System.* London: Runnymede Trust.

Smith, D., Visher, C., and Davidson, L. 1984. Equity and discretionary justice: The influence of race on police arrest decisions. *Journal of Criminal Law and Criminology,* 75: 234–249.

Solicitor General of Canada. *Basic Facts About Corrections in Canada: 1997 Edition.* Ottawa: Public Works and Government Services Canada.

Stenning, P. 2003. Policing the cultural kaleidoscope: Recent Canadian experience. *Police & Society,* 7: 21–87.

Stolzenberg, L., D'Alessio, S., and Eitle, D. 2004. A multilevel test of racial threat theory. *Criminology,* 42: 673–698.

Tanovich, D. 2006. *The Colour of Justice: Policing Race in Canada.* Toronto: Irwin Law.

Tator, C., and Henry, F. 2006. *Racial Profiling in Canada: Challenging the Myth of a Few Bad Apples.* Toronto: University of Toronto Press.

Tonry, M. 1995. *Malign Neglect: Race, Crime and Punishment in America.* New York: Oxford University Press.

Toronto Star. 2002. There is no racism. We do not do racial profiling. *Toronto Star.* October 19: A14.

Walker, S., Spohn, C., and Delone, M. 2004. *The Color of Justice: Race, Ethnicity and Crime in America.* Toronto: Wadsworth.

Wilbanks, W. 1987. *The Myth of a Racist Criminal Justice System.* Belmont, CA: Wadsworth.

Worthington, P. 2002. Oh, the deadly irony of it all: Violence shows cops right. *Toronto Sun.* October 30: 40.

Wortley, S. 2004. Hidden intersections: Research on race, crime and criminal justice in Canada. *Canadian Ethnic Studies Journal,* 35: 99–117.

Wortley, S. 2003. Misrepresentation or reality: The depiction of race and crime in the Canadian print media. In B. Schissel and C. Brooks (Eds.), *Marginality and Condemnation: Critical Criminology in Canada.* Halifax: Fernwood Press.

Wortley, S. 1999. A Northern Taboo: Research on race, crime, and criminal justice in Canada. *Canadian Journal of Criminology,* 41: 261–274.

Wortley, S. 1996. Justice for all? Race and perceptions of bias in the Ontario criminal justice system: A Toronto survey. *Canadian Journal of Criminology,* 38: 439–467.

Wortley, S., Macmillan R., and Hagan, J. 1997. Just des(s)erts? The racial polarization of perceptions of criminal injustice. *Law and Society Review,* 31: 637–676.

Wortley, S., and Marshall, L. 2005. *Police Stop Search Activities in Kingston, Ontario.* Kingston: Kingston Police Services Board.

Wortley, S., and Tanner, J. 2005. Inflammatory rhetoric? Baseless accusations? Responding to Gabor's critique of racial profiling research in Canada. *Canadian Journal of Criminology and Criminal Justice,* 47: 581–609.

Wortley, S., and Tanner, J. 2004a. Racial profiling in Canada: Survey evidence from Toronto. *The Canadian Review of Policing Research,* 1: 24–36.

Wortley, S., and Tanner, J. 2004b. Discrimination or good policing? The racial profiling debate in Canada. *Our Diverse Cities,* 1: 197–201.

Wortley, S., and Tanner, J. 2003. Data, denials and confusion: The racial profiling debate in Toronto. *Canadian Journal of Criminology and Criminal Justice,* 45: 367–389.

Wortley, S., and Kellough, G. 2004. Racializing risk: Police and Crown discretion and the overrepresentation of black people in the Ontario criminal justice system. In A. Harriott, F. Brathwaite and S. Wortley (Eds.), *Crime and Criminal Justice in the Caribbean and Among Caribbean Peoples.* Kingston, Jamaica: Arawak Publications.

CHAPTER 16
Aboriginal Overrepresentation: No Single Problem, No Simple Solution[1]

INTRODUCTION

Few problems in criminal justice have been discussed as much or attracted as much attention as the high number of Aboriginal Canadians in Canada's prisons. Relative to their numbers in the general population, Aboriginal Canadians have always accounted for a higher proportion of prisoners (see Roberts and Melchers, 2003, for trends). The issue has provoked a number of commissions of inquiry as well as a wealth of scholarship. Surveys of the Canadian public also indicate that although people know little about the workings of the justice system, most people are aware that Aboriginal peoples account for a disproportionate percentage of the prison population.

In this chapter, Carol La Prairie, one of the leading scholars in the field discusses this seemingly intractable problem and comes to the conclusion that the overrepresentation of Aboriginal peoples in Canadian prisons is a complex, multidimensional problem to which there is no simple or single solution.

Aboriginal Overrepresentation: No Single Problem, No Simple Solution
Carol La Prairie, Criminologist

Contrary to conventional wisdom, the greatest challenge in the area of Aboriginal justice is that no single solution or even a transition to an Aboriginal justice system can solve the justice problems facing Aboriginals in Canada. This is a bold statement, one that contradicts much of the Aboriginal and non-Aboriginal political and community rhetoric about self-government and its capacity for redressing justice problems. For two decades now, many advocates have maintained that if Aboriginal people had more or complete control over their own justice issues, the problem of Aboriginal overrepresentation in the criminal justice and correctional systems would solve itself. But this assumption may not be well founded.

This chapter explores some of the data pertaining to the problem of high rates of Aboriginal admissions to custody. The discussion begins with the issue of Aboriginal overrepresentation in the criminal justice system. From there, the chapter discusses Aboriginal crime and victimization, the characteristics of Aboriginal prison populations, and the factors contributing to the overrepresentation problem.

THE MEANING OF OVERREPRESENTATION

For the past 20 years, the overrepresentation of Aboriginal peoples in prison statistics has been the dominant Aboriginal criminal justice issue in Canada. It has generated royal commissions in Alberta, Saskatchewan, Manitoba, and Nova Scotia, with the inquiry into the wrongful conviction of Donald Marshall. Simply put, overrepresentation means that in relation to their numbers in the general population, Aboriginal populations in Canadian prisons are disproportionately high. Thus, while Aboriginals account for only 3.6 percent of the national population, they accounted for 18 percent of federal and 21 percent of provincial admissions to custody in 2003 (Canadian Centre for Justice Statistics, 2004). The issue of overrepresentation has also played a central role in criminal justice agendas in other countries with indigenous populations, such as New Zealand and Australia (Doone, 2000; Crime Research Centre, 2002).

However, understanding Aboriginal overrepresentation is not as straightforward as it appears at first glance for several reasons. First, Aboriginal admissions to custody have always been calculated as a percentage of the total number of sentenced admissions, even during the recent years during which total sentenced admissions have generally been declining.[2] This makes Aboriginal percentages look more extreme. Second, comparing the percentages of Aboriginal sentenced admissions with the percentage of Aboriginal people in the population of several jurisdictions is also problematic because Aboriginal people are generally undercounted in the census surveys. As a result, skewed census data tend to exaggerate the rate of Aboriginal prison admissions or prison populations. Third, there is considerable regional variation in overrepresentation in provincial and territorial institutions in Canada.

However, despite the weaknesses of these statistics, there is still very clearly a problem of Aboriginal overrepresentation in the criminal justice and correctional systems. If this problem is to be resolved and prevented in future generations, we need to develop a better understanding of the factors that contribute to it.

Across Canada, prison statistics show clear regional variations in the degree of overrepresentation. Table 16.1 provides some overrepresentation statistics. In Ontario, Aboriginals account for 1.7 percent of the general population but fully 9 percent of correctional admissions. This generates an "Overrepresentation Ratio" of 5.3. Table 16.1 reveals that the overrepresentation ratios are higher in the prairie provinces and the Territories and lower in Quebec, Ontario, and the Atlantic provinces. For example, in the Atlantic provinces and Quebec, overrepresentation is only slightly above what would be expected for the Aboriginal population in those provinces (Ratios of 1 to 3.5). However, in Manitoba, Ontario, Saskatchewan, and Alberta, the overrepresentation is higher (ratios of 5 to 7). This regional variation is significant, although it has not been adequately explained or even explored by researchers. One reason for the lack of attention is the endurance of the most widely used and most common explanation for overrepresentation—that the criminal justice system unfairly apprehends and processes Aboriginal people in relation to the way it treats non-Aboriginal people. But then one would have to assume that this unfairness has wide regional differences.

Table 16.1 *Aboriginal Population, Aboriginal Admissions to Federal/Provincial/ Territorial Institutions, and Overrepresentation Ratios (2001/03)*

Jurisdiction	Aboriginal % of General Population	Aboriginal % of Total Correctional Admissions	Overrepresentation Ratio
Alberta	5.3	39	7.3
Saskatchewan	13.5	80	5.9
Ontario	1.7	9	5.3
Manitoba	13.6	68	5.0
British Columbia	4.4	20	4.5
Nova Scotia	1.9	7	3.7
New Brunswick	2.4	9	3.7
Yukon	23.0	73	3.2
PEI	1.0	2	2.0
Quebec	1.1	2	1.8
Newfoundland	3.6	6	1.7
NWT	50.5	88	1.7
Nunavut	85.2	97	1.1
FEDERAL	3.6	18	5.5

Sources: Statistics Canada (2003) and CCJS (2004).

In addition to regional variations in overrepresentation levels, demographic differences influence the overrepresentation statistics. For example, the median age of the Aboriginal population in 2001 was 24.7 years, which was about 12 years lower than that of the Canadian population. Children aged 14 and under represented one-third of the Aboriginal population in 2001, far higher than the corresponding share of 19 percent in the non-Aboriginal population. Although the Aboriginal population accounted for only 3.6 percent of Canada's total population, Aboriginal children represented 5.6 percent of all children in Canada. Thus, in general, the Aboriginal population is younger than the non-Aboriginal population.

The comparative size of the Aboriginal and non-Aboriginal age groups between 15 and 24 is important for crime statistics because this age group is most likely to become involved in the criminal justice system. In 2001, 17.3 percent of the general Aboriginal population were in the 15–24 age group, compared to 13.6 percent of the non-Aboriginal population. This means that there was a larger Aboriginal "pool" of people in the most crime-prone age group. The Aboriginal population aged 24 and under in 2001 was 53 percent, compared to 31 percent in the non-Aboriginal population. There are also dramatic provincial and regional differences in the mean ages of the Aboriginal and non-Aboriginal populations. The mean age of the Aboriginal population in the three territories (Yukon, NWT, and Nunavut) is 24, compared to 36 for the non-Aboriginal population; in the prairie provinces, the figures are 22 and 37, respectively; in British Columbia, 27 and 39; in Ontario, 28 and 37; in Quebec, 28 and 38; and in the Atlantic Provinces and Newfoundland/Labrador, 26 and 38. The greatest difference is in the prairie provinces (22 and 37), which also have the highest levels of Aboriginal over-incarceration.

While discriminatory practices of the criminal justice system may constitute one explanation for Aboriginal overrepresentation, evidence suggests that the same factors that explain the presence of non-Aboriginal people in the criminal justice system also explain the presence of Aboriginal people. In Australia, Weatherburn et al. (2003) found that an important set of sociologicial factors distinguished Aboriginal people who come into conflict with the law and Aboriginal people who do not—alcohol use, early departure from school, unemployment, and removal from one's natural family. Similarly, among non-Aboriginal populations, these same four factors predispose people toward conflict with the law. American criminologist Michael Tonry, an expert on the issue of race and crime, has argued that class and socioeconomic disparities constitute more powerful explanations for minority overrepresentation in the criminal justice system in western countries than those based exclusively on discrimination. He writes: "a consensus is emerging among researchers in most countries that the disparities result primarily from racial differences in offending patterns" (Tonry, 1994, p. 158). In other words, the volume and type of offences have greater power to account for the overinvolvement of certain racial groups in the criminal justice system than overt or covert acts of discrimination on the part of criminal justice officials, such as police, prosecutors, and judges.

But Tonry also argues that these disparities are the consequence of historical experiences and contemporary social and economic circumstances. Thus, two fundamental questions from this research have relevance to the Canadian situation. First, what do we know about the relationship between Aboriginal offending patterns and Aboriginal socioeconomic conditions? Second, how do class and socioeconomic disparity explain both Aboriginal and non-Aboriginal patterns of incarceration?

ABORIGINAL CRIME AND VICTIMIZATION

Research documents several characteristics of Aboriginal crime in Canada. It reveals a consistent pattern of elevated levels of Aboriginal offending and victimization, as well as overrepresentation of Aboriginal people as offenders and as victims of interpersonal violence. Comparisons of Aboriginal and non-Aboriginal offence data in aggregate terms reveal some important and distinctive offence patterns. First, Aboriginal crime is quantitatively disproportionate to the amount of crime in the non-Aboriginal population (CCJS, 2000a; LaPrairie, 1996; Trevethan, 1991; Roberts and Doob, 1997; Dickson-Gilmore and LaPrairie, 2005)). In other words, the rate of crime by Aboriginal offenders (i.e., number of crimes committed by individual Aboriginal offenders per 100,000 members of the Aboriginal population) is considerably higher than the rates of crime by non-Aboriginal offenders. Second, there are significant qualitative differences between Aboriginal and non-Aboriginal crime. Crime by Aboriginal persons is more likely to involve violence (Moyer 1992; Silverman and Kennedy, 1993; Griffiths et al., 1995); and many of the Aboriginal crime problems that police and courts deal with are interpersonal in nature.

The criminal justice literature suggests that the incidence of Aboriginal crime and victimization varies widely by region; moreover, even within regions, Aboriginal and non-Aboriginal crime differs in both degree and kind (Roberts and Doob, 1997; Dickson-Gilmore and LaPrairie, 2005). For example, one study in Saskatchewan found that the Aboriginal crime rate was 11 times higher than the non-Aboriginal rate. In Saskatchewan, the on-reserve Aboriginal crime rate was five times higher than the Aboriginal crime rates in urban or rural areas; and in Regina and Prince Albert, 42 percent of victims of crime were Aboriginal, even though Aboriginal people comprised only 2 percent of the population. Victimization in this region was also predominately intraracial (CCJS, 2000b).

In addition, Aboriginal inmates in Canada are more likely to be incarcerated for crimes against the person and for offences against spouses and ex-spouses than for other crimes. Research in Canada, Australia, and the United States also documents the role alcohol plays in interpersonal crime committed by Aboriginal offenders (Moyer, 1992; Greenfield and Smith, 1995; Finn et al., 1999; Fitzgerald and Weatherburn, 2001; Dickson-Gilmore and La Prairie, 2005). Aboriginal victimization research in Canada presents a disturbing picture of disproportionate levels of violent victimization often involving Aboriginal females. In 1999, the General Social Survey (GSS) on victimization collected data on race and cultural status, including Aboriginal status. An analysis of the data showed that approximately 35 percent of the Aboriginal population reported having been the victim of at least one crime in the 12 months preceding the survey, compared to 26 percent of the non-Aboriginal population. Aboriginal people were also more likely to have been victimized more than once and to be victims of violent crime. While the rates of theft of personal property were similar for both Aboriginal and non-Aboriginal people, Aboriginal people experienced violent crime at a rate nearly three times that of non-Aboriginal people. (For visible minorities, the rates were similar to those of the general population; for the immigrant group, the rates were lower than for the general population.) Aboriginal people and Aboriginal women in particular were found to be at much greater risk for spousal violence (CCJS, 2001a).

This brief overview outlines characteristics particular to Aboriginal crime and victimization: disproportionate levels of crime, involvement of alcohol in the commission of crime, and the intraracial nature of crime. Understanding these factors is critical for understanding Aboriginal overinvolvement in the criminal justice system, because the volume and types of offences (and especially the disproportionate levels of family violence) and the influence of alcohol present judges with significant dilemmas at sentencing. The higher risk levels (based on seriousness of offences and prior records) of Aboriginal offenders may limit the use of community-based sanctions such as probation and conditional sentences and leave few options other than prison sentences.

CHARACTERISTICS OF ABORIGINAL AND NON-ABORIGINAL PRISON POPULATIONS IN CANADA

If class differences and socioeconomic disparities explain victimization and the involvement in the criminal justice system of some minority groups, they should also explain involvement of the non-Aboriginal population. When gender, age, employment, and education characteristics are compared for all inmates in correctional institutions in Canada, one finds that (a) males are vastly overrepresented in prison populations (i.e., males comprise 98 percent of the prison population but only 49 percent of the Canadian population); (b) young people are overrepresented in prison populations, (i.e., the mean age of inmates is 33, but the mean age of the general Canadian population is 41); (c) 49 percent of inmates were unemployed at admission to correctional institutions, compared to 10 percent of the Canadian population; and (d) the prison population is much less well-educated than the general population, (i.e., 37 percent of prison inmates had Grade 9 or less, compared to only 12 percent of adults in Canada) (see Table 16.2). These statistics tell us that the young, the poor, the uneducated, and males are all seriously overrepresented in general prison populations. Thus, it appears the real predictors of crime may not be race so much as gender, education level, and socioeconomic situation.

Table 16.2 *Characteristics of Canadian Prison and General Populations, 1996*

Characteristics	Prison Population %*	General Canadian Population %
Male gender	98%	49%
Mean age	33 years	41 years
Unemployed	49% (at time of admission)	10%
Less than Grade 9 education	37%	12%

combined for provincial and federal inmates; Source: Finn et al. (1999).

How does the Aboriginal population compare to the general non-Aboriginal population with respect to these factors? The variables most relevant for comparison purposes are gender, age, employment, and education (see Table 16.2). However, because the gender ratio is similar for the Canadian and the Aboriginal populations—49 percent male to 51 percent female—the comparison factors that are most relevant to this discussion are age, employment, education, and "being a child of single parents" (because of its oft-cited relationship to problems experienced by children). The age, education, unemployment, and "child of single parents" status data for the Aboriginal and non-Aboriginal populations are presented in Table 16.3.

These demographics reveal that the Aboriginal population is generally more disadvantaged than the non-Aboriginal population based on the prison population characteristics identified in Table 16.2. If the factors that characterize prison populations are similar to the general Aboriginal population, then

Table 16.3 *Select Canadian and Aboriginal Population Demographics*

Demographics	Canadian %	Aboriginal %
Ages 0–24	34%	53%
Ages 45+	33%	16%
Children living with single parents	15%	29%
Unemployed	10%	24%
Less than Grade 9	12%	20%

Sources: Statistics Canada (1996, 1997)

we should expect some overrepresentation of Aboriginals in the correctional system. But Aboriginal inmates are disadvantaged even within the inmate population itself, because Aboriginal inmates are even younger, have less education, and are more likely to be unemployed than their non-Aboriginal counterparts (CCJS, 2000a). They are considered at higher risk to reoffend (as a result of longer criminal records), have higher personal/emotional and marital/family needs, and have more employment and substance abuse problems (CCJS, 2000a).

The demographic differences between Aboriginal and non-Aboriginal populations in Canada suggest that more useful and accurate definitions and explanations of overrepresentation are possible. While overrepresentation has generally been described in racial terms, such as "Aboriginal overrepresentation," it might be described more accurately as the overrepresentation of the poor, the unemployed, and the uneducated. The Aboriginal population has a disproportionately higher number of people in these groups.

But do socioeconomic factors fully explain Aboriginal overrepresentation in prisons? Table 16.4 reveals that the Aboriginal population is generally more disadvantaged than the non-Aboriginal population, which would explain why Aboriginals are overrepresented in prison. But there is no reason to believe that middle-class, working, or educated Aboriginal people are any more vulnerable to being incarcerated than middle-class non-Aboriginal people. Moreover, incarceration data from those provinces with the largest proportion of adults to children in their Aboriginal populations support this assertion: while the Atlantic provinces and Eastern Canada have higher proportions of Aboriginal people 15 years of age and over, they also have among the lowest rates of Aboriginal incarceration. If being Aboriginal were the primary cause of overrepresentation, then the Atlantic provinces and Eastern Canada would have higher Aboriginal incarceration than they in fact do. By contrast, the provinces with the largest and youngest Aboriginal populations (the prairie provinces) also have the most Aboriginal youth involved in the criminal justice system.

Table 16.4 *Select Canadian, Aboriginal, and Inmate Demographics*

Demographics	Canadian Population %	General Provincial/ Federal Inmate Population %	Aboriginal Population %	Aboriginal Provincial/ Federal Inmate Population %*
Male gender	49%	98%	49%	91%
Mean age	41 years	34 years	31 years	30 years
Unemployed**	10%	49%	24%	70%
Less than Grade 9	12%	20%	37%	52%

* Note that the majority of Aboriginal inmates are Registered Indians.
** Those not employed but seeking work. Does not include those who have stopped searching for work.
Sources: CCJS (2001b); Finn et al. (1999).

CONCLUSION

Research suggests that Aboriginal overrepresentation in prisons cannot be explained simply by discriminatory practices embedded in the way criminal justice systems charge and process Aboriginal suspects, accused persons, and offenders. Therefore, calls for separate Aboriginal justice systems to solve the problem of Aboriginal overrepresentation in the criminal justice and correctional systems may be inadequate for solving the problem. In effect, any response to the problem that focuses solely on the criminal justice system itself is likely to fail: the same issues that plague the general justice system would migrate to an Aboriginal-controlled system (see Dickson-Gilmore and LaPrairie, 2005). Moreover, the socioeconomic differences between Registered Indians living on reserve and other Aboriginal groups (and in some cases Registered Indians living off-reserve) which show the former to be significantly lower on education and employment indicators, (see Maxim, 2002; LaPrairie, 2002) raise more questions about the nature of reserve life than about being Aboriginal.

To understand and respond appropriately to overrepresentation, Canadians have to learn more about the meaning of rates and levels, the role of cities and reserves as factors contributing to overrepresentation, the relationship between socioeconomic factors and involvement in the criminal justice system, criminal justice system policies and practices, and the impact of growing social stratification among Aboriginal people (for a discussion of social stratification in one province, see Hull, 2001). Until these critical issues have been researched, appropriate long-term solutions to the problem of Aboriginal overrepresentation in the criminal justice and correctional systems cannot be devised.

Moreover, other marginalized and disadvantaged people are vastly overrepresented in Canada's system of justice. Until issues of social and economic disparity are addressed more widely, overrepresentation of Aboriginal and of other disadvantaged and marginalized non-Aboriginal Canadians in the criminal justice and correctional systems will not be resolved. Criminal justice reforms must be considered for all disadvantaged offenders, not just for one group.

DISCUSSION QUESTIONS

1. *The Criminal Code contains a provision (s. 718.2(e)) that directs judges at sentencing to consider alternative sanctions for all offenders, but in particular Aboriginal offenders. The idea is that judges should make an extra effort to avoid imposing a term of custody if the offender is Aboriginal. Do you think this is an effective remedy to the problem of Aboriginal over-incarceration?*

2. *LaPrairie does not discuss in detail the kinds of reforms that might remedy the problem of high rates of incarceration among Aboriginal Canadians. What, in your view, can the federal or provincial/territorial governments do about this problem?*

FURTHER READINGS

Dickson-Gilmore, E. J., and LaPrairie, C. 2005. *Will the Circle be Unbroken: Aboriginal Communities, Restorative Justice and the Challenges of Conflict and Change.* Toronto: University of Toronto Press.

LaPrairie, C. 2002. Aboriginal over-representation in the criminal justice system: A tale of nine cities. *Canadian Journal of Criminology,* April: 181–202.

Stenning P., and Roberts, J.V. 2001. Empty promises: Parliament, the Supreme Court and the sentencing of Aboriginal offenders. *Saskatchewan Law Review,* 64 (1): 137–168.

REFERENCES

Canadian Centre for Justice Statistics. 2000a. *The Over-Representation of Aboriginal People in the Justice System.* Prepared for the Evaluation Unit, Department of Justice, Ottawa: Statistics Canada.

Canadian Centre for Justice Statistics. 2000b. *Police-Reported Aboriginal Crime in Saskatchewan.* Ottawa: Statistics Canada.

Canadian Centre for Justice Statistics. 2001a. *A Profile of Criminal Victimization: Results of the 1999 General Social Survey.* Ottawa: Statistics Canada.

Canadian Centre for Justice Statistics. 2001b. *Aboriginal Peoples in Canada,* Ottawa: Statistics Canada.

Canadian Centre for Justice Statistics. 2004. *Adult Correctional Services Survey and Integrated Correctional Services Survey, Statistics Canada.* Online at: http://estat.statcan.ca/cgi-win/CNSMCGI.EXE.

Crime Research Centre. 2002. *Executive Summary. Crime and Justice Statistics for WA: 2000.* Perth: University of Western Australia.

Dickson-Gilmore, E. J., and La Prairie, C. 2005. *Will the Circle be Unbroken: Aboriginal Communities, Restorative Justice and the Challenges of Conflict and Change.* Toronto: University of Toronto Press.

Doone, P. 2000. *Report on Combating and Preventing Maori Crime,* HEI WHAKARURUTANGA MO TE AO, Ministry of Justice, Crime Prevention Unit. Wellington NZ: Department of the Prime Minister and Cabinet.

Finn, A., Trevethan, S., Carriere, G., and Kowalski, M. 1999. Female inmates, Aboriginal inmates, and inmates serving life sentences: A one-day snapshot. *Juristat,* 19 (5). Ottawa: Statistics Canada, Canadian Centre for Justice Statistics.

Fitzgerald, Jacqueline and Weatherburn, Don. 2001. *Aboriginal Victimization and Offending: The Picture from Police Records.* Crime and Justice Statistics, NSW: Bureau of Crime Statistics and Research, 1–4.

Greenfield, Lawrence A. and. Smith, Steven K. 1995. *American Indians and Crime,* Bureau of Justice Statistics, Washington: U.S. Department of Justice, 1–13.

Griffiths, C., Zellerer, E., Wood, D., and Saville, G. 1995. *Crime, Law and Justice Among the Inuit in the Baffin Region, N.W.T. Canada.* Burnaby: Criminology Research Centre, Simon Fraser University.

Hull, J. 2001. *Aboriginal People and Social Class in Manitoba.* Winnipeg: Canadian Centre for Policy Alternatives, 1. Online at: http://www.policyalternatives.ca/manitoba/aboriginal-class.pdf.

La Prairie, C. 1996. *Examining Aboriginal Corrections in Canada.* Aboriginal Corrections Policy Unit. Ottawa: Ministry of the Solicitor General.

———. 2002. Aboriginal overrepresentation in the criminal justice system: A tale of nine cities. *Canadian Journal of Criminology*, 44 (2): 209–232.

Maxim, P. 2002. *A Sectoral Analysis of Aboriginal Women in the Labour Force.* London: University of Western Ontario (unpublished manuscript).

McCaskill, D. 1976. *A Study of Needs and Resources Related to Offenders of Native Origin in Manitoba: A Longitudinal Analysis.* Ottawa: Correctional Planning Branch, Ministry of the Solicitor General.

Moyer, S. 1992. *Race, Gender and Homicide: Comparisons between Aboriginals and Other Canadians.* Ottawa: Ministry of the Solicitor General.

Roberts, J.V., and Doob, A.N. 1997. Race, ethnicity and criminal justice in Canada. In M. Tonry (Ed.), *Ethnicity, Crime and Immigration: Crime and Justice: A Review of Research*, 21: 469–522. Chicago: University of Chicago Press.

Roberts, J.V., and Melchers, R. 2003. The incarceration of Aboriginal offenders: An analysis of trends, 1978–2001. *Canadian Journal of Criminology and Criminal Justice*, 45: 211–242.

Silverman, R., and Kennedy, L. 1993. Canadian Indian involvement in murder. In R. Silverman and L. Kennedy (Eds.), *Deadly Deeds: Murder in Canada.* Toronto: Nelson Canada.

Statistics Canada. 2003. *Aboriginal Peoples of Canada: A Demographic Profile, 2001 Census Analysis Series.* Ottawa: Census Operations Division,

Tonry, M. 1994. Editorial: Racial disparities in courts and prisons. *Criminal Behaviour and Mental Health*, 4: 158–162.

Trevethan, S. 1991. *Police-Reported Aboriginal Crime in Calgary, Regina and Saskatoon.* Ottawa: Canadian Centre for Justice Statistics.

Weatherburn, D., Fitzgerald, J., and Hua. J. 2004. Reducing Aboriginal overrepresentation in prison. *Australian Journal of Public Administration*, 62: 65–73.

ENDNOTES

[1] The *Constitution Act of 1982* recognizes that Aboriginal peoples include North American Indians, Métis, and Inuit. More specifically, Registered or Status Indians refers to those peoples who qualify for registration under *The Indian Act of 1985.* The "identity" concept was introduced in the 1996 Census, whereas previously there was only the "ancestry" concept. This change allows people to claim Aboriginal ancestry (i.e., their ancestral origins) and to identify themselves as Aboriginal (i.e., Aboriginal self-reporting). For example, in the 2001 Census, 1.2 million people claimed Aboriginal ancestry, whereas only 975,000 reported themselves as being Aboriginal.

2 An additional problem with using admissions data to calculate overrepresentation is that the same individual can be counted more than once over the same year. This is most likely in admissions to provincial and territorial institutions where short sentences are common. The consequence is that the statistics exaggerate the extent to which Aboriginal persons are overrepresented in prison admission statistics.

CHAPTER 17
When Justice Fails: Understanding Miscarriages of Justice

INTRODUCTION

A common perception among many members of the public is that the justice system tends to protect the rights of the accused, with the result that guilty parties too often escape conviction. However, the opposite can also occur: innocent accused persons are sometimes convicted of crimes that they did not commit. This is particularly disturbing when the conviction results in long prison sentences, as was the case for David Milgaard and several other individuals. Criminologists in Canada and elsewhere have explored the causes and consequences of wrongful convictions.

In this reading, two Canadian researchers who have examined this issue discuss the question of wrongful convictions.

When Justice Fails: Understanding Miscarriages of Justice
Myriam Denov and Kathryn Campbell, University of Ottawa

The Canadian criminal justice system is based on the adversarial model, in which two parties—the state and the accused—present their case before an impartial judge. The theory is that as a result of the criminal trial between competing parties, the truth eventually emerges. The numerous procedural safeguards in place are presumed to protect the innocent from both unintentional and/or intentional errors on the part of the police, prosecutors, and judges. Unfortunately, the cases of wrongful conviction in Canada call into question the ability of our criminal justice system to distinguish between the guilty and the innocent. The devastating ordeals of wrongly convicted Canadians, such as Donald Marshall, Jr., David Milgaard, Guy Paul Morin, Thomas Sophonow, and Jamie Nelson, serve as powerful reminders of the potential for error in the justice system. The media and lobby groups such as the Association in Defence of the Wrongly Convicted (AIDWYC) help in raising awareness about these cases.

The objective of this chapter is to explore the causes and consequences of wrongful convictions, as well as government responses to the problem. The chapter begins by examining the individual and systemic factors that appear to contribute to wrongful convictions. It then explores the effects of wrongful conviction on individuals and their families, based on in-depth interviews with two Canadians who have been wrongly convicted. Finally, it addresses state responses to wrongful conviction, including conviction review, commissions of inquiry, and government approaches to compensation.

THE PREVALENCE OF WRONGFUL CONVICTIONS

A miscarriage of justice can occur in two ways: an innocent person may be found guilty, or a guilty person may be acquitted. Until relatively recently, wrongful convictions were thought to be rare occurrences (Carrington, 1978). However, estimates of the frequency of such miscarriages range from very few cases each year to 20 percent of all convictions (Holmes, 2001). A study conducted at a maximum-security prison for the National Association of Parole Officers in Britain revealed that as many as 6 percent of the inmates may have been wrongly convicted. The association believed that this figure was typical of other British prisons (Carvel, 1992). An early study by Huff, Rattner, and Sagarin (1986) suggests that 0.5 percent of all convictions in the United States could be in error. There is no reason to believe that the rate of wrongful conviction is any lower in Canada.

Causes of Wrongful Conviction

Research has revealed that wrongful convictions do not occur as a result of one individual making a single grave mistake. Instead, several individual and systemic factors, either alone or in concert with one another, contribute to wrongful convictions (Castelle and Loftus, 2001). These factors include eyewitness error, erroneous forensic science, false confessions, the use of jailhouse informants, professional and institutional misconduct, and racial bias.

Eyewitness Error

Psychological research shows that due to normal deficiencies in the human memory process, eyewitness identification is inherently unreliable (Sanders, 1984). Eyewitness testimony is often the sole or major source of evidence leading to a conviction; for this reason, it is the single most important factor leading to wrongful convictions (Huff et al., 1986). According to a U.S. National Institute of Justice study of wrongful conviction cases (Conners et al., 1996), 24 out of the total 28 cases occurred at least in part from erroneous eyewitness identification.

Eyewitness errors may happen for several reasons, including suggestive police interviewing, unconscious transference, and the malleability of confidence (Castelle and Loftus, 2001). *Suggestive police interviewing* occurs if the police communicate information to eyewitnesses that subsequently influences and ultimately contaminates their testimony. In Canada, suggestive police interviewing led to the initial convictions of Donald Marshall, Jr., David Milgaard, and Thomas Sophonow. In each of these cases, witnesses were pressured by police until they abandoned their original testimony and gave false evidence (Anderson and Anderson, 1998). *Unconscious transference* is witness confusion between a person seen in one situation and one seen in another situation (Loftus, 1979). The term *malleability of confidence* refers to the pliable nature of a witness's certainty of their testimony. Research has demonstrated that witnesses who identify a suspect from a police line-up or group of photos are far more confident of their choice if they receive positive feedback from authorities (cf. Wells and Bradfield, 1998).

Because most jurors are unaware of the unreliability of eyewitness identification, they may place unwarranted faith in its accuracy (Sanders, 1984). In Ontario, defence lawyers are not permitted to call upon experts to discuss the weaknesses of eyewitness identification. While judges are supposed to inform the jury of the limitations of such evidence, they do so infrequently (Bayliss, 2002). The questionable accuracy of eyewitness testimony and the undue weight it receives from criminal justice personnel make eyewitness identifications a significant contributor to wrongful convictions.

Erroneous Forensic Science

Erroneous and fraudulent forensic science has also been cited as a cause of wrongful convictions. In some cases, inadvertent human error, sloppiness, exaggeration, misinterpretation, and bias may work to contaminate evidence, whether in the forensic laboratory or at the crime scene (Castelle and Loftus, 2001). More disturbing, however, are those cases in which forensic scientists deliberately tamper with evidence. For example, Stephanie Nyznyk, a laboratory technician working out of the Centre for Forensic Sciences in Ontario, suppressed information that hair and fibre samples used by the prosecution to successfully convict Guy Paul Morin of murder had been contaminated and should not have been entered as evidence (Anderson and Anderson, 1998).

False Confessions

A confession is often viewed as the most powerful piece of evidence that the prosecution can bring against an accused. Juries are said to believe a defendant who confesses to a crime, regardless of other evidence pointing to the contrary (Leo and Ofshe, 1998). While most people find it difficult to believe that anyone would confess to a crime they have not committed, research indicates that this may not be such a rare phenomenon. For example, Scheck, Neufeld, and Dwyer (2000) found that of 62 wrongly convicted individuals who were conclusively exonerated by DNA evidence in the United States, 15 had originally confessed to the crime. To understand how innocent people can come to confess to crimes that they did not commit, it is important to consider police interrogation techniques.

Christopher Bates was wrongly convicted of murder and spent five and a half years in a maximum-security prison after giving a false confession to police. Bates was arrested and charged with the murder of a shopkeeper who had been killed and robbed of $90. While in police custody, Bates was interrogated, threatened, and tortured for 17 hours. Furthermore, he was held without access to food, water, toilet facilities, and legal counsel for 72 hours. He was told that if he did not confess, his children would be taken by child protection authorities. After many hours of physical and psychological torture, Bates agreed to sign a declaration linking him to the robbery. Bates later explained that extreme fear for his life had led him to sign the declaration. His false confession played an important role in his conviction.

The Use of Jailhouse Informants

The use of jailhouse informants may also play an important role in the conviction of the innocent. Prisoner informants provide information to law enforcement officials in exchange for money, property, or the promise of leniency in sentencing. The practice is a popular means of securing a conviction. For example, of 13 Illinois death row inmates found to have been wrongfully convicted, 5 (or nearly 40 percent) had been prosecuted based on the testimony of jailhouse informants (Armstrong and Mills, 2000). Furthermore, jurors give great weight to such confessions. American studies indicate that to the average juror, there is not much difference between the manner in which they receive and weigh a confession given to a police officer and a confession given to a jailhouse informant (Cory, 2001).

In Canada, the case of Guy Paul Morin illustrates the serious dangers of relying on jailhouse informants. In 1985, Guy Paul Morin was arrested and charged with the murder of a young girl, Christine Jessop. While Morin was jailed without bail, two jailhouse informants who were facing charges of sexual assault and assault came forward claiming that Morin had confessed to the crime. This was the only direct evidence of Morin's guilt (Kaufman, 1998, p. 546). Both informants received more lenient sentences as a result of their testimonies. Morin was convicted in part because of their testimony, but his conviction was later reversed on appeal. The informants retestified at Morin's second trial, where he was convicted again. Through DNA evidence, Morin was later found to be innocent and was subsequently released from prison.

The risks involved with relying on jailhouse informants are obvious. In his report into the wrongful conviction of Thomas Sophonow, Justice Cory described jailhouse informants as a "uniquely evil group" who "should as far as it is possible, be excised and removed from our trial process" (Cory, 2001). Informants may have much to gain and little to lose by providing false testimonies to authorities. It is thus essential that this relatively common practice within the justice system be subject to limited use and informants be prohibited from testifying.

PROFESSIONAL AND INSTITUTIONAL MISCONDUCT

Unprofessional conduct on the part of police, the prosecution, and the judiciary is an important contributing factor to convicting the innocent (Huff et al., 1986). As a first point of entry into the criminal justice system, the police play a pivotal role in deciding whom to charge and in collecting evidence to support a charge. In building their case against a suspect, the police may suppress, lose, misinterpret, or overlook evidence that supports the defendant's claim of innocence. Such errors occur through prejudicial identification line-ups, misuse of informants, solicitation of false confessions, or reliance on poor forensic science. In addition, unprofessional behaviour may be well intentioned, motivated by a sincere desire to strengthen the case against a suspect whom professionals are convinced is guilty.

This set of process errors is often referred to as *tunnel vision*: the guilt of one suspect is assumed and evidence is then subconsciously manipulated to prove that guilt. Whether the tunnel vision occurs among police officers or the prosecution, the authorities may become so focused on one suspect that they may deliberately destroy that individual's alibi and eliminate all other potential suspects from the investigation (Schreck, 2002).

Professional misconduct also occurs through the withholding of evidence considered favourable to the defence. The Canadian justice system prohibits police and prosecutors from pursuing a prosecution while withholding evidence that supports a claim of innocence. A prosecutor has a duty to learn about evidence favourable to the defence that may be in police possession and ensure the disclosure of all such information to the defence (Lockyer, 2002). Withholding evidence not only raises ethical questions about prosecutorial conduct but may also contribute to wrongful convictions (Rosenberg, 2002).

The Canadian case of Donald Marshall, Jr., who was wrongly convicted of the murder of Sandy Seale in Nova Scotia in 1971, shows how the police and the prosecution can fail to disclose information crucial to an accused's defence. Ten days after Marshall's conviction for the murder of Sandy Seale, a witness (Jimmy MacNeil) told police that he had seen Roy Ebsary stab Seale, not Marshall. The police failed to thoroughly investigate this assertion. Moreover, according to the Marshall Inquiry (Royal Commission, 1989), MacNeil's claim was never disclosed by police to either Marshall's defence counsel or to the Halifax Crown counsel handling Marshall's appeal of his conviction. Had this information been presented to the Court of Appeal, a new trial would likely have been ordered (Royal Commission, 1989). In addition, the prosecution failed to inform Marshall's defence counsel of statements from several witnesses whose stories tended to corroborate Marshall's account of the events of the murder (Wall, 1992). Marshall spent 11 years in prison for a crime he did not commit. Roy Ebsary was tried and later convicted of this murder.

Wrongful convictions also occur in the larger institutional context. Martin (2001) identifies three institutional factors that contribute to convicting the innocent: the high-profile nature of the case that pressures authorities to make a quick arrest; the marginalized status of the accused (an "outsider"); and the unreliable nature of the evidence. When all three factors are present within the institutional context, authorities are more likely to overlook the initial reluctance of an eyewitness, believe an unreliable jailhouse informant, fail to disclose favourable evidence, or pressure a defendant into a false confession, all of which may precipitate a wrongful conviction.

The wrongful 22-year imprisonment of David Milgaard for the rape and murder of Gail Miller in 1970 involved police and institutional misconduct, as well as tunnel vision on the part of prosecutors. The high level of public anxiety over this brutal crime created pressure on the police to make a quick arrest. Milgaard, who had already been labeled as an impulsive and marginalized troublemaker, became the target. The case against him was based on questionable evidence obtained through police intimidation. Approximately six years following Milgaard's release from prison, DNA testing established his innocence. Larry Fisher, a serial rapist living blocks away from the murder scene, was subsequently convicted of the crime in 1999.

Racial Bias

Racism is a complex set of ideologies, attitudes, and beliefs claiming the superiority of one race over another, sometimes involving racial discrimination and disadvantage for ethnic minorities (Cashmore, 1996). Institutionalized racism is built into the structure of economic, political and legal institutions, thus contributing to differential opportunities and differential treatment of racialized groups within these institutions. Institutionalized racism places racial minorities at a severe disadvantage, because it makes them vulnerable to miscarriages of justice. Bedau and Radelet (1987) have shown that among 350 cases of documented wrongful convictions in the United States during the 20th century, 40 percent involved black defendants. Racial discrimination within the criminal justice system is particularly evident among blacks and Hispanics in the United States (Parker, Dewees and Radelet, 2001). Several factors, such as institutionalized racism, erroneous cross-racial identification, stereotyping, and extreme social disadvantage, can help to explain why racial minorities are disproportionately represented among those wrongly convicted.

While little Canadian research has addressed the link between race and wrongful conviction, the prominent case of Donald Marshall, Jr., a Mi'kmaw Aboriginal wrongly convicted of the murder of Sandy Seale, illustrates the ways that race is embedded in the Canadian criminal justice system. The Royal Commission on the prosecution of Marshall acknowledged that Marshall had been wrongly convicted and imprisoned because, *inter alia,* he is Mi'kmaw:

> The tragedy of the failure is compounded by the evidence that this miscarriage of justice could and should have been prevented, or at least corrected quickly, if those involved in the system had carried out their duties in a professional and/or competent manner. That they did not is due, in part at least, to the fact that Donald Marshall, Jr. is a Native (Royal Commission, 1989, p. 1).

The Royal Commissioners' report stated that a two-tier system of justice existed in Nova Scotia, a system that responds differently depending on the status, wealth, and race of the person investigated (Royal Commission, 1989). As a Mi'kmaw, Donald Marshall, Jr. was on the bottom of the second tier (Turpel/Aki-Kwe, 1992). The Commissioners note Marshall's second-class treatment and found that Marshall's defence counsel had failed to provide an adequate standard of professional representation to their client (Royal Commission, 1989). Despite having access to whatever financial resources they required, Marshall's lawyers had conducted no independent investigation, had interviewed no Crown witnesses, and had failed to ask for disclosure of the Crown's case against their client. The Marshall case demonstrates how stereotyping and social disadvantage can contribute to miscarriages of justice.

More recently, William Mullins-Johnson, an Aboriginal Canadian, was released on bail for a conviction review after serving 12 years of a life sentence for the murder and rape of his 4-year-old niece. Evidence indicates that Mullins-Johnson was a victim of a miscarriage of justice based to a great extent on false autopsy evidence.

EFFECTS OF WRONGFUL IMPRISONMENT

The negative effects of incarceration on those serving long terms of imprisonment have been well documented. According to Sykes (1958), the "pains of imprisonment" include the deprivation of liberty, goods and services, heterosexual relationships, autonomy, and security. However, not all prisoners experience these deprivations in the same way. This section draws upon in-depth interviews with two Canadians who were wrongly convicted. Jamie Nelson was wrongly convicted of a sexual assault and served over three years in prison, while Christopher Bates served over five years for a murder he did not commit. These interviews suggest that the negative effects of incarceration are often exacerbated by a miscarriage of justice.

Identity

A prison sentence constitutes a "massive assault" on the identity of those imprisoned (Berger, 1963). This assault is said to be especially difficult on first-time inmates who must contend with the sudden and abrupt shift in their social situation (Schmid and Jones, 1991). In order to protect themselves and their identity, prisoners are often compelled to adopt a provisional or "suspended identity" during the period of their incarceration (Schmid and Jones, 1991). Jamie Nelson explains the importance of taking on a new identity in prison to ensure his survival:

> I had to build up that extra protection in prison. The other layer of Jamie wasn't there ... I couldn't be Jamie. I had to be someone that I'm not, somebody that will fight, somebody that will push, somebody that doesn't give a fuck. I had to wear certain hats to survive.

Many inmates may attempt to suspend their pre-prison identity and formulate a provisional identity while incarcerated. However, the situation becomes highly complex for those wrongly convicted. Not only are these individuals forced to take on a prison identity that defines them as criminals when they are in fact innocent, but they may also be compelled to create a further identity given the nature of their conviction. Jamie Nelson, who was wrongly convicted of a sexual assault, explains:

> I developed a second story right away. I certainly didn't want anybody to know I was in custody for violently raping a woman. My second story was "I beat somebody up that was trying to break into my house." I had to create a good enough lie that could explain away me going to prison for 5 to 7 years ... so, it was a pretty grisly tale. I kicked him in the head a few times with steel boots, you know, I beat him up bad. That was my second story.

Nelson maintains that he could only show his true identity as an innocent man in the presence of parole board members who were to determine his fate:

> I had to wear a different hat when I was with the people that made the difference [prison administration]. That's when I wore the Jamie hat—when I was in front of the panel [parole board]. I never once deviated from my claim of being innocent. And that was the only time that I got to wear that

hat ... I could be Jamie, behind that door, because they could not release anything to the population. I knew I was safe in that room, in that environment. It was when I was living in the community as an inmate that I ... needed to wear those different hats.

Resistance

Being wrongly imprisoned appears to produce an unfaltering resistance to all aspects of prison life. Throughout their incarceration, both Nelson and Bates resisted being labeled as a criminal and maintained their innocence to the prison administration. The constant pronouncement that they had been wrongly convicted was frequently perceived by authorities as an inability to adapt to the prison environment and an example of the denial of their offence. As Bates notes:

> I was obsessed about my case ... I was wrongly convicted. [My case manager] kept on making reports "the guy just denies and denies and denies, he keeps talking to you about his case.... My classification officer told me, "Jesus, you've got to stop doing this, you're never going to get out.... The parole board takes this as if you're denying the crime ... that you're not healed ... you're not fixed.... You have to admit to the crime in order to fix your problems." Sorry! I'm not guilty! I'm not denying. I'm just telling you the truth.

This unwavering resistance often created further difficulties. Nelson, who was wrongly convicted of sexual assault, maintained his credibility and status as an innocent man by refusing to apply for parole and refusing to participate in prison programs for sexual offenders. He explains:

> I was clinging to my innocence ... I started to get myself in trouble because I wouldn't even apply for parole. You don't have to apply, it's a damn privilege last time I looked at it. I didn't want it, because I'd have to be that guilty man. So I wouldn't even apply, but then that started to go negatively against me. [They would say to me] "What are you hiding?

His refusal to self-identify as a sex offender and to participate in prison sex offender programs eventually led him to being placed in segregation:

> [The administration] told me that I was going to the sexual behaviour program ... and I said, no, I wasn't. I made it clear to them that the only way that they would have me go to that program was that somebody had to drag me to it. So they ended up keeping me in the hole six months.

Loss of Freedom and Consequences for the Prisoner's Family

The losses experienced by the wrongly convicted can be profound. For Jamie Nelson, these included loss of freedom and the loss of sense of self: "I lost me, is what I lost ... my identity, who I am.... The way I viewed life." However, the most significant loss appears to be the loss of family. Three of Nelson's four children were taken by child protection authorities when his wife suffered a breakdown during his incarceration. He explains the devastation of losing his family:

> What it affected was my nuclear family—wife and my children, my family.
> It completely devastated that. We lost our home ... I lost my kids ... I lost
> the care and guidance and companionship of my dad. We were extremely
> close ... the hardest part about being an inmate was the loss of the family.

Furthermore, the hardships that accompany losing one's family through incarceration also affect the families themselves. Not only are they deprived of the emotional support of their loved one and are forced to deal with the reality of having a family member in prison, but they may also be deprived of an essential source of income (Ferraro et al., 1983). As Nelson explains:

> [My wife] she was left living with the reality of being single, with four chil-
> dren, a mortgage, hydro, the groceries and other accoutrements that go
> with having four young children: one in school, needing to work, needing
> to deal with baby-sitters and, oh yeah, my husband's in prison.

The effects of a wrongful conviction and imprisonment are clearly devastating for the individual and their families. In response, the state has proposed several methods of redress, which will be outlined in the next section.

STATE RESPONSES TO WRONGFUL CONVICTION: ISSUES OF REDRESS AND COMPENSATION

When a miscarriage of justice has occurred, the wrongly convicted have levels of recourse available to them in order to rectify the miscarriage of justice. These areas of redress include conviction review through the *Criminal Code*, commissions of inquiry, and financial compensation.

Conviction Review

Currently, sections 696.1 through 696.6 of the Canadian *Criminal Code* allow individuals who maintain that they have been wrongly convicted to ask the federal Minister of Justice to review the circumstances of their case. Canada relies on the Criminal Conviction Review Group in the Department of Justice to undertake such reviews. The criteria of eligibility regarding application for a conviction review are quite narrow. First, while this right is available to all who have been convicted of an offence, it is considered to be an extraordinary measure (Campbell, 2005). Second, these individuals must also have exercised all of their rights of appeal through the various courts, a process that can take many years. Finally, there must be new matters of significance that were not previously considered by the courts or that arose after the conventional avenues of appeal had been exhausted (McFadyen, 2002).

The review process is lengthy and can take many years. Once all of the relevant information has been compiled and investigated, the Minister of Justice receives legal advice before making a decision. While the Minister does not make decisions regarding guilt or innocence, if he or she is satisfied that a miscarriage of justice has occurred, he or she makes a recommendation of one of the following remedies: (1) decline to make a remedy; (2) order a new trial or hearing; (3) order a new appeal proceeding; or (4) refer any question to the court of appeal for its opinion.

Few applications are made each year to the Minister of Justice. For example, for the years 2000/02, the Minister's office received a total of 109 applications: 22 decisions were taken, 20 cases were declined, and two referrals were made to the Court of Appeal (Denov and Campbell, 2005). One reason for these small numbers may be the arduous application process involved. Moreover, some wrongfully convicted individuals have challenged the relevancy of applying to the government for "mercy." As David Milgaard questions: "Why ask the Canadian government to give you mercy for something that you haven't done? I refuse." (Milgaard, 2002). Recent amendments (*Canada Gazette*, 2002) to this section of the *Criminal Code* came into effect on November 25, 2002. These amendments have clarified the process somewhat. The new provisions attempt to do the following:

- clearly state when a person is eligible for a review;
- specify the criteria under which a remedy may be granted;
- explain the process of review and how one applies for a review;
- expand the Minister's power to include the review of summary convictions; and
- provide investigative powers to those investigating cases on behalf of the Minister, allowing investigators to compel witnesses to testify and to compel the release of documents.

In addition, an independent senior individual from outside the Department of Justice, Bernard Grenier, a retired Quebec provincial court judge, was appointed to oversee certain applications. However, criticisms of the conviction review process remain:

1. It is a lengthy, costly process that takes place mainly in secrecy;
2. The principle of finality in law may contribute to reticence on the part of the Minister and Courts of Appeal to interfere with a conviction; and
3. There is a lack of established rules of procedure and a possibility of conflict of interest (Braiden and Brockman, 1999).

As a means of redress, conviction review may still be inaccessible to many and is limited in its application.

Commissions of Inquiry

Historically, the Canadian judiciary and public have become aware of flaws to the criminal justice process as a result of the work of various Royal Commissions or commissions of inquiry. To date, three commissions of inquiry have addressed the circumstances surrounding wrongful convictions, and at the time of writing, two other commissions are occurring (one in Newfoundland and one in Saskatchewan). The Marshall inquiry, which resulted from the wrongful conviction of Donald Marshall, Jr., had a broad mandate to review and assess the administration of criminal justice in Nova Scotia, and to "make recommendations" to help prevent such tragedies in the future (Royal Commission, 1989). The report contained findings of fact as well as specific recommendations that addressed the role of the police and Crown attorneys, ways to ensure more equitable treatment of blacks and Aboriginals in the criminal justice system, and new mechanisms to deal with future cases of wrongful convictions (Royal Commission, 1989).

Later, the Kaufman inquiry (into the wrongful conviction of Guy Paul Morin) and the Sophonow inquiry[1] examined police and forensic investigations and criminal proceedings that can lead to wrongful convictions. Together, these two inquiries recommended changes to police procedures regarding evidence gathering, reliance on jailhouse informants, and enhanced disclosure of evidence to the defence.

Compensation

When a wrongful conviction occurs, individuals often attempt to seek financial compensation for the harm they have suffered. While the awarding of compensation is an attempt by the government to rectify a miscarriage of justice, such awards are small consolation for the devastation to family, credibility, livelihood, and mental health that a wrongful conviction entails. In some cases of wrongful convictions, compensation was awarded by the courts in the absence of commissions of inquiry. The case of David Milgaard is such an example, since he served 22 years in prison for a murder he did not commit and received $10 million dollars in 1999 from the Saskatchewan and federal governments for pain and suffering, lost income, out-of-pocket expense, and legal fees.

In these cases, provinces have recognized errors in the administration of justice and have awarded compensation. However, these awards are difficult to obtain and come only after many years of legal and political wrangling. Canada has an obligation to provide compensation to the wrongly convicted. In addition to its obligations under national laws, Canada also has a binding obligation at international law, through ratification of the International Covenant on Civil and Political Rights in 1976. Moreover, in 1988, Canada adopted a set of Federal Provincial guidelines for compensation, conditions of eligibility, and criteria for quantum of compensation (Campbell, 2005). Problems regarding the kinds of cases deemed deserving of compensation as well as the amount of compensation deemed appropriate plague this process. Ultimately, financial compensation, regardless of the amount, does little to rectify the emotional, social, and financial damages wrought by a wrongful conviction.

CONCLUSION

Serious individual and systemic factors contribute to judicial errors in Canada. The complexities surrounding eyewitness error, false confessions, racial bias, jailhouse informants, and professional misconduct highlight the need for further in-depth research and study. Moreover, the existing state responses of redress appear unable to adequately confront and tackle these issues. For example, the recent amendments to the conviction review process of the *Criminal Code* fall short of achieving their stated goals of enhanced transparency and accountability. Commissions of inquiry, which seek to address the issue of prevention, are often disappointing, since their recommendations are rarely fully implemented. From time to time, the media draw attention to the issue of wrongful conviction through highly controversial and publicized cases; however, this attention is often fleeting and fails to result in long-term change.

Piecemeal reforms introduced to address individual errors are insufficient. There must be greater accountability among agents of the criminal justice system as a whole. Programs of education will allow these individuals to become more aware of the consequences of their actions and the ways they contribute to wrongful convictions. A recent report by the Department of Justice regarding the prevention of miscarriages of justice offers some hope in this regard (Department of Justice, 2005). As well, the voices of the wrongly convicted themselves need to be heard. It is only by listening to their accounts and experiences that the true extent and impact of the problem will be understood.

DISCUSSION QUESTIONS

1. *Parole authorities often require a prisoner to accept responsibility for "their" crime before he will be granted parole. Do you see the problem that this creates for prisoners serving time for crimes that they did not commit?*
2. *In light of what you have read in this chapter, do you think the Canadian criminal justice system does enough to prevent wrongful convictions?*

FURTHER READINGS

Anderson, B., and Anderson, D. 1998. *Manufacturing Guilt: Wrongful Convictions in Canada*. Halifax: Fernwood.

Huff, C.R., Rattner, A., and Sagarin, E. 1996. *Convicted but Innocent: Wrongful Conviction and Public Policy*. Thousand Oaks, California: Sage Publications.

Westervelt, S., and Humphrey, J. (Eds.) 2001. *Wrongly Convicted: Perspectives on Failed Justice*. New Jersey: Rutgers University Press.

REFERENCES

Anderson, B., and Anderson, D. 1998. *Manufacturing Guilt: Wrongful Convictions in Canada*. Halifax: Fernwood.

Armstrong, K., and Mills, S. 2000. Ryan: "Until I can be sure": Illinois is first state to suspend death penalty. *Chicago Tribune*, 1 February.

Bayliss, D. 2002. *The Impact of Canadian Inquiries into Wrongful Conviction*. Paper presented at the conference on Wrongful Conviction: Experiences, Implications and Working Towards Justice. Ottawa: University of Ottawa.

Bedau, H.A., and Radelet, M. 1987. Miscarriages of justice in potentially capital cases. *Stanford Law Review*, 40: 21–179.

Berger, P. 1963. *Invitation to Sociology: A Humanistic Perspective*. Garden City, New York: Doubleday Anchor Books.

Braiden, P., and Brockman, J. 1999. Remedying wrongful convictions through applications to the Minister of Justice under Section 690 of the *Criminal Code. Windsor Yearbook of Access to Justice*, 17: 3–34.

Campbell, K. 2005. Policy responses to wrongful conviction in Canada: The role of conviction review, public inquiries and compensation. *Criminal Law Bulletin*, 41: 145–168.

Canada Gazette 2002. *Regulations Respecting Applications for Ministerial Review—Miscarriages of Justice*. Part 1, Vol. 136, No. 39. The Queen's Printer for Canada.

Carrington, F. 1978. *Neither Cruel nor Unusual*. New Rochelle, New York: Arlington House.

Carvel, J. 1992. Many prisoners could be wrongly jailed. *Guardian Weekly*, April 5.

Cashmore, E. 1996. *Dictionary of Race and Ethnic Relations*. London: Routledge.

Castelle, G., and Loftus, E. 2001. Misinformation. In S. Westervelt and J. Humphrey (Eds.), *Wrongly Convicted: Perspectives on Failed Justice*. New Jersey: Rutgers University Press.

Conners, E., Lundregan, T., Miller, N., and McEwan, T. 1996. *Convicted by Juries, Exonerated by Science: Case Studies in the Use of DNA Evidence to Establish Innocence after Trial*. Washington, DC: National Institute of Justice.

Cory, P. 2001. *Commission of Inquiry Regarding Thomas Sophonow*. Manitoba Justice, Province of Manitoba.

Denov, M., and Campbell, K. 2005. Criminal injustice: Understanding the causes, effects, and responses to wrongful conviction in Canada. *Journal of Contemporary Criminal Justice*, 21: 1–26.

Department of Justice Canada 2005. *Report on the Prevention of Miscarriages of Justice*. Federal/Provincial/Territorial Heads of Prosecution Committee Working Group.

Ferraro, K.J., Johson, J.M., Jorgensen, S.R., and Bolton, F.G. 1983. Problems of prisoners' families: The hidden costs of imprisonment. *Journal of Family Issues*, 4: 575–591.

Holmes, W. 2001. Who are the Wrongly Convicted on Death Row? In
S. Westervelt and J. Humphrey (Eds.), *Wrongly Convicted: Perspectives on
Failed Justice*. New Jersey: Rutgers University Press.

Huff, R., Rattner, A., and Saragin, E. 1986. Guilty until proven innocent:
Wrongful conviction and public policy. *Crime and Delinquency*, 32:
518–544.

Kaufman, F. 1998. *Commission on Proceedings involving Guy Paul Morin.
Executive Summary and Recommendations*. Toronto. Report of
Commission on Proceedings involving Guy Paul Morin.

Leo, R., and Ofshe, R. 1998. The consequences of false confessions:
Deprivation of liberty and miscarriages of justice in the age of psychological interrogation. *Journal of Criminology and Criminal Law*, 88:
429–96.

Lockyer, J. 2002. *Disclosure of Evidence*. Innocents Behind Bars. November 17,
2002. Conference Presentation available from Association in Defence of
the Wrongly Convicted.

Loftus, E. 1979. *Eyewitness Testimony*. Cambridge: Harvard University Press.

McFadyen, M. 2002. *Criminal Conviction Review Group: 690 Review Clause*.
Paper presented at the conference on Wrongful Conviction:
Experiences, Implications and Working Towards Justice. Ottawa:
University of Ottawa.

Martin, D. 2001. The police role in wrongful convictions: An interna-
tional comparative study. In S. Westervelt and J. Humphrey (Eds.),
Wrongly Convicted: Perspectives on Failed Justice. New Jersey: Rutgers
University Press.

Milgaard, D. 2002. *The Voices of the Wrongly Convicted. Innocents Behind Bars*.
November 16, 2002. Conference presentation available from Association
in Defence of the Wrongly Convicted.

Parker, K., Dewees, M., and Radelet, M. 2001. Racial bias and the convic-
tion of the innocent. In S. Westervelt and J. Humphrey (Eds.),
Wrongly Convicted: Perspectives on Failed Justice. New Jersey: Rutgers
University Press.

Rosenberg, M. 2002. *Public Inquiries: The Process and the Value*. Innocents
Behind Bars. November 17, 2002. Conference Presentation available
from Association in Defence of the Wrongly Convicted.

Royal Commission on the Donald Marshall Jr. Prosecution. 1989.
Commissioners' Report. Halifax: Nova Scotia.

Sanders, R. 1984. Helping the jury evaluate eyewitness testimony: The need
for additional safeguards. *American Journal of Criminal Law*, 12: 189–220.

Scheck, B., Neufeld, P., and Dwyer, J. 2000. *Actual Innocence*. New York:
Doubleday.

Schmid, T., and Jones, R. 1991. Suspended identity: Identity transformation
in a maximum security prison. *Symbolic Interaction*, 14: 415–432.

Sykes, G. 1958. *The Society of Captives*. Princeton, NJ: Princeton University Press.

Turpel/Aki-Kwe, M. 1992. Further travails of Canada's Human Rights Record: The Marshall case. In J. Mannette (Ed.), *Elusive Justice: Beyond the Marshall Inquiry*. Halifax: Fernwood.

Wall, B. 1992. Analyzing the Marshall commission: Why it was established and how it functioned. In J. Mannette (Ed.), *Elusive Justice: Beyond the Marshall Inquiry*. Halifax: Fernwood.

Wells, G., and Bradfield, A. 1998. Good, you identified the suspect: Feedback to eyewitnesses distorts their reports of the witnesses' experience. *Journal of Applied Psychology*, 83: 360–376.

ENDNOTES

[1] Thomas Sophonow underwent three trials for the murder of Barbara Stoppel in 1981. After a mistrial and two successful appeals, Sophonow was acquitted and received an apology from the Saskatchewan government.

CHAPTER 18

Why Say Sorry When I Didn't Do It?: The Dilemma of the Wrongfully Convicted

INTRODUCTION

Most people expect wrongdoers to express remorse for their transgressions; it seems a natural way to make amends to the victim. When offenders do express remorse, it is appreciated by the victim as well as the community in general. For this reason, the corrections system tends to be more punitive towards offenders who fail to express remorse. The criminal law reflects this attitude to offenders by imposing more lenient sentences on remorseful offenders, such as those who plead guilty in court.

But what happens when the person charged with an offence is innocent? He or she can hardly be expected to express remorse for a crime that they did not commit. A dilemma arises for persons who are wrongfully convicted and then enter the correctional system: they are expected to express remorse and yet they remain adamant in their claim of innocence. As a result, they are treated more harshly by correctional authorities, who perceive them in negative terms simply because they refuse to accept responsibility and express remorse.

Drawing on examples from Canada and the United States, Richard Weisman explores the question of remorse and the wrongfully convicted individual.

Why Say Sorry When I Didn't Do It?: The Dilemma of the Wrongfully Convicted

Richard Weisman, York University

On June 19, 1998, a young man (Mr. W.) left a party with twice the legal limit of alcohol in his blood. He got behind the wheel of his car, having refused the offer of a friend to drive him home. After driving westbound on eastbound lanes for several kilometres, he collided with another vehicle, despite frantic attempts to get his attention. Three of the four passengers in the other car died and the other was critically injured (*Toronto Star*, May 29, 2001). A jury convicted Mr. W. of three counts of criminal negligence causing death, criminal negligence causing bodily harm, impaired driving causing bodily harm, and exceeding the legal blood- alcohol limit. When Mr. W. appeared in court to be sentenced, the Assistant Crown Attorney described him as unremorseful: "He expressed no remorse at any time throughout these proceedings" and asked the court to sentence Mr. W. to eight to 12 years in prison. Counsel for the defence asked for three to five years.

Prior to imposing sentence, the judge asked Mr. W. if he had anything to say. The reply was "No." The judge noted that the sentence was determined partly by the fact that Mr. W. had not shown "any remorse during the course of the trial." He added that when given the opportunity to make a statement, Mr. W had refused to say anything: "Mr. W. is not inarticulate. He's a well-spoken gentleman who could say he was sorry. But he didn't." After that preamble, the judge imposed a sentence of nine years to be served in a federal penitentiary.

But, unexpectedly, just after the judge had finished speaking, Mr. W. stood up and faced those who were in attendance declaring "I want to address the families and friends of the deceased." The Crown attorney told him to face the other way so the court reporter could take down his words. Mr. W. refused, saying "I'm not interested in what you guys put on the record. What I have to say is for the families." He then made the following statement:

> I've chosen to give my statement after the judgment because it was the only way I had to show you I meant what I was saying. Despite what has been said in prior hearings, it has never been my intention to deny the accident took place nor my part in the horrific and tragic loss of lives. I have no right to request your understanding, nor do I have the right to ask for your forgiveness. But I do ask that someday you search your hearts and find that I did not intend for this to happen. I would surely surrender my life if this could return your brother, your father, your husband, your friend, your son. I'm so very sorry for the grief and sorrow I have caused your family and friends. I am truly ashamed of my actions, and all I have to offer are these words: I'm sorry.

The reporter who witnessed these events then describes the reaction of those who were present: "Silence.... And as everyone else in the courtroom sat stunned, unsure of what to do, a young man broke the silence. 'Thank you,' he said" (*Toronto Star*, 2001).

I recount this remarkable vignette for two reasons. First, it reveals the importance that both the courts and the media place on expressions of remorse or their absence. People who show remorse are viewed as deserving of compassion and entitled to mitigation in the form of a more lenient punishment. Those like Mr. W. who do not show remorse (prior to being sentenced) are viewed more harshly and denied the benefits of mitigation. Second, because expressions of remorse are linked to mitigation, it is difficult to decide whether offenders say they are sorry because they mean it or because they want to obtain a more lenient sentence. Mr. W. went to great lengths to solve this problem by deliberately withholding his expression of remorse until he could not possibly obtain any benefit from it.

Long before their vindication if vindication ever occurs, the wrongfully convicted are designated as persons who lack remorse and they are separated from those who are characterized as having remorse. Just as in the case of Mr. W., they are perceived as not acknowledging responsibility for their crime and not having any feelings of sorrow or empathy for their victim(s). This chapter examines the impact of this designation on the identity and treatment of those who have been wrongfully convicted. People who have been wrongfully convicted often assert their innocence and, not surprisingly, refuse to express remorse for a crime they did not commit. The purpose of this chapter is to explore the consequences of failing to express remorse. For the purposes of this analysis, I will draw on both Canadian and American data.

The most widely publicized instances in which remorse makes a difference have involved the life and death decisions of jurors in capital trials in the United States. In 2003, in a trial that attracted international attention, a jury was charged to decide whether John Muhammad, convicted of six murders—the so-called "sniper" killings—should be executed. One juror was quoted in explaining why he had voted for the death penalty: "I tried to pay attention to his demeanor the whole time. I looked for something in him that might have shown remorse. But I never saw it." The jury foreman agreed that "the lack of emotion, his (Muhammad's) failure to even acknowledge what he had done, had played into" his decision to support the death penalty as well (*New York Times*, 2003.) A continuing research project set up in 1993—the National Capital Jury Project—used a sample of 1,155 real jurors from 340 capital trials in 14 states to establish that the offender's remorse is one of the most important determinants of whether a jury will decide in favour of death rather than a life sentence in capital trials (Sundby, 1998).

The social preoccupation with remorse is also illustrated in the public response to offenders who commit offenses that shock the sensibilities of their communities. No aspect of the execution of Timothy McVeigh—the man convicted of the notorious Oklahoma bombing that resulted in 168 deaths—was more thoroughly scrutinized than whether he had shown remorse prior to his death. Even his father was quoted as asking his son whether he would apologize and commenting that the "lack of remorse" was not "OK with me."(*Terre Haute Tribune-Star*, 2001). A search through Canadian newspapers using *Factiva* shows a similar interest in high-profile offenders, such as Karla Homolka, regarding whether she has felt remorse for her participation in the murders of her sister and the two young victims who were also kidnapped and raped by her husband. Thousands of news items appearing each week in North American mass media focus on whether or not convicted offenders show remorse for their wrongdoing. How a person feels about their wrongful act is as important to the courts and to the public as why they did it or that they did it.

JUSTIFICATIONS FOR BEING MORE LENIENT TOWARDS PEOPLE WHO EXPRESS REMORSE

One reason for this interest in remorse-related cases is that expressions of remorse tell us whether the person who has violated the norms of their community feels the same way about their misdeed as would someone who was law-abiding. Social psychologists have demonstrated that groups respond with empathy and compassion if they believe that a wrongdoer is sorry for his or her misconduct. People are likely to be far more punitive if they perceive that wrongdoers feel indifferent to the harm they have caused. In this sense, when judges denounce offenders who fail to show remorse while showing mercy to those who do, they are reflecting and affirming values that are shared by the community as a whole.

Another reason why courts pay so much attention to remorse is the widespread belief that offenders who feel remorse are less likely to offend again. Judges as well as members of the public tend to view remorse as an emotion that reveals one's true character. If at the deepest level of feeling, offenders condemn their own actions, then it is possible that the emotional pain that they experience may help deter them from further misconduct. Many correctional authorities also regard the expression of remorse as the first step towards rehabilitation.

But these justifications for leniency lose their force if the expression of remorse is strategic or insincere rather than genuine. Hence, judges and juries are interested not just in the expression of remorse but also whether, in their view, what is shown corresponds to what is felt. Since very few offenders are prepared to act as unstrategically as Mr. W., with all the risks that this entails, most expressions of remorse leave room for doubt whether appearance corresponds to reality.

As we shall see below in the case of the wrongfully convicted, this potential gap between appearance and reality can also work the other way. Just as a claim to feel remorse can be discredited if it seems rehearsed or unfelt, so also can a claim not to feel remorse be invalidated by what are perceived as underlying feelings of guilt or shame.

THE PROBLEM OF REMORSE FOR THE WRONGFULLY CONVICTED

There is much at stake in a wrongful conviction even apart from the rupture of the innocent person's life. As Huff, Rattner, and Sagarin have observed, wrongful convictions frequently involve a multiplicity of errors and occasional wrongdoings that may implicate different levels of the criminal justice system in "the ratification of error"(Huff et al., 1996). Well-known Canadian cases over the past 20 years have shown that the eventual unravelling of a wrongful conviction that restores the reputation of the innocent may also challenge the credibility of those police, defence and crown attorneys, judges, witnesses, jurors, correctional staff—even high-ranking political officials—who contributed to or condoned the injustice that led to the wrongful conviction. At the root of every wrongful conviction is a contest of credibility between an individual who asserts a claim of innocence and whose reputation and potential liberty depend upon this claim and the officials in the criminal justice system, who claim that a finding of guilt and the punishment that followed were justified.

Remorse is one of the issues that will determine whose definition of the situation will prevail. For the authorities, an assertion of innocence after conviction calls into question the credibility of the entire system of criminal justice, whereas a show of remorse is an affirmation that the institutions that imposed punishment did so with just cause. But for the person who has been convicted, any show of remorse subverts their claim to innocence. Even the momentary abandonment of this claim is enough to cast a lingering doubt as to its validity and thus compromise later attempts at exoneration should the opportunity arise. The net effect of this clash of purposes is to trigger a process in which correctional staff and other officials intensify their efforts to elicit a show of remorse from the individual, while those who wish to advance a claim of wrongful conviction must embark on a project of long-term resistance.

However, this contest is decidedly unequal. If the wrongfully convicted maintain their innocence, they are likely to be placed in the category of the unremorseful and subjected to the same deprivations as others who have been designated as lacking in remorse.[1] These deprivations are evident both in the sentencing process and in the way that the sentence is administered. Those who plead guilty to an offence are already credited with the most elemental demonstration of remorse—namely, that they have acknowledged their responsibility for the commission of the offence. Those who claim innocence but are nonetheless found guilty are not allowed this credit.

These presumptions pervade all forms of sentencing, from the least to the most severe of penalties. The person who pleads guilty is officially entitled to mitigation even though the absence of remorse (as reflected in a plea of not guilty) should not result in a harsher sentence (*R. v. Ambrose*). For sentencing, pleading guilty translates into measurable and tangible reductions in the severity of sentences.[2] But more recently, it has also come to fulfil what appears to be an emerging requirement for a conditional sentence of imprisonment (served in the community) and for sentencing by sentencing circles. Because remorse in the form of acknowledgement of responsibility is taken as a first step towards rehabilitation and towards renunciation of the offending criminal conduct, those who maintain their innocence after conviction are perceived as not having accepted responsibility for their actions and therefore, more likely to re-offend, more dangerous and more of a risk to the community.[3]

Moreover, the reluctance to express remorse, whatever its source, has deep cultural connotations in our society from which the law is not insulated. Individuals define themselves as members of a shared moral community to the extent that their feelings of remorse affirm the seriousness that others attach to moral transgressions. The findings of the Capital Jury Project show not only that jurors are more likely to impose a death sentence on persons who deny guilt on grounds of factual innocence or reasonable doubt (Sundby, 1998) but also that their responses indicate a strong negative characterization of the persons who raise these defences. Especially in cases involving the death of the victim, there is a cultural expectation that those perceived as perpetrators will experience regret commensurate with the gravity of the offence. Those who do not—even on the impeccable moral ground that they were wrongfully convicted—risk adverse characterization as "cold-hearted," or "utterly without feeling."[4] The moral career of the wrongfully convicted thus begins not just with a harsher sentence but with the ascription of qualities that define them as more of a risk than others similarly situated and as lacking the moral sentiments—the inner emotional life—that other members of the community share.

It is in the context of this asymmetrical struggle for credibility that it becomes possible to better understand the pressures placed on the wrongfully convicted to show remorse and the tenacity with which these pressures are often resisted. The most obvious pressures consist in the deprivations that are likely to be far greater for wrongly convicted persons who have been incarcerated than for other inmates. The annals of the wrongfully convicted in Canada list denial of parole and temporary absence because of continued assertions of innocence.[5] Even evidence that would normally favour a positive outcome, such as acquiring a skill, being active on committees, or having a record of no institutional violence, fails to outweigh the negative impact of a denial of guilt.

Moreover, the pressures to show remorse are also likely to be indirect. Programs of therapy that enhance a person's eligibility for parole and other benefits typically require as a first sign of rehabilitation that the prisoner admit responsibility for the crime, even though fulfilling such a condition negates a claim of innocence. The result is that the wrongfully convicted tend to accumulate a record that attests not only to their denial of guilt but to their nonparticipation in programs designed to make them safe to return to the community.

LACK OF REMORSE VIEWED AS PSYCHOPATHOLOGY

However, no occasion touches more directly on issues of credibility than the psychological assessment and treatment of those who maintain their innocence. Here the assertion of innocence is approached less as a factual claim to be contested or rejected than as a symptom that requires therapeutic intervention. From the standpoint of the specialists—whether psychiatrists, psychologists, parole officers, or others who favour this perspective—the unwillingness to take responsibility for the crime is less a matter of defiance than of denial. An excerpt from the *Royal Commission on the Donald Marshall, Jr. Prosecution* offers a revealing glimpse into how this framework was applied during Marshall's wrongful incarceration for the murder of Sandy Seale. In the following exchange, the commission explores a memo in which a parole officer had denied Marshall's request for a temporary absence "as it (was) felt that in light of his unstableness at the present time, he presents too high a security risk" (Hickman, 1989, p. 110):

Q. What was his unstableness?

A. This was a period of time when his behaviour in the institution was extremely aggressive towards the staff, towards myself, and towards the other members of the case management team where in one case he threw a chair at one of the staff members.

Q. Are you able to offer any insight as to what provoked that aggressiveness?

A. I suspect that it had a lot to do with the issue of whether he was guilty or innocent of the crime. Although I was not (putting) a lot of pressure on him to admit that he was guilty, some people were.

Q. Who would these people have been?

A. Some of the other people were members of his case management team who had contact with him far more frequently than I did on a daily basis.

Q. Was it your sense that his frustration in maintaining his innocence in the face of the response that he was guilty was causing this aggression to a degree?

A. In retrospect, yes. At the time, my belief was that he was coming close to admitting that he was involved in the crime and that it was starting to come out.

Because the officials presume guilt, they seek underlying disturbances that show a gap between appearance and reality in the expression of remorse and bely the claim of innocence. Just as overt claims of remorse can be challenged by inconsistencies between words and feelings or feelings and deeds, so also can a claim of innocence be invalidated by involuntary displays of conscience whether in the form of "aggression" or emotional turbulence.[6]

Similarly, the therapeutic approach used on Stephen Truscott during his wrongful conviction for the murder of Lynne Harper at age 14 also involved a search for "abnormal" reactions. When Truscott failed to break down and admit guilt even after being administered Sodium Pentothal and several doses of LSD over an extended period, the psychiatric notes read as follows: "he is so controlled, so pleasant, and so objective that certainly there must be in his subconscious a tremendous control for commanding details" (Sher, 2001, p. 376). In another log entry, the psychiatrist observes: "If he's guilty and is not admitting, then this implies that there is a complete repression of the problems involved" (Sher, 2001, p. 395).

Yet, paradoxically, the absence of these same "abnormal" reactions does not lead experts in forensic psychiatry to the conclusion that the person's claim of innocence might be credible. In one well-known American case of wrongful conviction, the prisoner's absence of affect resulted in the psychiatrist diagnosing the defendant as "a sociopathic personality disorder" because of "the absolute absence of any type of guilt or remorse" (Adams, 1991, p. 129). In another Canadian case in which the person incarcerated has long asserted his innocence, the psychologist performing the assessment observed that the defendant's "calm, confident, and remorseless exterior was consistent with the reaction of an innocent man" (Harris, 1996, pp. 397–398); but then added: "a similar presentation associated with heinous and egregious behaviour would represent a powerful indicator of psychopathy." It would seem that there is no psychological model of what would be a normal reaction to a wrongful conviction.

Biographies and interviews reveal how the wrongfully convicted resist these pressures to weaken their resolve. Despite maintaining their claim of innocence, most did attempt at some point to fashion a measure of relief from the restrictions, deprivations, and adverse characterizations to which they were subjected. These actions illustrate the challenge of meeting official expectations without forfeiting one's credibility. In one instance, a man who had been wrongfully convicted of sexual assault agreed to attend therapy sessions directed at sex offenders while refusing to sign a document admitting guilt (Liptak, 2002, Section 4, p. 4). For Donald Marshall, after unrelenting attempts by authorities to elicit a show of remorse, a compromise of sorts was achieved when he agreed to admit to his parole officer, after being asked, that, even if he may not have committed the murder for which he was convicted, "he was the sort of individual who could have committed a murder … a condition with which Marshall complied in hopes of improving his situation" (Harris, 1990, p. 285). Similarly, Truscott eventually produced a generalized statement in his application before a parole board in which he neither asserted his innocence nor explicitly claimed responsibility for the crime in an effort to win freedom without negating the original claim of innocence (Sher, 2001, p. 372).

The demand that all persons who are convicted of crimes demonstrate remorse by accepting responsibility for their offences has unintended consequences for those who have been wrongfully convicted. The self-same efforts to maintain one's integrity in opposition to external pressures—actions that under other circumstances might well be viewed as virtuous behaviour—result in what Goffman (1961) referred to as the *mortification of the self*—the process by which the self is stripped of its social and psychological supports so that a new identity can replace the identity that has been lost. The treatment of the wrongfully convicted illustrates this process in which the force of criminal justice and corrections is directed towards recasting the truths claimed by those who are innocent as pathology at best and defiance at worst.

DISCUSSION QUESTIONS

1. *What is the solution to the problem identified by the author? Should the justice system ignore expressions of remorse and treat all people charged or convicted of a crime in the same way, whether they are remorseful or not?*
2. *Victims often state that they appreciate the expression of remorse from the offender. Is this a good justification for imposing less severe punishments when the offender says he or she is sorry?*

FURTHER READINGS

Bibas, S., and Bierschbach, R. 2004. Integrating remorse and apology into criminal procedure. *Yale Law Journal*, Vol.114: 85.

Tavuchis, N. 1991. *Mea Culpa: A Sociology of Apology and Reconciliation.* Stanford, CA: Stanford University Press.

REFERENCES

Adams, R. (with Hoffer, W. and Hoffer, M.) 1991. *Adams v. Texas*. New York: St. Martin's Press.

Clairmont, S. 2001. "Unrepentant" drunk driver utters a stunning last word. *Toronto Star*, May 29, p. 5.

Dao, J., and Bacon, L. 2003. Death sentence for Muhammad: Sniper jury cites lack of sorrow. *New York Times*, November 25, p. A1.

Davis, S. 1997. The rape that wasn't. *Alberta Report*, June 2, p. 30.

Finkle, D. 1998. *No Claim to Mercy*. Toronto: Penguin Books.

Goffman, E. 1961. *Asylums: Essays on the Social Situation of Mental Patients and Other Inmates*. New York: Doubleday Anchor.

Harris, M. 1996. *The Judas Kiss*. Toronto: McClelland and Stewart.

Harris, M. 1990. *Justice Denied: The Law Versus Donald Marshall*. Toronto: HarperCollins.

Hickman, A. 1989. *Royal Commission on the Donald Marshall, Jr. Prosecution: Vol. 1: Findings and Recommendations*. Halifax: Province of Nova Scotia.

Huff, C., Rattner, A., and Sagarin, E. 1996. *Convicted But Innocent: Wrongful Conviction and Public Policy*. Thousand Oaks, California: Sage Publications.

Karp, C., and Rosner, C. 1991. *When Justice Fails: The David Milgaard Story*. Toronto: McClelland and Stewart.

Liptak, A. 2002. Not at all remorseful but not guilty either. *New York Times, News of the Week*, Nov. 3, p. 4.

Makin, K. 2001. Man jailed 29 years had alibi but police buried it. *Globe and Mail*, Nov. 8, p. 1.

Myers, L. 1997. An appeal for clemency: The case of Harold Lamont Otey. In H. Bedau (Ed.), *The Death Penalty in America,* pp. 361–383. New York: Oxford University Press.

O'Hear, M. 1997. Remorse, cooperation, and 'acceptance of responsibility': The structure, implementation, and reform of Section 3e1.1 of the Federal Sentencing Guidelines. *Northwestern University Law Review,* 91: 1507.

Sher, J. 2001. *"Until You are Dead" Stephen Truscott's Long Ride Into History.* Toronto: Alfred A. Knopf Canada.

Sundby, S. 1998. The Capital Jury and absolution: The intersection of trial strategy, remorse, and the death penalty. *Cornell Law Review,* 83: 1557.

Vandersnick, L. 1998. Lack of remorse versus persistence of innocence. *Illinois Bar Journal,* 86: 692.

Weisman, R. 1999. Detecting remorse and its absence in the criminal justice system. In A. Sarat and P. Ewick (Eds.), *Studies in Law, Politics, and Society,* Vol. 19.

Williamson, L. 2001. A Canadian tragedy: Money can never right the wrongs of the Thomas Sophonow case. *Calgary Sun,* Nov. 10, p. 15.

Young, N. 1989. *Innocence Regained.* Annandale, N.S.W.: Federation Press.

CASES CITED

R. v. Allard (1999) 43 W.C.B. (2nd) 296.

R. v. Ambrose (2000) 271 A.R., 164.

R. v. A.G.W. (1994) 117 Nfld. & P.E.I.R., 233.

R. v. Baltovich (1992) 18 W.C.B. (2nd) 215.

R. v Baltovich (2000) 47 O.R. (3rd) 761.

R. v. Layte (1983) 38 C.R. (3rd) 205.

R. v. Parent (1999) O.C.J. Lexis 47.

R. v. Taylor (1997) 122 C.C.C. (3rd) 376.

Riggins v. Nevada (1992) 112 S. Ct. 1810.

ENDNOTES

[1] Many wrongful convictions begin with a false confession rather than with a plea of not guilty. For purposes of this analysis, I am assuming that whether or not wrongfully convicted persons maintain their innocence from the outset, at some point they will have to assert their innocence in order to pursue the claim. Once they do so, they will experience the disadvantages arising from an assertion of innocence.

[2] One of the most candid statements of this principle is contained in *R. v. Layte* [1983] 38 C.R. (3rd) 205, in which two defendants were prosecuted on identical charges—the only difference being that one pleaded guilty and the other pleaded not guilty. In defending the disparity in sentence between the two co-accused who were convicted of the same crime, the court cited as one among several factors—"a plea of guilty is an indication and demonstration of the accused's remorse."

3 The equation of an absence of remorse with dangerousness is common-place in Canadian and American judgements. See, for example, *R. v. Allard,* [1999] (B.C.C.A.) at para 5: "The trial judge was quite properly concerned with protection of the public, and hence the extent to which the applicant constituted a continuing danger to those he had harmed and threatened to harm, as well as to others. For that purpose, the appellant's apparent lack of remorse was relevant...."

4 One example is the reaction of the court to Robert Baltovich's assertion of innocence after he was convicted of murder in 1992. See *R. v. Baltovich,* [1992]18 W.C.B. (2nd) 215 at para 25: "The record shows a cold, calculating person, and that person killed a person who had loved and trusted you"; or at para 26: "You have high intelligence, but you are totally devoid of heart and conscience." Baltovich has since been released from prison pending the outcome of his appeal from conviction (*R. v. Baltovich* [2000] 47 O.R. (3rd) 761). See also Derek Finkle, *No Claim to Mercy: Elizabeth Bain and Robert Baltovich. A Suburban Mystery,* 1998.

5 Examples include the following: Thomas Sophonow, wrongly convicted of second-degree murder who was refused parole and temporary absences (Williamson, 2001, p.15); Wilfred Beaulieu, who was wrongly convicted of sexual assault and denied temporary absence to attend the funerals of his brother and sister (Davis, 1997, p. 30); David Milgaard, wrongly convicted of sexual assault and murder who was turned down for parole and temporary absences many times during his 23 years in prison (Karp and Rosner, 1991, p. 129); Donald Marshall, wrongly convicted of murder, who was refused parole for the same reasons (Harris, *Justice Denied*, 1990, p.266). Romeo Phillion, who has served nearly 30 years for a conviction that is currently being challenged under a s.690 application and whose requests for parole have also been consistently denied, is not altogether mistaken when he was recently quoted as saying that "Parole is for the guilty, not for the innocent."(Makin, 2001, p.1).

6 Interestingly, from this vantage point, those family members and others who believe the claim of innocence are viewed as supporting the underlying pathology and hence continued contact is seen as problematic. Thus, one of Marshall's parole officers included in his appraisal: "there still remains the problem of Marshall himself denying his guilt and being supported in this by an overprotective mother" (Harris, *Justice Denied*, p. 283). Or in the case of David Milgaard, one case worker at Stony Mountain wrote: "this writer questions how constructive familial support is. First, if the subject is guilty, familial belief in his innocence provides a firm block to subject even admitting to or working through intrapsychic aspects of offence" (Karp and Rosner, 1991, p. 130).

CHAPTER 19

The Use of Court and Custody under the *Youth Criminal Justice Act*

INTRODUCTION

For many years, crime by young people has been a cause of great public concern. This is true in Canada as well as in many other western nations. This chapter by two leading youth justice researchers explores the impact of new legislation on the practice of the youth justice system. In this sense, the chapter tells an interesting story from two perspectives. First, it provides insight into the functioning of the system under the new law. Second, by comparing statistics from the pre-reform period with those of today, Sprott and Doob demonstrate how a change to the youth justice legislation can have an important impact on the practice of youth justice. In particular, they focus on the use of youth court and of custody for young offenders.

The Use of Court and Custody under the *Youth Criminal Justice Act*

Jane B. Sprott, University of Guelph and *Anthony N. Doob*, University of Toronto

In April 2003, the *Youth Criminal Justice Act* (*YCJA*) replaced the *Young Offenders Act* (*YOA*) as the legislation governing the manner in which youths age 12 to 17 (inclusive) charged with federal offences should be treated. Although the *YOA* had received all-party support on its final vote in the

House of Commons in 1982, the law was a focus of concern almost from the day it came into force in 1984. Much of the public criticism had to do with the perception of leniency of the Act. The professional criticisms, beginning in the late 1980s, focused on the large numbers of minor cases being tried in youth court and the large number of youths, in most provinces, who were being placed in custody (Doob and Cesaroni, 2004; Doob and Sprott, 2004; Cesaroni, this volume). These criticisms—from different groups of people— argued simultaneously that the YOA was too "soft" and indiscriminately "tough" and continued until the YOA was replaced by the YCJA.

While there have been debates over the nature and intent of the new law (see, for example, Hogeveen, 2005 and 2006; and for a response, Doob and Sprott, 2006a and 2006b), a careful read of the legislation reveals some important changes designed to reduce the use of court and custody. The preamble to the YCJA sets the tone for the legislation: "Canadian society should have a youth criminal justice system ... that reserves its most serious intervention for the most serious crimes and reduces the over-reliance on incarceration for non-violent young persons" (YCJA preamble). Clearly, then, one of the main goals of the legislation is to reduce the over-reliance on court and custody.

What impact has the new law had upon the use of youth court and of custody? This chapter examines recent statistics to determine whether the new law has resulted in any changes to the number of youths appearing in court and committed to custody by youth court judges.

ADDRESSING THE OVERUSE OF YOUTH COURT

Part of the problem with the YOA was its weak language (Doob and Sprott, 1999), which gave very little direction to decision makers. For example, although the YOA explicitly allowed cases to be resolved outside of the court system, it did so in a very nondirective fashion: "Where it is not inconsistent with the protection of society, taking no measures or taking measures other than judicial proceedings under this Act should be considered for dealing with young persons who have committed offences" (YOA, Section 3 (d)). Telling a police officer that something should be "considered" gives little direction on how a particular case should be dealt with.

In contrast, the YCJA states: "Extrajudicial measures [measures outside of the formal court structure] are *presumed* to be adequate to hold a young person accountable for his or her offending behaviour if the young person has committed a non-violent offence and has not previously been found guilty of an offence.... Extrajudicial measures *should be used* if they are adequate to hold a young person accountable for his or her offending behaviour and, if the use of extrajudicial measures is consistent with the principles set out in this section, nothing in this Act precludes their use in respect to a young person who (i) has been previously dealt with by the use of extrajudicial measures, or (ii) has previously been found guilty of an offence." (YCJA,

Section 4 (c) and (d), emphasis added). In other words, the *YCJA* explicitly tells a police officer that unless there are compelling reasons for doing otherwise, they should deal with certain youths outside of the youth court setting.

Furthermore, the *YCJA* states: "A police officer *shall*, before starting judicial proceedings or taking any other measures under this Act against a young person alleged to have committed an offence, consider whether it would be sufficient, having regard to the principles set out in section 4 [extrajudicial measures, or non-court alternatives to responding to youth crime], to take no further action, warn the young person, administer a caution ... or, with the consent of the young person, refer the young person to a program or agency in the community that may assist the young person not to commit offences." (*YCJA*, Section 6 (1), emphasis added).

Requiring the police officer to consider non-court alternatives in every case is obviously a much stronger requirement than that which existed in the *YOA*, which just gave general direction on the availability of non-court alternatives by indicating that they should be *considered* if they are "not inconsistent with the protection of society." Under the *YCJA*, non-court approaches are presumed to be adequate for a wide range of cases (cases where the youth has never been to court and is charged with something other than a violent offence). A presumption in favour of a non-court approach means that an argument needs to be made to bring the case to court; otherwise, the case should be resolved outside of the court. Moreover, as the second of these subsections points out, non-court alternatives *can* be used even if they have been used before or if on a previous occasion the youth had been taken to court and found guilty. Finally, Section 6 (1) appears to require police to consider non-court responses to youthful offending, although there are no formal consequences if it turns out that the police do not obey the law in this regard.

Given the stronger direction for police under the *YCJA*, was there a corresponding reduction in the number of cases in youth court during the first year of implementation? Figure 19.1 shows the rate (per 1,000 youths in the population) of cases in youth court (with guilt findings). It shows trends in the rate of violence cases from 1991/92 until 2003/04, the first year of the *YCJA*. Minor assaults are shown separately from all other types of violence.

This figure shows two important trends, the first relating to the *YOA* years. From 1993/94 onwards until the implementation of the *YCJA* at the end of 2002/03, the rate of minor assault cases (found guilty) in youth court was slowly declining. For other forms of violence, the rate had stabilized by the mid-1990s.

The second important finding is that during the first year of the *YCJA* (2003/04), the rate of these cases in youth court dropped substantially. This is true for minor assaults as well as other crimes of violence. Although such a reduction might be expected for minor assaults, why there is a parallel reduction for other forms of violence is less obvious. The reason for this reduction may be that some of these other offence categories involved a wide range of

Figure 19.1 *Rate of Violence Cases (found guilty) in Youth Court (Canada)*

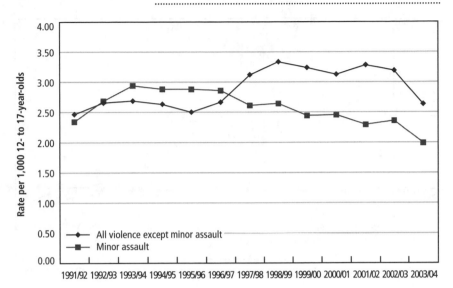

behaviours from very serious to barely worth noting. A robbery, for example, can range from holding up a convenience store with a firearm to grabbing a hat from the hand of another student in a schoolyard. Thus, the reduction in the use of court for "all other violence" may be the result of police officers' decisions to screen out minor instances of charges that sound more serious than they really are.

Figure 19.2 shows trends in the rate (per 1,000 12- to 17-year-olds in the population) of property cases (found guilty) in youth court. One sees a steady decline in the rates of these cases throughout the 1990s. Under the first year of the *YCJA*, there was a larger one-year reduction for "theft under" and "all other property" than in any other year. Specifically, the rate of "theft under" decreased by 0.68, and the rate for "all other property" decreased by 0.74. "Break and enter" decreased by 0.38, which was larger than the decrease the previous year, but not as large as other one-year decreases that occurred in other years throughout the 1990s.

Finally, Figure 19.3 presents the rate of criminal code administration of justice offences, drug offences, and *YOA/YCJA* offences (predominately the offence of failing to comply with a disposition). The relatively high—and increasing—rate of *YOA/YCJA* offences throughout the 1990s is immediately apparent. Not until 2000 does the rate of these cases start to fall. Clearly, however, there was a very striking one-year reduction under the *YCJA*: the rate dropped from 2.84 in 2002/03 to 2.05 in 2003/04. Drug offences and criminal code administration of justice offences also saw a larger one-year decrease under the *YCJA* than in any other year.

Figure 19.2 *Rate of Property Cases (found guilty) in Youth Court (Canada)*

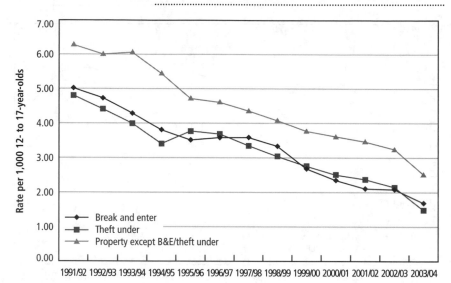

Figure 19.3 *Rate of "Other" Cases (found guilty) in Youth Court (Canada)*

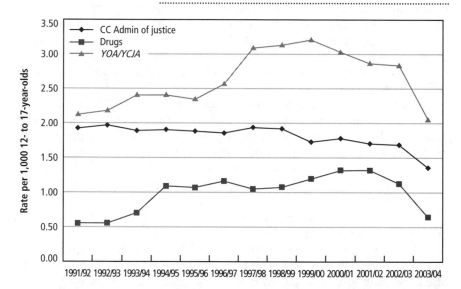

During the first year of the *YCJA*, then, substantial reductions in the rate of youth court cases (found guilty) were seen. The largest decreases were seen in relatively minor offences, though there were decreases even in the cases of more serious violence. However, as already noted, this difference could be due to police officers screening out the minor incidents of "serious sounding" charges.

ADDRESSING THE OVERUSE OF CUSTODY

The provisions in the *YOA* concerning the use of custody and those concerning ways of dealing with offending outside of court (see Section 24(1) to 24(1.1)(b) and (c)) were weak. Generally, the *YOA* told judges to use custody only if it was necessary for the protection of the public. But how were judges to determine whether it was necessary? Moreover, telling judges that non-custodial dispositions were to be used "wherever appropriate" and that custodial sentences were to be used only after the alternatives that were "reasonable in the circumstances" have been considered does not offer much guidance. A judge could easily conclude that she or he was not being told anything: the law merely said to refrain from using any alternatives to custodial sentences that the judge considered *inappropriate* or *unreasonable* in the circumstances. Thus, as long as the judge believed that a custodial sentence was appropriate and reasonable, it would have appeared to have met the *YOA* standard.

In contrast, the *YCJA* contains two explicit sections on sentencing. Section 38 sets out the principles that guide sentencing, while Section 39 lays out specific constraints on the use of custody. Section 38 states that the purpose of sentencing is to hold a young person accountable through "the imposition of just sanctions that have meaningful consequences for the young person and that promote his or her rehabilitation and reintegration into society, thereby contributing to the long-term protection of the public" (Section 38(1)). It then gives judges a list of seven principles to follow when sentencing: for example, the punishment must be proportionate to the seriousness of the offences and the degree of responsibility of the young person for the offence; and the sentence must be the least restrictive one available (*YCJA* Section 38(2)).

Section 39 of the *YCJA* creates further "hurdles" to be overcome before a court may commit a case to custody. Selected text from Section 39 is reproduced below:

> A youth justice court shall not commit a young person to custody under Section 42 (youth sentences) unless
>
> (a) the young person has committed a violent offence;
> (b) the young person has failed to comply with non-custodial sentences;
> (c) the young person has committed an indictable offence for which an adult would be liable to imprisonment for a term of more than two years and has a history that indicates a pattern of findings of guilt....
> (d) in exceptional cases where the young person has committed an indictable offence, the aggravating circumstances of the offence are such that the imposition of a non-custodial sentence would be inconsistent with the purpose and principles set out in section 38. (*YCJA*, Section 39(1)).

This last section appears to provide a rather broad exception. However, by focusing on the "aggravating circumstances" of the offence and referring to the purposes and principles in Section 38 (proportionality), this section clearly does not allow judges to give custodial sentences arbitrarily. For example, a judge would have a hard time ruling that a second-time shoplifter or a first-time break-and-enter offender would qualify for a custodial sentence.

Clearly, the language of the *YCJA* is stronger than the language of the *YOA*. For example, the *YCJA* requires that sentences be proportional to the seriousness of the offences, rather than simply suggesting that proportionality should be considered. In addition, Section 39 indicates that a case must meet at least one of four conditions for a judge to impose a custodial sanction. Certainly, the last of these (Section 39(1)(d)) is the least explicit of the four; however, this section also states that the circumstances must be "exceptional" and that a non-custodial sentence must be inconsistent with the purpose and principles of sentencing thereby requiring a custodial sentence. More importantly, a court which hands down a custodial sentence "shall state the reasons why it has determined that a non-custodial sentence is not adequate [to achieve the purposes of sentencing] ... including, if applicable the reasons why the case is an exceptional case [under the fourth condition for custody]" (Section 39(9)).

Figure 19.4 shows the number of cases throughout this period in which custody was imposed on one or more charges in the case. As this figure shows, the number of custody cases has been decreasing from 1997/98 onward. However,

Figure 19.4 *Number of Youth Cases in which Custody was Imposed (Canada)*

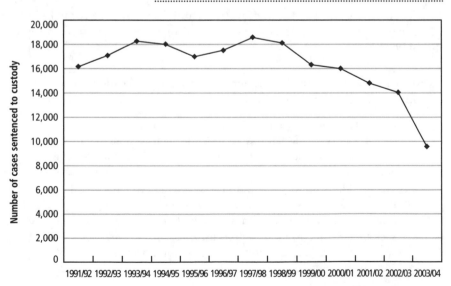

Source: Doob and Sprott (2005).

the decrease that occurred in the first year of the *YCJA* (from 14,118 cases in 2002/03 to 9,570 cases in 2003/04—a one-year drop of 32.2 percent) is the largest annual change since 1991/92.

This reduction in the use of custody is partly due to the reduced number of cases coming into court and being found guilty. Figures 19.5 through 19.7 show the rate of imposing custody (per 1,000 12- to 17-year-olds in the population) for violence, property, and "other" offences. Figure 19.5 shows a gradual but substantial reduction in the rate of imposing custody on minor assaults and "all other violence" since 1998/99. Yet the reductions under the *YCJA* are the largest one-year reductions throughout this time period.

Figure 19.6 shows the rate of sentencing youths to custody for property offences. These rates decline throughout the 1990s for both "break and enter" and "all other property" offences. But the rate for theft under $5,000 remained relatively stable throughout this time period until the first year of the *YCJA*. For both "theft under" and "all other property," the largest one-year reduction occurred in 2003/04, the first year of the *YCJA*. Custodial sentences for "break and enter" also decreased substantially in 2003/04—a rate decrease of 0.23. However, a similar one-year reduction occurred from 1994/95 to 1995/96 (a reduction of 0.21) and again from 1998/99 to 1999/00 (a reduction of 0.22). Not surprisingly then, the largest reductions were seen in the most minor offences.

Finally, Figure 19.7 shows the rate of sentencing youths to custody for "other" types of offences. One notices immediately a dramatic one-year change in sentencing *YOA/YCJA* cases to custody. In 2002/03, the rate of sentencing youths to custody was 1.13; but in 2003/04, the rate fell to 0.56,

Figure 19.5 *Rate of Sentencing Youth Violence Cases to Custody (Canada)*

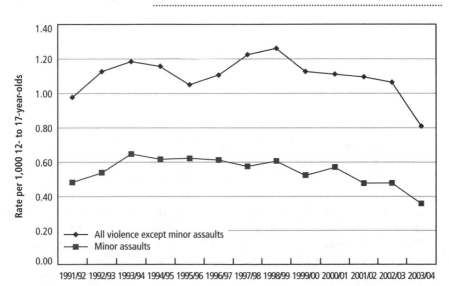

Figure 19.6 *Rate of Sentencing Youth Property Cases to Custody (Canada)*

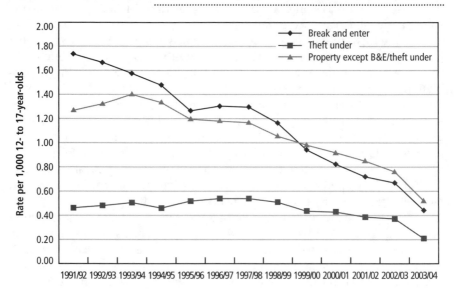

Figure 19.7 *Rate of Sentencing "Other" Youth Cases to Custody (Canada)*

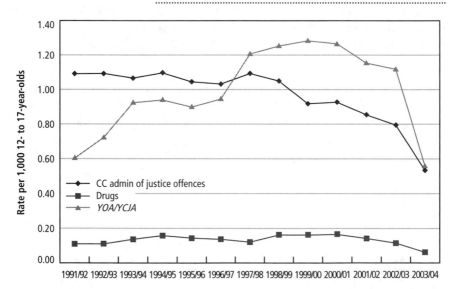

a one year reduction of 50 percent. Criminal Code administration of justice offences also saw a relatively large one-year reduction in the use of custody in 2003/04, larger than any other one-year decrease. Sentencing drug cases to custody also declined in the same year.

Comparisons across Provinces and Territories

Since the inception of the *YCJA*, the number of youth cases (found guilty) and sentenced to custody has fallen in all 13 jurisdictions across Canada. Table 19.1 shows the five-year average rate (per 1,000 12- to 17-year-olds) of cases found guilty and sentenced to custody and compares that to the one-year rate (2003/04) for each of the 13 jurisdictions with that of Canada as a whole. The table shows that in every jurisdiction, the rate of cases in youth

Table 19.1 *Rate (per 1,000 12- to 17-year-olds) of Cases in Youth Court (found guilty) and Sentenced to Custody: Five-year average compared to YCJA year (2003/04)*

	Rate (per 1,000 youths) of cases found guilty in youth court		Rate (per 1,000 youths) of sentencing cases to custody	
	Five year average: 1998/99– 2002/03	YCJA year: 2003/04	Five year average: 1998/99– 2002/03	YCJA year: 2003/04
Canada	21.79	16.18	6.40	3.78
NFLD and Labrador	25.02	20.61	8.70	4.70
PEI	15.67	10.00	6.54	2.11
Nova Scotia	21.69	13.13	6.74	2.09
New Brunswick	26.61	17.88	8.16	4.60
Quebec	12.84	9.97	3.03	1.66
Ontario	22.95	16.92	7.43	5.16
Manitoba	27.92	21.44	7.40	3.58
Saskatchewan	44.13	33.23	14.42	9.50
Alberta	29.09	20.69	6.14	3.00
BC	17.06	11.32	5.40	2.35
Yukon	41.90	15.86	19.32	4.83
NWT*	60.83	39.29	27.85	8.33
Nunavut**	38.56	38.16	10.09	9.47

*NWT: Northwest Territories included Nunavut in 1998/99 but not in 1999/00. For this reason, this table examines NWT only from 1999/00 onwards, so that the average is over the three years.
**Nunavut: Data were available only since 1999/00; therefore, the average is for three years. An unknown number of cases are missing from 1999/00 for the Nunavut data.

court (found guilty) and the rate of sentencing cases to custody fell during the *YCJA* year (2003/04) compared to the five-year average rates (from 1998/99 to 2002/03). These data strengthen the conclusion that the change that occurred in 2003/04 was due to a single national event—the implementation of the *YCJA*.

SUMMARY

In the first year of the *YCJA* there was a clear reduction in the total number of cases in youth court (found guilty). This reduction was larger than in previous years, suggesting that the *YCJA* reduced substantially the use of youth court. These decreases tended to be concentrated among the most minor offences. Similar patterns have been observed regarding the use of custodial sentences. These trends in the reduction of court and custody occurred across the country.

Whether they will persist is, of course, not known, especially given the more conservative political climate beginning in early 2006. During the 2006 federal election campaign, all three major political parties supported "toughening up" various aspects of both the youth and adult justice systems. However, it is difficult to predict what measures, if any, will actually be proposed. Given that the Conservatives have a minority government and the Bloc Québécois would undoubtedly object to radical changes of a punitive nature to the *YCJA*, any reforms may be limited in scope.

DISCUSSION QUESTIONS

1. *This chapter shows that in the first year under the new youth justice law, the use of custody declined significantly. Is there any danger that this will lead to calls to amend the legislation, as was the case with the previous youth justice law (the* YOA)?
2. *Sentencing under the Youth Criminal Justice Act is quite different from the sentencing of adults, which is regulated by other sections of the Criminal Code. What justifications exist for punishing young persons who break the law according to different principles? Why, for example, do we use custody more often for adults than for juveniles convicted of the same Criminal Code offence?*

FURTHER READINGS

Bala, N. 2002. *Youth Criminal Justice Act*. Toronto: Irwin Law.
Bala, N., and Anand, S. 2004. The first months under the Youth Criminal Justice Act: A survey and analysis of case law. *Canadian Journal of Criminology and Criminal Justice*, 46: 251–172.
Doob A.N., and Sprott, J.B. 2004. Changing models of youth justice in Canada. In M. Tonry and A. Doob (Eds.), *Crime and Justice: A Review of the Research*. Vol. 31. Chicago: University of Chicago Press.

REFERENCES

Doob A.N., and Cesaroni C. 2004. *Responding to Youth Crime in Canada.* Toronto: University of Toronto Press.

Doob A.N., and Sprott, J.B. 2004. Changing models of youth justice in Canada. In M. Tonry and A. Doob (Eds.), *Crime and Justice: A Review of the Research.* Vol. 31. Chicago: University of Chicago Press.

Doob, A.N., and Sprott, J.B. 2005. *The Use of Custody under the Youth Criminal Justice Act.* Ottawa: Department of Justice Canada.

Doob, A.N., and Sprott, J.B. 2006a. Punishing youth crime in Canada: The blind men and the elephant. *Punishment and Society,* 8: 223–233.

Doob, A.N., and Sprott, J.B. 2006b (in press). Assessing punitiveness in Canadian youth justice policy. *Punishment and Society.*

Hogeveen, B. 2005. "If we are tough on crime, if we punish crime, then people get the message": Constructing and governing the punishable young offender in Canada during the late 1990s. *Punishment and Society,* 7: 73–89.

Hogeveen, B. (in press). Memoir of the blind: A reply to Doob and Sprott. *Punishment and Society,* 8 (4).

CHAPTER 20
The Consequences of Incarceration for Young Offenders

INTRODUCTION

Custody is the most invasive and punitive disposition available to the Canadian justice system. Christie (1993) argues: "Next to killing, imprisonment is the strongest measure of power at the disposal of the state" (p. 23). This is one reason that many countries, including Canada, have provisions in their youth justice legislation suggesting that imprisonment should be used sparingly and only for very specific purposes. As noted in the previous chapter, the *Youth Criminal Justice Act* (*YCJA*) places important restrictions on the use of custody by a youth court, much greater than any restrictions in adult court; for example, youth court judges must overcome special "hurdles" before sentencing a youth to custody, whereas adult court judges simply follow a general principle that prison should be used only when no other sanction is appropriate.

Why should Canada be reluctant to send young offenders to prison? The principal reason is that imprisonment carries more adverse consequences for young offenders.[1] It is also believed to be a more severe sanction for youth. However, this belief needs to be substantiated by documented research, since many Canadians feel that judges should not sentence young people differently from adults.

This chapter by Carla Cesaroni explores the effects of incarceration upon young offenders. It considers the unique challenge that custody poses for young people and the kinds of young people who end up in custody.

The Consequences of Incarceration for Young Offenders

Carla Cesaroni, University of Ontario Institute of Technology

Research evidence suggests that young people experience custody in a unique way. Age is one of the most consistently established correlates of interpersonal violence in prison; for example, compared to adults, young prisoners are more likely to be involved in disciplinary infractions, including assaults on other inmates and staff (MacKenzie, 1987; McShane and Williams, 1989). Younger inmates are also less able to cope with the stress of imprisonment. They tend to experience much higher levels of anxiety as a result of being deprived of their families and social networks. Research suggests that custody ranks high amongst traumatic lifetime stressors for young people, right after the death or divorce of parents (Frydenberg, 1997). Unlike the suicide risk of older prisoners, which is often related to psychiatric illnesses, the suicide vulnerability of young prisoners is usually a function of their inability to cope with the prison environment itself (Liebling, 1999).

For many young offenders, incarceration is the first significant period that they have spent away from their family, friends, and home communities. A custodial sentence may increase disengagement from family, pro-social peers, and familial/social values at a critical stage of the young offender's development. In addition, custody removes youth from local schools and therefore may affect young people who already have little commitment to their school. This may place them at risk for reoffending, delinquency, and other problem behaviors (LeBlanc, Cote, and Loeber, 1991; Wasserman et al., 2003).

Adolescence itself generates developmental challenges to a young person's physical, intellectual, emotional, and social capabilities. These challenges become more difficult with the prospect of a custodial sentence. For example, establishing a stable, integrated identity is a central task of adolescent development. It is not hard to imagine the influence exerted on the development of personal identity by an onerous and very restrictive institutional environment (Greve, Enzmann, and Hosser, 2001).

In addition, peers play a much more important role in the life of an adolescent than in the life of an adult. Given the importance of peer relationships in adolescent development, it is not surprising that the friendships a young person makes while in custody are strong predictors of later adjustment. However, relationships amongst adolescent peers in custody tend to be volatile. Research suggests that friendships of delinquents involve more arguments, more aggressive and impulsive behaviors, and greater conflict and instability than other adolescent friendships (Markus, 1996). In addition, studies of delinquent friendships suggest that delinquents are more likely to ridicule, gang up on, or reject their friends (Claes and Simard, 1992).

Criminological literature on youths in custody focuses on *bullying*—the victimization of inmates by their peers (Mutchnick and Fawcett, 1991; Sheilds and Simourd, 1991; Beck, 1995; Connell and Farrington, 1996). Bullying is a common activity in young offender detention centres. Between 20 and 45 percent of prisoners in young offender institutions report they have been victimized during the course of their sentence (Adler, 1994; Beck, 1995; O'Donnell and Edgar, 1999).

In addition, youth in custody have difficulty dealing with negative peer relationships. Of course, peer victimization can also occur in schools and local neighborhoods; but peer abuse within custody centres differs significantly from peer abuse in other settings because it is much more difficult for youth in custody to escape their tormentors. Adolescents are also generally less likely than adults to solicit support directly and are more likely to use help-seeking behaviours that are more indirect and disguised (Gottlieb, 1991). Often they are afraid of damaging their reputation with their peers or appearing foolish (Gottlieb, 1991). In addition to the "adolescent code," imprisoned youth often have an "inmate code" to follow. In a recent study of incarcerated young offenders (Peterson-Badali and Koegl, 2001), half the sample reported that if something bad happened, there was an adult/staff/professional inside or outside of the institution they could ask for help. However, most said they would be unwilling to do so for fear of being labeled a "rat."

Thus, a custodial sentence represents a difficult challenge for any young person. The loss of freedom that custody entails and some of the other consequences that are an inevitable part of "doing time"—such as missing family and friends—may be felt more acutely by youth than by an adult inmate. Experiencing custody is particularly difficult for youth who are already vulnerable.

TYPES OF YOUNG OFFENDERS IN CUSTODY

Compared to other adolescents, youths in custody are vulnerable because of high levels of psychiatric problems and difficult family backgrounds. The prevalence of psychiatric disorders in incarcerated youth is high (Ulzen and Hamilton, 1998). These disorders include (but are not limited to) unipolar and bipolar depression, alcohol dependence, attention deficit hyperactivity disorder, conduct disorder, post-traumatic stress disorder, and separation anxiety disorder (Duclos et al., 1998; Ulzen and Hamilton, 1998). Several studies have attempted to estimate the prevalence rates of psychiatric diagnoses among young offenders in the youth justice system, but the results so far are highly variable (Kazdin, 2000). However, even the most conservative results suggest that the prevalence rate of mental disorder is much higher among young offenders than in community samples (Kazdin, 2000).

In addition, research has demonstrated that up to 75 percent of incarcerated young offenders may have a learning disability (Henteleff, 1999). Young offenders are also likely to have been involved with the child welfare system prior to custody (Doob, Marinos, and Varma, 1995). Moreover, many forms of family adversity are associated with youth incarceration, including physical abuse, family breakup, and violence between parents (Bortner and Williams, 1997).

A recent study of male youth in custodial institutions in Ontario (Cesaroni, 2005) found that over half the respondents reported having contact with child welfare authorities at some point during their childhood. This finding confirms previous research that there is often significant overlap between youths who are brought to court for offending and those with previous contact with child welfare or mental health agencies (for example, see Burt, Resnick, and Novick, 1998; Taussig, 2002). Approximately one third of the same sample had been removed from their family of origin by a Children's Aid Society; and almost a quarter had spent time in group homes. This finding is noteworthy, since it suggests that there is a strong relationship between placement in foster or group care and subsequent risk of incarceration for criminal behaviour (Johnson-Reid and Barth, 2000).

Youth in the same sample reported a relatively high exposure to violence both within the home and in their neighbourhoods. Thirty-nine percent of youth indicated that their parents always, often, or sometimes had violent arguments; and almost a quarter said that they had witnessed physical violence between their parents/guardians. In addition, almost three-quarters of respondents (72 percent) indicated that they had witnessed violence outside of their home at least once. The types of violence that youths witnessed outside of their homes varied considerably. For some youths, it was the "normal" violence of youths beating up other youths (albeit sometimes with baseball bats and pipes). Others witnessed a variety of forms of violence, including shootings, stabbings, and beatings in the course of drug deals or other criminal activity.

CANADIAN RESEARCH FINDINGS

Canadian research suggests that custodial sentences carry unique risks for young offenders. A great deal of research on youth in custody has resulted from official reports or inquiries into the conditions of confinement within Canadian youth custody facilities.[2] Many of these inquiries were responses to specific incidents within custodial facilities, including allegations of excessive use of force by staff and, in one extreme case, the death of a young person at the hands of another youth. These reports are useful because they include qualitative data that describe the youths' experiences in their own words. For example, youth who were interviewed about their first experiences in institutional facilities often spoke of "overwhelming sadness, fear of the unknown, anger, and a lack of information about what was happening to them" (Office of Child and Family Service Advocacy, 1998, p. 8). In the words of another young person: "I cried at night, felt kind of lost" (Office of Child and Family Service Advocacy, 1998, p.9).

Government reports and inquiries are also useful because they describe living conditions and treatment by staff that many youth may find stressful. They illustrate how the challenges of custody experienced by youth differ from those of adult inmates, particularly in regard to young offenders' relationships with and treatment by adult staff.

The physical environment of youth custody facilities has also been an area of concern since the youth justice system was first created. However, some descriptions of modern youth facilities do not even approximate the "standard" that was set out in the 1908 *Juvenile Delinquents Act*. That act stated that "the care and custody and discipline of a juvenile delinquent shall approximate as nearly as may be that which should be given by his parents" (s.38). In contrast, both government-operated and privately run youth agencies often house young people in run-down, decrepit buildings. Constant concerns have also been raised regarding the quality and quantity of food in youth facilities (often a cause of bullying), the lack of access to proper health care, and the inconsistent and substandard educational programming. In addition to concerns about basic needs and necessities, concerns regarding institutional risks have also been raised. These institutional risks include peer-on-peer violence, physical restraint, and placement in isolation. Peer abuse and inmate-on-inmate violence appear to be frequent features of custodial life for incarcerated youth.

However, abuse in youth detention centers is not necessarily restricted to peer abuse. Certainly, the use of extraordinary control measures with youth in custody is necessary at times to protect staff, restrict the movement of youth, stop a youth from acting in a dangerous or aggressive manner, or confirm suspicions about contraband. Intrusive procedures may include manual restraint, mechanical restraint, isolation, and personal searches. At a minimum, youth see these incidents as "scary," "unsafe," and "unfairly applied." However, it is important to note that youth frequently report injuries; incidents have been documented of youth being kicked, dragged, smashed against the floor or a table, choked, punched, or hit with batons or brooms while immobilized.

A review of reports on conditions in Canadian institutions confirms the high frequency of peer-on-peer victimization in youth facilities. These findings are consistent with research from other western countries and remain a constant concern in youth custody facilities across Canada. Peer-on-peer violence can occur in the context of intimidation, extortion, stealing, destruction of personal possessions, and/or verbal abuse. Youth in custody confirm the presence of several types of peer violence, including *soldiering, blowing bubbles*,[3] and degrading activity involving bodily fluids. Although the description of peer-on-peer violence in youth facilities is distressing, the descriptions of the degree of staff involvement in that violence are even more disturbing.

One researcher concluded: "From the perspective of those youth who found themselves in [these] secure facilities in Ontario, there not only is a fair amount of violence, but there is also a fair amount of staff involvement in creating or allowing this violence to occur" (Doob, 1999, p. 30). According to youth questioned in one survey, staff involvement in violence included putting inmates at risk by "letting bad things happen" (reported by 46 percent of the sample), putting an inmate's safety in jeopardy (47 percent), and bribing inmates to "discipline" other inmates (31 percent).

Inappropriate treatment of youth inmates by custodial staff is a disturbingly common aspect of institutional life, one that may be linked to the power dynamic inherent in adult–youth relationships. Certainly, there is a power dynamic between guards and inmates in most adult facilities; but in youth facilities, there is the additional power dynamic of *adult* guard and *adolescent* inmate. Being relegated to a child-like status during the age of individuation, independence, and control may create additional conflict for youth inmates with their adult guards, as it does between adolescents and their parents.

THE IMPACT OF CUSTODY ON YOUNG OFFENDERS

Custody remains the most punitive means of holding a young person accountable for his or her offences. Although many Canadians believe in "holding youths accountable" for their actions through imprisonment, it is not clear that the public would want youths to leave a correctional facility in worse condition than when they entered. In fact, many Canadians believe that assisting in the rehabilitation of a young offender is extremely important (Doob et al., 1998). Moreover, they would generally want youths not to suffer any long-term harm as a result of their time in custody. But as Steinberg, Chui, and Little (2004) argue, a rehabilitative perspective on young offenders provides challenges to both practitioners and policy makers because many custodial systems expose young offenders to harmful experiences (e.g., violence or trauma) that create more problems for the youth than they had when they entered (Steinberg, Chui, and Little, 2004).

Furthermore, the peer- or staff-induced harm that youth experience in custody has implications for institutional adjustment and for the likelihood of reoffending. Wasserman *et al.* (2003) argue that maladjustment to confinement may make rehabilitation much more difficult: "An untreated mental disorder or emotional impairment resulting from a negative reaction to confinement might result in poorer adjustment during confinement that would negatively affect both discipline and a youth's capacity to take advantage of available programs" (p. 314).

What are the key predictors of adjustment to custody? A study of an Ontario sample of incarcerated relatively younger inmates (those 12 to 15 years old when they offended) demonstrated that those young people who entered an institution with a higher number of vulnerabilities (e.g., child welfare involvement, problems in school, delinquent peers, instability in the home) were more likely to experience subsequent difficulties with adjustment and psychological well-being (Cesaroni and Peterson-Badali, 2005).

In addition, risk factors associated with institutional life appear to have an impact on adjustment. Prison stresses (e.g., missing freedom as well as family and friends) are aspects of adjustment to custody that the institution cannot necessarily control. As most frontline staff are likely aware, many youth get used to the common difficulties associated with entry to custody (Cesaroni, 2005). There, are however, two important predictors of prison adjustment over which staff do have some control.

First, staff can control the level of fear a youth experiences in an institution as a result of bullying or the fear of being bullied. The consequences for the victims include not only physical injury but also psychological distress, which manifests itself in insomnia, escape attempts, and in extreme cases, suicide (Leschied, Cunningham, and Mazaheri, 1997). A study by McCorkle (1993) suggests that a youth's level of fear is an extremely important predictor of his or her general well-being: high levels of fear in prison often undermine the correctional system's efforts to treat, educate, and train offenders. He argues that personal security is an essential requirement in any program designed to effect changes in prosocial attitudes or behaviours.

Second, staff internal support can affect a youth's adjustment. Having friends in an institution is important to a youth inmate for a number of reasons, the least of which is knowing that there are friends in the institution who will "watch your back" (Maitland and Sluder, 1996; Office of the Child and Family Advocacy of Ontario, 2003). A recent government inquiry concluded that young prisoners who are friendless within an institution are considered to be at serious risk of victimization (Office of Child and Family Advocacy, 2003). As one youth from that same inquiry suggests: "Alliances and friendships make you safe. Having no friends makes you unsafe" (Office of Child and Family Advocacy, 2003, p. 35).

Feelings of fear may be related to the turnover of youth in custody facilities and the constant renegotiation of alliances and friendships and of "sizing each other up." Many facilities in Canada have a high turnover of youth because of the number of short sentences imposed. Although some of the violence experienced by youth in custodial institutions is staff-related, dedicated staff play an important role in the adjustment process by providing internal support to youth in custody. Perhaps the most vital role that staff play is that of creating a climate in custody that fosters positive social interactions, a sense of stability, and a secure environment. Perhaps custodial facilities can learn from successful schools: some schools have been very successful in reducing student victimization and fostering positive relationships. Research suggests that the promotion of healthy relationships in school rests largely on developing a positive and supportive organizational climate (Mulvey and Cauffman, 2001).

LONG-TERM CONSEQUENCES OF YOUTH CUSTODY

Any psychological distress that a young person experiences while in custody could be considered relatively transient with no long-term implications for the youth's well-being. Although relatively few studies explore the long-term psychological consequences of the custodial experience on the life of a young person, some evidence points to long-term developmental effects. Sampson and Laub's (1997) reanalysis of the natural histories of 500 delinquents found that youth custody had significant negative effects on job stability at ages 25 to 32. According to Sampson and Laub (1997), "the structural disadvantages accorded institutionalized adolescents are so great (e.g., through dropping out of high school, record of confinement known to employers) that the influence lingers throughout adult development" (p. 149). Incarceration appears to cut off opportunities for employment later in life.

CONCLUSION

Given the short- and long-term implications of custody on a young person's future, custody should be imposed only with great restraint. The slogan "Do the crime, do the time" is often used to argue that youths should receive the same sentences as adults convicted of the same criminal behaviour. However, because of the impact of custodial sentences on youths, for young people custody is in fact *more* punishing than it is for adults. This conclusion provides an additional justification for treating youths differently from adults. This was undoubtedly the spirit behind the establishment of the first youth custody facilities in Canada and indeed the criteria for custody contained in the current youth justice law.

DISCUSSION QUESTIONS

1. *Some youth justice advocates argue that young offenders should only be imprisoned if they commit the most serious crimes such as murder. Is this a realistic position to take?*
2. *You may have heard of military-style "boot camps" for young offenders that are used in several American states. Do you think these kinds of institutions would be better than the correctional institutions currently in use here in Canada?*

FURTHER READINGS

Doob, A. N. 1999. *The Experiences of Phase II Male Young Offenders in Secure Facilities in the Province of Ontario.* Toronto: The Canadian Foundation for Children, Youth and the Law.

Frydenberg, E. 1997. *Adolescent Coping: Theoretical and Research Perspectives.* New York: Routledge.

REFERENCES

Adler, J. 1994. The incidence of fear: A survey of prisoners. *Prison Service Journal*, 96: 34–37.

Bala, N. 2003. *Youth Criminal Justice Law*. Toronto: Irwin Law Inc.

Beck, G. 1995. Bullying among young offenders in custody. *Issues in Criminological and Legal Psychology*, 22: 54–70.

Bortner, M. A., and Williams, L. M. 1997. *Youth in Prison: We the People of Unit Four*. New York: Routledge.

Burt, M. R., Resnick, G., and Novick, E. R. 1998. *Building Supportive Communities for At-Risk Adolescents*. Washington, DC: American Psychological Association.

Cesaroni, C. 2005. *The Stress and Adjustment of Youth in Custody*. Unpublished doctoral dissertation, University of Toronto, Centre of Criminology, Toronto.

Cesaroni, C., and Peterson-Badali, M. 2005. Young offenders in custody: Risk and adjustment. *Criminal Justice & Behavior*, 32: 251–277.

Christie, N. 1993. *Crime Control as Industry*. London: Routledge.

Claes, M., and Simard, R. 1992. Friendship characteristics of delinquent adolescents. *International Journal of Adolescence and Youth*, 3: 287–301.

Connell, A., and Farrington, D. 1996. Bullying among incarcerated young offenders: developing an interview schedule and some preliminary results. *Journal of Adolescence*, 19: 75–93.

Doob, A. N. 1999. *The Experiences of Phase II Male Young Offenders in Secure Facilities in the Province of Ontario*. Toronto: The Canadian Foundation for Children, Youth and the Law.

Doob, A. N., Marinos, V., and Varma, K. N. 1995. *Youth Crime and the Youth Justice System in Canada*. Toronto: Centre of Criminology, University of Toronto.

Doob, A. N., Sprott, J. B., Marinos, V., and Varma, K. N. 1998. *An Exploration of Ontario Residents' Views of Crime and the Criminal Justice System*. Toronto: Centre of Criminology, University of Toronto.

Duclos, C. W., et al. 1998. Prevalence of common psychiatric disorders among American Indian adolescent detainees. *Journal of American Academy of Child and Adolescent Psychiatry*, 37: 866–873.

Frydenberg, E. 1997. *Adolescent Coping: Theoretical and Research Perspectives*. New York: Routledge.

Gottlieb, B. H. 1991. Social support in adolescence. In M. E. Colten and S. Gore (Eds.), *Adolescent Stress: Causes and Consequences*. New York: Aldine de Gruyter.

Greve, W., Enzmann, D., and Hosser, D. 2001. The stabilization of self-esteem among incarcerated adolescents: Accommodative and immunizing processes. *International Journal of Offender Therapy and Comparative Criminology*, 45: 749–768.

Henteleff, Y. 1999. *The Learning Disabled Child-at-Risk: Why Youth Service Systems have So Badly Failed Them.* Paper presented at the Working Together for Children: Protection and Prevention Conference, Ottawa.

Johnson-Reid, M., and Barth, R. P. 2000. From placement to prison: The path to adolescent incarceration from child welfare supervised or group care. *Children and Youth Services Review*, 22: 493–517.

Juvenile Delinquents Act, R.S.C.1970, c J-3.

Kazdin, A. 2000. Adolescent development, mental disorders, and decision making of delinquent youths. In T. Grisso & R. Schwartz (Eds.), *Youth on Trial: A Developmental Perspective on Youth Justice.* Chicago: University of Chicago Press.

Law Commission of Canada 2000. *Restoring Dignity: Responding to Child Abuse in Canadian Institutions.* Ottawa: Law Commission of Canada.

Le Blanc, M., Cote, G., and Locber, R. 1991. Temporal paths in delinquency: Stability, regression and progression analyzed with panel data from an adolescent and delinquent sample. *Canadian Journal of Criminology*, 33: 23–44.

Leon, J. 1977. The development of Canadian juvenile justice: A background for reform. *Osgood Hall Law Journal*, 15: 71–106.

Leschied, A. W., Cunningham, A., and Mazaheri, N. 1997. *Safe and Secure: Eliminating Peer-to-Peer Violence in Ontario's Phase II Secure Detention Centres.* North Bay: Ministry of Solicitor General and Correctional Services.

Liebling, A. 1999. Prison suicide and prison coping. In M. Tonry and J. Petersilia (Eds.), *Prisons: Crime and Justice: A Review of Research.* Chicago: University of Chicago Press.

MacKenzie, D. 1987. Age and adjustment in prison: Interactions with attitudes and anxiety. *Criminal Justice and Behavior*, 14: 427–447.

Maitland, A., and Sluder R. D. 1996. Victimization in prisons: A study of factors related to general well-being of youthful inmates. *Federal Probation*, 60: 24–31.

Markus, Robert F. 1996. The friendships of delinquents. *Adolescence*, 31: 145–158.

McCorkle, R. C. 1993. Living on the edge: Fear in a maximum security prison. *Journal of Offender Rehabilitation*, 20: 73–91.

McShane, M. D., and Williams III, F. P. 1989. The prison adjustment of juvenile offenders. *Crime and Delinquency*, 35: 254–269.

Mulvey, E. P., and Cauffman, E. 2001. The inherent limits of predicting school violence. *American Psychologist*, 797–802.

Mutchnick, R. J., and Fawcett, M. 1991. Group home environments and victimization of resident juveniles. *International Journal of Offender Therapy & Comparative Criminology*, 25: 126–142.

O'Donnell, I., and Edgar, K. 1999. Fear in prison. *The Prison Journal*, 79: 90–99.

Office of the Child and Family Service Advocacy. 2003. *Review of Toronto Youth Assessment Centre (TYAC)*. Toronto: Author.

Office of the Child and Family Service Advocacy. 1998. *Voices from Within: Youth in Care in Ontario*. Toronto: Queen's Printer for Ontario.

Office of the Child and Family Service Advocacy. 1992. *Care of Youth at Thistletown Regional Centre, Syl Apps Campus*. Toronto: Office of the Child and Family Service Advocacy.

Ombudsman Province of British Columbia. 1994. *Building Respect: A Review of Youth Custody Centres in British Columbia*. Public Report Bo. 34, June.

Ontario Ministry of the Solicitor General. 1999. *Verdict of the Jury at the Inquest in the Death of James Preston Lonnee*. Toronto: Ontario Ministry of the Solicitor General.

Peterson-Badali, M., and Koegl, C. J. 2001. Juveniles' experiences of incarceration: The role of correctional staff in peer violence. *Journal of Criminal Justice*, 29: 1–9.

Sampson, R.J., and Laub, J. H. 1997. A life-course theory of cumulative disadvantage and the stability of delinquency. In T. P. Thornberry (Ed.), *Developmental Theories of Crime and Delinquency*. New Brunswick, NJ: Transaction Publishers.

Saskatchewan Children's Advocate Office. 1999. *Issues Affecting Youth in Conflict with the Law: A Review of Issues Raised with Saskatchewan Children's Advocacy Office*. Saskatoon: Saskatchewan Children's Advocate Office.

Shields, I. W., and Simourd, D. J. 1991. Predicting predatory behaviour in a population of incarcerated young offenders. *Criminal Justice and Behaviour*, 18: 180–194.

Steinberg, L., Chui Len, H., and Little, M. 2004. Re-entry of young offenders from the justice system: A developmental perspective. *Youth Violence and Juvenile Justice*, 2: 21–38.

Taussig, H. N. 2002. Risk behaviors in maltreated youth placed in foster care: A longitudinal study of protective and vulnerability factors. *Child Abuse and Neglect*, 26: 1179–1199.

Ulzen, T., and Hamilton, H. 1998. Psychiatric disorders in incarcerated youth. *Youth Update*, 16: 4–5.

Wasserman, G.A. *et al.* 2003. Risk and protective factors of child delinquency. *Child Delinquency Bulletin Series*. April. Washington, DC: Office of Juvenile Justice and Delinquency Prevention, U.S. Department of Justice.

ENDNOTES

[1] Indeed, there is agreement around the world that custody affects young offenders more than it does adults. Historically, one of the prime rationales for establishing a separate youth justice system and separate custodial facilities was a belief that youth are more vulnerable than adults

(Bala, 2003). Recognition of young people's special needs, their vulnerabilities, and their need to avoid stigmatization were the original impetus for the establishment of youth custody facilities in Canada (Leon, 1977).

2   See Doob, 1999; Law Commission of Canada, 2000; Office of Child and Family Service Advocacy, 1992, 1998, 2003; Ombudsman Province of British Columbia, 1994; Ontario Ministry of Solicitor General, 1999; Saskatchewan Children's Advocate Office, 1999.

3   *Soldiering* is defined as one youth demanding that another youth assault a third youth. The weakest youth or new arrivals to the unit are selected as soldiers. *Blowing bubbles* involves submerging a youth's head in a toilet and making them blow bubbles. Acts of degradation include forcing youth to drink urine or forcing youth to lick spit or semen off the walls or floors.

CHAPTER 21
Responding to Intimate Partner Violence

INTRODUCTION

Violence against intimate partners has become one of the most important problems that the criminal justice system attempts to address. It is only in recent years, with the creation of victimization surveys such as the "Violence Against Women" survey conducted by Statistics Canada, that Canadians have come to appreciate the full scope of the problem. Until the advent of victimization surveys, the true extent of domestic violence was unknown, since only a small proportion of incidents was ever reported to the police. Devising appropriate responses to intimate partner violence has proved challenging for all western systems of criminal justice.

In this chapter, two experts in the field of law and sociology review the principal criminal and civil law responses to this grave social problem.

Responding to Intimate Partner Violence

Gillian Blackell, Department of Justice Canada and
Holly Johnson, Canadian Centre for Justice Statistics[1]

Intimate partner violence affects a substantial number of victims each year in Canada and commands the attention and resources of the criminal justice, health, and social service systems. For the purposes of this article, *intimate partner relationships* refer to marital or common-law spousal as well as dating relationships, including same-sex relationships. In 2004, through a national telephone survey on crime victimization, Statistics Canada estimated that 196,000 women and 174,000 men had been victims of spousal violence in that year alone (spousal violence does not include violence in dating relationships) (AuCoin, 2005). Approximately 653,000 women and 546,000 men reported violence by a spouse (common-law or marital partner) in the preceding 5-year period. In addition, between 1991 and 2004, 929 women and 238 men were murdered by intimate partners in Canada. Police recorded a history of family violence in 55 percent of spousal homicides against women and 72 percent of spousal homicides against men (Johnson, 2006).

Although women and men report similar prevalence rates of spousal violence committed against them, the impacts and consequences differ sharply for female and male victims (Johnson, 2006). Women were twice as likely as men to be injured, six times as likely to require medical attention, five times as likely to be hospitalized, and three times as likely to fear for their lives. They were also more likely to experience ten or more assaults and to take time off from paid or unpaid work as a result of the violence.

The risk of violence remains higher for Aboriginal women than for non-Aboriginal women. For example, according to the 2004 victimization survey, 24 percent of Aboriginal women reported being victims of spousal violence over the previous 5-year period, more than 3 times the rate for non-Aboriginal women (7 percent) and higher than the rate for Aboriginal men (18 percent). Moreover, Aboriginal women experience more severe violence and more serious consequences: spousal homicide rates are almost 8 times higher for Aboriginal women than for non-Aboriginal women (4.6 and 0.6 per 100,000 population, respectively; Johnson, 2006).

Public awareness of intimate partner violence dates back to the 1970s. Domestic violence and sexual assaults in intimate relationships were historically viewed as private matters that did not necessarily warrant intervention from the criminal justice system. Over the past few decades, however, a wide range of interventions including legislation, policies, and services have been implemented by federal, provincial, and municipal level governments as well as community organizations in Canada to respond to the problem of intimate partner violence. These include shelters and other supports for victims, treatment for abusive partners, interagency collaboration at the community level, prevention and public awareness campaigns, specialized court processes, changes to both the criminal and civil law, pro-charging policies for police, and pro-prosecution policies for Crown prosecutors. Without exploring the full range of interventions to address intimate partner violence, this article summarizes some of the means by which criminal and civil law have been utilized to improve the legal response to intimate partner violence.

CRIMINAL LAW RESPONSES

While the *Criminal Code* does not contain a specific offence called *domestic* or *intimate partner violence*, a wide range of criminal offences cover violence within relationships. These include the offences of assault, sexual assault, homicide (murder, manslaughter), criminal negligence, forcible confinement, uttering threats, and criminal harassment. In 1983, the crimes of rape and indecent assault were replaced by the current three-tiered sexual assault provisions (ss.271, 272 and 273). The same reforms repealed spousal immunity from sexual assault charges. In addition to substantive offences, the *Criminal Code* now provides procedural protections, preventative measures, and sentencing principles applicable in qualifying spousal violence cases.

Addressing Criminal Harassment

The offence of *criminal harassment*, commonly known as *stalking*, was enacted in 1993 following several heinous incidents of estranged male partners harassing and stalking female victims, eventually leading to their death. Although prior to 1993 police were able to charge stalkers for other offences (such as mischief, uttering threats, or making harassing phone calls), the new offence captured seemingly innocuous acts, such as watching someone's place of residence or leaving unwanted gifts on someone's doorstep. Yet in the context of a stalking, these acts can be highly threatening for the victim and often serve as a precursor to physical violence. Thus, the criminal harassment offence under section 264 of the *Criminal Code* enables police to intervene if the behaviour is repetitive or threatening and causes the victim to fear for his or her safety or that of someone known to him or her. This offence was modeled on similar offences in the United States (California was the first state to criminalize stalking, in 1990).

The offence is particularly relevant in circumstances of intimate partner abuse, where the risks of violence or the escalation of violence are often heightened during or immediately following separation. For example, according to Statistics Canada's 2004 victimization survey, half of the women who were assaulted by a past partner said the violence occurred after the couple separated; and in one-third of post-separation assaults, the violence began or became more severe after the separation. Moreover, women have a heightened risk of spousal homicide after marital separation; ex-marital partners are responsible for 26 percent of all spousal homicides perpetrated against women, but only 10 percent of homicides perpetrated against men (Johnson, 2006).

More recent statutes have sharpened the focus of Canada's stalking laws. A 1996 amendment to the *Criminal Code* included a lifetime prohibition of firearms after a conviction for criminal harassment. A 1997 amendment made a conviction for criminal harassment while under a restraining order an aggravating factor that should be reflected in sentencing (section 264(5)); and a homicide committed in conjunction with the commission of an offence of criminal harassment became first degree murder, regardless of whether the murder was planned and deliberate (section 231(6)). In addition, in 2002 the maximum penalty for criminal harassment upon indictment was also doubled from five to ten years. As a result, offenders convicted of criminal harassment offences can be subjected to dangerous offender applications under section 759 of the *Criminal Code*. Finally, amendments to the *Code* in 2005 enhanced the provisions facilitating testimony by children and other vulnerable persons, including victims of criminal harassment (discussed further below).

Estimates of the number of women and men who have been stalked over a five-year period are available through Statistics Canada's 2004 national crime victimization survey. Based on a module of questions that conform to *Criminal Code* definitions of criminal harassment, this survey found that 11 percent of women and 7 percent of men had been stalked over the previous 5-year period. Women were twice as likely as men to report being stalked by intimate partners (current or former spouse or boyfriend): 21 percent of female victims compared with 11 percent of male victims. A strong association between stalking and intimate partner violence and homicide has been found in other research studies (Tjaden and Thoennes, 1998; McFarlane et al., 1999). In the 2004 Statistics Canada study, three-quarters of women who were stalked by an ex-partner also had been physically or sexually assaulted by that partner. Ex-partner stalkers were also found to be more dangerous and threatening than other categories of stalkers. Higher proportions of ex-partner stalkers intimidated, threatened, grabbed, or attacked their victims. Sixty percent of women stalked by ex-partners feared their lives were in danger (Johnson, 2006).

In addition to the traditional means of harassment is the relatively recent phenomenon of *cyber-stalking*—criminal harassment conducted through the Internet or other electronic means, such as harassing e-mail communications, posting offensive or threatening information about the victim on the Internet, or sabotaging the victim's computer. Cyber-stalkers can also incite others to harass their victims by posting personal advertisements or images in the victim's name. While some of the conduct involved does fall under the criminal harassment offence, some does not. Other offences such as the *unauthorized use of a computer* (s.342.1) or *mischief in relation to data* (s.430 (1.1)) might be applicable. The challenges for combating cyber-stalking are multiple, including the anonymity and lack of accountability of the perpetrator and cross-jurisdictional barriers.

Battered Women and Self-Defence

Sections 34 to 37 of the *Criminal Code* define the law on self-defence. According to these provisions, a person who is attacked is not criminally responsible for using a reasonable or proportionate amount of force against his or her attacker. A person can also use defensive force against an apprehended assault or attack because a threat to apply force also constitutes an assault under the *Code*. In addition, the law permits the use of reasonable force to defend someone else from harm or death. A successful claim of self-defence results in an acquittal for the assault or homicide. However, in all cases, the law does not permit the use of excessive or unreasonable force.

Prior to the Supreme Court of Canada's (SCC) groundbreaking decision in *R. v. Lavallée*, [1990] 1 S.C.R. 854, the law of self-defence in Canada was difficult to apply successfully in cases where battered women killed their abusive partners in self-defence. Lyn Lavallée was charged with the murder of her violent common-law partner, Kevin Rust, who had regularly subjected her to physical abuse. She shot him in the back of the head as he was leaving the room after he beat her and told her that if she didn't kill him, he would kill her when their guests left. Expert evidence was introduced to demonstrate that Lavallée had been terrorized by Rust, and that as a battered woman, her actions were based on a "reasonable" belief that she had no other option but to shoot him. In order to explain the perspective of the accused, the expert referred to the "battered woman syndrome," which is based on the work of Dr. Lenore Walker (1979).

Walker identified three phases of the cycle of domestic violence. The first phase, known as the *tension building phase*, is characterized by a series of minor assaults and verbal abuse. During the second phase, known as the *acute battering phase*, the batterer is unable to control the rage and severely beats the woman. This is followed by the third phase, the *kindness and contrite loving behaviour phase*, during which the batterer behaves kindly towards the woman, asking her forgiveness and promising never to repeat the violence. This final phase provides the woman with positive reinforcement for staying in the relationship. To explain why women remain in violent relationships after the cycle has been repeated more than once, Walker argued that battered women are psychologically paralyzed because they have learned from the repeated beatings that they cannot control their circumstances. This is known as "learned helplessness."

Based on the battered woman syndrome, Walker testified that Lavallée's actions constituted the final desperate act of someone who sincerely believed that she would be killed that night. The jury then acquitted Lavallée. The decision was appealed to the Supreme Court of Canada, which decided unanimously to acquit her of the charge of murder.

The *Lavallée* ruling was significant for a number of reasons: (1) it made admissible expert evidence related to the *battered women's syndrome*, which in turn helped to dispel myths about why battered women remain in violent relationships; (2) this evidence impacted the *imminency requirement* (the requirement that the risk of attack must be imminent); and (3) the Court accepted that women's experiences and perspectives in relation to self-defence may be different from those of men and that courts must now make their judgments based on the "objective" standard of the actions of a "reasonable person," rather than on the actions of the traditional legal standard, the "reasonable man" (*R. v. Malott*, [1998] 1 S.C.R 123).

While the *Lavallée* decision was lauded by those who work with abused women, some feminist scholars expressed concern that it might lead to the "syndromization" of women's experiences, as had been the case in the United States (Boyle, 1990; Grant, 1991; Comack, 1993; Noonan, 1993; Shaffer, 1997; Sheehy, 2001). The concerns regarding the battered women syndrome included the risk that this would portray battered women as dysfunctional, deviant, and even pathological. Likewise, concerns were also expressed regarding the creation of a new stereotype of the "authentic" battered woman, thereby restricting the applicability of the syndrome evidence to women who fought back or did not otherwise fit the passive victim profile. While some authors indicate that cases subsequent to *Lavallée* have fallen prey to the syndromization of battered women (Shaffer, 1997; Sheehy, 2001), the Supreme Court was careful in both *Lavallée* and in *Malott* (another battered women's syndrome case) to indicate that the battered women's syndrome is not a defence in itself, but rather a tool for understanding the "reasonableness" of a battered woman's actions. The *Lavallée* ruling has contributed significantly to raising awareness of the realities of battered women among the judiciary and other criminal justice personnel and is regularly cited in court decisions.

Following *Lavallée*, in October 1995 the Minister of Justice and the Solicitor General of Canada established the Self Defence Review (SDR) to discover whether any women who had been convicted prior to or after *Lavallée* should have benefited from a self-defence claim. The SDR, under the lead of Judge Ratushny, reviewed the cases of women convicted of murdering their intimate partners. The SDR Final Report, released in July 1997, recommended relief in seven cases and included recommendations for reforming the self-defence provision in the *Criminal Code*. In the end, redress was granted in just five of the cases examined; however, no woman was actually released from jail as a result of the SDR (Trotter, 2001).

Preventive Measures

A number of provisions in the *Criminal Code* can be used to help prevent intimate partner violence. For instance, section 810 allows a Justice of the Peace or a judge to issue *recognizances* (peace bonds or protective court orders) to protect someone from possible criminal offences. Recognizances require alleged offenders to adhere to conditions, such as staying away from the victim's residence or place of work, and surrendering any firearms they may possess. Although the standard of proof is a civil standard—meaning only that on a balance of probabilities, there may be future violence—a breach of conditions is an offence under the *Criminal Code*.

In 1995, these provisions were amended to facilitate obtaining peace bonds, to make those peace bonds more effective, and to increase the maximum penalty for a breach from six months to two years (section 811). In light of pro-charging policies in domestic violence cases, peace bonds are generally not used if there are reasonable and probable grounds to arrest the abuser for a criminal offence.

In addition to peace bonds, the *Criminal Code* allows the justice or judge at a bail hearing to make recognizance orders or undertakings with conditions to prevent the accused from communicating with or harassing the victim or witness, in addition to other relevant conditions. In response to concerns regarding violent occurrences during the 24-hour period between arrest and the bail hearing in domestic violence cases, the *Code* was amended in 1999 to permit a justice of the peace who remands arrested persons into custody to order the person not to communicate with any witness or other person between the time he or she is detained and his or her first bail hearing. A 1999 amendment also requires police officers and judges to consider a victim's safety in all bail decisions.

Following the mass killings at the Ecole Polytechnique in Montreal on December 6, 1989, public pressure to update gun control legislation was significantly increased. In 1991, screening checks and safety courses for *Firearms Acquisition Certificates* (FAC) applicants were added to those certificates. Then in 1995, the federal government introduced the *Firearms Act,* which created licences for the possession of firearms, a national registration system for all firearms, and mandatory minimum sentences of four years of prison and lifetime prohibitions against the possession of restricted or prohibited firearms upon conviction of specific violent offences, including sexual assault with a weapon and aggravated sexual assault. The registration of firearms permits police to be alerted to the presence of firearms in scenes of family violence. Moreover, FACs ensure that risk factors associated with incidents of family violence are considered, especially through the requirement of spousal consent.

Protective Procedural Measures

It is trite to say that the criminal trial process can be gruelling for both the accused and the victim or witness. Concerns about the potential for re-victimization of intimate partner violence victims have led to the introduction of many protective procedural measures over the past two decades. In order to protect sexual assault complainants from having irrelevant evidence of prior sexual activity admitted at trial, revised *rape shield* legislation was introduced in 1992. These amendments to the *Criminal Code* also included a definition of consent for the purposes of the sexual assault provisions. The amendments clearly state that the defence of mistaken belief in consent could not be used if the belief stemmed from the accused's drunkenness, recklessness, or willful blindness, or if the accused did not take reasonable steps to determine whether the victim was, in fact, consenting.

The *Criminal Code* also contains a number of other provisions to facilitate the testimony of vulnerable victims and witnesses. For example, a court can exclude some or all of the members of the public from the proceedings; as well, it can prohibit the publication or transmission of information that could identify a victim in cases where the victim is under 18 years of age and in cases where such a ban is deemed necessary for the proper administration of justice (s.486). Moreover, victims or witnesses under the age of 18 or those who suffer mental or physical disabilities may be permitted to give evidence by way of a video recording (ss.715.1 and 715.2).

In addition, a wide range of testimonial aids are available to allow victims to testify, including closed circuit television and screens (to avoid seeing the accused). The victim can also be accompanied by a support person at trial. As well, a court-appointed lawyer can be asked to cross-examine the victim if the accused is self-represented. While many of these testimonial aids have been available since 1999 for young victims and witnesses of specified violence and sexual offences, in 2005 they were made available upon application for adult victims of spousal abuse and sexual assault (s.486). The new subsection 486.3(4) specifically provides for the presumptive appointment of a lawyer for cross-examination of the victim in criminal harassment cases where the accused is self-represented.

For sentencing in spousal assault cases, the *Criminal Code* provides for victim impact statements and requires that these statements be considered by courts. Moreover, in 1995, the sentencing provisions of the *Criminal Code* were amended to provide that where an offender, in committing the offence, abuses his spouse or child or any position of trust or authority, this shall be considered an aggravating factor for sentencing purposes. Amendments were also made to the restitution provisions of the *Code* to entitle a victim to seek restitution for actual and reasonable expenses for moving out of the offender's home to avoid bodily harm.

Domestic Violence Policies and Courts

One cornerstone of the criminal justice response to intimate partner violence has been the implementation since the 1980s in all provinces and territories of directives or guidelines for police and Crown prosecutors. These are referred to as *pro-charging* or *pro-prosecution* policies. They generally require police to lay charges in cases of domestic violence where there are legal grounds to do so. Some policies require Crown prosecutors to prosecute domestic violence cases regardless of the victim's alleged desire to withdraw charges. The original aim of these directives was to send a message to abusers that spousal violence is a crime and to ensure that victims are supported and offenders treated seriously by the criminal justice system.

But in September 2000, the Federal-Provincial-Territorial (F/P/T) Ministers Responsible for Justice requested a review of these policies, the first comprehensive review since their inception, in order to assess the effectiveness of these policies and their application and to strengthen the government response to domestic violence. The resulting 2003 report recommended the retention of pro-charging and pro-prosecution policies in spousal abuse cases, as well as the development and enhancement of supporting programs, services and structures, including a multi-sectoral response to spousal violence.

In addition, in order to improve the justice system's response to partner violence, several jurisdictions have instituted domestic or family violence courts, which provide a range of specialized services, such as advocacy and support for victims and their children, specially trained Crown prosecutors, translation services, and treatment for abusers. The first specialized family violence court was established in Winnipeg, Manitoba, in 1990. Since 1996, the Ontario government has introduced a domestic violence court program in 49 court sites, and it plans to expand these programs province-wide in 2006. Dedicated courts and specially trained prosecutors can also be found in five cities in Alberta since 2000 (Calgary, Edmonton, Lethbridge, Red Deer, and Medicine Hat). In addition, almost all of these Alberta cities now have police units trained in domestic violence. Yukon introduced a Domestic Violence Treatment Option in 2000. Saskatchewan is the latest jurisdiction to open a domestic violence court (in Saskatoon).

The primary goals of these courts are to expedite court processing, to increase victim cooperation and improve conviction rates, to provide better support to victims throughout the criminal justice process, and to provide appropriate sentencing, such as treatment for abusers. It appears that the Winnipeg Court has had some success with these goals. The number of spousal violence cases coming before the Court more than doubled between 1990 and 1998 (Ursel, 2000). The most common sentence is supervised probation and treatment for abusers. In response to a sharp increase in the number of court-mandated treatment orders, Manitoba Corrections department created a special probation unit to deliver treatment programs to batterers (Ursel, 1998).[2] All provincial correctional institutions also operate batterer's treatment groups for incarcerated offenders.

Feminist scholars have raised important questions about the potential for mandatory charging and prosecution policies to disempower victims by removing control of the situation from them once a report is made to police (Currie, 1990; Snider, 1998). The primary need of victims when calling the police is to receive protection and to stop the violence from continuing. For many reasons, including financial, emotional or child-related factors, the victim may be reluctant to have the abuser arrested and incarcerated. However, regardless of the victim's wishes, calling the police puts in motion the weight of the entire criminal justice process. To deal with this difficulty, the Winnipeg Family Violence Court has changed its culture to ensure that the process does not re-victimize victims, while giving them some decision-making power over the outcome of cases (Ursel, 2002).

One important development in spousal abuse cases is a shift away from the notion that success in a spousal abuse case requires a conviction. Rather than defining success on this single event, prosecutors have begun to place greater emphasis on the process and on providing a service to victims. Victims are encouraged and supported when testifying against an abusive spouse; but the Crown does not proceed with the prosecution without the victim's cooperation, except in cases where there is a serious risk to the victim or the community. Reluctant victims are encouraged to consider testifying at another time. According to Ursel (2002): "It is important that the Crown leave the message with the victim that she will not be harassed with warrants for failing to appear and she will not be treated as a hostile victim if she recants."

In some ways, family violence does not fit the traditional model of criminal justice. Ursel (2002, p. 58) argues that the high rate of stays of proceedings in Family Violence Courts is the result of the "single-incident framework" of the criminal justice system. Some spousal violence cases can appear several times as stays in court statistics, but one conviction can be based on an accumulation of charges over time. She argues that it is important that the victim knows that the system is there to help her and that she will be taken seriously and treated with respect if she reports to the police and charges are laid in future. This follows more closely the philosophy of shelters for battered women, where the focus is on providing support, and where efforts are not considered failures when these women return to an abusive partner.

CIVIL LAW RESPONSES

In addition to criminal sanctions that apply across Canada, several remedies for intimate partner violence are available through the civil law. Civil remedies are provided for either through legislation or through the common law. Torts such as assault, battery, trespass, and nuisance could apply to a claim for damages from intimate violence. Tort law has not been applied often to domestic violence cases in Canada due in part to vicitms' fear of their aggressors (Christopher, 2005). In addition to remedies for damages through the common law, many jurisdictions have criminal compensation recovery legislation that victims can access following the conviction of the offender.

Civil Domestic Violence Legislation

Eight provinces and territories have introduced civil legislation to better protect victims in situations of domestic violence: Saskatchewan (enacted in 1995), Prince Edward Island (1996), Yukon (1999), Manitoba (1999), Alberta (1999), Nova Scotia (2003), Northwest Territories (2005) and Newfoundland and Labrador (passed in 2005, in force July 1, 2006). These civil statutes are intended to compliment the criminal law process, and jurisdictions are encouraged to proceed with criminal charges where applicable. The civil remedies available include emergency protection orders, orders providing temporary exclusive possession of the family home, civil restraining orders, and other provisions necessary for the protection of victims and their children.

The primary value of civil domestic violence legislation is the immediacy of protection and the practical intervention it offers through remedies to victims and their children. Although the orders are civil, a violation of an order can result in a criminal charge under s.127 of the *Criminal Code* in the absence of a specified penalty for a breach in the civil legislation.

The Impact of Intimate Partner Violence on Custody and Access of Children

A considerable body of clinical research identifies the negative impact on children of witnessing spousal abuse (Jaffe, Crooks and Bala, 2006). Courts in five jurisdictions (Newfoundland, Northwest Territories, Nunavut, Alberta and Ontario) currently consider the impact of living with domestic or family violence as a factor in determining the best interests for the child for the purposes of custody and access (called *parenting orders* in Alberta). Moreover, even in the absence of specific legislation, the courts have considered evidence of family violence to be a relevant factor in post-separation or divorce custodial arrangements. Researchers have indicated that child access is often used as a window of opportunity for a partner to continue the violence, intimidate, or harass a former partner (Jaffe, Lemon and Poisson, 2003).

Exposing a child to spousal violence may also be grounds for intervention of child protection authorities on the grounds of emotional harm or a risk of emotional harm to the child (Wilson, 2003). Moreover, child protection legislation in seven jurisdictions explicitly identifies exposure to domestic violence as a factor to be considered when determining whether a child is in need of protection. Child protection orders supersede custody and access orders in a divorce or separation proceeding (Wilson, 2003, §3.73); therefore, exposure to post-separation violence could have an impact on the ability of a victimized parent to retain custody of his or her child. However, according to the Canadian Incidence Study of Reported Child Abuse and Neglect (CIS-2003), only 2 percent of cases involving exposure to domestic violence in 2003 resulted in a child welfare placement. An additional 2 percent resulted in informal kinship care placement (Black et al., 2005).

CONCLUSIONS

Over the past 20 years, Canada's legal system has witnessed a form of dialogue between feminists and community organizations, the courts, researchers, and governments concerning the harms of intimate partner violence. Effectively addressing intimate partner violence requires multiple interventions from health, social, community and justice service providers. As indicated in this chapter, intimate partner violence continues to be a persistent and pervasive problem in Canada, and the responses of the criminal and civil law continue to evolve, adapting to the growing body of social science research and case law on this important social problem.

DISCUSSION QUESTIONS

1. *Do you think that the reforms to the law described in this chapter are likely to increase the level of confidence that victims have in the criminal justice system?*
2. *Can you think of any other steps that the justice system can take to more effectively respond to the problem of violence between intimates?*

FURTHER READINGS

Johnson, H. 1996. *Dangerous Domains: Violence Against Women in Canada.* Toronto: Nelson Canada.

Bonnycastle, K., and Rigakos, G. 1998. *Unsettling Truths: Battered Women, Policy, Politics and Contemporary Research in Canada.* Vancouver: Collective Press.

McKenna, K., and Larkin, J. 2002. *Violence Against Women: New Canadian Perspectives.* Toronto: Inanna Publications and Education, Inc.

REFERENCES

Ad Hoc Federal-Provincial-Territorial Working Group Reviewing Spousal Abuse Policies and Legislation 2003. *Final Report of the Ad Hoc Federal-Provincial-Territorial Working Group Reviewing Spousal Abuse Policies and Legislation Prepared for Federal-Provincial-Territorial Ministers Responsible for Justice.* Ottawa: Department of Justice Canada.

AuCoin, K. 2005. *Family Violence in Canada: A Statistical Profile, 2005.* Catalogue 85-224-XIE. Ottawa: Statistics Canada.

Bala, N., and Ringseis, E. 2002. Review of Yukon's *Family Violence Prevention Act.* Under contract with the Canadian Research Institute for Law and the Family for the Victim Services Office of the Department of Justice, Yukon Territory.

Black, T., Trocmé, N., Fallon, B., MacLaurin B., Roy, C., and Lajoie, J. 2005. *Children's Exposure to Domestic Violence in Canada.* CECW Information Sheet #28E. Montreal: University of McGill University, School of Social Work.

Boyle, C. 1990. The battered wife syndrome and self-defence: *Lavallée* v. *R. Canadian Journal of Family Law,* 9: 171–179.

Christopher, C. 2005. *Law of Domestic Conflict in Canada.* Toronto: Carswell.

Comack, E. 1993. Feminist engagement with the law: The legal recognition of battered woman syndrome. *The CRIAW Papers.* Ottawa: Canadian Research Institute for the Advancement of Women.

Currie, D. 1990. Battered women and the state: From the failure of theory to a theory of failure. *Journal of Human Justice,* 1: 77–96.

Dawson, M. 2004. *Criminal Justice Outcomes in Intimate and Non-intimate Partner Homicide Cases.* Ottawa: Department of Justice Canada.

Department of Justice Canada 2004. *Criminal Harassment: A Handbook for Police and Crown Prosecutors.* Ottawa: Department of Justice Canada.

Feder, L., and Dugan, L. 2002. A test of the efficacy of court-mandated counseling for domestic violence offenders: The Broward experiment. *Justice Quarterly,* 19: 343–375.

Gotell, L. 2002. The ideal victim, the hysterical complainant, and the disclosure of confidential records: The implications of the Charter for Sexual Assault Law. *Osgoode Hall Law Journal,* 40: 251–295.

Gotell, L. 2005. Review of Manfredi, C. Feminist activism in the Supreme Court: Legal mobilization and the Women's Legal Education and Action Fund (Vancouver: University of British Columbia Press, 2004). *Queen's Law Journal*, 30: 883–889.

Grant, I. 1991. The "syndromization" of women's experience. *University of British Columbia Law Review*, 25: 51–59.

Jaffe, P., Crooks, C., and Bala, N. 2006. *Making Appropriate Parenting Arrangements in Family Violence Cases: Applying the Literature to Identify Promising Practices*. Research Report, 2005-FCY-3E. Ottawa: Department of Justice Canada.

Jaffe, P., Lemon, N., and Poisson, S. 2003. *Child Custody and Domestic Violence*. Thousand Oaks, CA: Sage.

Johnson, H. 2006. *Measuring Violence Against Women: Statistical Trends, 2006*. Catalogue 85-561-MWE. Ottawa: Statistics Canada.

McCallum, T. 2000. Ontario Domestic Violence Courts Initiative. In V. Pottie Bunge and D. Locke (Eds.), *Family Violence in Canada: A Statistical Profile, 2000*. Catalogue 85-224-XPE. Ottawa: Statistics Canada.

McFarlane, J, Campbell, J., Wilt, S., Sachs, C., Ulrick Y., and Xu, X. 1999. Stalking and intimate partner femicide. *Homicide Studies*, 3: 300-316.

Noonan, S. 1993. Strategies of survival: Moving beyond the battered woman syndrome. In E. Adelberg and C. Currie (Eds.), *In Conflict with the Law: Women and the Canadian Justice System*. Vancouver: Press Gang Publishers.

Pottie Bunge, V. 2002. National trends in partner homicides, 1974–2000. *Juristat*, 22 (5), Catalogue 85-002-XIE. Ottawa: Statistics Canada.

R. v. Lavallée (1990), 1 S.C.R. 852-9000.

Sampson, F. 2001. Mandatory minimum sentences and women with disabilities. *Osgoode Hall Law Journal*, 39: 589–609.

Shaffer, M. 1997. The battered women syndrome revisited: Some complicating thoughts five years after *R. v. Lavallée*. *University of Toronto Law Journal*, 47: 1–33.

Sheehy, E. 2001. Battered women and mandatory minimum sentences. *Osgoode Hall Law Journal*, 39: 529–555.

Snider, L. 1998. Struggles for social justice: Criminalization and alternatives. In K. Bonnycastle and G. Rigakos (Eds.), *Unsettling Truths: Battered Women, Policy, Politics and Contemporary Research in Canada*. Vancouver: Collective Press.

Tjaden, P., and Thoennes, N. 1998. *Stalking in America: Findings from the National Violence against Women Survey*. Washington: U.S. Department of Justice.

Trotter, G. T. 2001. Justice, politics and the royal prerogative of mercy: Examining the self-defence Review. *Queen's Law Journal*, 26: 339–395.

Ursel, J. 1998. Mandatory charging: The Manitoba Model. In K. Bonnycastle and G. Rigakos (Eds.), *Unsettling Truths: Battered Women, Policy, Politics and Contemporary Research in Canada*. Vancouver: Collective Press.

Ursel, J. 2000. Winnipeg Family Violence Court Report. In V. Pottie Bunge and D. Locke (Eds.), *Family Violence in Canada: A Statistical Profile, 2000*. Catalogue 85-224-XPE. Ottawa: Statistics Canada.

Ursel, J. 2002. "His sentence is my freedom": Processing domestic violence cases in the Winnipeg Family Violence Court. In L. Tutty and C. Goard (Eds.), *Reclaiming Self: Issues and Resources for Women Abused by Intimate Partners*. Halifax, NS: Fernwood.

Walker, L. 1979. *The Battered Woman*. New York: Harper Perennial.

Wilson, J. 2003. *Wilson on Children and the Law*. Markham: Butterworths.

ENDNOTES

1 The views expressed in this chapter represent those of the authors and do not necessarily reflect the views of Justice Canada or Statistics Canada.

2 The rise in pro-charging policies and Domestic Violence Courts has brought about a rise in court-mandated treatment for batterers, even though the evidence concerning the effectiveness of treatment programs is mixed (Feder and Dugan, 2002).

CHAPTER 22
Victims of Crime and the Justice System

INTRODUCTION

For many years, crime victims have been overlooked by the criminal justice system. More recently, they have come to play an increasingly important role in the criminal process. This is true in Canada as well as in other common-law jurisdictions, such as England, Wales, and New Zealand, and at the level of international criminal justice. Both the federal and provincial governments in Canada have introduced legislation to provide victims with more services and more "voice" in the processing of criminal cases.

In this chapter, Michelle Grossman and Catherine Kane, two authors who have worked in the area of victims' policy and practice for many years, explore ways that the Canadian criminal justice system has created a role for victims.

Victims of Crime and the Justice System

Michelle G. Grossman, University of Oxford, and *Catherine Kane*, Policy Centre for Victim Issues, Department of Justice Canada[1]

In recent years, both the federal and provincial levels of government in Canada have made significant efforts to improve the experiences of crime victims in the criminal justice system. Despite these efforts, many issues related to victims' needs and expectations in the criminal justice system require additional attention. This chapter explores several key issues relating to crime victims and the criminal justice system in Canada by examining relevant Canadian legislation and the findings from research conducted for the Policy Centre for Victim Issues in the Department of Justice Canada (PCVI).

While this chapter does not address the impact of victimization, it is important to recognize that people react differently to crimes committed against them. For example, some victims can end up traumatized and fearful following the theft of a car; others will only feel annoyed and inconvenienced and will seek information from the police and others. More serious and personal violence offences have far greater impact on and longer-term consequences for victims. Victims are thrown into an unfamiliar justice system where they do not have a clearly articulated or understood role. For a judge or Crown attorney, a victim may be simply one more "case" or one more "witness"; but for the victim, this case is usually his or her only case.

When asked to identify the "players" in the criminal justice system, most people would likely identify the police, Crown attorney, defence counsel, judge, and probation or parole officers. The legal system generally refers to the "parties" in a proceeding. In a civil proceeding (e.g., a claim for damages for negligence), the parties are referred to as the "plaintiff" (the person "complaining" or alleging a wrong and seeking damages) and the "defendant" (the accused). In criminal proceedings, the parties are the Crown and the accused. It is the Crown that is complaining on behalf of the state about a wrong (i.e., a crime) committed by the accused. The roles or duties of all these "parties" are clear and defined. The victim (the person who actually suffered because of this wrong) is not a party in the proceedings.

THE EVOLUTION OF VICTIM "RIGHTS" IN CANADA

In Canada, the emergence of the victim's voice and recognition of the concerns of victims dates back to the early 1970s. Criminal injuries compensation programs, which provided financial awards to victims of crime, originated in some jurisdictions as compensation to police officers injured in the course of their duties and grew to provide limited compensation from the state (i.e., the province) to other eligible victims of violent crime. Then, in an effort to encourage the development of such programs in all provinces, the federal government provided financial contributions to provinces and established minimum criteria for compensation programs. The federal support for these programs that benefited some victims coincided with government funding for legal aid programs that benefited some accused persons.

By the early 1980s, all Canadian provinces and territories had criminal injuries compensation programs. These programs varied in terms of eligibility and the scope of financial awards. But by the early 1990s, many provinces and territories were exploring the effectiveness of criminal injuries compensation programs in meeting the needs of victims in general. Although most victims found the financial assistance beneficial, many were ineligible, and many other needs of crime victims did not receive attention. Even more important than statutory reforms were services and assistance for victims of crime, including emergency or crisis response services, shelters, counselling, victim-witness assistance programs, and specialized services for children and for sexual assault survivors.

The current victim-related provisions in both the *Criminal Code* and the *Corrections and Conditional Release Act* are set out below. Keep in mind the distinction between the roles of the federal government and those of the provincial governments. The federal government is responsible for enacting the criminal law, while the provinces are responsible for the enforcement of the criminal law, the prosecution of offences, and the administration of justice, which includes the provision of services to victims. Thus, all provinces and territories have enacted victim-related legislation addressing matters of provincial responsibility. For example, Manitoba, the first province to enact comprehensive victim legislation in 1986, has *The Victim's Bill of Rights* to define a victim's rights and specify the obligations of the police, Crown, and other criminal justice professionals toward victims.

At the federal level, the development of victims' rights in the *Criminal Code* has largely occurred since 1988, even though the *Criminal Code* has included provisions to permit restitution orders since the 1950s. In addition, the significant reforms to Canada's sexual assault laws in the early 1980s recognized that sexual offence complainants needed special considerations. Following Canada's sponsorship of the *U.N. Declaration of Basic Principles of Justice for Victims of Crime* and its endorsement of the *Canadian Statement of Basic Principles of Justice for Victims of Crime,* both the federal and provincial levels of government pursued victim-specific legislative reforms. The description of key *Code* provisions below follows the stages of the criminal process—pretrial, trial, and/or preliminary inquiry, sentencing, and post-sentencing.

CRIMINAL CODE PROVISIONS OF BENEFIT TO VICTIMS

Definition of *Victim*

In the *Criminal Code,* a crime victim has been broadly defined as "the victim of an alleged offence." The definition is non-exhaustive and makes no distinction between primary victims (i.e., the actual victim), secondary victims (i.e., spouse, parent, co-worker, etc.), and indirect victims of crime. It only clarifies that the term may properly be used even when the crime is still alleged, acknowledging that the term "victim" does not presume the guilt of the accused.

Consideration of Victim's Safety in Bail Decisions

When a suspect is arrested, the police determine whether or not the suspect should be detained in custody or released with a promise to appear for trial, sometimes with conditions (commonly referred to as *bail*). In some cases, police make these decisions; in others, a justice of the peace or a judge makes them. Regardless of who makes the decisions, most victims want to know the outcome and seek assurance that their safety has been taken into account in the bail decision.

Amendments to the *Criminal Code* enacted in 1999 require the decision maker to ensure "the safety and security of any victim of or to the offence" at various points in the criminal justice process. Decision makers must take the following factors into consideration:

- The responsible judicial officer (officer in charge, justice of the peace, or judge) must consider the safety and security of the victim.
- Where an accused is released pending trial, the judge must consider whether to make as a condition of bail that the accused abstain from any direct or indirect communication with the victim, as well as any other condition necessary to ensure the safety and security of the victim.
- The judge must consider particular concerns of the victim and highlight them in decisions when imposing special bail conditions, including in firearms prohibitions and criminal harassment measures.

Facilitating Testimony

For some victims and witnesses, participating in the judicial proceedings can be intimidating or even frightening. The *Criminal Code* includes several provisions for assisting victims and reducing their anxiety. Recent amendments to the *Code* proclaimed in January 2006 strengthen these provisions for children under 18 and for other more vulnerable adult victims and witnesses. For example:

- providing discretion for the judge to exclude members of the public from the courtroom when necessary for the proper administration of justice;
- allowing a victim or witness who is under 18 years of age, or who may have difficulty communicating the evidence by reason of mental or physical disability, to testify outside the courtroom or behind a screen or device that would prevent a view of the accused;
- allowing the admission of videotaped testimony of the victim or witness who is under the age of 18 in specified proceedings, including sexual offences;
- permitting a support person to accompany a witness or victim who is disabled or young (under 14 years of age); and
- restricting personal cross-examination of young sexual offence victims and personal violence offence victims (under 18 years of age) by a self-represented accused (e.g., the Crown can apply for an order appointing counsel to conduct the cross-examination of the victim).

The 2006 amendments also make testimonial aids available for all child victims and witnesses under the age of 18 years, on application, unless such aids would interfere with the proper administration of justice.

In addition, other vulnerable victims and witnesses, such as victims of spousal abuse and sexual assault, may apply for a testimonial aid, where the person can show that due to the circumstances (including the nature of the offence and any relationship between the victim/witness and the accused), he or she would not be able to provide a full and candid account without the aid.

Publication Bans

While the general rule is that all criminal proceedings against an accused are held in open court, the *Criminal Code* sets out several exceptions to facilitate victims' or witnesses' participation and to protect their privacy. Sexual offence complainants, young victims, and young witnesses are the primary beneficiaries of these special provisions. A judge can order a publication ban on the identity of a victim or witness and on any information that could disclose that person's identity, if the judge is satisfied that the order is "necessary for the proper administration of justice" (see s.486(4.1)). The victim, witness, or Crown can apply to the court for a publication ban, stating why the order is required. The hearing to determine whether the publication ban should be granted may be held in private.

In addition, a judge must order a publication ban (on application) to protect the identity of all victims of sexual offences and of all witnesses of sexual offences who are under 18 years of age (s.486(3), s.486(4)). In these cases, the judge advises the victim, witness, or Crown prosecutor in advance that they may request this protection.

Provisions for Sexual Offence Victims

In addition to provisions that benefit victims, legislative reforms also recognize the unique nature of sexual assault offences, the trauma suffered by victims of these offences, and the re-victimization often caused by participating in the criminal justice system in such cases. The *Criminal Code* provides a clear and common sense definition of *consent* for the purpose of sexual assault offences. Any nonconsensual sexual activity is a sexual assault; hence, proof of lack of consent is an essential element of the offence. Subsection 273.1(1) defines *consent* as the voluntary agreement of the complainant to engage in the sexual activity in question. Conduct short of a voluntary agreement to engage in sexual activity does not constitute consent as a matter of law. For greater certainty, subsection 273.1(2) sets out specific situations where there is no consent in law.

Section 273.2 limits the scope of the defence of honest belief in consent to sexual activity by providing that the defence is not available where the accused's belief arose from the accused's self-induced intoxication, or where the accused's belief arose from the accused's recklessness or willful blindness, or where the accused failed to take reasonable steps to ascertain whether the complainant was consenting.

Moreover, sections 276 to 276.5 of the *Criminal Code* protect the complainant from undue interrogation about the complainant's other sexual activity. The *Code* makes it clear that evidence that a complainant has engaged in sexual activity with others is not admissible to suggest that the victim was more likely to have consented to the sexual activity that is the subject matter of the current charge. The provisions restrict the admissibility of evidence to specific instances of sexual activity—those relevant to an issue at trial—and to evidence that has "significant probative value which is not substantially outweighed by the danger of prejudice to the administration of justice." The judge is required to consider a range of factors set out in the *Code* in making this determination. The *Code* also sets out the procedure to be followed and includes provisions to safeguard the victim's privacy, including provisions for an *in camera* (closed) hearing, non-compellability of the victim at the hearing, and a publication ban on the proceedings. These provisions are sometimes referred to as the *rape shield* laws.

Finally, sections 278.1 to 278.9 of the *Code* protect the sexual offence victim and witnesses from requests for personal records. These provisions place the onus on the accused to establish that the records sought are likely to be relevant to an issue at trial. In addition, the trial judge is required to carefully scrutinize applications and make a decision in accordance with a two-part process that balances consideration of both the accused's rights to a defence and the victim's rights to privacy and equality. The procedure is also set out in the *Code* and includes safeguards for the victim's privacy, including an *in camera* hearing, non-compellability of the victim at the hearing, a publication ban on the proceedings and the contents of the application, editing of the records (where ordered to be produced) to delete irrelevant personal information, and the imposition of other appropriate conditions.

Sentencing

Reforms to the sentencing provisions of the *Criminal Code* enacted in 1996 defined the purposes and principles of sentencing. Judges are directed to consider a number of objectives when sentencing offenders. Two of these are directly relevant to the interests of victims:

- to provide reparations for harm done to victims or to the community; and
- to promote a sense of responsibility in offenders and acknowledgement of the harm done to victims and to the community.

Victim Impact Statements:

Although there are only two parties in a sentencing hearing—the offender, represented by defence counsel, and the state, represented by the Crown—the victim of the crime nevertheless has a role to play. Most countries permit crime victims to submit a statement to the court detailing the impact that the crime has had upon their lives. Some American states go even further and allow victims to make recommendations to the court about specific sentences. This is not permitted in Canada.

In 1988, the *Criminal Code* was amended to permit the court to consider *victim impact statements* (VISs); since 1995, the *Code* requires the court to consider a VIS at the time of sentencing. The VIS describes the harm done to or loss suffered by the victim of the offence. The form of the statement must be in accordance with procedures established by a victim impact statement program designated by the lieutenant governor in council of the province. The 1999 amendments to the *Criminal Code* do the following to improve the usefulness of VISs:

- ensure that the victim is permitted to read a VIS at the time of sentencing if he or she wishes to do so;
- require the judge to ask, before imposing sentence, whether the victim has been informed of the opportunity to prepare a victim impact statement;
- authorize adjournments to permit a victim to prepare a statement or to submit other evidence to the court about the impact of the crime;
- require that victim impact statements be considered by courts and review boards following a verdict of not criminally responsible on account of mental disorder; and
- clarify that oral or written information may be provided by a victim at any proceedings to determine whether an offender sentenced to life in prison should have an earlier parole eligibility date (s.745.6 hearings).

Victim Surcharge:

A *victim surcharge* is an additional financial penalty automatically imposed on offenders at the time of sentencing (unless the accused seeks an exception due to undue hardship). It is collected and retained by the provincial and territorial governments and used to help fund programs, services, and assistance to victims of crime within their jurisdiction. The victim surcharge was included in the 1988 amendments to the *Criminal Code* and proclaimed in 1989, along with regulations setting out the applicable amount. Amendments in 1999 fixed the amount of the surcharge and provided for automatic imposition upon conviction. The surcharge is 15 percent of any fine imposed on the offender. If no fine is imposed, the surcharge is $50 in the case of an offence punishable by summary conviction and $100 in the case of an offence punishable by indictment; or a higher surcharge is permissible at the discretion of the judge in appropriate circumstances.

Restitution:

The court may order the offender to pay restitution in addition to any other sentence imposed on the offender. Restitution may be ordered by the court on its own motion or on application by the Crown or victim to cover easily ascertainable monetary damages, including those resulting from bodily injury (but not for pain and suffering). However, there are no criminal enforcement provisions; enforcement of restitution is the victim's responsibility. The victim may file the restitution order as if it were a judgment in civil proceedings and pursue civil remedies.

Victims and the Correctional System

The *Corrections and Conditional Release Act (CCRA)* governs Correctional Service Canada (CSC), which is responsible for supervising offenders sentenced to more than two years in custody, and the National Parole Board (NPB), which determines whether to release offenders into the community. This act contains specific provisions authorizing the release of some offender-related information to victims who register with CSC and request information.

Anyone can request publicly available information, such as a description of the offence for which an offender was convicted, the sentence length, and eligibility dates for temporary absences, day parole, or full parole. But victims of crime, as defined in the *CCRA,* may register and request additional information that may include the penitentiary where the offender is serving the sentence; the date of a Parole Board hearing; the nature of the conditions attached to any work release, parole, statutory release, or temporary absences; as well as whether the offender is in custody. Victims may request ongoing information and must ensure that CSC and the NPB have their current address for this purpose.

Victims may also request information from CSC and the NPB. Victim liaison officers within CSC generally receive requests for information from victims and provide information to them. Victims may request to attend Parole Board hearings as observers and may also have access to the decision registry of the NPB. Victims may prepare and submit victim impact statements describing the physical, emotional, and financial impact of the offence upon them to the Parole Board. NPB policy permits victims to read or otherwise present the victim impact statement at the hearing.

Victims and Life Sentences

Offenders convicted of murder are sentenced to imprisonment for life; however, most become eligible for parole after serving part of their sentence. In many cases, victims and/or their families want to know when the offender becomes eligible for parole or has a parole hearing. Most prisoners serving life sentences with no parole for at least 15 years are eligible to apply for a jury review of their parole eligibility date. The provision in the *Code* that permits such an application is sometimes referred to as the *faint hope clause.* Often the families of murder victims express a desire to know when the offender in their case makes an application under this provision.

To ensure that information is provided to victims about life sentences, the *Criminal Code* requires a judge to state, for the record and for the benefit of surviving victims, that an offender convicted of murder who has received a life sentence may apply for a reduction in the waiting period before his or her parole application may be made. In addition, at proceedings to determine whether an offender should have his or her parole ineligibility period reduced (s.745.6 or *faint hope clause* hearings), oral or written information may be provided by the victim.

RESEARCH ON VICTIMS IN THE CRIMINAL JUSTICE SYSTEM

Legislative reform has addressed some victim needs, and while further reforms are necessary, such reforms should be supported by research that examines both the effectiveness of the existing legislation and the broader needs of victims. An exhaustive review of all research relating to victims of crime is beyond the scope of this chapter; however, a selection of key issues is presented below.

Victim Needs

The needs of crime victims range from the general to the specific and may depend on the type of victimization experienced and the characteristics of the individual victim. Victims identify financial needs, emotional needs, practical needs, and needs related to personal safety and security to varying degrees and in varying circumstances. However, research indicates that the need for information is one of the most critical and universal needs expressed by victims of crime (e.g., Wemmers, 2002; Fattah, 1997). For example, faced with a very unfamiliar and complex criminal justice process, victims frequently do not know how to navigate the system. Accused persons have defence lawyers who ensure that defendants know the details of the case; but while many victims may mistakenly believe the Crown attorney is their personal lawyer, the Crown acts on behalf of the state, not the victim. Victims should not have to hire their own lawyers to protect their interests or assist them as the case proceeds through the system. However, as victims do not have a lawyer, they must rely on criminal justice system officials to provide appropriate information about how their case is proceeding and progressing.

Plea Negotiations

Plea negotiations (or plea bargains) may not seem like a topic related to victims; however, the practice of such negotiations has a significant impact on crime victims. *Plea bargaining* is defined as a "negotiation between the Crown prosecutor, defence counsel, and the accused to determine which charge will be laid or what sentence will be recommended. Typically, this negotiation is undertaken in an effort to have the accused plead guilty and avoid the need for a trial" (Drislane and Parkinson, 2005, p. 106). Plea bargaining is important since about 90 percent of criminal cases are resolved through guilty pleas, many of which are the direct outcome of plea negotiations between Crown and defence (Verdun-Jones and Tijerino, 2002). But as Verdun-Jones and Tijerino (2002) note, a victim's role in plea bargaining in Canada is virtually nonexistent, despite the fact that the results of a plea bargain arrangement may have direct consequences for the victim. Verdun-Jones and Tijerino explain that although plea negotiations play an integral role in the criminal justice process in Canada, they in fact "have no formal legal status and are not subject to direct judicial regulation" (p. 5).

A victim's exclusion from plea bargaining may well affect his or her perception of the criminal justice process. Agreements made between the Crown and the defence without the input or, at a minimum, the knowledge of the concerned crime victim may contribute directly to a victim's dissatisfaction with the criminal justice system. On the other hand, a guilty plea avoids the need for victims to participate in trial proceedings, an activity that some crime victims may find traumatizing.

In 1987, the Canadian Sentencing Commission made several recommendations related to the issue of plea negotiations, a number of which address victim involvement in the process; however, to date, none of these recommendations have been implemented (Verdun-Jones and Tijerino, 2002). The recommendations included simple steps such as informing victims of the plea negotiation before it takes place, as well as representing a victim's views via the Crown at the time of the plea negotiation. Both these recommendations may serve to satisfy the wishes of many crime victims regarding plea bargaining (Verdun-Jones and Tijerino, 2002).

Victim Impact Statements

A 2001 exploratory study conducted by Meredith and Paquette for the PCVI examined victims' experiences with VISs. This study held six focus groups in six Canadian provinces. Although each focus group was small (thereby limiting generalization of the findings), the study raised several important issues about victim impact statements and the need for further exploration of this provision. A summary of the report notes that "participants' perceptions of what victim impact statements are supposed to accomplish were twofold. The first perceived goal was that the statements should allow victims to have a say in the sentencing process by presenting to the court how the crime has affected their lives" (2001, p. 6). The second perceived goal was to "have an effect on the sentence actually imposed in their cases" (p. 6). The latest research into victim impact statements revealed that another important reason for submitting a VIS was to make the offender understand the effect of the crime (Prairie Research Associates, 2006).

Many of the participants in the Meredith and Paquette study acknowledged "that judges must take into account a number of factors in reaching their decisions on sentencing," and some participants reported "a cathartic effect from preparing their statements" (p. 6). Most participants were aware of their right to read their statements aloud (there was strong support among participants for this right); and participants in five of the six groups were generally positive about their experiences with victim impact statements, "despite frequent doubt that these statements had any significant effect on the sentences imposed" (p. 10).

The following were cited as benefits of the process of completing and submitting a VIS:

- It allows victims to express their anger.
- It allows victims to confront the accused in a safe environment.
- It enables victims to include in their statements information that they were prevented from providing in their testimony.
- It allows victims to bring to the court's attention the total impact of the offence regardless of the specific charges.
- Some offenders, as a result of hearing the victim impact statement, may come to think more seriously about the harm they have done (p. 10).

Significantly, in one of the five groups, almost all of the participants of that group expressed dissatisfaction with their experiences of completing a victim impact statement. In analyzing this response, the summary report of the study noted: "Some group participants reported considerable frustration with the court process when sentences were imposed that they perceived to have been negotiated prior to submission of their VISs. In these cases, they were confident that no account had been taken of their experiences as victims, and resented the system's seeming disregard for the effort which went into preparing their VISs" (p. 12).

Further exploration and research is needed to define the intended purpose and actual use of VIS, and to determine the overall satisfaction of victims, offenders, and criminal justice professionals with VISs (see Roberts, 2003, for a review of research on victim impact statements at sentencing).

CONCLUSION

The criminal justice system needs to consider justice proceedings from the perspective of the victim. While the role that crime victims play in this system is not as clear as those of other participants in the criminal justice process, crime victims need to be considered. Although the involvement of the victim in the justice system has received increased attention in both the research literature and in policy and legislation, more work remains. Further exploration of the needs and concerns of victims is necessary, as are continuing efforts to evaluate the benefits of the progress already made (or initiatives already taken) to improve the criminal justice system with respect to victims of crime.

DISCUSSION QUESTIONS

1. *Do you think that the legislative provisions described in the chapter provide an adequate level of involvement for victims, or should the role of the victim be further expanded?*

2. *Some victims' rights advocates suggest that crime victims should be able to include a recommendation about the sentence in their victim impact statement. Others respond that victims should not have this right since it would lead to more variability in sentencing. What do you think?*

FURTHER READINGS

Barrett, Joan M. 2000. *Balancing Charter Interests: Victims' Rights and Third Party Remedies*. Toronto: Carswell.

Prairie Research Associates. 2006. *Multi-site Survey of Victims of Crime and Criminal Justice Professionals across Canada*. Ottawa: Department of Justice Canada, Policy Centre for Victim Issues.

Roach, K. 1999. *Due Process and Victims' Rights: The New Law and Politics of Criminal Justice*. Toronto: University of Toronto Press.

REFERENCES

Canadian Sentencing Commission. 1987. *Sentencing Reform: A Canadian Approach*. Ottawa: Supply and Services Canada.

Drislane, R., and Parkinson, G. 2005. *Nelson Criminology Dictionary*. Toronto: Thomson Nelson Canada Limited.

Fattah, E.A. 1997. From crime policy to victim policy: The need for a fundamental policy change. In M. McShane and F.P. Williams III (Eds.), *Criminal Justice: Contemporary Literature in Theory and Practice*. New York and London: Garland Publishing, Inc.

Meredith, C., and Paquette, C. 2001. *Summary Report on Victim Impact Statement Focus Groups*. Victims of Crime Research Series. Ottawa: Department of Justice Canada.

Prairie Research Associates. 2006. *Multi-site Survey of Victims of Crime and Criminal Justice Professionals across Canada*. Ottawa: Department of Justice Canada, Policy Centre for Victim Issues.

Roberts, J.V. 2003. Victim impact statements and the sentencing process: Recent developments and research findings. *Criminal Law Quarterly*, 47: 365–396.

Verdun-Jones, S., and Tijerino, A. 2002. *Victim Participation in the Plea Negotiation Process in Canada: A Review of the Literature and Four Models for Law Reform*. Report for the Policy Centre for Victim Issues. Ottawa: Department of Justice Canada.

ENDNOTES

[1] The views expressed in this chapter are those of the authors and do not necessarily represent those of the organizations with which they are affiliated.

CHAPTER 23

Sex Offender Registries: Sign Here Please, and Don't Forget to Stay in Touch

INTRODUCTION

Sex offenders provoke more concern among members of the public than any other category of offender. This is particularly true for the worst kinds of offending—for example when the crime is murder and the victim a child. When terrible crimes such as these occur, they attract intense media attention, and politicians seek to make changes to the criminal justice system to ensure that society is adequately protected. Of the reforms launched in recent years, few have attracted as much attention as the concept of sex offender registries. The Canadian criminal justice system now has sex offender registries at the federal and provincial levels.

In this chapter, Mary Campbell, a correctional policy expert, describes the sex offender registries that have been created in Canada within the past few years.

Sex Offender Registries: Sign Here Please, and Don't Forget to Stay in Touch
Mary E. Campbell of the Ontario Bar

Great public and political concern about sex offenders has resulted in several policies designed to reduce the risk to society. One such policy is the creation of a database of known sex offenders so that authorities know where these ex-offenders are living. Prior to the mid-1980s, sex offender registries were a largely unknown concept in Canada and abroad—a handful of American states had adopted registration schemes in the 1960s but with little fanfare (e.g., California 1944, Nevada 1961, Ohio 1963, and Alabama 1967). Before the registry began, sex offenders were tried and sentenced, completed their sentences, and then resumed some degree of anonymity in their daily lives. But the offender's criminal record remained in existence even without the registry, subject to any later pardon or form of executive clemency. In Canada, criminal records are maintained in the Canadian Police Information Centre (CPIC), an electronic database that can be accessed only by police for investigative purposes or for court proceedings. In a very real sense, CPIC has functioned as a "registry" of all criminal records.

However, in the early 1990s, three events occurred, one in Canada and two in the United States, that changed the ways in which the public thought about the reintegration of sex offenders into the community. The Canadian event was the tragic abduction and murder of a young boy named Christopher Stephenson. He was lured away from a shopping centre, sexually assaulted, and murdered by Joseph Fredericks, a known sex offender who had spent most of his life bouncing back and forth between the mental health and criminal justice systems. At the time of the murder, Fredericks was on a "registry": he had been released from penitentiary under the form of conditional release then known as *mandatory supervision* (now called *statutory release*) and was under a requirement to report to the police and to a parole supervisor. Thus, Fredericks was effectively on two "registries": CPIC (by virtue of having a criminal record) and the rosters of both Correctional Service Canada (CSC) and the National Parole Board (by virtue of being a conditionally released inmate). But one afternoon, he headed to the mall and committed his terrible crime. The community and the country were understandably outraged.

At the same time that the Coroner's Inquest into the death of Christopher Stephenson was unfolding in Ontario, two other pivotal events occurred. The first was the 1990 Washington State passage of several highly publicized reforms to the management of sex offenders, including a sex offender registry. The other was the creation of a similar registry in 1994 in New Jersey, following the death of young Megan Kanka at the hands of a convicted sex offender who had been living next door to the victim at the time of the crime. Taken together, these events contributed to growing public concern about the problem of sex offenders in North America. There was enormous pressure in Canada to strengthen Canadian laws controlling sex offenders and to adopt the American responses, including registries.

FEDERAL ACTION

The Canadian response to sexual offenders followed the American response; however, the American and Canadian criminal justice systems have two key differences.

The first, as noted above, is the existence of CPIC in Canada, which has no national counterpart in the United States. Thus, in effect, Canada has been operating a national "registry" of all convicted offenders since 1962. Any police officer can enter an individual's name and obtain a record of all convictions, not just sex offences. Confirmation of the match can be made through fingerprints.

The other key distinction is the existence (since 1949) of Canadian legislation that allows for the indefinite (or lifetime) incarceration of offenders who are deemed a serious risk to society. These provisions, now known as the Dangerous Offender (DO) sections of the *Criminal Code,* allow courts at the time of sentencing to order the indefinite incarceration of high-risk offenders if the case meets certain criteria. The vast majority of DO detainees are sex offenders. Washington State had no such legislation when it adopted its legislative measures in 1990 to control sex offenders; offenders there could be sentenced only to a fixed term of imprisonment.

Thus, while there was significant pressure to adopt the American reforms, an examination of the Canadian system indicated that there was less need to do so. Nonetheless, federal, provincial, and territorial ministers responsible for criminal justice asked their officials to examine ways in which the Canadian system could be improved. In 1993, an interdepartmental working group of officials from the justice and health departments and the Solicitor General's office undertook an extensive review of issues relating to child sexual abuse. A federal/provincial/territorial working group on high-risk offenders formed the same year developed a 16-point action plan. Recommendations from these two groups resulted in the following reforms:

- the development of a "screening system" (CPIC checks) for use by voluntary sector agencies and other groups working with children, to better screen potential volunteers and employees who would be working with children;
- the creation of a *Long-Term Offender* designation in the *Criminal Code* to allow postsentence community supervision of sex offenders for up to 10 years, recognizing that sex offender recidivism tends to occur over longer periods of time than non-sex offending;
- amendments to the Dangerous Offender provisions to streamline and focus the proceedings; and
- the creation of a new *peace bond* in s. 810.1 of the *Criminal Code,* to permit supervision of persons suspected of being at risk to commit a sex offence against a child.

At this time, the specific issue of creating a sex offender registry along the lines of the American models was researched, reviewed, and rejected.

PROVINCIAL REGISTRIES

The public and political pressure to create a national sex offender registry did not disappear with the 1993 reforms. By 2001, six provinces had created or announced their intention to create a registry. The registries were largely directed at sex offenders, although in at least one region the registry was aimed at any "high-risk offenders." However, even among those aimed exclusively at sex offenders, the proposals were not entirely consistent in their interpretations of this term.

Ontario was the only province to fully operationalize a registry system. *Christopher's Law*, named after Christopher Stephenson, came in force in Ontario on April 23, 2001. The preamble to the act stated its purpose:

> The people of Ontario believe that there is a need to ensure the safety and
> security of all persons in Ontario and that police forces require access to
> information about the whereabouts of sex offenders in order to assist them
> in the important work of maintaining community safety. The people of
> Ontario further believe that a registry of sex offenders will provide the infor-
> mation and investigative tools that their police forces require in order to
> prevent and solve crimes of a sexual nature.

The act requires any person living in Ontario who has been convicted of a specified sex offence to register with local police. Other persons required to register are those found guilty of such an offence but given an absolute or conditional discharge, and those persons charged but found not criminally responsible on account of mental disorder.

According to new legislation, offenders have 15 days in which to register after moving to the province, completing their custodial sentence, or leaving their final court appearance if it results in a non-custodial disposition. However, there is no obligation in the act for police, courts, or corrections officials to notify offenders of the registration requirement. But failure to register (without lawful excuse) is punishable on first offence by a fine of up to $25,000 and/or imprisonment for up to one year; and on second or subsequent offence by a fine of up to $25,000 and/or imprisonment for up to two years less a day. Depending on the nature of the "registrable offence," the required registration period is either 10 years or life. Re-registration is required annually or upon moving. Information in the registry is intended primarily for police use but can be used as the basis for public notification of the presence of a sex offender in the community. Anecdotal reports so far indicate a high uptake in initial registration.

In April 2001, British Columbia passed the *Sex Offender Registry Act* just prior to dissolution of the legislature for an election. The new government indicated its intention to pursue similar legislation; but as of the fall of 2002, it had not done so. The April 2001 legislation was intended to proceed in two phases. Phase One was to compile in one database information from courts and corrections databases about sex offenders. Phase Two was to include mandatory registration by convicted sex offenders—the same coverage as Ontario but also extended to persons with outstanding charges for sex offences, persons convicted by a court outside Canada, and young offenders. The list of sex offences was also broader than Ontario's list, including nonsexual offences with a sexual motive or nature, such as some kinds of break and enter, trespassing at night, criminal harassment, and kidnapping and forcible confinement. The objectives of the act were summarized in s. 3, which stated that the minister "may establish a sex offender registry for the purposes of (a) law enforcement, (b) crime prevention, and (c) public safety."

Since then, Alberta also announced its intention to create a registry, although references were to a somewhat ambiguous "high-risk offender" registry as well as to a "pedophile registry." On May 15, 2001, the premier announced that a registry of convicted offenders would be established "if the concept is deemed feasible following a two-week review" by the provincial Solicitor General. As with many other registries, the impetus for Alberta's declaration came from a case where a young girl had been murdered. However, in this case, the person charged was a family friend with no reported record of sexual offences. The utility of a sex offender registry in such a case would have therefore been somewhat unclear.

The two weeks then passed with no further announcement; but Aberta's continuing interest in the matter was evidenced by a May 31, 2001, press release from a meeting of Western premiers:

> Premiers expressed concern about violent sexual offenders. They highlighted the importance of providing the police with the tools they need to protect our communities—and particularly our children—from high-risk sex offenders. They noted that since sexual offenders often move, there is a need to keep track of their movements. Premiers agreed that a national sex offender registry would be the most effective solution to this problem. In the absence of a federal commitment to a national registry, Premiers agreed that provinces and territories should take action on this matter.

Alberta did not ultimately create a sex offender registry but instead created a "high-risk offender Web page." The Solicitor General may post the photograph of and personal information about offenders who have completed their sentence but are considered a risk of significant harm to the public. The offender is not afforded any hearing or other opportunity to contest the notification. The information may remain on the Web site indefinitely, although offenders may apply after one year to have it removed, if they are able to demonstrate they are no longer a threat to the community.

In addition to Ontario and the western provinces, Nova Scotia has also signaled its interest in creating a registry. By the time federal, provincial, and territorial justice ministers met in September 2001 at their annual meeting, there was even more consensus among the provinces and territories that a national registry was needed, even though there was less than complete agreement on the precise details.

OTHER JURISDICTIONS

Similar pressure to create registries had peaked a few years earlier in the United States. Only eight states had registration schemes in the mid-1980s; but by 1998, all states had sex offender registry legislation (Travis, 2002). The *Jacob Wetterling Crimes Against Children and Sexually Violent Offender Registration Program* (*Wetterling Act*) established the minimum national standards for registration and community notification, allowing states the freedom to tailor particular requirements. But it is important to examine the details of this apparent unanimous support across the country. Travis (2002) explains: "the 1994 *Crime Act* required each state to enact a sex offender registration law within 3 years or lose 10 percent of its federal funding for criminal justice programs" (p. 24). Consequently, it is difficult to know how many states adopted registry legislation out of a firm belief in its effectiveness or out of fear of losing funding.

The United Kingdom also enacted sex offender registration in 1997. Persons convicted of specified sex offences are required to register for a period of time linked to the sentence length. While the registry is not proactively available for public access, police have the authority to use the information from the registry to issue public warnings that a particular sex offender is living in a particular neighbourhood. Within a year of the legislation coming into force, 95 percent of those required to register had done so (Plotnikoff and Woolfson, 2000). By the time of the first evaluation in 2000, this already high rate was even higher, with only 4 percent of the 8,600 individuals required to register being in noncompliance.

NATIONAL CANADIAN SEX OFFENDER REGISTRY

In the fall of 2002, the Canadian federal government announced its intention to create a national sex offender registry, based in CPIC and administered and enforced locally by police. When the final bill was proclaimed law on December 15, 2004, the registry was made available only to police in order to provide a rapid tool to investigate sex offences by identifying possible suspects known to reside near the offence occurrence. Like sex offender registries elsewhere, the federal registry is an offence-based system with no assessment of individual risk. Sex offences that may trigger a registration order are listed in law. After an offender is convicted of one of the specified offences, the Crown attorney can apply to the court for a registration order.

The length of the registration is tied to the maximum penalty available for the offence, with up to lifetime registration where the offence carries a maximum of life or the offender has a prior sex offence. Offenders must reregister annually while the order is in force or whenever they change address.

Offenders are able to apply for a judicial review at set times during the order if they wish to argue that it should be lifted. It is an offence to fail to register after an order has been issued. It is also an offence for anyone to disclose information from the registry for any purpose other than a police investigation.

RESEARCH ON THE EFFECTIVENESS OF SEX OFFENDER REGISTRIES

Assessing the usefulness of registries requires knowing their differences in scope and purpose. These differences include the types of offenders who must register, the process for registration, and the enforcement mechanisms. The purposes also vary and may include the following: improved crime prevention through increased tracking of offenders in the community, including using the registration information as a basis for community notification of offenders' whereabouts; more efficient criminal investigation when a crime has occurred; and (in theory at least) a deterrent effect that arises from the fact that offenders know that registration will be a consequence of committing certain crimes.

To date, the research has shown a fairly high rate of initial compliance in registering in a new program. However, the evidence also reveals that there is little systematic follow-up to verify addresses and other particulars and that enforcement is almost entirely reactive. There is only limited and anecdotal evidence of crime prevention or investigation benefits. The costs of sex offender registries have generally not been tracked, as registries have usually been implemented within existing resources. This lack of tracking and updating is often cited as the reason for failures in implementing adequate verification, monitoring, or enforcement measures (Plotnikoff and Woolfson, 2000). As a result, high rates of initial compliance with registration requirements do not necessarily mean that the program is effective.

CONCLUSION

Sex offender registries are the latest in a series of recent initiatives aimed at controlling the behaviour of certain categories of offenders. While popular with many groups, their effectiveness is not yet clear from evaluations done to date, nor is their legal viability fully assessed by the courts (both the Ontario and the national Canadian registries are still before the courts and will almost certainly find their way to the Supreme Court of Canada). In determining effectiveness, it is important to bear in mind distinct differences among the various registry models and the purposes behind them. Some are narrowly cast, with access only by police and only for quickly investigating a suspected crime. Others, particularly those that are disclosed to the public, are ostensibly oriented toward crime prevention. Moreover, considerations of effectiveness might also take into account whether treatment is provided to the registrant or whether only surveillance is provided.

Questions of fairness and legal rights are also raised in the different models, since some operate automatically upon conviction for specified sex offences while others provide a court hearing. These issues are important on their own; but they are also important because they are linked to the question of risk in individual cases: few registries allow for an assessment of the current dangerousness of the individual offender, but rather presume a level of risk based on the offence that was committed.

Finally, sex offender registries should be evaluated as one element in a continuum of responses that could be made to the problem of sex offenders. The effectiveness and legality of registries should ultimately be assessed not only on their own merits but also in comparison to other actions that could be taken to prevent and respond to sex offending. Comprehensive, research-based strategies may provide the best means of responding to public concerns about these offenders.

DISCUSSION QUESTIONS

1. *In your opinion, are sex offender registries a good idea or not? Do you think they are a reasonable response to the problem of sex offenders?*
2. *Some American states permit members of the public to access information about someone's criminal record from the criminal record database. What problems can you see arising from this expanded access to the database?*

FURTHER READINGS

Coflin, J. 2001. *Sex Offender Registration Programs—A Status Report*. Ottawa: Solicitor General Canada.

Jenkins, P. 1998. *Moral Panic: Changing Concepts of the Child Molester in Modern America*. New Haven, CT: Yale University Press.

Petrunik, M. 2002. Managing unacceptable risk: Sex offenders, community response, and social policy in the United States and Canada. *International Journal of Offender Therapy and Comparative Criminology*, 46: 483–512.

Petrunik, M. 2003 (in press). The hare and the tortoise: Dangerousness and sex offender policy in the United States and Canada. *Canadian Journal of Criminology and Criminal Justice*, 45: 43–72.

REFERENCES

Statutes

Sex Offender Information Registration Act, S.C. 2004, c. 10.

An Act in Memory of Christopher Stephenson, to Establish and Maintain a Registry of Sex Offenders to Protect Children and Communities ("Christopher's Law") S.O., Ch. 1, 2000.

Jacob Wetterling Crimes Against Children and Sexually Violent Offender Registration Program (Wetterling Act) 42 U.S.C. 14071 (1994 and Supp. V 1999).

Sex Offenders Act 1997 (U.K.), 1997, c. 51.

Cases

Connecticut Department of Public Safety et al. v. John Doe et al., 538 U.S. ___
(2003).
Smith et al. v. John Doe et al., 538 U.S. ___ (2003).

Texts

Plotnikoff, J., and Woolfson, R. 2000. *Where Are They Now? An Evaluation of
Sex Offender Registration in England and Wales,* Police Research Series,
Paper 126. London: Home Office.
Travis, J. 2002. Invisible punishment: An instrument of social exclusion. In
M. Mauer and M. Chesney-Lind (Eds.), *Invisible Punishment: The Collat-
eral Consequences of Mass Imprisonment.* New York: The New Press.

CHAPTER 24
Restorative Justice in Canada

INTRODUCTION

The traditional model of criminal justice in Canada is largely *retributive* in nature; *retributive justice* focuses on punishing offenders in proportion to the seriousness of their crimes. But an alternative model, called *restorative justice*, is becoming popular in many countries. Under a restorative justice model, the goal is not to punish offenders but rather to seek reconciliation between the offender and the victim and to restore the offender to the community. The emphasis is on achieving some tangible benefit for the victim rather than simply punishing the offender. The restorative response to crime is therefore said to be more victim-oriented than the conventional criminal justice system, in which victims' interests are often neglected.

In this chapter, Liz Elliott discusses the nature of restorative justice and describes some specific restorative justice programs.

Restorative Justice in Canada
Liz Elliott, Simon Fraser University

Restorative justice is a concept with several different meanings. One common perspective is that restorative justice is a program, one that diverts non-violent, first-time lawbreakers from jail to community-based measures. However, this kind of restorative justice is based on the same assumptions as those of the retributive justice system and is invariably little more than an "add-on" program to that system. Practitioners who begin with this understanding of restorative justice may eventually develop an appreciation for the more inclusive and egalitarian processes of these programs. But without a shift in our framework of understanding crime itself, we lose the opportunity to develop new ways of understanding problems and developing solutions.

Howard Zehr, one of the leaders of the late twentieth-century restorative justice movement, suggests: "The framework: it makes a difference. How do we interpret what has happened? What factors are relevant? What responses are possible and appropriate? The lens we look through determines how we frame both the problem and the "solution."[1] Without this change of lens, the appreciation of valuable aspects of restorative processes remains limited to the realm of conventional criminal justice systems.

In this chapter, I make a case for a vision of restorative justice based on such a paradigm shift. As a result, restorative justice can be visualized through the lenses of peacemaking and social justice. I also provide an overview of restorative process models found in current practice.

RESTORATIVE JUSTICE AS PEACEMAKING

When seen through the retributive lens, justice focuses on identifying which laws have been broken, proving who the perpetrators are, and then punishing them according to the seriousness of the crimes. The "justice as scales" metaphor conveys the idea of balancing, equalizing, and measuring. From this perspective, equality in the relationship between the parties (e.g., victim, accused, Crown, legal counsel) affected by a crime is generally sought through punishment (Llewellyn and Howse, 1999). Punishment "intends inflicting pain, suffering or loss" (Haan, 1990, p. 112) on an offender; its purpose in inflicting harm on the offender is to "equalize" the harm suffered by the victim. Justice is achieved through the finding of guilt, the imposition of a proportionate sentence, and its subsequent implementation.

This justice system at the beginning of twenty-first-century Canada revolves around images of police, courtrooms and lawyers, jails and prisons, and parole officers. Justice is the domain of professionals and institutions acting on behalf of the people involved in the conflict, criminal or otherwise. This institutionalization of justice appears to have increased the dependency of citizens on professionals to solve conflicts, undermining the ability of communities to handle their own personal and local problems.

But justice viewed through a restorative lens replaces the metaphorical image of the scales of retributive justice with the image of a circle. Through the restorative lens, justice begins with a focus on harms suffered by victims, then attends meaningfully to the needs of all the affected parties, and tries to restore and/or build relationships among the parties themselves, their families/friends, and the community at large. There is no definable "end" or destination in a circle, just as there is no definable beginning. Restorative justice can be understood as an ongoing process of righting relationships damaged by the harm and involves the pursuit of peaceful relations.

The implications of "peace as practice" are significant in restorative justice. The idea that "process is product" means that restorative justice practices need to *emulate* peaceful ways of resolving conflict. Recently, Howard Zehr has described restorative justice as "a kind of coherent value system that gives us a vision of the good, how we want to be together" (in Cobden and Harley, 2004, p. 268). Consequently, seasoned practitioners of restorative justice speak of *values-based processes*, where the means used to address conflicts embody the guiding values of the community at large. Examples of typical community values are respect, equality, inclusion, caring, and honesty; thus, restorative justice programs upholding these values develop processes for handling conflicts that are respectful of every participant, treat each equally, are inclusive of all relevant interests, care for everyone, and permit the honest expression of each participant's truth and needs.

The idea of criminal justice as peacemaking reflects but is not restricted to traditional Aboriginal ways of dispute resolution. Many Aboriginal communities have started to reclaim their traditional ways of dealing with offenders.[2] Circle processes and an attention to harm-doing that includes participation of offender, victim, and community are evident in the procedures used by the jurisdictions of Hollow Water, Manitoba,[3] and Carcross, Yukon Territory.

Restorative justice proponents who operate from a peacemaking perspective often find themselves in a similar position to Aboriginal people whose traditional ways conflict with the formal legal system. Familiarity with the conventional criminal justice system and the tendency to include some restorative justice programs within that system make the task of developing values-based restorative processes a challenging one. Moreover, values-based restorative justice needs to avoid the fate of the many alternatives to incarceration developed in the 1980s, all of which simply helped to widen the formal criminal justice system. Restorative justice approaches can still operate within the formal system, as long as the integrity of the processes is not compromised by conventional expectations.

RESTORATIVE JUSTICE AS SOCIAL JUSTICE

Criminological theory and research from the beginning of the 1900s has attempted to define the factors that contribute to harm-producing behaviours. The factors affecting criminal actions have been considered historically by theorists such as Sutherland (1947) and Hirshi (1969), who spoke of the influence of social learning, labelling, and basic social arrangements (such as the family). More recently, Canada has improved crime prevention through the reduction of opportunities[4] and through social development.[5] Prevention is considered to be in the best interest of the individual, the community, and the larger society.

However, the capacity of the criminal justice system to prevent crime is limited. Classical theory holds that people will be deterred from committing crimes by the fear and anticipation of punishment.[6] For this deterrent effect to occur, however, the punishment must be swift and certain. In reality, sentences are imposed long after the crime was committed, and there is a considerable amount of uncertainty regarding the nature of the sentence that will be imposed. The problem of trial delays is also a common criticism of the legal system. Apart from the general difficulty in enumerating how many people are, in fact, deterred from crimes, there is also the difficulty of demonstrating exactly what prevents people from committing crimes—the fear of punishment or their own values. The only certain crime prevention function of the criminal justice system is the incapacitation of detected offenders for the duration of their incarceration; but even this notion is undermined by the argument that the prison experience itself often exacerbates criminal behaviour.[7]

Positivist[8] theories consider factors that increase individual conditions favourable to crime. While the Canadian legal system begins with classical school assumptions, it also incorporates positivist ideas when it determines mitigating and exacerbating factors during sentencing, factors that are later revisited by the corrections system in "treatment" programs. However, a justice system that is only mandated to intervene *after* the commission of crimes is unlikely to prevent many crimes. Moreover, since most crime prevention through social development is likely to occur *outside* of the criminal justice system, these programs generally do not receive criminal justice funding. For example, the connections between criminal justice, public schools, the family, and social welfare are often obscured by discrete departmental mandates that inhibit collaboration of agencies towards crime prevention. Particularly troubling is the focus on the needs of the offender only, with minimal attention to the needs of the victim.[9]

In restorative justice processes, the obligations and needs of both the offender and the victim are given full attention. The active involvement of community members—as supporters of both victims and offenders, as professionals, or as interested parties—extends the understanding of these obligations and needs, case after case, into the community itself. The *experience* of restorative values can further shift the community culture. The community has its own needs as well, primarily the need for a restored sense of safety (Sharpe, 1998). As an important source of informal social controls, the community also plays a key role in crime prevention (Clear and Karp, 1999, pp. 37–57). Restorative processes focus on what is not working in the community, creating opportunities for its members to remedy specific deficits and to continue supporting certain community assets. These processes can also help to build the capacity of individual members to address conflicts in peaceful ways without the intervention (and expense) of large governing institutions.

By focusing on needs, restorative justice increases community awareness of its social problems. These problems—which typically include substance abuse, family violence, sexual abuse, and the neglect and abandonment of children—require remedies within the community itself. If a community begins to recognize child neglect, for example, it can then determine the extent of that problem in that community and develop strategies to respond to it. Governments are a necessary part of that process; but it takes the community, neighbour by neighbour, to attend to the needs of neglected children.

While the social problems revealed by criminal justice processes are generally interpreted to be the problems of the individual offender, restorative justice processes look for deeper causes. Restorative justice can be useful in helping individuals explore their own behaviours as part of crime prevention (Haley, 1996); but they have much greater potential to explore aggregate problems as symptoms of larger social injustices, such as poverty, racism, and sexism. The greater the community involvement in responding to conflict and harm, the greater the awareness of social justice issues present within the community itself. Crime prevention, then, is not merely about erecting more streetlights and reporting suspicious behaviour, but also about attending to deeper social inequities that are reflected in individual acts of harm. For example, youth gang violence might be viewed as a symptom of a larger problem of racism in high schools. Thus, community members involved in such cases may be motivated to develop strategies in local schools to address the roots of racism.

Criticisms of Restorative Justice

A common criticism of restorative justice is that it emphasizes the notion of the *community* in an idealistic rather than realistic form, particularly for communities in larger urban centres. In restorative justice, the *community* is not a simple geographic entity (although it could be), but a place as defined by interests. As such, people generally belong to several different communities of interest at the same time (McCold and Wachtel, 1998), based on work, school, recreation, neighbourhoods, families, and friendships. Since crime is a product of dysfunction in a community, the community must be part of the solution. Weak communities can be strengthened by the involvement of members in conflict resolution processes (Crawford and Clear, 2001). Indeed, social injustices may be related to the "arms-length" position of the community from conflict resolution processes. But the professionalization of criminal justice has clouded the idea that conflicts are the property of those most affected by them (Christie, 1977). In contrast, when communities are involved in their own conflicts and problems, issues of social justice remain personal and real as opposed to general and abstract. Crime prevention through social justice affords a human and ethical approach to harm reduction in communities.

FROM PHILOSOPHY TO PRACTICE: EXAMPLES OF RESTORATIVE JUSTICE PRACTICES

There are three basic models of restorative justice practice: *victim-offender meetings*, *family group conferences*, and *circle peacemaking* (Zehr, 2002). All of these models include an encounter between the victim and the offender, and many also extend to key participants, such as family and community members. The processes are led by volunteer or professional facilitators trained to organize and run the encounters in a way that balances the concern for everyone involved. These models generally include three discussion components: the facts about the crime (what happened?), the way the parties felt as a result of the crime (how was everyone affected?), and possible resolutions that might be pursued in order to meet the obligations created by the harm (what can be done?). The parties involved create agreements, which are expected to respect the healing mandate of restorative justice.

VICTIM-OFFENDER RECONCILIATION PROGRAMS

Victim-offender meetings were first used in Canada in Kitchener-Waterloo, Ontario, as part of the Victim-Offender Reconciliation Program (VORP).[10] This model involves a face-to-face meeting between a victim and an offender that is mediated by a trained community volunteer (Gilman and Bowler, 1995). VORP is a pioneer restorative program which has inspired formalized consideration of restorative justice theory in Canada. While the Kitchener-Waterloo program used it exclusively for property crimes, British Columbia extended the VORP concept to include victims and offenders of serious personal crimes. Under the title of Victim Offender Mediation Program (VOMP), the B.C. restorative process began in 1991 as a pilot project of the Correctional Service of Canada for federal offenders and their victims.[11] VOMP and VORP differ in some ways, especially regarding the seriousness of the offences that each program deals with and the amount of preparation and aftercare necessary.

Victim-offender encounters are used for healing and reconciliation. The process begins when the mediator receives a referral and contacts the victims and offenders to hear their stories. If the victim and offender agree to meet, the mediator arranges an encounter, but only when the mediator senses that an encounter will be helpful to both of the parties. The amount of time needed for pre-meeting counselling varies according to the needs of the parties—because the needs of victims and offenders in serious cases are usually greater than those in minor cases. For example, a meeting between the victim of a car theft and the teenage boy who stole the car might require a few weeks of preparation; but a meeting between a victim of serious sexual assault and her assailant may take several months or years to arrange. This time lag can pose problems for cases that are constrained by court schedules; but in general, violent offence mediations occur soon after the offender has been sentenced.

FAMILY GROUP CONFERENCING

Family group conferencing was developed in New Zealand through the *Children, Young Persons and Their Families Act* (1989). Family group conferences deal with both child protection cases and youth justice cases and include the youth in question, as well as family members and community professionals

(Hassall, 1996). Family group conferencing is based on restorative justice values such as respect and sensitivity, with a particular criminal justice emphasis on victim inclusion and offender accountability. Australia adapted the family group conference model into a program developed by the police, one that uses a scripted model of facilitation, paying particular attention to the restorative and rehabilitative power of shame (Zehr, 2002).

A similar model was developed in Canada by the RCMP in 1995, when RCMP and Crown counsel implemented a process in Sparwood, B.C., that later became known as *community justice forums* (CJFs) (Shaw and Jané, 1999). The RCMP officially adopted this model in 1997; and by the end of 1998, it had trained about 1,700 police officers across Canada to use the program (Chatterjee and Elliott, 2003). Also called *conferencing*, this process brings together the victim, the offender, their supporters, and other community stakeholders to talk about the harm resulting from the crime and possible solutions to it. This model often relies on a script that guides the facilitators through the process. The offenders are usually young, and the outcomes generally involve material restitution and an agreement to deal with certain presenting problems, such as substance abuse or truancy. In Newfoundland and Labrador, pilot conferencing projects have even been used in cases of domestic violence (Shaw and Jané, 1999), which helps bring the problem to the community's attention. Similar programs exist in schools, generally in place of conventional disciplinary penalties, such as detentions and suspensions.

CIRCLE PEACEMAKING

Circle peacemaking is strongly rooted in indigenous cultures and came to the broader North American society from northern Canadian cultures. In a circle program, participants sit in a circle and pass a "talking piece" to ensure that each person has an opportunity to speak. There is a strong emphasis in circle peacemaking on values such as integrity and truth telling (Pranis et al., 2002). The circle includes not only the victim, offender, and their supporters, but also other community members. In criminal justice programs, circles are used for sentencing (*sentencing circles*), as well as for healing and general community dialogue.

Interest in circles began when judges recognized the limited impact of the conventional process in northern Aboriginal communities. As a result, they adapted circles to the demands of the formal court system for these cultural groups. In circle sentencing, the community and the victim have active roles in the offender's hearing in order to build connections to and within communities (Stuart, 1996b). In cases where the victim's safety is compromised by the offender's liberty, imprisonment may be a component of a sentencing outcome. When carefully deployed, the circle process may be useful in cases of domestic violence, where the community can take stringent measures to deal with power imbalances in intimate relationships.[12] Circle sentencing is used for a range of offences, generally in cases where the offender pleads guilty.

COMMON FEATURES OF RESTORATIVE PROCESSES

Regardless of the specific restorative process model, all restorative justice programs share several common characteristics. First, referrals come through negotiated agreements with partnering agencies, such as the police, the courts, schools or social service agencies; or they may come directly from the community itself. Decisions about whether or not to accept a case for restorative intervention vary according to mandates, agreements, the specific factors of the case, or the particular circumstances of the main parties to the conflict. These variations depend on the parameters of the restorative resolution service itself; for example, police-run programs may be restricted to minor criminal cases, while school programs might only address disciplinary cases where the conflict is non-criminal. A common distinction is made between services that work with youth only (Morris and Maxwell, 2003) and those that accept cases with primary stakeholders of all ages.

Second, all restorative models begin with preparatory casework, which receives variable attention depending on the model and the nature of the cases accepted. Victim-offender mediation processes emphasize pre-mediation meetings with each party to the conflict; as Umbreit (1994) notes: "having the mediator meet with both [parties] individually before even scheduling the mediation is extremely important. It tends to humanize the justice process and results in a higher 'getting-to-the-table' rate of actual mediation participation" (pp. 7–8). Given its wider capture of "stakeholder" input, family group conferencing entails pre-conference meetings with a larger number of participants, often constrained by court schedules and legal imperatives. These meetings generally focus on the purpose and process of the conferencing, as well as assessing the offender's acceptance of responsibility and willingness to participate (Hudson et al., 1996). In circle processes, the referral and pre-encounter stages might take the form of circles, particularly when the key parties need support people. In these preparatory circles, the facilitators ensure that both victim and offender support groups are balanced, that both have received relevant resources, and that both are working on healing plans (Pranis et al., 2003).

Restorative processes are also characterized by a post-encounter phase. All models include a subsequent monitoring phase during which either volunteers or professionals assess the agreements created in the encounter phase of the process to ensure that the parties act on the recommendations. The depth and breadth of these interventions generally depend on the seriousness of the offence and the needs of the participants involved. In Canada, conferencing agreements and those generated from relatively minor victim-offender mediation cases tend to be more simple and time-constrained. Post-sentence victim-offender mediation and circle processes for serious crime cases may involve open-ended, evolving supervision and facilitation of agreements. The difference tends to be based on the motivation for the restorative justice process; some are criminal justice mandated and concerned with clearing cases, whereas others are more primarily concerned with the healing of those affected by the harm.

Whatever the model, several principles must guide the process. These are itemized in Mika and Zehr's "Signposts of Restorative Justice" (see Figure 24.1). A summarizing adage might be to "do no harm" in restorative endeavours, whether in criminal justice or the schools, whether for minor disputes or major crimes.

CHALLENGES AND CONCERNS

Seasoned practitioners of restorative justice have noted several areas of concern that require attention as restorative justice programs become more popular. One major issue is the role of victims and the attention paid to their needs. For example, conferencing tends to focus on the offender, with victims often used simply as a means of dealing with the offender (albeit in ways that are more inclusive than the formal criminal justice system). Certainly, research shows that victims participating in restorative justice processes are more satisfied with the results than are victims who participate in the formal

Figure 24.1 *Signposts of Restorative Justice*

1. Focus on the harms of crime rather than on the rules that have been broken.

2. Show equal concern and commitment to victims and offenders, involving both in the process of justice.

3. Work toward the restoration of victims, empowering them and responding to their needs as they see them.

4. Support offenders while encouraging them to understand, accept, and carry out their obligations.

5. Recognize that while obligations may be difficult for offenders, those obligations should not be intended as harms; moreover, they must be achievable.

6. Provide opportunities for dialogue (direct or indirect) between victim and offender as appropriate.

7. Find meaningful ways to involve the community and to respond to the community bases of crime.

8. Encourage collaboration and reintegration of victims and offenders, rather than coercion and isolation.

9. Give attention to the unintended consequences of your actions and program.

10. Show respect to all parties—victims, offenders, and justice colleagues.

Source: Mika and Zehr, 1998.

criminal justice processes (Strang, 2002; Daly, 2005; Dignan, 2005). However, restitution agreements may offer only material compensation for victims (which can be sufficient in some cases), without meaningful attention to the victim's personal healing needs (Herman, 2004). This concern is particularly strong in restorative processes that are "add-ons" to the formal criminal justice system, as opposed to programs that operate autonomously.

Another concern relates to the potential for coercion and consequent lack of safety for participants. While safety may be a concern for offenders, the problem for victims may often be more subtle and potentially more dangerous. The problem of victim safety was raised first in Canada by practitioners and advocates working with victims of familial violence, where power imbalances in close intimate relationships can hide the vulnerability of victims from proper scrutiny. While restorative justice has been used effectively in cases of domestic violence (Mills, 2006) and child abuse (Pennell and Burford, 1996), there are many situations in which restorative processes are not appropriate for these kinds of offences. For example, Aboriginal women and children in isolated communities may be silenced by local political leadership and unhealthy kinship relationships (Stewart et al., 2001). Some advocates argue that contemporary sexism in Aboriginal communities prevents safety for women and children in restorative processes, and they recommend that restorative practices be discontinued until further research is conducted (Cameron, 2006).

Restorative practices have been very effective in drawing attention to the emotional and psychological implications of crime—features which are ignored or minimized by the traditional legalistic response to crime. For example, shame is a key concept in restorative justice theory. *Shame* is an innate human emotion which acts as a spotlight of conscience on behaviour; if processed in a healthy way by the individual experiencing it, shame can help govern behaviour. In effect, shame (as a noun denoting a specific human affect) is significant to informal social control. However, criminal justice officials and community members influenced by retributive ways of thinking tend to use the term *shaming* (as a verb denoting an action) to mean *stigmatizing*, despite Braithwaite's careful definition of shaming as a *reintegrative* process (1989). In addition, the tendency of some restorative process facilitators to remain grounded in retributive habits rather than restorative values means that they see shaming as a process of humiliation, which can result in violence. But thoughtful and thorough training of facilitators with a focus on values can help address this problem. Without such training and without improvements to the chronic problem of under-resourcing of restorative justice programs, the potential for abuse of the process remains high.

CONCLUSION

Can restorative justice ever replace the existing punitive justice system? The question is probably premature. Current efforts in restorative justice are more concerned with preventing its absorption into the existing justice system.

Perhaps in time, restorative justice will become the first option for criminal justice interventions, with the conventional system playing a back-up role. A more likely scenario is for restorative justice processes to become established alongside traditional justice systems, as an option for offenders who want to take responsibility for their actions and for victims who want a restorative encounter as part of their own healing. The few evaluations of the effectiveness of restorative justice programs to date have been promising (e.g., Flaten, 1996; Latimer et al., 2001; Umbreit, 1994).

Restorative justice challenges Canadians to consider what we want from justice and what kind of world we want to live in. If the purpose of justice is peace and safety in our communities, then we need to find the means to get us there. To do so requires us to challenge primary concepts about criminal justice, such as punishment and formal criminal justice institutions. Perhaps the simple availability of other response options to harm-doing afforded by restorative justice will help broaden this perspective; if the only tool we have is a hammer, every problem looks like a nail.

DISCUSSION QUESTIONS

1. *In your view, what is the most important advantage of restorative responses to offending over the conventional criminal justice system?*
2. *Critics of the restorative justice movement have identified a number of problems associated with this new paradigm. Do you see any difficulties with the restorative response?*

FURTHER READINGS

Braithwaite, J. 1999. Restorative justice: Pessimistic and optimistic accounts. In M. Tonry (Ed.), *Crime and Justice: A Review of Research*. Chicago: University of Chicago Press.

Roberts, J. V., and Roach, R. 2003. Restorative justice in Canada: From sentencing circles to sentencing principles. In von Hirsch, A., Roberts, J.V., Bottoms, A., and Roach, K. (Eds.), *Restorative Justice and Criminal Justice*. Oxford: Hart Publishing.

Roach, K. 2000. Changing punishment at the turn of the century: Restorative justice on the rise. *Canadian Journal of Criminology*, 42: 249–280.

REFERENCES

Beccaria, C. 1985 (orig. 1764). *On Crimes and Punishments*. New York: Macmillan Publishing Company.

Braithwaite, J. 1989. *Crime, Shame and Reintegration*. New York: Cambridge University Press.

Brandt, C. 1990. Native ethics and rules of behaviour. *The Canadian Journal of Psychiatry*, 35: 534–539.

Brantingham, P., and Brantingham, P. 1990. Situational crime prevention in practice. *Canadian Journal of Criminology*, 32: 17–40.

Cameron, A. 2006. Stopping the violence: Canadian feminist debates on restorative justice and intimate violence. *Theoretical Criminology*, 10: 49–66.

Chatterjee, J., and Elliott, L. 2003. Restorative policing in Canada: The Royal Canadian Mounted Police, community justice forums, and the *Youth Criminal Justice Act. Police Practice and Research*, 4: 347–359.

Christie, N. 1977. Conflicts as property. *British Journal of Criminology*, 17: 1–14.

Clear, T., and Karp, D. 1999. *The Community Justice Ideal: Preventing Crime and Achieving Justice*. Boulder, CO: Westview Press.

Clemmer, D. 1958. (orig. 1940). *The Prison Community*. Toronto: Holt, Rinehart and Winston.

Cobden, J., and Harley, P. 2004. Intentional conversations about restorative justice, mediation and the practice of Law. *Hamline Journal of Public Law and Policy*, 25: 235–334.

Cohen, S., and Taylor, L. 1972. *Psychological Survival: The Experience of Long-Term Imprisonment*. New York: Pantheon Books.

Coker, D. 2006. Restorative justice, Navajo peacemaking and domestic violence. *Theoretical Criminology*, 10: 67–85.

Crawford, A., and Clear, T. 2001 Community justice: Transforming communities through restorative justice? In G. Bazemore and M. Schiff (Eds.), *Restorative Community Justice: Repairing Harm and Transforming Communities*. Cincinnati, OH: Anderson Publishing Company.

Daly, K. 2005. A tale of two studies: Restorative justice from a victim's perspective. In E. Elliott and R. Gordon (Eds.), *New Directions in Restorative Justice: Issues, Practice, Evaluation*. Portland, OR: Willan Publishing.

Dignan, J. 2005. *Understanding Victims and Restorative Justice*. New York: Open University Press.

Flaten, C. 1996. Victim-offender mediation: Application with serious offences committed by juveniles. In B. Galaway and J. Hudson (Eds.), *Restorative Justice: International Perspectives*. Monsey, NY: Criminal Justice Press.

Felson, M. 1994. *Crime and Everyday Life*. Newbury Park, CA: Pine Forge Press.

Gilman, E., and Bowler, C. 1995. *Victim Offender Mediation Training Program, Revised Edition, Training and Resource Manual*. Langley, BC: Fraser Region Community Justice Initiatives Association.

Goffman, E. 1961. *Asylums*. New York: Anchor.

Gustafson, D. 2005. Exploring treatment and trauma recovery implications of facilitating victim-offender encounters in crimes of severe violence: Lessons from the Canadian experience. In E. Elliott and R. Gordon (Eds.), *New Directions in Restorative Justice: Issues, Practice, Evaluation*. Portland, OR: Willan Publishing.

Haan, W. 1990. *The Politics of Redress: Crime, Punishment and Penal Abolition*. Boston, MA: Unwin Hyman.

Haley, J. 1996. Crime prevention through restorative justice: Lessons from Japan. In B. Galaway & J. Hudson (Eds.), *Restorative Justice: International Perspectives*. Monsey, NY: Criminal Justice Press.

Hassall, I. 1996. Origin and development of family group conferences. In J. Hudson, A. Morris, G. Maxwell and B. Galaway (Eds.), *Family Group Conferences: Perspectives on Policy and Practice*. Monsey, NY: Criminal Justice Press.

Herman, S. 2004. Is restorative justice possible without a parallel system for victims? In H. Zehr and B. Toews (Eds.), *Critical Issues in Restorative Justice*. Monsey, NY: Criminal Justice Press.

Hirshi, T. 1969. *Causes of Delinquency*. Berkeley: University of California Press.

Hudson, J., Galaway, B., Morris, A., and Maxwell, G. 1996. Introduction. In J. Hudson, A. Morris, G. Maxwell and B. Galaway (Eds.), *Family Group Conferences: Perspectives on Policy and Practice*. Monsey, NY: Criminal Justice Press.

Latimer, J., Dowden, C., and Muise, D. 2001.*The Effectiveness of Restorative Justice Practices: A Meta-Analysis*. Ottawa: Department of Justice Canada, Research and Statistics Division.

Llewellyn, J., and Howse, R. 1999. *Restorative Justice: A Conceptual Framework*. Ottawa: The Law Commission of Canada. Online at: www.lcc.gc.ca.

McCold, P., and Wachtel, P. 1998. Community is not a place: A new look at community justice initiatives. *Contemporary Justice Review*, 1: 71–85.

Mika, H., and Zehr, H. 1998. Fundamental principles of restorative justice. *The Contemporary Justice Review*, 1: 47–55.

Mills, L. 2006. *From Insult to Injury: Rethinking Our Responses to Intimate Abuse*. Princeton, NJ: Princeton University Press.

Morris, A., and Maxwell, G. (Eds.). 2003. *Restorative Justice for Juveniles: Conferencing, Mediation & Circles*. Portland, OR: Hart Publishing.

Pennell, J., and Burford, G. 1996. Attending to context: Family group decision making in Canada. In J. Hudson, A. Morris, G. Maxwell and B. Galaway (Eds.), *Family Group Conferences: Perspectives on Policy and Practice*. Monsey, N.Y.: Criminal Justice Press.

Pranis, K., Stuart, B., and Wedge, M. 2003. *Using Peacemaking Circles in the Justice System*. Minnesota: Living Justice Press.

Roberts, T. 1995. *Evaluation of the Victim Offender Mediation Project*. Langley, B.C., Ottawa: Solicitor General of Canada.

Ross, R. 1996. *Returning to the Teachings: Exploring Aboriginal Justice*. Toronto: Penguin Books.

Sacco, V., and Kennedy, L. 1998. *The Criminal Event*, 2nd ed. Toronto: ITP Nelson.

Sharpe, S. 1998. *Restorative Justice: A Vision for Healing and Change*. Edmonton: Edmonton Victim Offender Mediation Society.

Shaw, M., and Jané, F. 1999. *Family Group Conferencing with Children Under Twelve: A Discussion Paper*. Ottawa: Department of Justice Canada.

Stewart, W., Huntley, A., and Blaney, F. 2001. *The Implications of Restorative Justice for Aboriginal Women and Children Survivors of Violence: A Comparative Overview of Five Communities in British Columbia.* Ottawa: Law Commission of Canada.

Stuart, B. 1996. Circle sentencing: Turning swords into plowshares. In B. Galaway and J. Hudson (Eds.), *Restorative Justice: International Perspectives.* Monsey, NY: Criminal Justice Press.

Stewart, W., Huntley, A., and Blaney, F. 2001. *The Implications of Restorative Justice for Aboriginal Women and Children Survivors of Violence: A Comparative Overview of Five Communities in British Columbia.* Unpublished paper prepared for the Aboriginal Women's Action Network in their Aboriginal Women, Violence and the Law Participatory Action Research Project, July.

Strang, H. 2002. *Repair or Revenge: Victims and Restorative Justice.* Oxford: Clarendon Press.

Sutherland, E. 1947. *Criminology,* 4th ed. Philadelphia: Lippincott.

Sykes, G. 1958. *The Society of Captives: A Study of a Maximum Security Prison.* Princeton, NJ: Princeton University Press.

Umbreit, M. 1994. *Victim Meets Offender: The Impact of Restorative Justice and Mediation.* Monsey, NY: Criminal Justice Press.

Vold, G., Bernard, T., and Snipes, J. 2002. *Theoretical Criminology,* 5th ed. New York: Oxford University Press.

Zehr, H. 2002. *The Little Book of Restorative Justice.* Intercourse, PA: Good Books.

_____. 1990. *Changing Lenses.* Waterloo: Herald Press.

ENDNOTES

[1] From *Changing Lenses* (1990), pp. 177–178. Zehr also suggested that restorative justice may be a paradigm shift (pp. 83–94), which presents a limitation of the "restorative justice as add-on program" perspective.

[2] For a basic discussion of Aboriginal ways of social conduct, see Brandt (1990).

[3] See Ross (1996), Chapter 2.

[4] See, for example, Brantingham and Brantingham (1990) and Felson (1994).

[5] This refers mainly to early intervention strategies and social welfare policies.

[6] The classical school sees the law-breaker as a rational person governed by pleasure and pain, who can be deterred only by the threat of sanction (Sacco and Kennedy, 1998). For a full explication of the classical school of criminology, see Beccaria (orig. 1764).

[7] Literature on the sociology of imprisonment, especially those outlining the concepts of the prison community (Clemmer, 1958), maximum-security prison culture (Sykes, 1958), the "total institution" (Goffman, 1961), and the psychological impacts of incarceration (Cohen and Taylor, 1972), provides useful insights into the effects of prison on reoffending.

8 The term *positivism* refers to the "philosophical position, developed by Auguste Comte that scientific knowledge can come only from direct observation, experimentation, and provision of quantitative data" (Sacco and Kennedy, 1998, p. 420). Positivist criminology sees behaviour as determined by factors beyond the individual. Criminal behaviour is caused by biological, psychological and social factors (Vold et al., 2002).

9 For a discussion of the effects of victimization on future criminal behaviour, see http://www.prevention.gc.ca/english/publications/youth/mobilize/contex_e.html.

10 VORP began in 1974 for a case in which two young men pleaded guilty to 22 counts of vandalizing properties in the Kitchener area. It was the result of a collaborative effort between the Mennonite Central Committee and the local probation department. The two offenders met with individual victims to work out restitution agreements, launching a program that is still in effect. VORP is also offered in British Columbia, Saskatchewan, and Manitoba. The history of VORP is outlined in Zehr (1990) Chapter 9.

11 A more detailed explication of VOMP is found in Roberts (1995).

12 In her study of Navajo peacemaking and domestic violence, Coker (2006) argues that restorative processes may be beneficial if they meet five criteria: "prioritize victim safety over batterer rehabilitation; offer material as well as social supports for victims; work as part of a coordinated community response; engage normative judgments that oppose gendered domination as well as violence; and do not make forgiveness a goal of the process" (p. 67).

COPYRIGHTS AND ACKNOWLEDGMENTS

We wish to thank the publishers and copyright holders for permission to reprint the selections in this book. These are listed below in order of appearance.

"Criminal Justice Trends in Canada," by Karen Mihorean and Rebecca Kong. Used by permission of the authors.

"The Role of the Prosecutor," by Brian Manarin. Used by permission of the author.

"The Role of a Defence Counsel," by Paul Burstein. Used by permission of the author.

"A Day in the Life of a Provincial Court Judge," by Judge David P. Cole. Used by permission of the author.

"The Probation Officer's Report," by Karen Middlecoat. Used by permission of the author.

"The Professional Life of a Federal Parole Officer," by Sheldon Schwartz. Used by permission of the author.

"A Life Prisoner's Story," Extract from *Paroled for Life: Interviews with Parolees Serving Life Sentences*, by P.J. Murphy, Loyd Johnsen and Jennifer Murphy (New Star Books, 2002). Used by permission of New Star Books.

"Community Policing in Canada: The Broad Blue Line," by Barry N. Leighton. Used by permission of the author.

"Plea Bargaining," by Simon Verdun-Jones. Used by permission of the author.

"Preventing Gun Crime," by Thomas Gabor. Used by permission of the author.

"Serving Time at Home," by Julian Roberts. Used by permission of the author.

"Treatment of Prisoners," by Shereen H. Benzvy Miller. Used by permission of the author.